PRESENTED TO

____

ON

____

BY

____

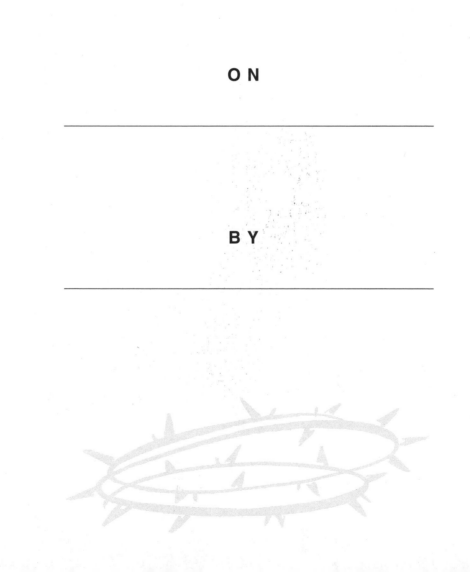

OVER THE EDGE

Youth Devotional

OVER THE EDGE

Youth Devotional

Kenneth and Gloria Copeland

"I am not ashamed of the gospel of Christ, for it is the power of God to salvation for everyone who believes, for the Jew first and also for the Greek. For in it the righteousness of God is revealed from faith to faith; as it is written, 'The just shall live by faith.'"
(Romans 1:16-17, NKJV)

Harrison House
Tulsa, Oklahoma

Unless otherwise indicated, all Scripture references are taken from the *New International Version* of the Bible.

Scripture quotations marked (NKJV) are taken from *The New King James Version*. Copyright © 1979, 1980, 1982, Thomas Nelson, Inc.

Scripture quotations marked (ICB) are taken from the *International Children's Bible, New Century Version*, copyright © 1986, 1988 by Word Publishing, Dallas, Texas 75234. Used by permission.

Scripture quotations marked (AMP) are taken from *The Amplified Bible, Old Testament*. Copyright © 1965, 1987 by Zondervan Corporation, Grand Rapids, Michigan. Used by permission.

Scripture quotations marked (NEB) are taken from *The New English Bible*. Copyright © The Delegates of the Oxford University Press and the Syndics of the Cambridge University Press 1961, 1970. Reprinted by permission.

4th Printing

Over the Edge
Youth Devotional
ISBN 1-57794-138-1

Kenneth Copeland Ministries
Fort Worth, Texas 76192-0001

Published by Harrison House, Inc.
P.O. Box 35035
Tulsa, OK 74153

PREFACE

The world tries to sell you a lie that living *on the edge* is the "ultimate experience." But there is a higher way...a more powerful way... a more exciting way. The *true* ultimate experience is going *Over The Edge* with God!

Gloria and I first determined to go *over the edge* and live by faith more than 30 years ago—and let me be the first to tell you, it's the best decision we ever made. Since then, life has been a nonstop adventure with Him.

We have discovered that the Bible is packed with promises for victory—spiritually, mentally, physically, financially, socially—in every area of life. And when we act on God's promises by faith, the miraculous takes place!

Now is the time to set the course of your life. Now is the time to determine to go up and over with God and live by faith every step of the way. In God, you have unlimited resources to do all that He's called you to do. No one else is like you, and no one else is called to do what you are called to do. No one but God can bring you to that place.

So fulfill you destiny. Spend time in God's Word and get to know Him every day. Seek Him and let His plans for your life unfold before you. That's the reason we created *Over the Edge*—to help you draw closer to God and receive what you need to succeed.

Our prayer is that your spirit, soul and body will grow stronger each day so that you can live a victorious life of power and purpose and, ultimately, share that life with others. God *will* use you to influence your world. So take the plunge into the real Xtremescene today—go *Over the Edge* with God!

Kenneth and Gloria Copeland

HOW TO USE OVER THE EDGE

1. After reading each devotion, take a moment to think about what you read and how it directly applies to your life *today*. You can write notes directly on the page!

2. Speak God's Word aloud in faith each day and watch the circumstances change in your life. **talk the truth**

3. Study more about each devotion by reading and meditating on the **study the truth** passage every day.

4. Set a goal of reading through the Bible in a year. By following the Read Through the Bible Plan **read the truth** you can read a portion every day. By the end of the year, you'll have read all of God's Word!

5. Learn to take the Bible literally as God speaking to you. God's Words are victory words. Following God's way of doing things ensures success in every area of life.

6. Take hold of Psalm 145:9 for the rest of your life. Don't allow yourself to deviate from this truth. "The Lord is good to all: and his tender mercies are over all his works." This will keep your thinking straight about God when the devil tries to separate you from Him. God is always good. God is always right. God always desires good for you.

January 1

Kenneth

A HAPPY NEW YEAR

"Everyone who calls on the name of the Lord will be saved."

ROMANS 10:13

People everywhere are gathering to celebrate the first bright moments of the new year...yet for thousands, this day will be the toughest 24 hours of their lives.

You probably know classmates who partied all night, did things they knew they shouldn't do and now regret every moment of it. For them, New Year's will simply mark the beginning of another year of failure.

What about you? You may appear to be happy enough. But inside, you may be hurt and disappointed. *You* may be the one who regrets last night's actions. You may even feel like you can't go on.

Have you ever said to yourself, *If I could do it again, I'd do it all differently?* Well, Jesus has actually made that *possible.* He paid the price for all your sins and the penalty for all your mistakes—no matter what you've done. That's the reason He came to earth—so you could start over and make this New Year's Day the best day of your life!

How can you make a new start? Romans 10:9 says that "if you confess with your mouth, 'Jesus is Lord,' and believe in your heart that God raised him from the dead, you will be saved."

It's as easy as saying, "Jesus, I'm turning my life over to You. From this day forward I'm Yours. At home, in school, around my friends—everywhere—I will follow You."

What better time to turn your life around than on this first day of the new year? Even if you've given your life to Jesus before but feel like you've lost your focus, you can commit yourself to Him again. Right now, wherever you are, just give your life to Jesus once and for all. And find out what it *really* means to have a happy new year!

talk the truth

"Today I am brand new. I call on the name of the Lord and I am saved." (Romans 10:13)

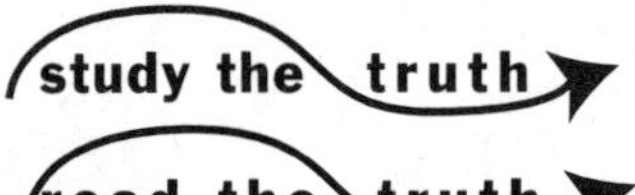
study the truth
read the truth

Romans 10:1-13

Genesis 1,2,3; Matthew 1,2

LOOK UP!

"Think about Jesus. He held on patiently while sinful men were doing evil things against him. Look at Jesus' example so that you will not get tired and stop trying."

HEBREWS 12:3, ICB

Some time ago, the Lord showed me how Satan tries to work tiredness into our lives through all the pressures that surround us.

Perhaps you have friends who have tried to pressure you into drinking. Perhaps you've been with a date who attempted to push you into an uncomfortable situation. Or perhaps you've just turned on the television and felt pressured to be someone other than who you are. Whatever kind of pressure you're facing, it's this kind of bombardment of negative things that allows tiredness to work its way into your life. It tries to take your eyes off God's Word by forcing you to look down at defeat instead of up at Jesus.

If you let that happen, it will be harder for you to see yourself as the person God created you to be...you will "get tired and stop trying."

Jesus said that when everyday worries and problems enter into your heart and mind, they'll stop the Word and cause it to have no effect in your life (Mark 4). And since your faith comes from God's Word, that means your faith will weaken. Once that happens, you're headed for disaster.

What can you do to stop this chain reaction?

Look up! Get your eyes back on Jesus.

When my school participated in athletic events, we learned that once an opponent allowed himself to drop his head, he could very easily be defeated. So keep your head up. Get your eyes on Jesus instead of the worries and problems that come against you. Think about what God has promised you in His Word. Remind yourself that He has a great future planned for you (Jeremiah 29:11).

If you've felt worn-out lately—if you've felt tired and like you don't want to try anymore—just lift your eyes to Him today. Raise your head up. God is up. Jesus is up. Satan is down—under your feet. Look up!

talk the truth

"I look to Jesus, Who held on patiently under pressure. I will not get tired or stop trying." (Hebrews 12:3, ICB)

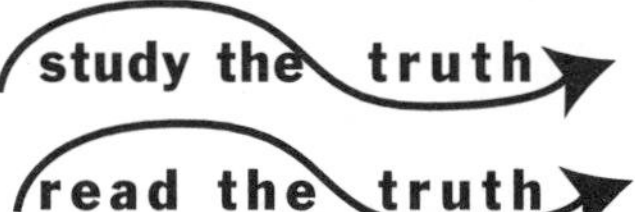
study the truth
read the truth

Isaiah 40:21-31

Genesis 4,5; Matthew 3

Kenneth

January 3

BE A BLESSING

"May those who delight in my vindication shout for joy and gladness; may they always say, 'The Lord be exalted, who delights in the well-being of his servant.'"

Psalm 35:27

If you've ever heard that God wants you poor, weak and loaded down with problems, I have good news. The Bible says God *delights* in your well-being. God *wants* you to have a rich life!

I'm not saying He just wants you to have money—He wants you to be rich in every area of your life...spirit, soul and body.

God wants to see you win in every situation that comes against you. He wants you to be strong in faith. He wants you to have outstanding grades. He wants you to be physically fit.

Why? Because He loves you and He has a job for you to do. He wants you to help meet the needs of others, and He knows that you can't give away what you don't have. You can't give to spread God's Word or buy food for the hungry when you're broke. You can't go out and lay hands on the sick when you're lying in a hospital bed. You can't help your classmates find joy when you're being held captive by depression. No! You have to be blessed to be a blessing.

If you really want to tap into the riches God has for you today, make up your mind to start giving to others, and before you know it, you'll be receiving more from God than you ever dreamed.

Become His servant today. Become a giver—lay down your time and your money and your love for those who need it—and God will *delight* in making sure your being is well!

talk the truth **"I am a giver and I praise God Who delights in my well-being." (Psalm 35:27)**

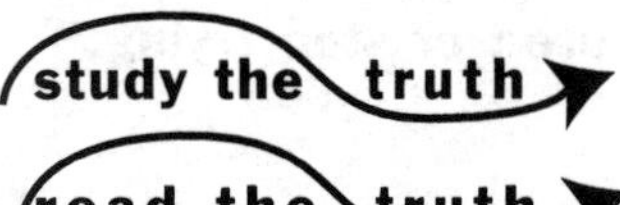

Genesis 12:1-4; 13:1-4

read the truth **Genesis 6,7; Matthew 4**

LET THE WORLD KNOW

"My prayer is not for them alone. I pray also for those who will believe in me through their message...that they may be one as we are one: I in them and you in me. May they be brought to complete unity to let the world know that you sent me."

JOHN 17:20,22,23

Do you know Jesus gave us the key to winning the world? Most Christians don't even realize it, but He did. Right before He went to the Cross, He asked His Father to bring us into a place of such "complete unity" with each other and with Him that the *world would know* He had been sent from God.

If you and I, and all the other Christians around the world, would work together, we could spread the message of God's Word so fast it would make your head spin. It's true! But until recently, we've been too busy fighting with one another to give it much thought.

The good news is that Christians like you are beginning to realize that fighting like this is ridiculous. They're beginning to understand that we need to start treating Jesus' command to "love one another" as a *command* instead of a *choice.*

Do you want to take a step toward spreading God's salvation message to the world today? Then become one of the powerful young men and women who pray for unity. Make up your mind that you'll start loving other Christians instead of criticizing, complaining and talking ugly about them.

Start praying that Christians everywhere will rise up in faith and love as one Body driven by the power of Jesus Himself. We are, you know. Jesus prayed that it would happen, and it's beginning to happen all over the world.

Satan can't stop it. It's far more powerful than he is—and it's sure to blast a hole in his operation big enough to drive a train through. It will let the whole world know that Jesus truly is Lord!

talk the truth

"Jesus is in me, and I am in Him. I am in complete union with Him and others so the world will know Jesus is Lord." (John 17:20,22,23)

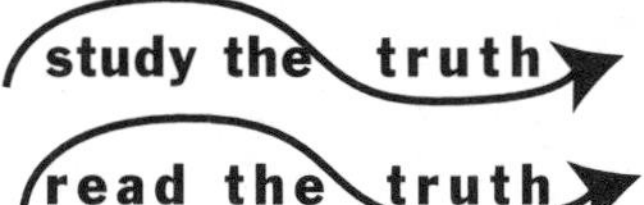
study the truth
read the truth

John 17:9-26

Genesis 8,9; Matthew 5

January 5

YOU ARE RIGHTEOUS

"Not having a righteousness of my own that comes from the law, but that which is through faith in Christ—the righteousness that comes from God and is by faith."

PHILIPPIANS 3:9

I don't care how much you messed things up by gossiping yesterday, or how many bad words you let slip, I want you to begin this day knowing *you are righteous!* It's not because of anything you've done, but it's because God made you right with Him when you made Jesus the Lord of your life.

Righteousness literally means *right-standing with God*—it means that you're in "good standing" with Him. The best thing about righteousness is that it's God's gift to you. It's not something you earn by being good. Even if you make mistakes, He sees you as righteous.

Now, just look at the benefits God's Word says standing right with Him brings:

- "The righteous will flourish like a palm tree" (Psalm 92:12).
- "Those who are righteous will go free" (Proverbs 11:21).
- "For the eyes of the Lord are on the righteous and his ears are attentive to their prayer" (1 Peter 3:12).
- "For surely, O Lord, you bless the righteous; you surround them with your favor as with a shield" (Psalm 5:12).
- "The righteous cry out, and the Lord hears them; he delivers [rescues] them from all their troubles" (Psalm 34:17).
- "The righteous will inherit the land and dwell in it forever" (Psalm 37:29).
- "The Lord loves the righteous" (Psalm 146:8).

Don't let Satan rob you of even one of these benefits by telling you that you're unworthy of them. Let him know you are in right-standing with God. Then, with faith, step out and enjoy all these excellent benefits God has for you!

talk the truth

"I am in right-standing with God—and my righteousness comes from God by faith. I am righteous!" (Philippians 3:9)

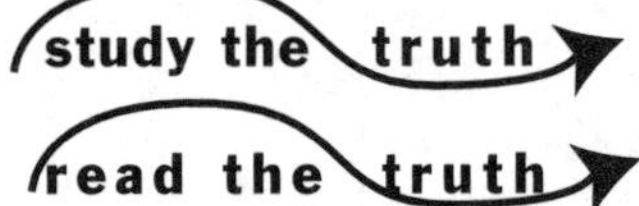
study the truth
read the truth

Romans 3:21-28

Genesis 10,11; Matthew 6

WATCH AND PRAY

"Watch and pray so that you will not fall into temptation. The spirit is willing, but the body is weak."

MATTHEW 26:41

Have you ever been frustrated because you felt weak? Have you ever promised yourself you'd stop sinning and then sinned again?

It's happened to all of us. It even happened to Peter, Jesus' disciple. He swore he would never deny Jesus...but he did it anyway, time and time again.

There is, however, something we can do to keep from falling into sin. We can "watch and pray." That's what Jesus told Peter and the other disciples to do just before He went to the cross. He knew they were about to be tempted, and He knew that they would give in to their weaknesses if they didn't strengthen themselves through prayer.

That's true for you and me too. That's why in Jude 20 and 21, God says, "Build yourselves up [founded] on your most holy faith...praying in the Holy Spirit; Guard and keep yourselves in the love of God" (AMP). God knows even better than we do that before we made Jesus our Lord, we weren't trained to live by faith. And He knows that even though we're following Him, our old, sinful ways will sneak up and try to pull us into sin.

Because of that, God has given us a special gift. It's a gift that will strengthen our spirit and give us victory over those old, sinful ways. That gift is the ability to pray in other tongues—the ability to let His Spirit pray through us. As we pray in tongues, Romans 8:26 tells us, the Holy Spirit "helps us in our weakness. We do not know what we ought to pray for, but the Spirit himself intercedes for us...."

Is it any wonder the Apostle Paul said, "I thank God that I speak in tongues more than all of you"? (See 1 Corinthians 14:18.) It's one of the most powerful tools God has given us. If you've never prayed in tongues, just ask the Holy Spirit to fill you now! (You can use the prayer in the back of this devotional as a guide.) When you ask Him for help, He won't let you down.

Then don't forget to pray in the spirit every day. Don't make the mistake that Peter made. When temptation comes to your door, don't let it surprise you. Make sure your spirit is strong enough to keep you from that sin.

talk the truth

"I watch and pray so I won't fall into temptation." (Matthew 26:41)

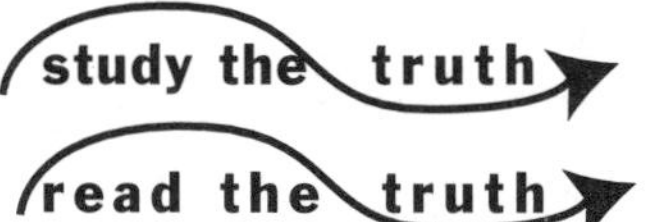
study the truth
read the truth

Ephesians 3:16; 6:18

Genesis 12,13; Matthew 7

January 7

GOD HAS SOMETHING TO SAY

"The sheep listen to his [the Shepherd's] voice and heed it, and he calls his own sheep by name and brings (leads) them out."

JOHN 10:3, AMP

Don't ever be so afraid of making a mistake that you miss out on following God's voice. Instead, trust Him to show you what His voice sounds like.

When Gloria and I first became Christians, we didn't have any idea how to hear God. But since the Bible promised we could do it, we began to *expect* to hear God's direction—and He began to give it.

I'll never forget the first time it happened to Gloria. She'd been reading the Bible and she just stopped for a few minutes to see if God would say something to her. Suddenly, down inside her, she heard Him say, *The light is on in your car.*

Of course, she didn't expect God to talk to her about something so unimportant, so she just ignored the thought and went on listening. Pretty soon, He said the same thing again. *The light is on in your car.* Finally, she got up and walked out to the car. Sure enough, the light was on.

Why would God bother with something as insignificant as a car light? Because He cares! He knew Gloria would have been stuck home alone with two small children if that battery had run down. God was looking out for her.

At the same time, He knew she was just learning to hear His voice, so He gave her an instruction she could follow without much risk. I mean, what if she'd made a mistake and it wasn't God's voice? She would have felt silly, but that's all. That's the way the Holy Spirit works. He will lead you one step at a time in a way that will help you, not hurt you. He will start out with little things and move on to larger ones when you know His voice better.

The biggest mistake you can make is to be afraid to follow that still, small voice, which is the number one way God leads you (Romans 8:14). So take time to listen today. Expect to hear His voice inside...because God has something to say!

talk the truth

"I listen to God's voice and follow it. He calls me by name and leads me." (John 10:3, AMP)

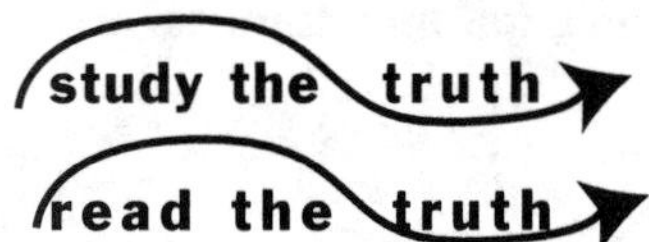
study the truth
read the truth

1 Corinthians 2:6-16

Genesis 14,15; Matthew 8

STEP ACROSS THE FAITH LINE

"Without weakening in his faith, he [Abraham] faced the fact that his body was as good as dead—since he was about a hundred years old—and that Sarah's womb was also dead. Yet he did not waver through unbelief regarding the promise of God, but was strengthened in his faith and gave glory to God."

ROMANS 4:19,20

Does someone in your family need Jesus? Do you need help getting rid of an addiction to drugs, alcohol or eating too much? Do you need strength to stand up in faith around your friends? If you have an "impossible" situation, you may be interested in something I've learned that I call "stepping over the faith line."

A *faith line* is what you need when you want God to do something that's "impossible" in your life. It's what you need when you want to be rock solid in your faith, and yet you have a difficult time staying focused on God's promises instead of the circumstances.

It's what can make you like faithful Abraham. He knew there was no natural way for God's promise to him—the promise for a son—to come true. Yet the Bible says Abraham ignored the natural evidence (that he and Sarah were so old) and believed only God's promise that they would have a child.

Somewhere he stepped across the line of faith. He made a solid decision to go with what God had said. And if you and I ever want to see God do the impossible in our lives, we will have to do the same thing!

How do you draw that faith line? First, search the Bible for God's promises and make a decision to believe what He says. Focus your attention on those promises until your faith becomes strong.

Then draw the line of faith in your mind and heart. Pray about the impossible problem and say, "In Jesus' Name, I'm stepping across the line of faith. From this moment on, I consider this matter done and I give God thanks for answering my prayer."

From then on, speak only as if your miracle has already happened. Turn your back on the doubts. God *will* do the impossible in your life when you dare to step across the faith line!

talk the truth

"I step over the faith line regarding God's promises to me. I believe them all!" (Romans 4:19,20)

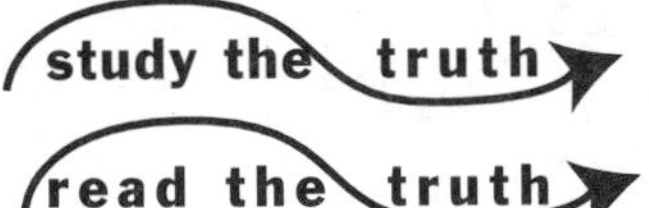
study the truth
read the truth

Romans 4:13-21

Genesis 16,17,18; Matthew 9,10

NO TIME FOR CLAY POTS

"In a large house there are things [vessels] made of gold and silver. But also there are things [pots] made of wood and clay. Some things are used for special purposes, and others are made for ordinary jobs."

2 Timothy 2:20, ICB

Are you destined for greatness?

Some Christians will humbly assure you they're not. "We can't all be golden vessels," they'll say. "The Bible says some of us are just called to be little clay pots." But the Bible doesn't say that!

Certainly some people will be "golden vessels" and some will be "clay pots," but we are the ones—not God—who determine which kind we will be. Second Timothy 2:21—the verse following the one quoted above—says, "If anyone makes him clean from evil things, he will be used for special purposes. He will be made holy, and the Master can use him. He will be ready to do any good work" (ICB).

Golden vessel or clay pot—destined for greatness or not—the choice is up to you!

Why then are so many Christians content to remain clay pots?

Because they lack one thing every golden vessel must have: commitment. They haven't made a lasting decision to separate themselves from worldly influences. They haven't been willing to follow the dreams God has for their lives.

But you don't have to be a clay pot! If you haven't yet made a commitment that will turn you into a golden vessel, admit it. Then take the time to get before God and study His Word—get your desires in line with His desires. Let the Holy Spirit deal with you until you're willing to leave the way of the world behind and walk in a better, higher way—God's way.

talk the truth

"I commit to be a vessel of gold, ready to do any good work. God uses me for special purposes!" (2 Timothy 2:20, ICB)

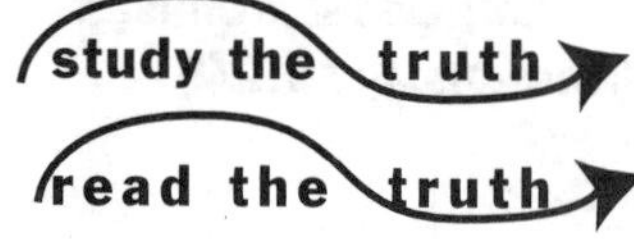
study the truth
read the truth

2 Timothy 2:15-26

Genesis 19,20; Matthew 11

REMEMBER GOD'S COMPASSION

"Yet this I call to mind and therefore I have hope: Because of the Lord's great love we are not consumed, for his compassions never fail. They are new every morning; great is your faithfulness."

Lamentations 3:21-23

God is faithful and full of compassion. He never runs out of it. Sure, you may already know that...but for it to do you any good, you have to remember it. You have to remember it again and again in order to ignite your faith and hope in God. As it becomes a part of you, you'll be preparing yourself for any difficult situation you might run into at home, school, work or anywhere else you might go.

So, make it a point—every morning—to remind yourself about God's faithfulness to you. Remind yourself of the promises that are yours in Jesus.

What are those promises? You'll find some of them in Psalm 103. Say them aloud to yourself now:

- He forgives all my sins.
- He heals all my diseases.
- He redeems my life from destruction.
- He crowns me with love and compassion.
- He satisfies my desires with good things so that my youth is renewed like the eagle's.
- He executes righteousness and justice for me against oppression. He sets me free.
- He makes His ways known to me.
- He gives me His grace and mercy when I need it.

Make it a point every morning this year to come back to this devotion and say those eight promises aloud, prayerfully. Turn the top corner of this page down right now as a reminder. Keep reading these promises, and by the end of this year, you'll be stronger in faith and more confident of God's love than you've ever been.

Don't just settle for *knowing* God's promises. *Remember* them every day and watch them come alive in you!

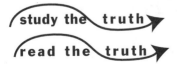

talk the truth

"I remember God's promises toward me today. He is faithful!" (Lamentations 3:21-23)

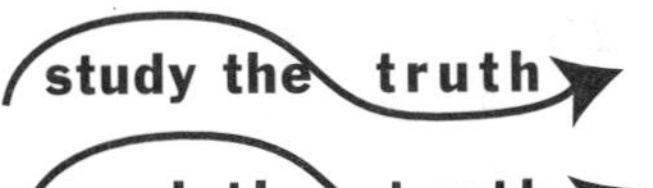
study the truth
read the truth

Psalm 103:1-17

Genesis 21,22; Matthew 12

January 11

DON'T LOOK AT THE STORM

"But when he saw the wind, he was afraid and, beginning to sink, cried out, 'Lord, save me!' Immediately Jesus reached out his hand and caught him. 'You of little faith,' he said, 'why did you doubt?'"

MATTHEW 14:30,31

If there's any way Satan can get your eyes away from God's promises to you, he'll do it. He'll cause trouble. He'll try to get you in a relationship with someone who doesn't serve the Lord. He'll try to make you think your parents don't love you. Satan will do anything he can to get your eyes off God's promises, because he knows that if he doesn't, you'll take those promises and beat his brains out with them.

That's what he did to Peter. Read the story in Matthew 14:22-32. What happened when Peter first jumped out of the boat after Jesus said, "Come!"? He walked right across the water without a problem. His faith was rock solid on the word Jesus had spoken to him.

But when he took his eyes off that word, he started looking at the storm. He started looking at the impossible thing he was doing. After all, he was a fisherman. All his training and experience told him when the waves were that high, you were going *under*. He started to focus on the circumstances instead of what Jesus said. When he did that, his faith slipped out of gear and he started to sink.

Don't let that happen to you. Once you get a promise from the Bible, hang on to it. Don't focus on anything else.

Satan will do everything he can to get you to let go of it. He'll stir up trouble around you. But don't let go of God's promises. Keep your eyes on God's Word until it's more real inside you than anything else. If you do, you'll be able to walk across the water just fine.

talk the truth

"I will not let go of God's promises. They are more real to me than anything else." (Matthew 14:30,31)

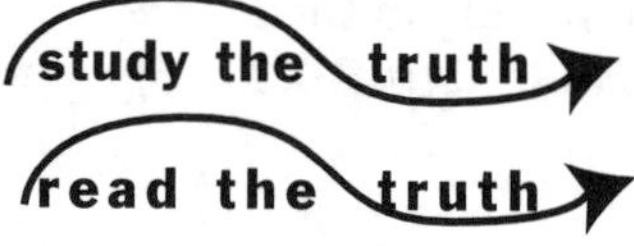
study the truth
read the truth

Matthew 14:22-33

Genesis 23,24; Matthew 13

OUR ONLY HOPE IS JESUS

"Therefore my heart is glad and my tongue rejoices; my body also will live in hope, because you will not abandon me to the grave, nor will you let your Holy One see decay."

ACTS 2:26,27

Some years ago, God said something to me that will impact my ministry forever. It was this: *The only hope that anyone has—anywhere in the world—is faith in Jesus Christ.*

In light of what's happening around us today, the truth of that statement is easier to see than ever before. There are diseases no person can heal and problems no person can solve. Even the brief successes people have are quickly overtaken by new and greater crises.

All too often, that's as true for Christians as it is for non-Christians. It shouldn't be, but it is. Christians are being killed by the same diseases that are devastating the rest of the world. They're being troubled by the same problems. And what's really sad is that many are walking around without hope—just like the rest of the world.

Why? Because the *only* hope that *anyone* has is faith in Jesus Christ. And many Christians don't know how to live by faith.

Instead of being filled with faith and knowing God's Word, they've been stuffed full of passed-down beliefs and superstitions. And they're suffering. When Satan hits them with sickness, disease, poverty, depression or pain, they often stand by helplessly as it destroys them. They simply don't know what else to do.

But *you* know. You're taking a higher way...your hope is in Jesus! So trust Him. And tell your friends—because they're longing to know—that their hope is in Him too.

talk the truth

"My hope is in Jesus." (Acts 2:26,27)

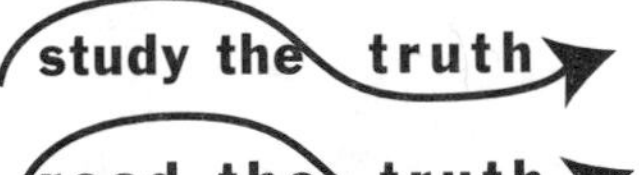
study the truth
read the truth

Mark 4:35-41

Genesis 25,26; Matthew 14

January 13

Gloria

IN GOOD TIMES AND BAD

"The Lord says, 'If someone loves me, I will save him. I will protect those who know me. They will call to me, and I will answer them. I will be with them in trouble. I will rescue them and honor them.'"

PSALM 91:14,15, ICB

God is called by many names. He is the Lord our Healer, our Provider and our Righteousness. He also promises to be our Rescuer. And in this troubled world, that may very well be what we need Him to be most often.

But there are many Christians who never experience God's mighty rescuing power because, instead of walking closely with Him day by day, they wait until danger strikes to call upon Him. That just doesn't work. If you want God to rescue you in the bad times, you have to spend time with Him in the good times. Why? Because God responds to your faith. Your faith, not your need, is what causes Him to act on your behalf. And you'll never be able to develop that kind of faith—that kind of trust and confidence in Him—if you don't spend enough time just getting to know Him.

First John 3:20-22 tells us that we can go to God without fear when we obey His commands and do what pleases Him. If we only serve God halfheartedly, then we won't have confidence that He will rescue us from trouble. When danger surrounds us, instead of being filled with faith, we'll find ourselves paralyzed with fear.

Love and serve God with your whole heart. Walk closely with Him in the good times. Then, when you need Him to be your Rescuer, you'll know without a doubt you can trust Him to care for you. And He will!

talk the truth

"I love and serve God with all my heart. He is always there to protect and rescue me." (Psalm 91:14,15, ICB)

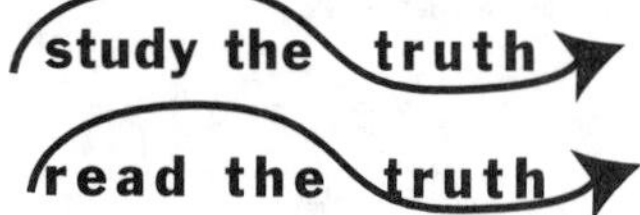
study the truth
read the truth

Psalm 108:1-6

Genesis 27,28; Matthew 15

UNDER YOUR FEET

> ***"The Lord said to my Lord: 'Sit at my right hand until I make your enemies a footstool for your feet.'"***
>
> **Acts 2:34,35**

Satan lost all his authority the day Jesus rose from the dead. Yet for the past 2,000 years, he's been running around as a spiritual outlaw—continuing to kill, steal and destroy anyone and anything he can.

But his time is running out. There's coming a day when God will completely put him out of business.

Most Christians know that's true, but they haven't really understood how it will happen. They haven't realized that *they* are the foot that will squash the works of Satan! *They* are the ones God will use to trample Satan's works.

The Bible clearly states that Jesus is the Head of the Church. You and I are the feet. We are the ones who will take His authority and power and stomp on sin and sickness and every demonic thing in this earth. We are the ones God will use, as Acts 2:35 says, to make Jesus' enemies "a footstool" for His feet.

That's what Jesus was telling us when He said, "Go into all the world and preach the good news.... In my name they will drive out demons...they will place their hands on sick people, and they will get well" (Mark 16:15-18). He was saying, "Go and be My feet." He was saying, "All power and authority everywhere has been given to Me. So take it and use it to put Satan under."

But instead of obeying Him, we've waited around wondering when God will stop thieves from stealing, gangs from fighting and bullies from bullying.

We are the reason it's taking so long! Jesus is waiting on us to step out in His power, put Satan in his place and win the world. So start putting the works of Satan under your feet—and let's kick that spiritual outlaw out of the earth's affairs!

talk the truth

"Satan and his works are under my feet!" (Acts 2:34,35)

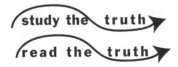

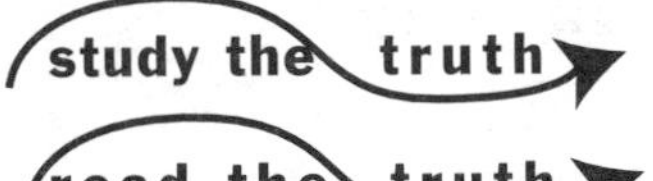
study the truth
read the truth

Genesis 3:1-14

Genesis 29,30; Matthew 16

Kenneth

DON'T WORRY

"Therefore do not worry and be anxious."

MATTHEW 6:31, AMP

God hates worry. Jesus preached against it. The Apostle Paul preached against it. The whole Bible speaks against worry because it was designed by Satan to produce stress, pain and death.

Yet many people act as if we're free to worry if we want to. But we're not! Worrying is a sin. It's one of those things the Bible directly commands us not to do.

What are you supposed to do then with all your concerns? In 1 Peter 5:7, God says you should "give *all* your worries to him" (ICB). *All.* Not 75 percent of them. Not all of them but the ones about dating. All of them!

Let me illustrate how that works. Let's say you were standing about 10 feet away from me and I tossed my car keys to you. If someone else were to come to me and say, "Hey, I need the keys to your car," I would say, "I can't help you. I gave them to my friend here. I don't have them anymore."

That's what you need to do with your worries. You need to toss them over to the Lord and not take them back. If Satan brings a worried thought to your mind, saying, *What if this terrible thing happens?* then you can tell him to talk to God about it. It's in His hands, not yours!

Once you do that, problems you've been worrying about for weeks will start to be solved. You'll no longer be tying God's hands with your worrying.

Remember, though, God will not take your worries away from you. You have to give them to Him and replace those worries with the promises in His Word. You are the one who has to keep your thoughts under control. But you can do it. The Greater One lives in you...and He is able to put you over to victory!

talk the truth

"I am not worried or anxious. I give all my worries to God." (Matthew 6:31, AMP)

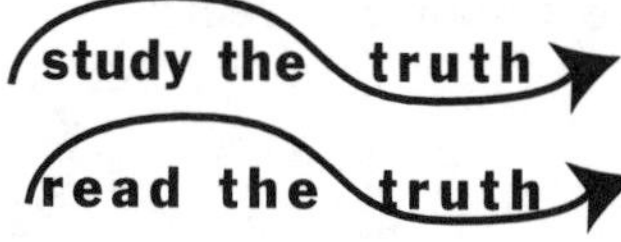
study the truth
read the truth

Psalm 55

Genesis 31,32,33; Matthew 17,18

January 16

JESUS CAN SET THEM FREE

"As you go, preach this message: 'The kingdom of heaven is near.' Heal the sick, raise the dead, cleanse those who have leprosy, drive out demons. Freely you have received, freely give."

MATTHEW 10:7,8

Some people say that some of the diseases on the rampage right now—diseases such as AIDS and cancer—are God's way of punishing sinful people. But there is absolutely no scriptural basis for that!

God doesn't bring disease on us. In fact, if there's anyone Who hates sickness and disease, it's Him. Satan is the one who's shouting a lie, trying to get us to believe God is the One Who's putting diseases on people. He knows that if the victims believe that, it will drive them further from God than ever...and that's his aim.

It's time you and I put a stop to that lie. Some time ago, the Lord told me, *Reach out to those who are suffering. Let them know I didn't do this to them. Let them know I'm the One Who can rescue them from it.*

That word was not just for me—it was for every one of us. It was for you. If you know someone at school, work or in your family with AIDS, cancer or any other disease, don't be afraid to approach them. Don't be afraid to let them know Jesus is Lord over it! Tell them God loves them, and He has the desire and the power to heal them.

God is not responsible for the suffering we're seeing around us. That's just a lie Satan is passing around. But if we do our job right, very soon another word will start spreading through our schools, hospitals and streets. The news will get out that Jesus Christ is not the captor—He's the One Who can set everyone free!

talk the truth

"I reach out to the suffering and let them know about God's love. He is the only One Who can rescue them." (Matthew 10:7,8)

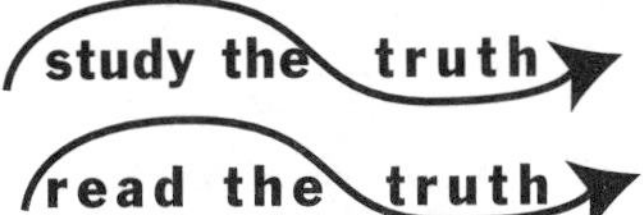
study the truth
read the truth

Matthew 9:18-26

Genesis 34,35; Matthew 19

January 17

Kenneth

LET GOD DO IT HIS WAY

"Elisha sent a messenger to say to him [Naaman], 'Go, wash yourself seven times in the Jordan, and your flesh will be restored and you will be cleansed.' But Naaman went away angry and said, 'I thought that he would surely come out to me and stand and call on the name of the Lord his God, wave his hand over the spot and cure me of my leprosy.'"

2 Kings 5:10,11

Too often we miss out on what God wants to do for us because He doesn't do it the way we think He should. We get an idea in our mind about how He could heal us, for instance. We think He might send some famous preacher to pray for us or that maybe He will knock us off our feet with a blast of His power. When He doesn't, we lose faith and foul up what He had actually planned to do.

That's what Naaman did. Naaman went to Elisha expecting to be healed in a certain way...and what Elisha told him to do was simple: "Wash yourself seven times in the Jordan." But Naaman didn't think his healing should come that way. He thought Elisha should heal him by waving his hand and praying to God.

Naaman stormed away angrily, and he wouldn't have been healed if one of his servants hadn't talked him into giving Elisha's instructions a try.

I used to be like that. I wanted spectacular experiences so much that I was missing out on the adventures God had for me. Once I realized that, I quit looking for feelings and dramatic displays and just began expecting God to keep His Word.

I remember I went to a meeting one night with my ankle messed up terribly. The pain was so sharp that it went from my foot all the way up to my shoulders. But I was expecting God to heal me.

During the praise time, I just worshiped God and ignored the pain in my foot. When the preaching started, I opened my Bible and listened intently. Sure enough, the next thing I knew, I was healed. The funny thing is that I don't know when it happened. I didn't feel anything. I didn't see any fireworks. It wasn't until I got about halfway to the door after the service and realized, *Glory to God, my foot's healed.*

Don't let your own ideas about how God works rob you of healing, prosperity or even hearing God's voice. Just trust Him and let Him do things His way!

talk the truth

"I commit my way to the Lord and trust in Him. God knows what's best for me!" (2 Kings 5:10,11)

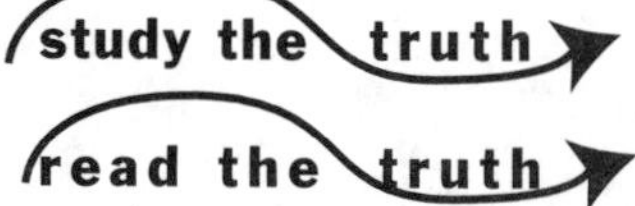
study the truth
read the truth

2 Kings 5:1-14

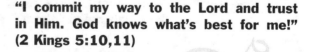

Genesis 36,37; Matthew 20

GET YOURSELF TOGETHER

"Do two walk together unless they have agreed to do so?"

Amos 3:3

When it comes to growing in faith, a lot of Christians feel like no matter how hard they try, they just can't seem to go any further.

If you'll watch them, you can see why. It's because they literally can't "get themselves together." One minute they'll be telling you, "Of course, I believe the Bible," and the next minute they'll be speaking something contrary to it. "I know God says He'll give me wisdom, but my grades in geometry are so bad, I'll probably flunk out."

Dig a little deeper, and you may find out that they've pulled their actions out of line with God's Word as well. "Well, you know, I can't possibly find time to pray, with all the activities I have!"

Faith just won't work for a person like that.

You see, you're a three-part being. You are a spirit. You have a soul (which is your mind, will and emotions), and you live in a body. You have to get all three to work together before you can grow in faith at all!

Start by feeding your spirit with God's Word. Just like your body produces physical strength when you feed it with food, your spirit produces spiritual strength when you feed it with His Word. That spiritual strength is called faith.

Next, bring your soul in line. Make a decision to not think bad, lustful or discouraging things. Think about God's promises and what the Bible says until your own thoughts agree with it.

Finally, bring your body in line. Once you truly get your spirit and soul focused on God's Word, that won't be hard. Begin teaching your body to act on the truth you've put in your mind and spirit, and it will follow right along.

So get yourself together! Bring your spirit, soul and body into harmony—and God's Word will take you as far as you want to go.

talk the truth

"I bring my spirit, soul and body in line with God's Word." (Amos 3:3)

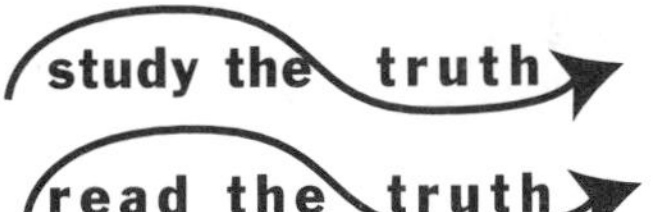
study the truth
read the truth

1 Thessalonians 5:14-24

Genesis 38,39; Matthew 21

January 19

Kenneth

FROM MESSES TO MIRACLES

"A fool's mouth is his undoing, and his lips are a snare to his soul."

PROVERBS 18:7

We have what we say. As Christians, we must understand that's an important biblical truth. We see it in Mark 11:23, Matthew 21:21, James 3:2 and many other verses. Yet we often let it slip.

Sometimes we talk like we have no hope instead of saying what's written in the Bible. And eventually we get what we've been asking for—a big mess.

If that's happened to you, remember—your life is a product of what you've been saying. If you feel like you have no friends, ask yourself what you've been saying. If you feel like your grades are at an all-time low, ask yourself what's been coming out of your mouth.

In order to change what you have, you must change what you're saying. Sure, it's easier said than done—but it must be said in order to be done!

How do you start? First, realize that it's something that you can't do by yourself. This is a spiritual principle, so it must be handled with spiritual power.

James 3:7-8 says the tongue can't be tamed like a wild animal. It takes God's wisdom—and His Word is His wisdom (Proverbs 2:6). It takes God's Word to get what we say in line.

Second, don't allow what you say to be influenced by anyone except the Holy Spirit. Be determined that everything you speak is full of love, faith and peace.

The third thing to do is what Jesus said in Mark 4:24: Pay attention to what you hear. Listen to yourself! Think, *Do I want what I just said to come true?* If the answer is no, then stop and correct yourself. Replace negative words with words that give God praise (Ephesians 5:4). Put the power that's in words to work *for* you instead of *against* you.

Change everything by changing your words. Ask God to help you be careful about what you say (Psalm 141:3). Stop making messes, and start making miracles!

talk the truth **"I watch my words, asking God to help me be careful about what I say." (Proverbs 18:7)**

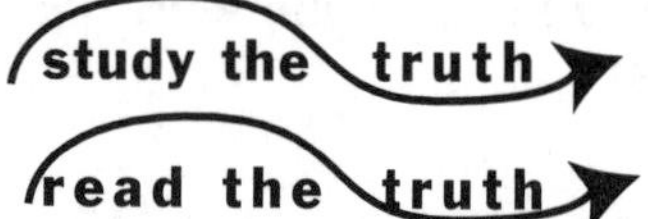

study the truth **James 3:1-13**

read the truth **Genesis 40,41; Matthew 22**

BELIEVE THE LOVE

"And so we know and rely on the love God has for us."

1 John 4:16

One day while praying, I asked God a simple question, "Lord, what do You want me to tell Your people?"

Without a moment's hesitation, He said: *Tell them how much I love them.*

He said it with so much love and compassion that mere words can't fully express it. For days afterward all I could think of was 1 John 4:16: "And so we know and rely on the love God has for us."

We've read and heard about God's love, but I don't think many of us have really believed how much He really loves us. If we did, it would totally change everything about us and everything around us.

It's that love that caused Jesus to lay down His life for us and to experience all the pains and weaknesses we experience. It's that love that says to us, even when we feel so unworthy, "Come to Me and get what you need. Don't be shy about it. I've been there. Come right to Me and receive help."

God is in love with you—so in love, He's given you everything He has! He's given you *all* the health, wisdom, prosperity and strength you'll *ever* need!

"But what about all the terrible things I've done?" you may ask.

That's what His compassion is for! It has taken care of your past and covered every sin and failure you ever had. All you have to do now is accept His love.

Think about 1 John 4:16 over and over. Say it to yourself again and again. "I believe the love Jesus has for me." Once it gets down into your heart, you'll never be the same again.

talk the truth **"I know and I believe the love God has for me." (1 John 4:16)**

study the truth **Psalm 139:1-18**

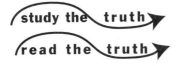

read the truth **Genesis 42,43; Matthew 23**

January 21

Kenneth

HEAVEN'S ECONOMY

"Giving thanks to the Father, who has... rescued us from the dominion of darkness and brought us into the kingdom of the Son he loves."

Colossians 1:12,13

If—in spite of all the Bible's promises about your prosperity and all the prayers you've prayed—you are still wondering how you'll have enough money for next week...or for college...or for the future, consider this: *Where do you think God will get the resources to meet your needs?*

Many Christians limit God without even knowing it—somehow they think all God can bless them with is the limited resources of this world. Their faith fails when they think of the troubled economy on earth, of the shortages and scarcity that surround them. They wonder, *How can God bless me in the middle of all this?*

If that's what you've been thinking, here's some news that will turn those thoughts around!

The Bible says God has "rescued us from the dominion of darkness and *brought us into the kingdom of the Son he loves."* This verse says He has literally taken us out of one place and put us into another. In other words, you're not just a citizen of this earth. You are not just American or Canadian or Australian, for example—you are first and foremost a citizen of God's kingdom.

That means this planet doesn't have any right to dictate to you whether or not you have everything you need. The Bible says God will meet your needs according to His glorious riches in Jesus! (Philippians 4:19). You can live by heaven's economy—rather than earth's—and in heaven there is always more than enough.

Wake up to all that's been made yours through Jesus. Wake up to the fact that you've been brought out of a world of poverty and into a kingdom where there's more than enough. Heaven's unlimited resources have been made available to you!

talk the truth

"God has rescued me from the dominion of darkness and brought me into His kingdom!" (Colossians 1:12,13)

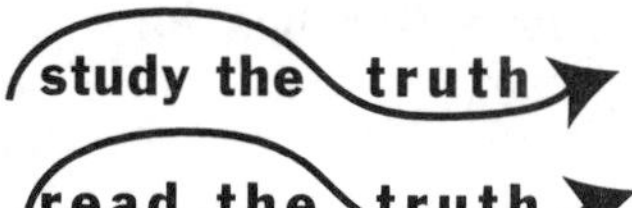
study the truth
read the truth

Psalm 105:37-45

Genesis 44,45; Matthew 24

LIVE LIKE JESUS

"But [Jesus] made himself nothing, taking the very nature of a servant, being made in human likeness."

PHILIPPIANS 2:7

Many people mistakenly think that Jesus was able to perform miracles and live without sin because He had divine powers that we don't have. Because of that, they have never really tried to live like He lived.

What they don't realize is that when Jesus came to earth, He chose to give up that advantage. He lived on earth not as God, but as a man. He had no ability to perform miracles until after the Holy Spirit came upon Him (Luke 3:22). When He worked wonders, it was by God's power—not His own (John 14:10).

When He prayed, He didn't pray like He was as powerful as God, but He prayed as a man who obeyed and walked *with* God. And, as Hebrews 5:7 says, His prayers were heard not because of His deity, but "because of His reverence toward God" (AMP).

Jesus, God's Son, put aside His privileges and powers while He lived as a man on earth. Once you grasp that, you can't help but get excited! Why? Because it means that you, as a Christian, filled with the same Holy Spirit as Jesus, have the same opportunity to live as He lived on earth. In fact, that's exactly what He wants. In John 17:18 He said to the Father, "As you sent me into the world, I have sent them into the world."

Jesus has sent *you* into the world to live as He lived. He's given you the ability (and the command) to live above sin, to live in close friendship with the Father, to preach God's Word, to heal the sick, to drive out evil spirits and to train others to spread His Word.

Once you realize that, you'll get rid of any doubting thoughts and insecure feelings that have held you back. You'll begin to live as Jesus meant for you to live—not as a sin-filled person, but as a sinless child of God. Then those around you will actually begin to see Jesus *in you*.

talk the truth

"I live the same way Jesus lived in the world — sinless, in close friendship with God, following His commands." (Philippians 2:7)

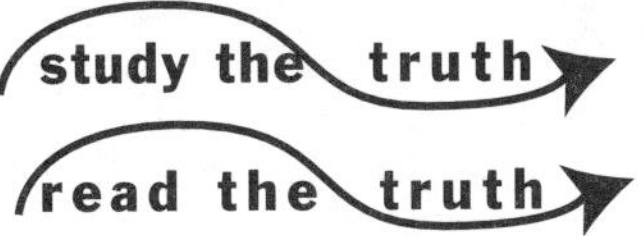
study the truth
read the truth

1 John 3:1-8

Genesis 46,47,48; Matthew 25,26

GROW UP!

"Like newborn babies, crave pure spiritual milk, so that by it you may grow up in your salvation."

1 PETER 2:2

Have you ever been in a room full of babies, or baby-sat several infants at once? Well, you can get your hands full really fast. Some babies will start crying and screaming for no reason whatsoever. And toddlers will push and whine to get their way...

The sad thing is that when a bunch of "spiritual babies" get together, it's just about the same way! Of course, there's nothing wrong with being a spiritual baby. All of us start out that way. When we first make Jesus the Lord of our life, we're much like newborn babies. We're not very strong or well-developed. We curiously try to learn how to operate in our new life. That's how we all have to begin. But God never meant for us to stay that way.

That's why in 1 Peter 2:2 He says we should "crave pure spiritual milk, so that by it you may grow up...." He expects us to grow up! He intends for us to feed on His Word, eventually developing teeth so we can eat solid food instead of simple milk. He wants us to become mature sons and daughters.

Start finding the nutrition in His Word and enjoy the reward of growing up in Him today!

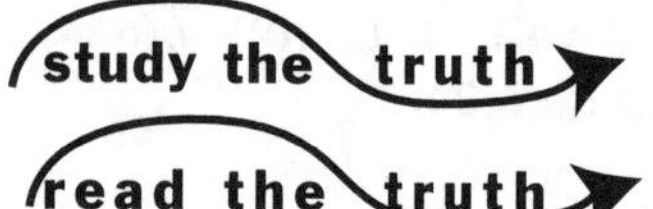

talk the truth **"I crave the pure spiritual milk of the Word and grow up in the Lord." (1 Peter 2:2)**

study the truth **Ephesians 4:12-16**

read the truth **Genesis 49,50; Matthew 27**

DO YOUR OWN PRAYING

"Is any one of you in trouble? He should pray."

JAMES 5:13

If you're in trouble, you need to pray. That's what the Bible says. Notice it doesn't say your pastor or a friend needs to pray for you. It says *you* need to pray.

Too often we try to find a "quick fix" to our problems by asking everyone else to pray for us. There's nothing wrong with having others pray for you, but you'll never get to a place of lasting victory until you begin to pray yourself.

The biggest church in the world is in Seoul, Korea. It's pastored by Dr. David Cho, and the last I heard it had more than 700,000 members—it's huge! How did that church grow to be so large? According to Dr. Cho, the key is the prayers of the people. Praying is a way of life in that church.

I've even heard that when their church members have family problems or problems in their personal lives, before anything else is done, the members are told to fast and pray for 24 hours.

We need to do more of that in our churches. We need to train people to do their own praying instead of expecting others to pray for them all the time.

You see, if I pray for God to solve a problem for you, you may enjoy success for a while, but then another problem will come along because you'll still be making the same mistakes that got you in trouble the first time. If, however, you stop and pray *yourself*—if you train yourself to start seeking God and all He has for your life—you'll get lasting answers. You'll learn how to make changes in your life that will keep the problems from coming up again.

You have the privilege to go to God any time you want. He has every solution to every problem you'll ever have, and He's just waiting for you to come to Him so He can give you the answer. It may take some private time alone with Him for you to hear it, but He will never let you down.

talk the truth

"I will always remember to pray—for God always answers." (James 5:13)

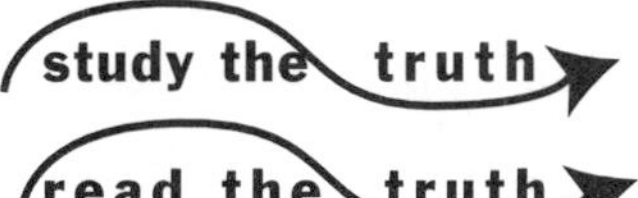
study the truth
read the truth

Psalm 5

Exodus 1,2; Matthew 28

January 25

USE YOUR AUTHORITY!

"I pursued my enemies and overtook them... they fell beneath my feet."

Psalm 18:37,38

If you've been worrying about what Satan is planning to do to you, it's time you made a switch. It's time you put Satan under your feet!

Jesus has already given you everything you need to do it. He's given you the power to speak God's Word and stop evil spirits from hindering you. You can even speak what the Bible says and instruct angels to work on your behalf (Matthew 16:19).

What's more, you've been given the power to use the mighty Name of Jesus. His Name will cause every knee to bow—in heaven, on earth and under the earth (Philippians 2:9,10).

So don't waste time worrying about Satan and his forces. Stand up with the authority God's given to you. Stop the evil spirits that try to destroy your home, your friends, your school, your church and your nation. Speak God's Word and enforce it with the Name of Jesus.

You have the authority. Learn to use it, and before long Satan will be worrying about *you!*

talk the truth **"I use the authority God gave me by speaking God's Word and standing in the Name of Jesus." (Psalm 18:37,38)**

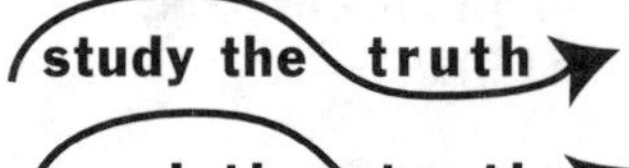

study the truth **Matthew 16:13-27**

read the truth **Exodus 3,4; Mark 1**

January 26

CHRIST IN YOU!

One time years ago, I was praying in our little house in Tulsa, Oklahoma. I was repeating 1 John 4:4, "Greater is He that is in me, than he that is in the world" (KJV). Suddenly, I realized something extraordinary—*God is in me!*

It hit me like someone slapped me on the face. Suddenly I wasn't just a poor preacher living in a tiny, run-down house anymore! God lives in me! That changed my thinking about so many things. I looked at my hands and it hit me. *His fingers are in my fingers.* I looked at my legs. *His legs are in my legs. His feet are even in my feet...so if I walk into danger, He walks into danger.*

Now, when I hear people say, "My prayers don't even get out of my room," I am shocked. I just want to say, "Out of your room? They don't need to get any farther from you than your nose! *He's inside you!* The Creator of the world has 'moved in' to your life!"

"God decided to let his people know this rich and glorious truth which he has for all people. This truth is Christ himself, who is in you. He is our only hope for glory."

COLOSSIANS 1:27, ICB

Wow! If you'll spend some time thinking about it, it'll really hit you. It will eventually change your whole life. Think about it—when you go to school, He goes with you. When you go out with your friends, He goes with you. "As God has said: 'I will live with them and walk among them, and I will be their God, and they will be my people'" (2 Corinthians 6:16).

Jesus is in you. That's the most magnificent truth in the Bible. Let it become a reality to you today.

talk the truth

"The Creator of the universe is in my life!" (Colossians 1:27, ICB)

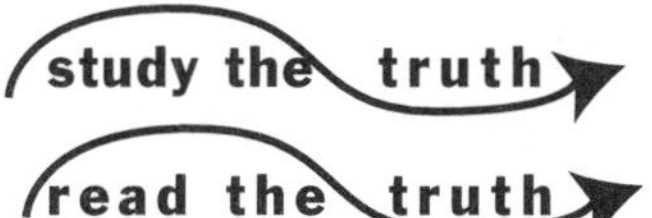
study the truth
read the truth

Colossians 1:13-27

Exodus 5,6; Mark 2

January 27

GOD WANTS YOU WELL

"'But I will restore you to health and heal your wounds,' declares the Lord."

JEREMIAH 30:17

God wants you well! He wants you healthy and strong in every area of your life. First, He wants you to be spiritually strong. Strong in faith. Strong in His Word. Strong in who Jesus has made you to be. Strong in His love.

He also wants you to be well in your mind—to be strong and in control of your emotions. He wants you to make healthy choices that are in line with what He desires for you. He wants you to be free from worries about home, school and activities.

Finally, He wants your body to be well. He wants you free from pain, sickness and disease.

Your Heavenly Father wants you well!

What's more, He *needs* you well. He needs you living in victory and health so that you can teach others how to do it. We're living in a time when this is absolutely necessary. There's no more time for Christians to limp along, uninformed and unprepared for Satan's attacks.

In fact, here's what the Lord has told me:

As the days go by, life in the earth will become more dangerous. People will have to grow in their understanding of what Jesus has done for them. They'll also have to grow in the "how-to's" of living by faith in order to live in the great, overcoming way I have planned for them.

Jesus wants us to be healthy and strong as a living example to a world that's filled with fear—an example of His love, kindness and power. So commit yourself to getting well and growing strong in every area of your life today!

talk the truth

"The Lord restores my health and heals my wounds." (Jeremiah 30:17)

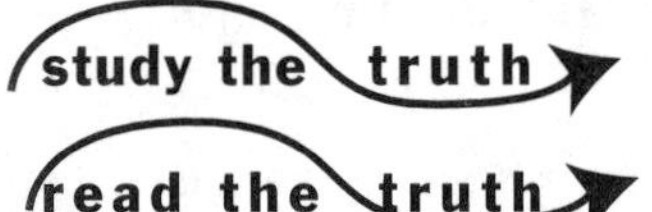
study the truth
read the truth

Psalm 107

Exodus 7,8; Mark 3

DON'T BE ROCKY GROUND

There seem to be a whole lot of "rocky" Christians these days. Initially, they get excited about the Bible. They'll hear someone talk about prayer, for instance, and they'll go home saying, "Yes! God will answer all my prayers!" But then, somehow, things don't work out like they thought.

Their friends don't all become Christians overnight. They go through some disappointments. Classmates make fun of them. Then, before you know it, their faith has faded away.

If you don't want that to happen to you, make up your mind right now that you won't let the rough times defeat you. Decide now that you will hang on to God's Word even when hard days and criticism come—because, I guarantee you, they *will* come.

"Others, like seed sown on rocky places, hear the word and at once receive it with joy. But since they have no root, they last only a short time. When trouble or persecution comes because of the word, they quickly fall away."

MARK 4:16,17

When you decide to live a life of faith, you don't get rid of trouble. You learn to overcome it. You'll have problems, but the difference is *now* you have the answer—God's Word.

So thank God that through Jesus you have the power to defeat Satan. When he brings problems and disappointments your way, you don't have to surrender and let them run you down. Just keep standing in faith until you win.

If you get knocked down, get back up and say, "Look here, Satan. God's Word is in my heart and I say what it says. I'll believe it and act on it until God's promises show up all around me. If you don't believe me, just hide and watch!"

If you'll take that attitude, no matter what Satan does, he'll never make a "rocky" Christian out of you!

talk the truth

"God's Word is in my heart and I can't be kept down. God always causes me to win in Jesus!" (Mark 4:20; Romans 8:37)

study the truth
read the truth

2 Corinthians 4:6-18

Exodus 9,10; Mark 4

Kenneth

January 29

JUST DO IT

"Indignant because Jesus had healed on the Sabbath, the synagogue ruler said to the people, 'There are six days for work. So come and be healed on those days, not on the Sabbath.'"

LUKE 13:14

Religion—trying to follow God without having a relationship with Him—is dangerous. Many of the young men and women you know may be turned off to Christianity because that's what they think it is. But the difference is that religion would rather debate about healing than see someone healed. Religion would rather argue about God's power to set people free than actually see someone set free.

There's an example of that in Luke 13. Jesus healed a woman who had been crippled for 18 years. Think of it—a woman set free after being caught in Satan's grasp for nearly two decades. You'd think the temple rulers would have been thrilled at what Jesus had done. But, no! They were angry because He'd done it *on the wrong day* (the Sabbath).

Do you know what's worse? Those very same religious leaders who criticized Jesus for healing on the Sabbath could have prayed for healing for that woman themselves on any of the other six days of the week, if they'd cared enough to do it.

That's why Jesus was so aggravated with them. They had the covenant of Abraham that Jesus was ministering on. But their religion had kept that woman crippled instead of setting her free. It always does.

Remember that next time someone tries to sidetrack you into a debate about healing or God's power. If someone needs God's power to rescue them, just stop what you're doing and pray right there...don't debate about it!

That's the difference between religion and God's love. Religion argues. Love acts. Choose love today.

talk the truth **"I have a *relationship* with God today, so I will move out in love." (Luke 13:14)**

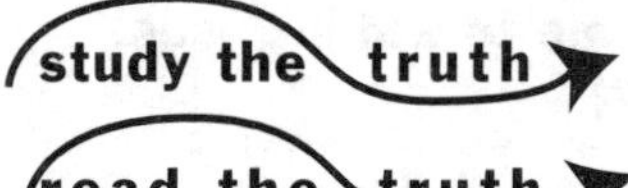
study the truth
read the truth

study the truth **Luke 13:11-17**

read the truth **Exodus 11,12,13; Mark 5,6**

MAKE HIS WORD THE LAST WORD

"I am the Alpha and the Omega, the Beginning and the End," says the Lord, "who is and who was and who is to come, the Almighty."

REVELATION 1:8, NKJV

Jesus is the beginning and the ending of all. When He told us that in the book of Revelation, He wasn't just giving us some information about Himself. He was giving us a powerful truth we can apply today!

Let me show you how. He said He is the beginning. So no matter what challenge or situation you may be facing right now, you need to start with Him. John 1:1 says Jesus is the Word (AMP). That means, if you're going to start with Jesus, you have to start with the Word. Don't do anything until you find out what the Bible has to say about your situation.

Then, continue to stand on the Word. As Colossians 1:23 says, "Continue strong and sure in your faith. You must not be moved away from the hope that Good News gave you" (ICB).

Continue in faith. Everything Satan does, every challenge he brings you, is intended to make you throw away God's promises and doubt His Word. So don't let go of them, no matter what may happen. Settle it with God in prayer and hold on to those promises forever.

Then end with the Word. Jesus said He was the first and the last. That means the doctor's word is not the last word. Even the word of your pastor is not the last word. The Word of Jesus is the last Word!

Remember this: You are now what the Bible says you are. You have what the Bible says you have. And you can do what the Bible says you can do. You just need to begin to believe it and say it aloud in faith.

Now celebrate the victory. Yes, now! You don't have to wait to see the outcome to celebrate. You have Jesus' Word on the matter, so you know beyond any doubt that your answer —your victory—is coming. Once you've settled it by believing God, you can be sure that He will have the last word!

talk the truth

"Whatever situations I face, I will start, continue and finish them with God's Word." (Revelation 1:8, NKJV)

study the truth
read the truth

Proverbs 1:1-9

Exodus 14,15; Mark 7

Kenneth

January 31

FOUR WORDS THAT WORK

"Therefore I tell you, whatever you ask for in prayer, believe that you have received it, and it will be yours."

MARK 11:24

Believing. That's the key to everything in the Christian life. It's the way we tap into the very power of God Himself. You might already know that, but do you know how to put it into action?

It's as simple as doing what Mark 11:24 says to do. Simply believe you receive. Say that: "I believe I receive."

Something happens inside you when you say those words. I don't understand how, but it does. I don't understand how my digestive system knows what to do when I swallow something, but it does. All I have to do is take a bite of food and it goes to work. It just happens. That's the way the body is made.

In much the same way, when you feed on the promises in God's Word and "swallow" them into your spirit by saying, "I believe I receive," faith is released. It just happens.

When you constantly say, "I believe I receive my healing" or "I believe I receive my needs met," *and then quote the scriptures that back those words,* faith is released. And faith brings power to meet those needs.

Say those words when you pray. Say them when you read the Bible. And be sure to say them in the face of darkness, when it looks like nothing is happening. When everything looks the worst, say it the loudest. *I believe I receive!*

Activate your faith today—by making those four key words the most important words in your vocabulary.

talk the truth **"*I believe I receive* what I ask for in prayer." (Mark 11:24)**

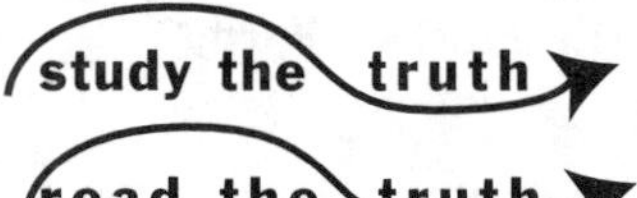
study the truth
read the truth

Mark 11:12-24

Exodus 16,17; Mark 8

HIT HIM WITH THE ROCK

"The Lord is my shepherd, I shall not be in want. He makes me lie down in green pastures, he leads me beside quiet waters."

PSALM 23:1,2

Have you ever thought about David and wondered how a shepherd boy could become a man the Bible says was "after God's own heart?" A man so spiritually strong that God chose him to be king? I have.

In fact, I asked God about it, and He showed me that David was such a powerhouse because he saw things the way God saw them. He received wisdom through hours of praying and focusing on His Word. I imagine the day he wrote Psalm 23, he was just spending time with God, when suddenly supernatural understanding came to him and he said, "The Lord is *my* Shepherd!"

He thought about taking care of the sheep when he was a boy and he started to get excited. *That time when that lion and bear came, God gave me victory,* he thought. *My God will fight for me! The* Lord *is my Shepherd! I have everything I need!*

That revelation was so strong in David that when Goliath tried to make a fool out of Israel, David went after him. Goliath couldn't intimidate David because David understood the situation as God saw it. That supernatural understanding enabled David to say, "You come against me with sword and spear and javelin, but I come against you in the Name of the Lord Almighty!" (1 Samuel 17:45). That supernatural understanding enabled David to send a rock sailing into that giant's brain.

Is Satan out to destroy you? Do what David did. Pray and study God's Word. Sing praises to Him. Spend time with Him until you get a supernatural understanding of Who He is. Then tell Satan, "You can't kill me. The Lord is my Shepherd!" Hit him with the rock of supernatural knowledge, and you'll knock him flat every time.

talk the truth

"The Lord is my shepherd, I shall not be in want. He makes me lie down in green pastures. He leads me beside quiet waters." (Psalm 23:1,2)

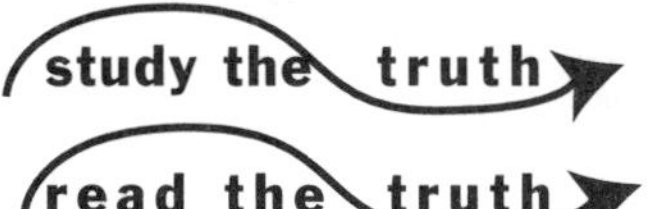
study the truth
read the truth

Psalm 23

Exodus 18,19; Mark 9

February 2

THANK YOU, LORD

"Give thanks in all circumstances, for this is God's will for you in Christ Jesus."

1 Thessalonians 5:18

Notice that this scripture tells us to give thanks *in* all circumstances, not *for* all circumstances. When tragedy or temptation strikes, God doesn't want us to thank Him for them. He's not the one who brings trouble. He's the One Who provides a way to escape from it...and *that's* what we thank Him for.

If you read Matthew, Mark, Luke and John, you'll find that Jesus never gave thanks for sickness or death. Instead, when He found them, He overcame them with God's power.

Say, for instance, that your family is having difficulty coming up with the money to pay the monthly electric bill. Now that could be a real problem. But don't thank God for it. Instead, give Him thanks *in* it. Thank Him that the spirit of poverty cannot stay in your house. Thank Him that He will supply your family with everything they need—whether it be the electricity itself, the money for the electric bill or wisdom for the way the finances are spent. Thank Him that when you rely on Him, He won't let you down.

So give thanks the way Jesus gave thanks—not for the trouble Satan brings, but for the victory God has given you over it!

talk the truth **"I give thanks *in* all circumstances—for God has given me victory!" (1 Thessalonians 5:18)**

study the truth **John 11:1-48**

read the truth **Exodus 20,21; Mark 10**

OUT OF THE SHADOW

Jesus came to *take away* sin. Do you realize what that means? It means that God, through the blood of Jesus, has so completely done away with the power of sin that you, as a Christian, can live as if it never existed.

Sure, you'll still make mistakes sometimes. But you don't have to live under the shadow of that sin five seconds if you'll receive God's forgiveness and turn away from it.

"But I just feel awful about that time I..."

It doesn't make any difference how you feel. Do it by faith. Learn to be quick to ask forgiveness and turn away from doing it again.

"The next day John saw Jesus coming toward him. John said, 'Look, the Lamb of God, who takes away the sin of the world!'"

JOHN 1:29

I remember one time in particular when I was in a situation like that. I'd made a huge mistake, and I was supposed to go preach that night. I felt so guilty that I just told the Lord I wouldn't preach.

Suddenly the Holy Spirit spoke up inside me. *Did you confess that sin before Me, Kenneth?*

"Yes, I did."

Do you think Jesus' blood doesn't do any good anymore? Do you think it can't set you free and make you holy?

"No! Absolutely not!" I answered. "I would never think that!"

Well, that's what you're doing, He said. *I gave you My Word that when you admit your wrong before Me, I would not only forgive you of it, but I'd wash it away and forget about it forever. It's disrespectful for you to keep bringing it up.*

I'm telling you, I dropped the matter right then and there, and I went into that service and preached for two and a half hours on God's forgiveness!

Don't let feelings of guilt rob you of the power of the victory Jesus has won for you. Ask for forgiveness and turn away from what you did that was wrong. Step out by faith from under the shadow of sin and into the bright light of God's forgiveness today!

talk the truth

"I step away from any sin in my life and receive God's forgiveness." (John 1:29)

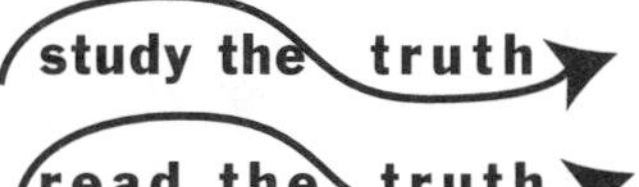
study the truth
read the truth

John 1:1-34

Exodus 22,23; Mark 11

Gloria

February 4

LET PEACE RULE

"And let the peace (soul harmony which comes) from the Christ rule (act as umpire continually) in your hearts—deciding and settling with finality all questions that arise in your minds.... And be thankful—appreciative, giving praise to God always."

Colossians 3:15, AMP

Have you been praying that God will show you whether something you want to do is all right with Him or not? Have you been wondering if it's all right to date a certain someone? Have you questioned whether you're friends with the right people? Let the peace of Jesus be your guide. Let it help you find the answer. If you're ready to do something and you realize you don't have peace, don't do it.

Remember, though, that this leading of the Holy Spirit on the inside of you is something you have to be careful to watch and listen for. He'll give you either a subtle sense of uneasiness or a subtle sense of peace. He generally won't just come up and knock you against your locker at school and tell you what you need to do. The main way He speaks to you is by what the Bible calls an "inward witness."

So you have to listen. You can't just stay busy doing the things of the world all the time and expect to hear. You have to take time to *carefully* listen.

Also, watch out for strife. If you're irritated and upset about things in your life, it will be very hard to receive that quiet guidance from the Holy Spirit. So pay close attention to the instructions at the end of this scripture and "be thankful—appreciative, giving praise to God always." Always have a thankful, grateful heart. You'll find it much easier to hear the "umpire of peace" when He makes a call.

talk the truth

"I let Jesus' peace rule as an umpire in my heart. It settles every question for me." (Colossians 3:15, AMP)

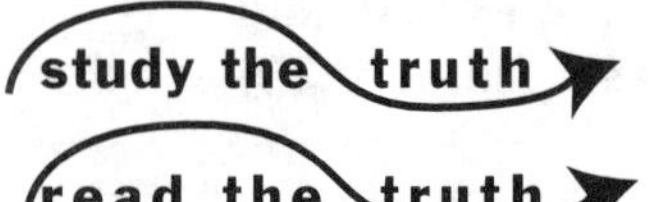
study the truth
read the truth

Psalm 95:1-7

Exodus 24,25; Mark 12

February 5

UNCOMMON PROTECTION

"The thief comes only to steal and kill and destroy."

JOHN 10:10

Considering how much Satan hates people and how determined he is to destroy them, it's no wonder we see so much tragedy and disaster in the world. In fact, it's surprising we don't see *more!*

I asked the Lord about that one time, and He told me it takes the forces of darkness a long time to set up major disasters. Take the airplane industry, for example. It has many rigid rules and it works hard to keep safety first—because otherwise no one would fly in planes. In a system like that, Satan has to work extremely hard to cause disasters.

He can't just come roaring in and start tearing things apart whenever he wants. If he could, he'd blow every plane out of the sky tonight. But he can't do it.

Why? Because he's limited. The Bible says he's limited to using things that are "common to mankind" (1 Corinthians 10:13). He has to line up certain things in this natural, human realm before he can lay a finger on you. He has to use people to get his work done.

But—this is the great part—*we're* not bound to what's "common to mankind." We're free to use what's common to *God!* We fight spiritual wars with "uncommon" weapons. What does that mean? It means you ought to tie Satan to the train tracks.

Satan can't come in and start destroying things and stealing from you unless he can get you into a place of sin, doubt, ignorance, unforgiveness or disobedience. So if he's been giving you trouble, ask the Holy Spirit to show you where you've let those things in. Then ask for forgiveness and turn from those sins.

Once you've done that, pull out the weapons God has given you and fire away on automatic. Pull out His Word. Pull out prayer. Pull out faith and use it to tie Satan to the tracks. Use the "uncommon" power of God to keep Satan tied up and he won't be able to put anything over on you.

talk the truth

"I operate in the 'uncommon' power of God today. I read His Word, pray and stand in faith...and Satan can't touch me!" (John 10:10)

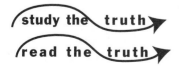

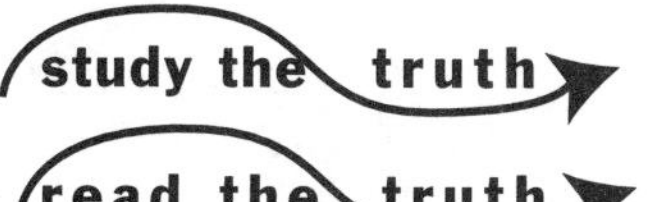
study the truth
read the truth

Ephesians 6:10-18

Exodus 26,27,28; Mark 13,14

February 6

YOUR FINAL AUTHORITY

"For I am the Lord, I do not change."

MALACHI 3:6, NKJV

The way the world does things is unreliable and unstable. Desperate words of uncertainty are crying out every day through radio, television and newspapers. Everything around us seems to be out of control.

But the good news is that if you're a Christian, you have something you can depend on: the unchanging Word of God!

God doesn't talk out of both sides of His mouth. He doesn't say one thing today and something else tomorrow. He is the same yesterday, today and forever (Hebrews 13:8).

If you make His Word the final say in your life, it will give you a solid place to stand when everything else around you falls away. If you'll let what God says settle the issue, you'll be confident when others are confused. You'll be at peace when others are under pressure. You'll be overcoming when others are being overcome!

What does it mean to make God's Word the final say? It means believing what the Bible says instead of believing what people say. It means believing what God says instead of what Satan says. It means believing what His promises say instead of what the circumstances say.

Make a decision in your heart to do that today. Make up your mind to live by faith in what God says and not by what you see happening. Fearlessly commit yourself to what's written in the Bible, and there won't be anything in this unstable world that can steal your security.

talk the truth — **"I make God's Word the *final* word for every area of my life." (Malachi 3:6, NKJV)**

Psalm 9:1-10

read the truth — **Exodus 29,30; Mark 15**

THANK GOD INSTEAD

> ***"If it is possible, as far as it depends on you, live at peace with everyone."***
>
> **ROMANS 12:18**

When I first became a Christian, it was almost impossible for me to live at peace with anyone! Almost every time I opened my mouth, I said something mean. I was constantly hurting the people closest to me. In fact, I spoke more harshly to them than to anyone else.

I criticized Gloria's driving so much that she nearly refused to drive when I was with her. I criticized my family so much that they began to avoid me. I didn't want to be so heartless, but I couldn't help it. I had a long-developed habit of speaking harshly and didn't know how to change it.

Then I found Ephesians 5:4. It said, "[Let there be] no coarse, stupid, or flippant talk; these things are out of place; you should rather be thanking God" (NEB). When I read that, I realized I needed to replace the words I was used to saying with words that gave thanks to God. That would solve my problem. I realized I couldn't criticize those around me if I was always thanking God for them.

Immediately I decided to put this to work in my life. I was rushing into my son's room one day, ready to give him a piece of my mind about something he had done, when I recognized that old behavior coming back. I just stopped myself and said, "The Bible says this kind of behavior is wrong, so I'm going to stop and thank God." I wasn't nearly as angry after I spent a few minutes praising and thanking Him.

If you've developed the habit of speaking harshly, start changing that habit today. When someone angers you at school, at home, on the job or wherever, and you're tempted to tear into them, stop! Instead, take a few moments to give thanks and praise to God. Once you begin thinking about how good God is, those harsh, angry words will just slip away unspoken.

talk the truth

"Before acting out, I will stop to praise and thank God so that I may live in peace." (Romans 12:18)

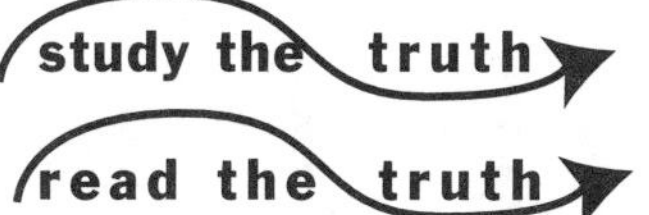
study the truth
read the truth

Ephesians 4:26-32; 5:1-4

Exodus 31,32; Mark 16

February 8

TITHE WITH JOY

"Soon you will go into the land the Lord your God is giving you to own.... You must take some of the first harvest of crops.... Go to the place where the Lord your God will choose to be worshiped."

DEUTERONOMY 26:1,2, ICB

Tithing is giving 10 percent of your income to God. Most Christians aren't very excited about it. But they should be—and they *would* be if they understood how to do it properly.

Tithing stirs up your faith. It activates God's power in your life when you do it thankfully and joyfully, expecting God to meet your needs.

In Deuteronomy 26:8-9, God told the Israelites exactly what to say when they brought their tithes. He instructed them to recognize the fact that He brought them out of the bondage of Egypt and to say:

"So the Lord brought us out of Egypt with a mighty hand and an outstretched arm, with great terror and with miraculous signs and wonders. He brought us to this place and gave us this land, a land flowing with milk and honey."

What does that have to do with you and me? God has done the same thing for us! He's brought us out of a life of bondage and poverty into a life that's filled with the fullness of God.

So when you bring your tithe to the Lord—whether you're tithing from an allowance, a paycheck or a gift—follow the example set by the Israelites. Make it a time of joy, a time of remembering again the wonderful things Jesus has done for you.

Thank Him for rescuing you from a land of darkness and bringing you into His promised land. Thank Him that it is a land of mercy, joy, peace and prosperity.

Tithe in faith, expecting the rich promises God has given you to become even more evident in your life. You may soon find tithing to be one of the most exciting things you do.

talk the truth

"I faithfully bring my tithe to God, thanking Him for all He has done for me." (Deuteronomy 26:1,2, ICB)

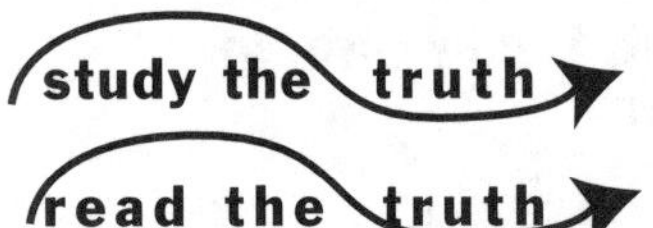
study the truth
read the truth

Deuteronomy 26

Exodus 33,34; Luke 1

CALLED TO INTERCESSION

"Blessed are those who mourn, for they will be comforted."

Matthew 5:4

Do you know what Jesus was talking about when He said those words? He was talking about the yearning of a person who prays. He was teaching about the comfort that comes to the one who prays when he is assured by the Holy Spirit that he has *prayed through.*

To *pray through* means "to break through the barriers that have stopped God's work in the lives of others." It means praying until you've pushed back the forces of darkness that surround them.

There's a desperate need for young men and women who are willing to do that today. There's a need for young people who will go before God and reach out with His compassion and love for the lost, the sick and the hurting people in this world. There's a need for warriors in prayer who will stick with it until they have the confidence and peace—in their spirits—that every wall is broken and every bit of captivity has been destroyed. There's a need for warriors who will *pray through.*

God is looking for young men and women like that—and there are certain things that won't happen on this earth until He finds them. There are moves of God that won't come until someone prays for them to come.

If you're wondering if you're one of those who's been called to prayer, then you probably are. God is calling young people everywhere to experience that unique kind of yearning and comfort that only the one who prays knows.

Somewhere in the world, someone needs you to pray for him or her. Pray them through to victory today.

talk the truth

"I will *pray through* the barriers that have stopped God's work in the lives of others." (Matthew 5:4)

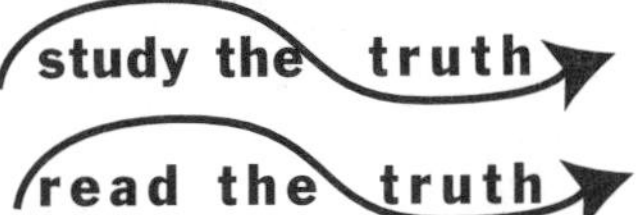
study the truth
read the truth

Luke 2:1-38

Exodus 35,36; Luke 2

February 10

PUNCH A HOLE IN THE DAM

"So [Israel] came up to Baal-perazim, and David smote the [Philistines] there. Then David said, God has broken my enemies by my hand, like the bursting forth of waters; therefore they called the name of that place Baal-perazim (Lord of breaking through)."

1 CHRONICLES 14:11, AMP

"*Like the bursting forth of waters*"...I love that phrase! It paints such a powerful and true picture of victory.

Do you remember the story of the little boy who saw a leak in the dam and plugged up the hole with his finger? He knew that the force of the water flowing through that one tiny hole would have enlarged the leak with every second that passed. And, as the dam gave way to the pressure, that tiny trickle would have quickly become a raging flood.

So all you have to do is the opposite of that little boy. Instead of plugging up the hole with your finger, use your spiritual fist to punch a big hole into that wall of problems—that dam of trouble—that's been holding you back. Dig a hole in it with God's Word.

Then keep tearing away at that single hole by speaking out your faith, day after day. Don't quit! Because God's forces are backed up behind you like an ocean of water. Each time you speak His Word in faith, they leak through. The more you speak and the more you pray, the bigger that leak will get until one day—POW!—that dam of trouble will break.

Begin your victory by breaking through right now. Say, *"Jesus, it's so good to know that today You are Lord of my breakthrough. I thank You that a flood of Your power is about to sweep through my life. I know there is no problem that can stand against it. Family problems can't stand against it. Lack of money can't stand against it. Nothing Satan can do can stop my victory. I thank You for it NOW! In Jesus' Name. Amen."*

Keep praying that. Keep believing that. And before long, God's forces will come bursting through, demolishing every obstacle in their path!

talk the truth

"Jesus is the Lord of my breakthrough!" (1 Chronicles 14:11, AMP)

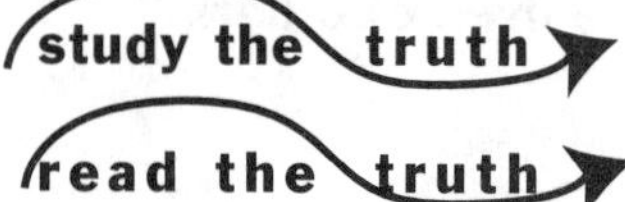
study the truth
read the truth

1 Chronicles 14:8-17

Exodus 37,38; Luke 3

PRAY BEYOND WHAT YOU KNOW

"I thank God that I speak in tongues more than all of you."

1 CORINTHIANS 14:18

Speaking in tongues has created more debates than just about any other issue in the Bible. Churches have been ruined over it. People have been ridiculed for doing it. People have even been killed for it.

Who's behind all the trouble? Satan himself, of course. He's so frightened of our ability to pray in tongues that he's continually trying to steal it from us.

You see, Satan knows that praying in tongues is the only way you and I can pray beyond what we know. When we pray in tongues, the Holy Spirit within us begins to teach us and show us things.

If you want to see a living example of what praying in tongues can do, look at the Apostle Paul. He said he prayed in tongues more than anyone in the whole Corinthian church, and he was responsible for writing most of the New Testament!

Another example is the first church at Jerusalem. At that time, they didn't have any of the New Testament to read. They just had to pray in tongues until the supernatural knowledge of God lit up in their hearts. That's all they could do. So they did it and turned the world upside down.

If you haven't made a commitment to spend some time each day praying in tongues, make one now. Set aside all the disagreements and confusion Satan has stirred up about it and just say, *"Lord, I'll do it. I don't care what Satan says. I don't care what anyone says. I know You have plans for me that are so good, my mind hasn't even been able to comprehend them yet. And by praying in the spirit, I will receive them."*

Now begin to pray in tongues every morning and every evening. Pray under your breath as you walk your school hall. Pray during a football game. And, of course, pray before taking a test! Pray in tongues whenever you can…it will stir up your faith and put Satan on the run!

talk the truth

"I build myself up daily by praying in tongues." (1 Corinthians 14:18)

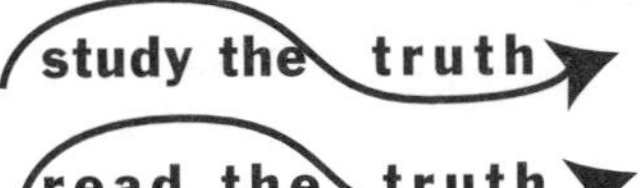
study the truth
read the truth

Isaiah 28:9-12

Exodus 39,40; Luke 4

February 12

WEARY OF WORRY

"But thanks be to God, who always leads us in triumphal procession in Christ and through us spreads everywhere the fragrance of the knowledge of him."

2 Corinthians 2:14

As you fight the good fight of faith today, remember this: Your mind is where the battle will take place. Whatever you allow yourself to think about will rule your life. Will you allow God's Word or Satan's lies to rule?

The decision is yours.

If you want God's Word to rule, make up your mind to resist Satan when he comes to make you doubt that what it says is true. Refuse to give in to the pressure of circumstances he brings your way. Decide before you're faced with it that you will not give in. Dig your heels in and stand rock solid upon God's promises.

When thoughts come that are opposite to what God would accept, throw them away. And above all, don't worry. Worrying is thinking about the thoughts Satan gives you. The second you realize you are worrying, stop it. Replace worried, fearful and doubtful thoughts with what the Bible says.

This is certain: Satan will continually try to tell you that your situation is hopeless. He will continually attack your mind with doubt, defeat and discouragement. But if you won't allow him to sell you his merchandise, he won't make any profit. If you don't buy his lies, he can't cause them to come true in your life.

God has promised that He will *always* give you the victory in Jesus—it's guaranteed over any enemy you face today. Make up your mind right now to be a winner and you'll spread the message of victory in Jesus everywhere you go.

talk the truth

"I replace worried, fearful and doubtful thoughts with promises from God's Word." (2 Corinthians 2:14)

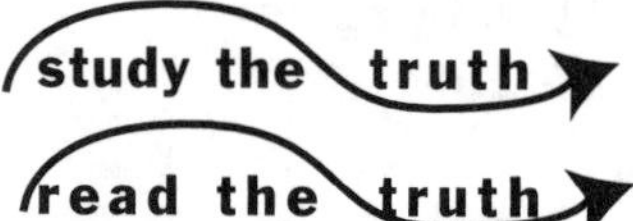
study the truth
read the truth

Philippians 4:1-9

Leviticus 1,2,3; Luke 5,6

YOU CAN OPEN THAT DOOR

"Ask and it will be given to you; seek and you will find; knock and the door will be opened to you."

MATTHEW 7:7

How long has it been since you were backed into a corner, hedged in by a problem that seemed unbeatable? Some spend all their teenage years trying to gain enough boldness to share Jesus with their friends, only to end up more bound by fear than ever. Others work hard to really love their parents, yet despite their best efforts, the relationships grow worse from year to year. Still others fight battles against alcohol or depression, drugs or disease.

Deep within our hearts, each of us knows there must be an answer to the problems we face. But often it seems to be out of reach, hidden behind a tightly locked door.

What I want you to know today, however, is this: *We can open that door!* Jesus Himself has given us the keys.

Right now you may be facing a situation that looks totally hopeless, but God has a ring full of keys that will unlock *any* situation. No matter how hard Satan tries to trap you, if you'll get hold of the right key, you can find your way out.

God's Word is full of keys to heavenly principles—keys to stopping Satan's operations and keys to getting free from his traps. God has a key that will unravel any knot Satan can tie. He also has a key that will lock up Satan's operation so tightly that he won't be able to move.

Remember this: There's no situation so dark and so cleverly designed by Satan that there's not a biblical key that will unlock it with God's power.

There *is* an answer to your situation. Keep digging for it. If you've been digging at one spot in the Bible and haven't found your answer, then look at another chapter, a different verse. Keep digging until you find the key. Keep knocking at every door until you find the one that opens.

talk the truth

"The answer to any situation is in God's Word. I will study it to find the keys I need." (Matthew 7:7)

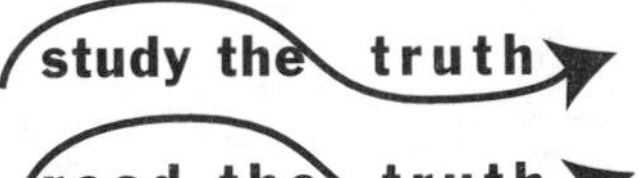
study the truth
read the truth

Psalm 63

Leviticus 4,5; Luke 7

Kenneth

February 14

LOVE IS THE POWER CHARGE

"My command is this: Love each other as I have loved you. Greater love has no one than this, that he lay down his life for his friends."

John 15:12,13

Love. It is the first and foremost command Jesus gave us, yet all too many Christians neglect to follow it.

I'm talking about Christians who can quote tremendous amounts of Scripture and who may speak the Name of Jesus all day long, yet they're harsh and insensitive to the needs of their family and friends. They're so busy "serving God," they don't have time to serve people. They're known for how much strife they cause.

You may have been a Christian since you were 3 years old, you may speak in tongues all day long, but if you have strife in your heart and you're not living by the love commandment of Jesus, spiritual things are foolishness to you.

When you're in that condition, Jesus' Name won't work. Faith won't work, because the Bible says that faith works by love. In fact, none of the gifts of the Spirit will work if you don't have love. First Corinthians 13 says so.

Do you want to see God's awesome power released through your life? Do you want to change the atmosphere around you wherever you go…from the halls in your school to the halls in your house? Then start putting the love command into action. Start loving those around you.

Love is the power charge. God's power package just won't work without it. That's why we've seen so many power failures in the Church. But starting today, you and I can turn those failures around. We can make up our minds to let God's Word live strong within us. We can set our hearts on keeping Jesus' commands and speak His Name with confidence and authority. And, most important of all, we can begin to love one another. Then we will truly see the power of God begin to flow.

talk the truth **"As I walk in love, I see God's awesome power released in my life." (John 15:12,13)**

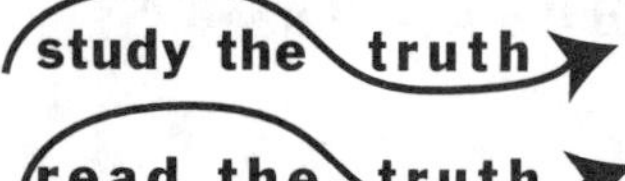
study the truth
read the truth

1 Corinthians 13:1-8

Leviticus 6,7; Luke 8

A PROVEN SUCCESS

Prove yourself. In today's world, isn't that what you constantly feel you have to do? At school, among friends, sometimes even at home, you work to win the approval you need. You work to convince those around you that you deserve the freedom, the friendship and even the love they give you.

But there is an escape from all that! It's called grace—unearned and undeserved favor and acceptance. And there's only one place you can find it—in the heart of God Himself.

There's no better picture of God's grace in action than in the story of the prodigal son. Few of us today can really feel the impact of that story like those who heard Jesus tell it firsthand. You see, by their standards the prodigal son had done some incredibly detestable things. He'd not only taken advantage of his father and spent his inheritance living recklessly, but he'd also left the nation of Israel and made a covenant with a foreigner.

"The son said to him, 'Father, I have sinned against heaven and against you. I am no longer worthy to be called your son.' But the father said to his servants, 'Quick! Bring the best robe and put it on him. Put a ring on his finger and sandals on his feet.... For this son of mine... was lost and is found.'"

Luke 15:21,22,24

In their eyes, that kid's rebellion was so serious, his father's only choice was to disown him.

But that's not what this father did! He welcomed his repentant son home with open arms. He offered him grace—unearned favor and acceptance—that was based on the father's love, rather than on the son's performance.

Next time you catch yourself working to win God's approval, remember the story of the prodigal son. Let it remind you that—in spite of your sins—your Father has received you with open arms.

Do you feel unworthy of that? Sure you do. You *were* unworthy of it. But God hasn't based His relationship with you on your worthiness. He's based it on His love and on *Jesus'* worthiness. You don't have to struggle to prove yourself to Him. As far as He's concerned, you're a proven success.

talk the truth

"I am saved by grace through faith, which is God's gift to me. It wasn't anything I did—it was all God's work." (Ephesians 2:8,9)

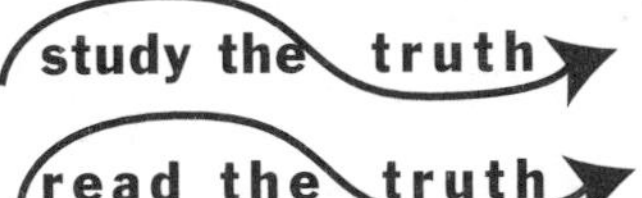
study the truth
read the truth

Luke 15:11-32

Leviticus 8,9; Luke 9

Kenneth

February 16

A HIDDEN TREASURE

"The farmer sows the word."

MARK 4:14

At this very moment you have a hidden treasure inside you. It's a treasure that can change the world. A treasure that can change a person's destiny—that can take him to heaven and save him from hell. A treasure that can turn a person's hate into love, sickness into health, sadness into joy.

You have within you the all-powerful Word of God.

Don't keep it to yourself. Spread it wherever you go! Put it in the hearts of everyone you meet. Share it at every opportunity.

"But I don't know how!" you may say.

Then let these three steps guide your way.

1. **Make a decision.** Make up your mind today that you will share God's Word with others no matter what! Determine right now that it's the most important thing you'll ever do. Commit to it. Once you've done that, you'll find the rest is easy.
2. **Prepare yourself.** Spend time in the Bible each day. Study and think about what you read. Allow the Holy Spirit to minister to you. That will make it easy for you to minister to others. You'll be open to the Holy Spirit and be able to hear His voice. He'll help you know what to say in each situation.
3. **Stay in faith.** Once you've shared God's Word with someone, trust Him to finish the work. His Word is never ineffective. Even if they seem like they don't care, even if no change seems to take place, keep believing. Your faith will keep that Word alive inside them, and eventually, it will do its transforming work.

You have hidden within you a treasure that can change the world. What will you do with it?

talk the truth

"I make the decision and prepare myself to share God's Word. I trust the Word I share will continue to work in others." (Mark 4:14)

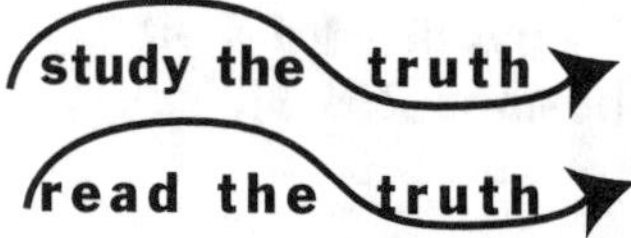
study the truth
read the truth

2 Corinthians 4:1-7

Leviticus 10,11; Luke 10

WELCOME TO THE BIG LEAGUE

When people start to mistreat you because of your faith, don't sit around and whine about it. Don't waste your time feeling sorry for yourself. Despite what you may think, that mistreatment hasn't come because Satan gets a kick out of picking on you. It comes because you've become a threat to him. It comes because you've put God's Word in your heart, and he knows if he doesn't get it out, you will cause him more trouble than he can handle.

So be happy! And when you're mistreated because of your faith, it means you've made it to the big league. It means Satan is taking you so seriously that he's sending in his best players in an effort to get you out of the game!

The players who make it to the Super Bowl don't look for some way out of it, do they? They don't say, "Man, I sure wish I didn't have to be in the Super Bowl. Those guys are the biggest, meanest players in the country. Maybe I'll get sick so I don't have to play." No! They *look forward* to the opportunity. "Let me at 'em!" they say. "I've worked all my life to get here and now I'm determined to prove I'm the best!"

"Blessed are you when people insult you, persecute you and falsely say all kinds of evil against you because of me. Rejoice and be glad, because great is your reward in heaven, for in the same way they persecuted the prophets who were before you."

MATTHEW 5:11,12

That's how you should be when Satan challenges you. You should accept the challenge with joy—because you *know* you'll come out a winner. After all, God is on your side. And He never stops to wonder if He will have enough resources to get you through your problems. He knows He can beat anything Satan brings against you.

So, when trouble comes, trust God and get excited—you've made it to the big league!

talk the truth

"When people insult me because I follow Christ, I am blessed. I've made it to the big league!" (Matthew 5:11,12)

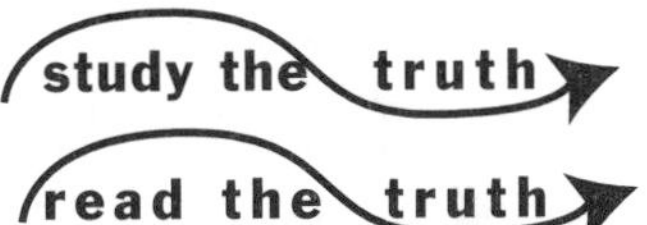
study the truth
read the truth

1 Peter 4:12-19

Leviticus 12,13; Luke 11

February 18

SIN-STAINED...OR BLOOD-WASHED?

"'This is the covenant I will make with them after that time, says the Lord. I will put my laws in their hearts, and I will write them on their minds.' Then he adds: 'Their sins and lawless acts I will remember no more.'"

HEBREWS 10:16,17

The Bible tells us that under the Old Covenant God had with man, an animal had to be offered every year to *cover* the sins of the people.

But let me tell you something exciting. Your sins aren't just "covered." What Jesus did for you on the cross is different altogether. He didn't just "cover" your sins...*He completely did away with them.*

Do you know what that means? It means they no longer exist. It means there is no longer a sin problem. Jesus solved it! He no longer remembers that you used to gossip or lie. He no longer remembers those times you were involved with alcohol, drugs or the wrong crowd. He doesn't even remember that big mistake you made.

When you made Jesus your Lord, He didn't just cover your sins—He put you into right-standing with God and re-created you by the Holy Spirit as if your sin *never* existed.

But if you're like many Christians, you haven't fully realized what a powerful truth that is. You're caught up in what I call "sin-consciousness." You keep thinking of yourself as marked by sin instead of cleaned by Jesus' blood.

"Well, after all, I'm just a sinner who's become a Christian."

No, you're not. You *were* a sinner, but God changed you forever and put you in right-standing with Him when you made Jesus your Lord. He has made you everything you are—He's re-created you in Jesus! As far as God is concerned, your past life is forgotten. It died on the cross with Jesus.

Think about that. Let it sink into you until you rise up and boldly receive the freedom from sin that's yours in Jesus. Receive the right-standing with God that only Jesus can give.

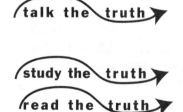

talk the truth **"Jesus became sin for me. Now I have been made right with God through Jesus." (2 Corinthians 5:21)**

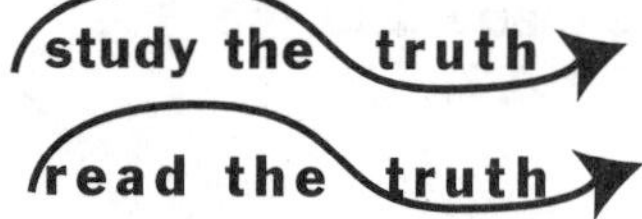
study the truth
read the truth

Hebrews 9:11-26

Leviticus 14,15; Luke 12

THE WORD MAKES YOU A WINNER

"Get wisdom, get understanding; do not forget my words or swerve from them. Do not forsake wisdom, and she will protect you; love her, and she will watch over you."

PROVERBS 4:5,6

Recently, God has been raising up an ever-growing number of young men and women who are hungry to know their God in a deeper way. Hungry to serve Him—at church, in school, on mission fields and anywhere else He might choose to send them.

These are young people who simply aren't content to find the easiest path and coast their way into heaven. No, they're determined to run the race...to run, as the Apostle Paul said, to win the prize (1 Corinthians 9:24). Spiritually speaking, they are on the road to excellence.

Are you one of them?

If so, I want to share four simple words that, I believe, will enable you to run the race like a winner: *Put the Word first.*

Whether your future goal is to be an excellent evangelist or a first-rate lawyer serving the Lord, it is the wisdom that comes from the Bible that will get you there.

Jesus said it this way: "The thing you should want most is God's kingdom and doing what God wants. Then all these other things you need will be given to you" (Matthew 6:33, ICB).

So commit yourself right now to do whatever it takes to totally fill yourself with God's Word. Use every available moment to read it, study it, listen to it and think about it.

I know it won't be easy, but if you've made a definite decision to reach your full potential as a Christian, and you are determined to take Jesus' commission seriously, then keep at it. Put the Word first and there will definitely be wonderful victories ahead.

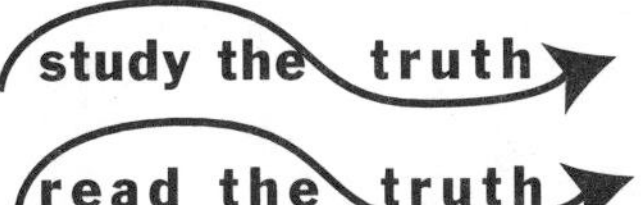

"I put the Word first. The thing I want most is God's kingdom and doing what God wants." (Matthew 6:33)

study the truth

Proverbs 4:1-18

read the truth

Leviticus 16,17,18; Luke 13,14

February 20

JOY—A VERY REAL FORCE

"The joy of the Lord is your strength."

NEHEMIAH 8:10, KJV

Joy. It's not a warm, happy feeling you're supposed to have now and then when things are going well. It's much more than that. Joy is one of the most powerful spiritual forces in the world.

Look again at Nehemiah 8:10 and I'll show you why. If, in English class, you were to diagram a sentence and remove the phrase, "of the Lord," you would find what it's saying is this: Joy is strength. The two are the same.

That's what makes joy so important. You can't live a life of faith without being strong in the Lord—and when God wants to make you strong, joy is what He uses to do the job!

Joy is not just a state of mind. It's not an emotion. Joy is a very real force, and Satan doesn't have anything that can stand up against it. Just as fear has to surrender to faith, discouragement has to surrender to joy.

Since joy is one of the fruits of the spirit, you already have it living within you (Galatians 5:22). But you must develop it and live it out if you want to enjoy its power.

Whatever circumstances you are facing today, you can be full of joy. You can be strong in the Lord. You can draw on this force the Holy Spirit has put within you and come out on top!

talk the truth **"The joy of the Lord is my strength." (Nehemiah 8:10, KJV)**

study the truth **Psalm 18:28-50**

read the truth **Leviticus 19,20; Luke 15**

Gloria

CHANGED!

Inside, you're perfect—re-created in the image of Jesus Himself. But on the outside do you find yourself falling short of that perfection? Is there a solution? Yes! The secret lies in "a new way of thinking."

"Do not change yourselves to be like the people of this world. But be changed within by a new way of thinking."

ROMANS 12:2, ICB

Romans 12:2 tells us that if you'll take on a new way of thinking, you can actually be "changed." That word "changed" is translated in the Bible from the Greek word from which we get the term "metamorphosis." It means to be transformed from one state to another. It's what the Bible is talking about in 2 Corinthians 3:18 when it says, "We all show the Lord's glory, and we are being changed to be like him. This change in us brings more and more glory. And it comes from the Lord, who is the Spirit" (ICB).

Changed! That's a powerful, exciting word—and it describes what will happen to you as you spend time in God's Word and in prayer. As you spend time learning a new way of thinking, your "outside" will be transformed in much the same way as a caterpillar is changed into a butterfly. Instead of changing to be like the people of this world, you'll begin to change to the image of the re-created spirit within you—which is created in true holiness and right-standing with God.

Take time to get away from the world and study the Bible. Pray and think about it. Be changed by a new way of thinking and, like a caterpillar that changes to a butterfly, you'll be changed from the inside out!

talk the truth

"I don't change myself to be like the world. I am changed from within by a new way of thinking." (Romans 12:2, ICB)

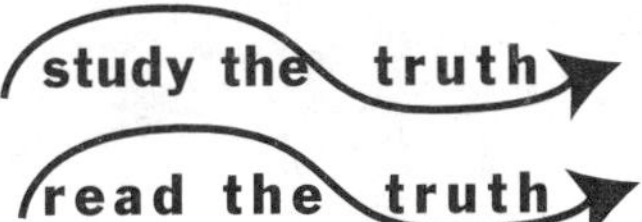
study the truth
read the truth

2 Corinthians 3:6-18

Leviticus 21,22; Luke 16

February 22

Gloria

BE WILLING TO WAIT

"He who guards his mouth and his tongue keeps himself from troubles."

PROVERBS 21:23, AMP

There are just no two ways about it. To live a victorious Christian life, you have to make your words agree with what God says. Not just for a few hours or a few days, but all the time.

And, if you've ever done that, you know it's not easy. As time wears on and the circumstances around you appear to be staying in the same miserable condition they've always been in, it's hard to keep speaking God's Word. But you have to do it if you ever want to see His promises come alive in your life.

When Kenneth started preaching about how God loves to see us living well in every area of life, I sat in the audience and listened to him with holes in the bottom of my shoes. We had terrible money problems. But we knew those problems didn't change what the Bible said. We knew His promises were true even if we hadn't been able to tap into them yet. So, even though we felt foolish at times, we just kept on talking about how much God takes care of His children.

I realized later that God's Word went to work for us from the first day we began to believe it and speak it and live like it was true. It just took time for those seeds of believing to grow.

The problem is, most Christians don't last that long. They start planting those seeds, but when they don't see immediate results they get discouraged and begin to speak about how they'll never make it. They tear up their crop with their words, and they never get to enjoy the benefits of it.

The next time you move out in faith, no matter what area it's in—financially, physically, socially or another area—keep that in mind. Make a decision from the beginning that you won't let that waiting period discourage you. Then hang on until God's promises are seen in your life. Be patient and watch what you say. You *will* receive your harvest.

talk the truth

"I am patient. I guard the words I say, keeping myself from trouble." (Proverbs 21:23, AMP)

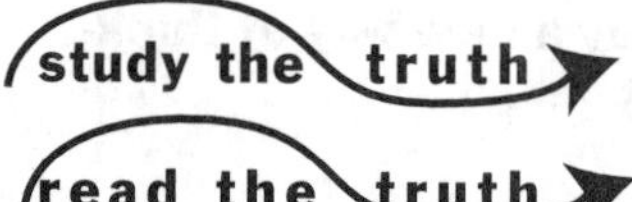
study the truth
read the truth

Proverbs 18:4-8,20,21

Leviticus 23,24; Luke 17

APPROACH THE THRONE

"Let us then approach the throne of grace with confidence, so that we may receive mercy and find grace to help us in our time of need."

HEBREWS 4:16

When you made Jesus your Lord, one of the privileges you received was the right, through prayer, to approach His throne any time you want. Think about that! You have the right to boldly go before God and receive whatever you need.

Even though that's clearly what the Bible says, most people don't act like they believe it. They don't feel very sure about going directly before God. Instead they think, *I'm so far away from where God is—way up in heaven in His throne room. I just hope He hears me.* I used to do that myself!

I remember one day I was in prayer, begging and pleading for revival. After I'd been at it a little while, the Lord spoke to me. *What are you doing?* He said.

"I'm bombarding the gates of heaven with prayer for revival," I answered.

Kenneth, how big is My city? He asked me.

"As far as I can tell from what the Bible says, it's about 1500 miles square and 1500 miles high."

Then why are you bombarding the gates? Assuming that My throne is in the middle of the city, that leaves you about 750 miles short! And, by the way, He added, *those gates aren't locked. Why don't you quit bombarding them and just come on in?*

After I asked God to forgive me, I remembered that the Bible says, "Let us then *approach the throne* of grace with confidence," and I've been coming with boldness ever since.

Do you need to receive something from God today? Don't waste time standing around, hoping that God will hear you. Through Jesus, you belong right before God's throne. So come on in. The door is always open.

talk the truth

"I approach God's throne of grace with confidence. I receive mercy and find grace to help me." (Hebrews 4:16)

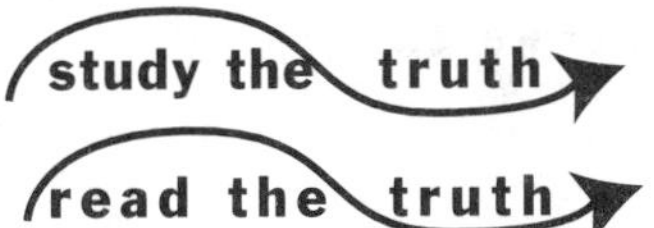
study the truth
read the truth

Hebrews 4:14-16; 5:1-9

Leviticus 25,26; Luke 18

February 24

Kenneth

PEACE AT HOME

"For where you have envy and selfish ambition, there you find disorder and every evil practice."

JAMES 3:16

Have you ever noticed that the easiest place to remain selfish is at home? It's easy to find a reason to be nice to others, but with your family you're tempted to allow yourself to be more selfish—as if it didn't count there.

Before I was a Christian, I was kinder and nicer to my friends than to my own family. I was more demanding and less forgiving with those I loved the most.

But after I made Jesus the Lord of my life, I realized all that had to change.

Gloria and I began to learn through the Bible how important friendship and harmony are within our family. We learned that we couldn't allow strife in our home if we wanted the power of prayer to work in our lives (see Matthew 18:19).

Strife drops the shield of faith, stops prayer results and invites Satan and his cohorts into your life. Strife is deadly. It paralyzes God's power in your life.

Don't allow the enemy to stop you at your own front door by allowing strife in your home. If you do, you'll be no threat to him anywhere else.

Put the power of love and friendship to work in your family instead!

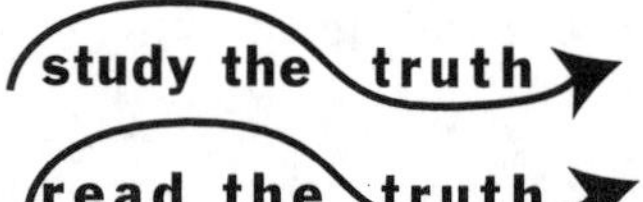

"I don't do anything through strife. I humbly esteem others better than myself." (Philippians 2:3)

study the truth — **Philippians 2:1-13**

read the truth — **Leviticus 27; Numbers 1; Luke 19**

THE CHOICE IS YOURS

"Choose for yourselves this day whom you will serve."

Joshua 24:15

Choosing to side with God's Word is a continual challenge. It's not something you do just once. It's a process of choosing to believe and act upon it over and over in every circumstance.

That's what everyone has to do. Years ago I decided to choose Jesus. Since then I've had to choose Him again and again in situations every day. I've chosen Him as my Lord. I've chosen Him as my Healer. I've chosen Him as my Money-Manager. I've chosen Him as head of my household. I've chosen Him as head of my ministry. And I still have to choose Him moment by moment.

Sometimes the choosing gets tough, but God has promised it will never get too tough. In 1 Corinthians 10:13, He says, "No temptation has seized you except what is common to man. And God is faithful; he will not let you be tempted beyond what you can bear." What the Lord is saying is that He will not allow you to be tempted with something you're unable to overcome. That scripture goes on to say that with every temptation, He'll make a way of escape. He'll *always* make sure you have a choice.

Satan doesn't tempt you while God is off somewhere else, unaware of what is happening to you. The Holy Spirit is always with you, providing you with the way to overcome. In other words, God matches even the toughest temptations with the weapons and power you need to conquer them. He always makes it possible for you to choose the right way.

So choose to walk in love. Choose to walk by faith. Choose to live by God's Word. Choose Him!

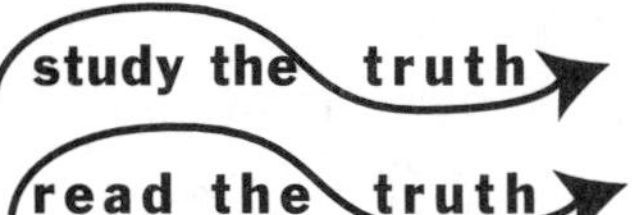

"I choose to serve the Lord!" (Joshua 24:15)

study the truth **Joshua 24:14-24**

read the truth **Numbers 2,3; Luke 20**

February 26

HIS EXTRAVAGANT LOVE

"All these blessings shall come upon you and overtake you, because you obey the voice of the Lord your God."

Deuteronomy 28:2, NKJV

Some people have very low expectations of what God will provide for them. They trust Him for basic needs like food and clothes…but they don't trust Him to feed and clothe them very well!

Somehow they have the idea that God's an old Scrooge who will do nothing more than put rags on their backs and beans on their plates. But that's not what Jesus told us. He said in Matthew 6 that God would clothe us better than He clothed rich King Solomon. That one statement alone proves that God wants to do more than just meet our basic needs. He wants to give to us generously.

Several years ago I came home and found two expensive automobiles parked in my driveway. They were given to me to use by men who'd been touched by God through my ministry.

I was surprised. "Lord," I said, "I didn't need these cars. I didn't ask You for them. I wasn't praying for them. What are they doing here?"

That's when the Lord spoke. *Have you ever read the scripture in Deuteronomy that says blessings shall come upon you and overtake you when you obey My voice?*

"Yes," I answered.

Well, son, He said, *you've just been overtaken.*

Am I saying God gave me those expensive cars just so I could enjoy them? Yes! That's exactly what I'm saying.

First Timothy 6:17 says, "God...richly provides us with everything for our enjoyment." God is a loving Father. He gets great pleasure from generously giving to His kids. He's extravagant when it comes to us.

Once you truly believe that and begin to obey His voice, it won't be long before His blessings will be overtaking you.

talk the truth

"Because I obey the Lord, His blessings come on me and overtake me." (Deuteronomy 28:2, NKJV)

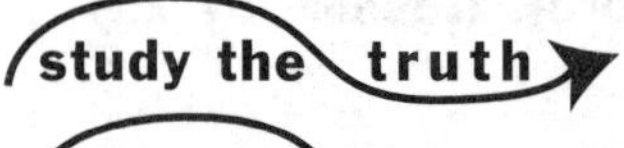
study the truth

1 Kings 10:1-24

read the truth

Numbers 4,5,6; Luke 21,22

February 27

A WINNING SPIRIT

"It is written, 'I believed, and therefore have I spoken; we also believe, and therefore speak."

2 CORINTHIANS 4:13

The spirit of faith speaks! It speaks about things that don't exist as though they do exist. It can't keep its mouth shut because it's expecting God to do something extraordinary! The spirit of faith says, "No matter what it takes, I know God will change this situation for me." Do you have a spirit of faith like that?

Every time I talk about the spirit of faith, I think about my high school football team. For years the school had losing teams. But something happened to the bunch on my team. A winning spirit—a spirit of faith—got into them.

When we were sophomores, we were on the "B-squad." *B-squad* was a nice term for "the football wanna-bes" a/k/a "the nothings." Every year the B-squad would have to scrimmage the varsity team, and 99.9 percent of the time, the varsity just beat the daylights out of the sophomores. And they enjoyed doing it.

But the year *our* B-squad played them, that changed. Somehow we got the idea that we could win. And do you know what? Before you knew it, we had them down by several touchdowns. We were winning, but good! We were just daring them to get the ball, when all of a sudden the coach called off the game. He was so mad at the varsity team, he didn't even let us finish!

So what happened to our little B-squad? We reached the point where we *expected* to win. On the inside, we saw ourselves as winners, and it eventually took the best team in the state to beat us.

If a varsity giant is staring you in the face today, get that winning spirit inside you. See yourself as the real winner. Ignite your spirit of faith. Speak the truth about whatever situation you're facing. Say, "I don't care what God has to do—He'll turn the world upside down if He has to—but I know He will change this situation for me. Because of what Jesus did for me, I am more than a conqueror and I have the victory!" And then celebrate...because you're a winner!

talk the truth **"Jesus has made me a winner today and no situation can beat me. I speak my victory aloud by the spirit of faith!" (Isaiah 54:17; 2 Corinthians 4:13)**

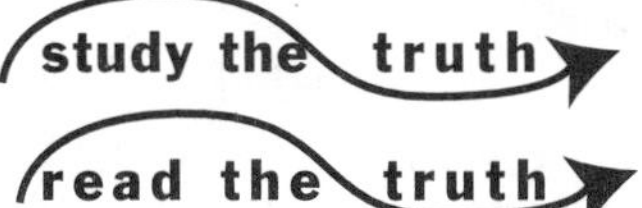

Romans 4:16-21

read the truth **Numbers 7:1-48; Luke 23**

February 28

Gloria

HE WILL LEAD YOU

"So I tell you: Live by following the Spirit. Then you will not do what your sinful selves want."

GALATIANS 5:16, ICB

Live by following the Spirit. That's the key to overcoming sinful habits. If you follow the leading of the Holy Spirit within you, you won't be ruled by the pressure your "old, sinful self" tries to put on you.

As you read God's Word and follow what the Holy Spirit tells you to do, you'll constantly be making little adjustments in your life to agree with what He says. Now those adjustments may not seem monumental. You may simply feel Him prompting you to decrease the amount of TV you watch. Or maybe He's prompting you to stop whispering under-the-breath put-downs to your sister. No, they may not seem like earthshaking changes, but those little adjustments will keep sin from overtaking you.

God knows just what you need. He can look ahead in your life and see the traps and pressures Satan is laying for you. So follow the Holy Spirit's leading and He will move you safely around them to victory.

talk the truth

"I live by following the Spirit. I will not do what the sinful nature wants." (Galatians 5:16, ICB)

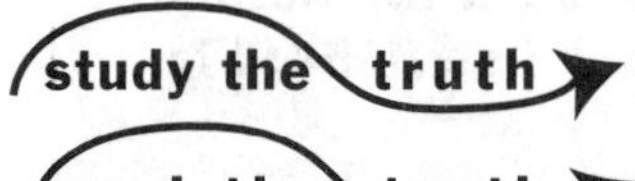
study the truth
read the truth

1 Corinthians 10:1-14

Numbers 7:49-78; Luke 24

NOW, *THAT'S* GOOD NEWS!

"And it shall come to pass in that day, that his burden shall be taken away from off thy shoulder, and his yoke from off thy neck, and the yoke shall be destroyed because of the anointing."

ISAIAH 10:27, KJV

Ever since man first sinned, Satan has been trying to make people his slaves. He has clamped his yoke around their necks and loaded them down with sin, sickness, addictions, failure, lack of what they needed and every other evil thing hell could devise.

Every person who has ever been born—except Jesus—has felt the terrible weight of that yoke. We've all experienced the pain and frustration that comes from struggling free from something just to have Satan trip us up one more time.

For thousands of years, that yoke of bondage was the one thing that plagued mankind day in and day out. It looked like there would never be a way to break free. But, with the help of the Holy Spirit, the prophet Isaiah looked forward in time and saw Someone coming. He saw Someone coming Who would finally free us from Satan's slavery. He saw Jesus.

Now, to get the full impact of how much Jesus has freed you, read the verse above again. Notice it says that the yoke will literally be *destroyed.* That means it will be absolutely useless. It can't be repaired and put back on you. In fact, Isaiah was saying that Jesus would so annihilate the yoke, that there would no longer be *any* evidence that it was ever on your neck in the first place!

That means that every time you allow God's power to destroy a yoke in your life—whether it's an addiction, your need for money, bad relationships or some mistake you made—it is literally, *utterly* destroyed and cannot be used against you again. Satan can't pick it up and hold you in bondage with it anymore. It's been destroyed!

Now, *that's* good news!

talk the truth

"The burden is taken off my shoulder and the yoke from my neck. The yoke is destroyed because of the anointing!" (Isaiah 10:27, KJV)

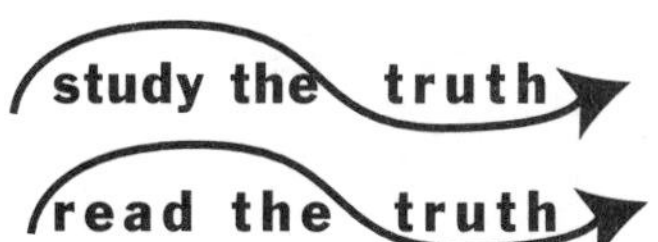
study the truth
read the truth

Psalm 18; Galatians 5

Luke 4

Gloria

March 1

LET GOD RUB OFF ON YOU

"God knew them before he made the world. And God decided that they would be like his Son. Then Jesus would be the firstborn of many brothers."

ROMANS 8:29, ICB

Look at yourself in the mirror. Now think about this: You are destined to grow up spiritually until you look just like Jesus. God's power began the process of spiritual growth within you the moment you made Him the Lord of your life. You were instantly changed inside. Now, the amount of success you have in allowing yourself to become like Jesus on the *outside* is mostly up to you.

So what can you do to speed up this growing process?

First, spend more time doing spiritual things than you spend doing worldly things. Become dedicated to reading and learning God's Word and spending time with Him in prayer. Be willing to put aside the busy things of life and get alone with Him, so He can guide you, teach you and share His character with you.

Have you ever noticed that if you spend time around people who have strong personalities, you're automatically affected by them? You'll find yourself doing the things they do. Their mannerisms will rub off on you. They could even be actors you watch on television or in the movies a lot. You can't help it. They just influence you, especially if they are people you respect and admire.

The same thing is true in your relationship with God. If you spend enough time with Him, He'll rub off on you! The way He does things will become the way you do things.

So make yourself available to Him by praying in the spirit and worshiping and loving Him. Hang around His Word and other people who love His Word and live it.

Before you know it, you'll begin to notice yourself changing. You'll find your character becoming more like His. Others will begin to see Him in you!

talk the truth

"I am destined to grow up spiritually until I look just like Jesus!" (Romans 8:29, ICB)

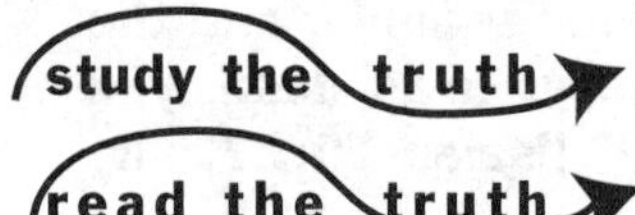
study the truth
read the truth

1 Corinthians 3:5-18

Numbers 7:79-89; 8; John 1

DEFEAT YOUR GIANT

"Goliath is a Philistine. He is not circumcised. Why does he think he can speak against the armies of the living God?"

1 Samuel 17:26, ICB

You may be facing a giant today. He may be a giant of sickness, insecurity or another kind of trouble. But don't let him scare you. You have a secret weapon. It's a weapon that once turned a puny shepherd boy into a bear-busting, lion-killing, giant-slaying champion. That weapon was a "blood covenant" with God.

Back in David's day, circumcision was the sign of that promise—or covenant—with God. So, when David called Goliath "uncircumcised," David was saying: This guy may be a giant and he may be strong—but he has no promise with God and that's why I can kill him.

Just like David, you, too, have a covenant with God. But yours is better. You see, the covenant David had gave tons of benefits to those who kept it, but it also included curses for those who broke it.

Yours doesn't. Yours is a New Covenant that Jesus paid for with His own blood. It doesn't depend on your ability to keep it or not. It only depends on what Jesus has already done—and He has done it all! All you have to do is believe it and accept it.

Right now, read Deuteronomy 28:16-68. It's a list of the curses Jesus has freed you from. (You can read about being made free from the curse in Galatians 3:13-14.) You might even call it a list of the "giants" Jesus has already killed for you. It contains every evil thing Satan could ever use to destroy you.

So don't let those giants intimidate you. You have a blood covenant—a new promise—with Almighty God. And there's no circumstance on the face of this earth that can take your victory away from you now.

talk the truth

"Christ set me free from the curse of the law once and for all when he became a curse for me." (Galatians 3:13)

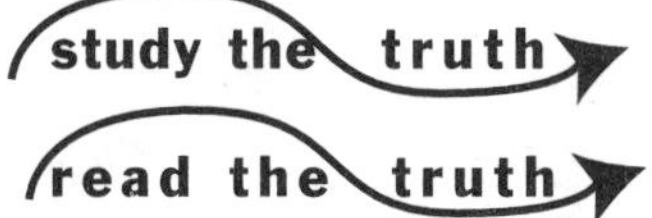
study the truth
read the truth

Galatians 3:13-29

Numbers 9,10; John 2

Gloria

March 3

CALLED TO BE DIFFERENT

"My prayer is not that you take them out of the world but that you protect them from the evil one. They are not of the world, even as I am not of it."

John 17:15,16

Being different. That's not something most people want to be, is it? Sure, some teenagers dress differently or act differently—many times they do it to be part of a certain crowd. But within that crowd, they're still all the same. God, however, wants you to be radically different from the world. He wants you to find your identity *in Him*. He has called you to be *set apart* and *stand out* from any crowd as living proof of His power and His love (1 Peter 2:9).

He gave us a real-life illustration of that during the time the nation of Israel was held captive in Egypt. Pharaoh refused to set the Israelites free, so God allowed a thick darkness—pitch black—to cover the whole land. The darkness was so dreadful throughout Egypt that no one moved for three days.

"Yet," reads Exodus 10:23, "all the Israelites had light in the places where they lived."

What an excellent example of how God wants us to live. We should give God Glory by the supernatural lives of victory we lead. We should always have people telling us, "I've heard how God protected you," or "I've heard how God healed you and saved your parents!"

So don't hold back. Put the promises in the Bible to work in your life, and dare to receive the great benefits that belong to those who believe. Start using God's Word to draw boundaries around your life, to create warning signs for Satan. Create signs that say: *Off Limits! According to the Bible, I don't belong to you anymore. My family doesn't belong to you. My health doesn't belong to you. My grades don't belong to you. My social life doesn't belong to you. I'm different! Now, back off in Jesus' Name.*

If that sounds a little different—that's all right. That's exactly what God's called you to be!

talk the truth

"I am not of this world, even as Jesus is not of this world." (John 17:15,16)

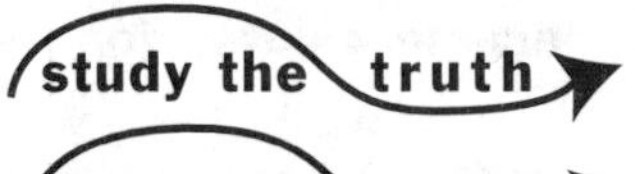
study the truth
read the truth

Exodus 10:20-29

Numbers 11,12; John 3

KNOW THE TRUTH

People go to a lot of trouble trying to get answers and wisdom from God when all they need to do is go to the Bible. God's not holding out. It's His will for everyone to walk in His truth.

"God...wants all men to be saved and to come to a knowledge of the truth."

1 Timothy 2:3,4

"Well now," some say, "God won't reveal the truth to all those sinners out there." Really? Why do you think He sends evangelists to preach to them? Why do you think He sends teenagers on missionary trips? Why do you think He sent His Word? To reveal the truth!

So, if you want to know that truth, just open the Bible and read it. All of it. He said absolutely everything that's in the Old Testament *and* the New Testament.

You'll even find that Jesus—the Word Himself—based His ministry on what was written in God's Word. Those promises brought Him to earth. Those promises enabled Him to heal and rescue people. He didn't minister by some special power no one else could have.

When Satan came to tempt Him, Jesus didn't fight him off with an army of angels assigned to protect Him because He was God's Son. He fought him off with the words, "It is written" (Matthew 4).

God has equipped you to do the same. He's given you His written Word, and He's given you His Holy Spirit to help you understand it. He's more than ready to give you the wisdom you need. You don't have to force it out of Him—just open the Book and let the truth be revealed.

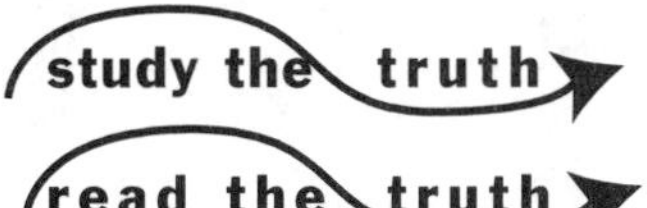

"I will base everything I do on God's Word. And I know the Holy Spirit Who lives in me will guide me into all truth." (John 16:13)

study the truth **John 16:7-15**

read the truth **Numbers 13,14; John 4**

March 5

BE CONSISTENT

"Jesus Christ is the same yesterday and today and forever."

HEBREWS 13:8

Some time ago, God spoke some words to Gloria that I've never forgotten. She'd been asking Him to teach her to walk and live more fully in His power.

He said to her, *The power is in consistency.*

When she told me that, hearing those words was tough for me. On my own, I'm anything *but* consistent. My human nature is to be up one day and down the next. But, praise God, I don't have to depend on my human nature to get by. I have Jesus living in me and He's the same yesterday, today and forever!

Jesus isn't inconsistent. He doesn't change His mind from one day to another. He's constant. And when you get to know Him, you'll become that way too.

Most Christians aren't consistent. That's why there are so many "faith failures" around. They stand on God's Word one day and fall off it the next.

What we need to do is "continue." Jesus said if we'd continue to obey His Word, then we'd be His followers. He said if we'd continue, we'd know the truth and it would make us free (John 8:31-32). There's a supernatural understanding of Who God is that comes when you're consistent...an understanding that the inconsistent person will never have.

So make a decision today to be consistent. Don't try to live today on yesterday's Bible study. Live today on *today's* Bible study. Start the day with God's Word, stay on His Word all day and end the day with His Word. Then get up tomorrow and do it all again!

There's power in consistency. So don't be an "off again, on again" Christian. *Continue* in the Word every day.

talk the truth

"Jesus is the same yesterday, today and forever. Because He lives in me, I am consistent in all I do." (Hebrews 13:8)

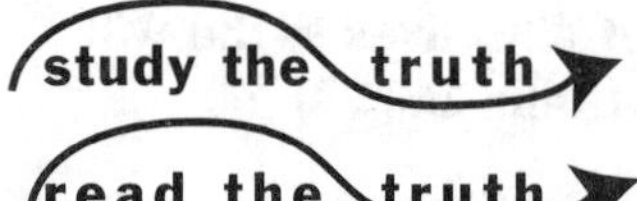
study the truth
read the truth

Colossians 1:14-23

Numbers 15,16,17; John 5,6

VICTORIOUS PRAISE

Praise comes before victory!

You can see a perfect example of that in 2 Chronicles 20. There, the Bible tells us that a huge army was marching against Israel. Israel's army was so outnumbered, they literally didn't know what to do. So they fasted and prayed until they heard direction from God: "Do not be afraid or discouraged because of this vast army. For the battle is not yours, but God's" (verse 15).

Do you know what they did when they heard that? They put together a choir! That's right. They appointed singers and praisers and sent them out *in front of the army!* And when that choir began to sing, the Bible tells us that "the Lord set ambushes against the men...who were invading Judah, and they were defeated" (verse 22).

"After consulting the people, Jehoshaphat appointed men to sing to the Lord and to praise him for the splendor of his holiness as they went out at the head of the army, saying: 'Give thanks to the Lord, for his love endures forever.'"

2 Chronicles 20:21

When it was all over, not *one* Israelite had fallen—and not *one* of their enemies had escaped. What's more, when they came to take the goods left from the defeated army, they found so many cattle, possessions, garments and other precious things, it took them three whole days to haul it all home.

Now *that's* victory! And it all began with praise.

Are you looking for that kind of victory today? Then you ought to be ready to shout because you're in the same situation those Israelites were in. You may have an army marching against you, but Jesus has already defeated it. He won that battle for you when He rose from the grave.

All that's left for you to do is trust Him and begin to praise Him. Praise Him today. Speak, sing and shout your praise to God in the enemy's face. Once he hears it, he'll know he doesn't have a prayer.

talk the truth

"I praise God today and trust Him—for He gives me the victory through Jesus!" (2 Corinthians 2:14)

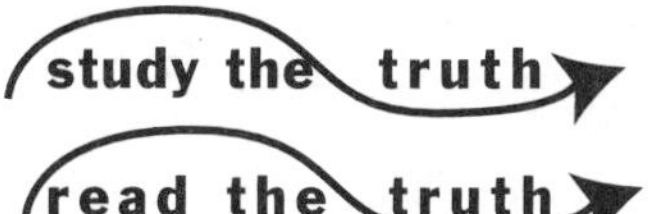
study the truth
read the truth

2 Chronicles 20:1-22

Numbers 18,19; John 7

March 7

EXPECT TO HEAR HIS VOICE

"My sheep listen to my voice; I know them, and they follow me."

John 10:27

Many young men and women are unsure of their ability to hear God or their ability to know His voice when they do hear it. They're always afraid that they won't be able to tell when the Holy Spirit is talking to them.

What they don't realize is this: Hearing the voice of the Spirit is a privilege that belongs to every Christian (Romans 8:14). All you have to do is accept that truth by faith and get ready to hear. Jesus said His sheep will know His voice and they won't follow the voice of a stranger. That's a promise from God to you today. Remember that the next time Satan tries to tell you that you can't hear God's voice.

The best way to learn to hear Him is to get to know the Bible. You see, the Holy Spirit will never say anything that contradicts the written Word (John 16:13). So, if you're not sure what the Bible says, you'll find it more difficult to know His leading.

When your friends call you on the phone, how do you know who it is if they don't say their name? Well, you've spent enough time with each of them that you're familiar with their voices. Get familiar with God's voice by studying His Word. Follow God's instruction to Joshua (Joshua 1:8): study and think about it day and night. Act on what you find in the Bible, not just when it's easy, but every time. Obey Him even in small things.

That consistent obedience to His Word will make you mature and tune your spirit to the voice of His Spirit. You'll soon be able to recognize it as easily as you recognize the voice of your best friend.

So, instead of wondering, start *expecting* to hear from Him...then start sharpening your spirit by spending time in His Word.

talk the truth

"I listen to the voice of Jesus. He knows me and I follow Him." (John 10:27)

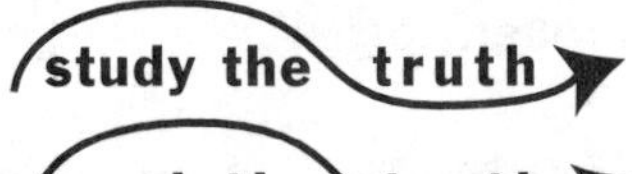
study the truth
read the truth

John 10:1-9

Numbers 20,21; John 8

MEET THE LIVING WORD

"For the word of God is living and active. Sharper than any double-edged sword, it penetrates even to dividing soul and spirit, joints and marrow; it judges the thoughts and attitudes of the heart."

HEBREWS 4:12

The living Word of God is the only power strong enough to discipline every part of you. It's the only power that can cause you to think, look, talk and act like a person who's been truly changed.

When I became a Christian, I had a horrible smoking habit. I tried to quit every way I could think of, but nothing worked. After months of struggling and failing, I decided to attend some church meetings in Houston, Texas. Before I went into those meetings, I tucked my cigarettes above the sun visor in my car and left them there.

Up to that time, I hadn't learned much of anything about the Bible, and I'd never been exposed to God's power. So when I began to hear the preachers preach in the power of the Holy Spirit, it surprised me. I was caught up in the living Word...and my desires changed. All I wanted was more of God. For the first time in my life, the Scriptures became real to me.

When those meetings ended (days later) and I started driving back home, I found those old, stale cigarettes tucked up in my sun visor and realized I hadn't even missed them.

What happened? God's Word separated me from the desire to smoke. It gave me the power to discipline myself. When I saw Jesus in the Word with the power of Almighty God, I was totally set free, not only of the habit but of the *desire!*

If you have a habit—or even a desire—of smoking, alcohol, pornography or any type of drug, you can get rid of it. Maybe you find yourself in the habit of cussing, cheating, lying or getting into wrong relationships. Well, get caught up in the living Word today and discover the power that can set you free...forever!

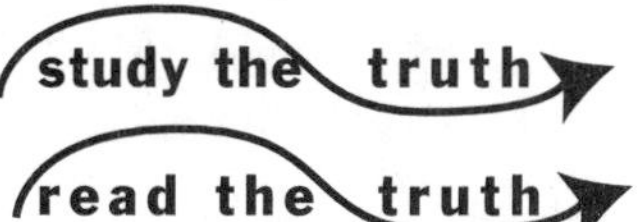

"God's Word is living and active. It is sharper than any double-edged sword. The power of the Word sets me free!" (Hebrews 4:12)

study the truth **Psalm 119:1-9**

read the truth **Numbers 22,23; John 9**

March 9

THE HABIT OF HOLINESS

"Whoever has my commands and obeys them, he is the one who loves me. He who loves me will be loved by my Father, and I too will love him and show myself to him."

JOHN 14:21

There's a way of life you can only experience when you make a decision to please God in everything you do. At that point, Jesus becomes real to you and shows Himself to you.

In the early 1900s, God started a spiritual awakening in America at a place called Azusa Street in Los Angeles, California. It was an incredible time when people's entire lives were turned inside out. Everything else in their world lost importance. Supernatural things were happening. God was showing Himself to them.

The people involved in that revival soon began to be known to the world as "holiness" people. They got that title because they were so obviously different from everyone else. They'd let go of anything they thought didn't please God. They were so caught up in the spiritual things, they lost interest in everything else.

Few Christians today even know what "holiness" means. Even fewer understand the power of God that comes to those who dare to be holy.

Holiness simply means to be separated to God. It's what you do with your life day by day. It's doing only what the Bible and the prompting of the Holy Spirit say to do. Holiness is the habit of believing God's Word, of turning away from the ways of the world and living the way God wants you to live. Holiness doesn't happen to anyone by accident. It requires a decision.

So love God with all your heart by keeping His commandments. He'll show His love to you by showing *Himself* to you in powerful new ways. He'll touch you just like He did those Christians at Azusa Street…and revival will truly begin in you.

talk the truth

"I believe God's Word, turn away from the world's ways and live the way God wants me to live. I love the Lord and He shows Himself to me." (John 14:21)

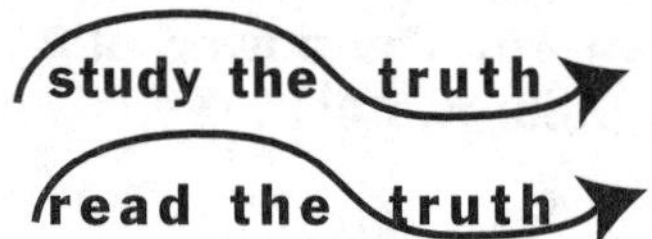
study the truth
read the truth

1 Thessalonians 4:1-8

Numbers 24,25; John 10

WATCH YOUR LANGUAGE

"When words are many, sin is not absent, but he who holds his tongue is wise."

PROVERBS 10:19

We need to start watching our language. We need to quit throwing words around like they weren't important and start using them like our lives depended on them—because, according to the Bible, they do (Proverbs 18:21)!

Too many of us have what Proverbs 19:1 calls a *perverted mouth.* Having a perverted mouth means more than just lying and cussing. It means saying things that are out of line with God's Word.

All of us have done that at one time or another. We'll say, for instance, that we're believing God will heal us, and then we turn right around to someone and make a statement like, "This pain is about to *kill* me!"

That's perverted! It's backward from what God's Word says.

"Oh well, I know I said that, but it's not really what I meant."

Listen, spiritual things don't work on what you *mean.* They work on what you *say.* Mark 11:23 tells us that "If anyone says to this mountain, 'Go, throw yourself into the sea,' and does not doubt in his heart but believes that what he says will happen, it will be done for him."

Check that verse out. It didn't say you will have what you *mean.* It says you will have what you *say.* It's what you say that counts.

Now, I'm not suggesting you should get tied up in knots all the time worrying about what comes out of your mouth. Just use the wisdom God has given you. Train yourself to obey His Word in what you say. Then, when you need it most, you'll find that Word inside you.

talk the truth

"Death and life are in the power of my tongue. I make sure my words agree with God's!" (James 3:10)

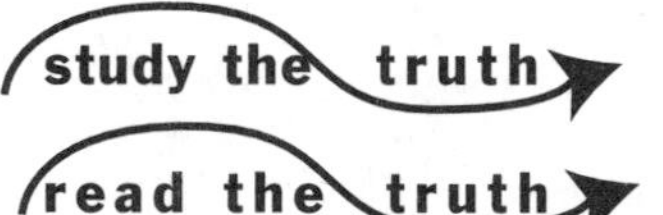
study the truth
read the truth

Proverbs 10:11-21

Numbers 26; John 11

Kenneth

March 11

A PROMISE OF LOVE

"For God so loved the world that he gave his one and only Son."

JOHN 3:16

God loved the world so much that He gave...and He gave...and He gave.

That's the message the Bible brings us from beginning to end. It sounds simple enough, but few people really understand it. Almighty God loves you so much that He desires, above all, to give to you! Even if you find that hard to believe, it's true.

For thousands of years, God has been working to put the truth of His love into people's hearts. But He's always faced the same obstacle—people who just couldn't get themselves to believe His loving promises were true.

The story of Abram is an example of this. God's promises shocked Abram so much that he couldn't believe them. "Lord God," he asked, "how can I be sure that I will own this land?" (Genesis 15:8, ICB).

Do you know how God answered him? By making a blood covenant with him. That forever settled any question Abram could have about God's love and loyalty. Once blood had been shed, he knew God meant what He said.

God did the same thing for you. He made a promise—a covenant in blood—with you. And He sacrificed His own Son to do it. Jesus' broken body and shed blood have become the eternal proof of God's love for you.

Get understanding of God's love for you by thinking about this covenant He's made with you. Get out a piece of bread and a cup of juice. Take Communion thinking about the body and blood of Jesus that have made you a member of God's family. Let them once and for all settle the question of God's love for you. When you do, you'll never again have to doubt His promises.

talk the truth

"God loves me so much that He gave His one and only Son so that I might have eternal life." (John 3:16)

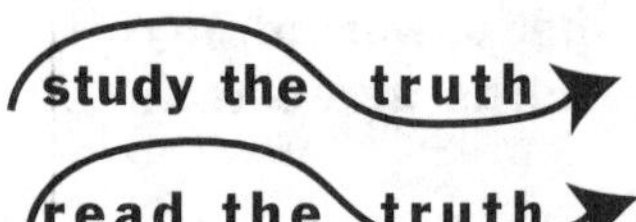
study the truth
read the truth

Genesis 15

Numbers 27,28; John 12

March 12

AS YOUR SOUL GETS ALONG WELL

"Dear friend, I pray that you may enjoy good health and that all may go well with you, even as your soul is getting along well."

3 John 2

Once you begin to believe God really wants you to live well in every area of life, you can't help but wonder how He will bless your day-to-day living. Will you win the Publisher's Clearing House sweepstakes? Or will someone you never met leave you a multimillion-dollar inheritance?!

Not likely. He'll do it by prospering your soul. Your soul is your mind, your will and your emotions. And that's where He will plant the seeds of prosperity, so they will grow and produce a great harvest.

Go to the book of Genesis and read the story of Joseph (Genesis 37-50). It's a perfect example of what I'm talking about.

When Joseph was sold as a slave to the Egyptians, he didn't have a dime to his name. He didn't even have his freedom. But, right in the middle of his slavery, God gave Joseph such wisdom and ability that he made his owner prosper. As a result, the man put Joseph in charge of everything he owned.

Later, Joseph was put in prison. There's really not much opportunity for advancement in prison, is there? But God gave him insight that no other man in Egypt had. That insight landed him a position on Pharaoh's staff. Not as a slave, but as the most honored man in the entire country next to Pharaoh himself.

He rode in a chariot and people literally bowed down before him. During a worldwide famine, Joseph was in charge of all the food. Now that's good living!

How did God accomplish all that? By prospering Joseph's soul. No matter how hard his situation became, no matter how impossible his problems, God was able to reveal the spiritual secrets that would open the door of success.

That's what makes God's method of prospering so exciting. It works anywhere and everywhere. And you can be sure that it will work for you!

talk the truth

"As my soul prospers, I enjoy good health and all goes well with me." (3 John 2)

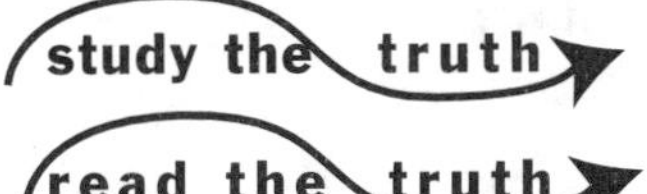
study the truth
read the truth

Genesis 39

Numbers 29,30; 31:24; John 13,14

March 13

LIVING BY FAITH—IT'S A LIFESTYLE

"Endure hardship with us like a good soldier of Christ Jesus."

2 Timothy 2:3

Hard times will come. You need to know that. It's true that we've been rescued from evil, and there's nothing Satan can do to change that...but he is sure to challenge you on it.

So don't be surprised when things get tough. Times will come when you have to stand strictly by faith, when you'll have to speak and act as though what God says is true even when you can't see it happening. There will be times when everything looks terrible. Your grades may seem bad, your friends may seem distant or your family is going through a difficult time. But that's when you must "endure hardship" like a good soldier in the military.

So many people hear messages about healing or prayer and they think, *Hey! I'll try that.* Then when the hard times come, they give up and cave in.

Let me warn you, living by faith is not something you *try*. It's a *lifestyle*. You do it when it's hard. You do it when it's easy. You do it all the time because you're not doing it just to get in on the benefits. You're doing it because you know faith pleases God (Hebrews 11:6).

Things may get a little rough at times, but let me assure you, you'll always come out on top if you endure the hard times. If you refuse to get tired and fall away, you will have the victory. After all, the only defeated Christian is the one who quits!

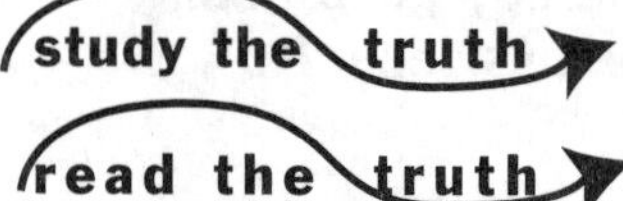

"I endure hardship as a good soldier of Christ." (2 Timothy 2:3)

study the truth **Numbers 14:1-24**

read the truth **Numbers 31:25-54; 32; John 15**

ACTIVATE THE POWER

"Now to him who is able to do immeasurably more than all we ask or imagine, according to his power that is at work within us."

Ephesians 3:20

As a Christian, you have the power of the Holy Spirit inside you. But that power won't go to work until you put it to work! The Holy Spirit won't just force Himself on you. He won't come in, turn off your stereo, throw you up against the wall and say, "Listen to Me!"

No, He's a Gentleman. He's sent to help you do what God wants, to give you strength and to guide you. The Holy Spirit is waiting for you to call on Him...but He won't do a thing until He's asked.

I'll tell you, if Jesus came into your house and sat down in your room, you'd drop everything to talk to Him, wouldn't you? You wouldn't just say, "Jesus, I'm so glad to see You. I wish I had the energy to talk, but between being forced to eat what the school cafeteria served for lunch and everything else that went wrong, I'm just too tired to do anything but sit here and watch TV. Maybe we can spend some time together later."

You wouldn't do that, would you? No! If Jesus were sitting there in your room where you could see Him, you'd drop to your knees and worship Him. You wouldn't care how tired you were, and you wouldn't spend a moment complaining about what the cafeteria served for lunch. You'd jump at the opportunity to spend time with Him.

Well, the Holy Spirit is in you saying, *I'm here to help you and strengthen you. I want to comfort you today. You know that problem you've been having with worrying? I want to help you get that out of your life.*

The Holy Spirit has things He wants to show you—things you've been beating your head against the wall trying to figure out. He's waiting there with the power to overcome every problem you come up against. Take time to pray. Pray in the spirit. Pray in your own language. Pray and activate God's power in you today.

talk the truth

"I call on the Holy Spirit and pray in the spirit—and His power works in me!" (Ephesians 3:20)

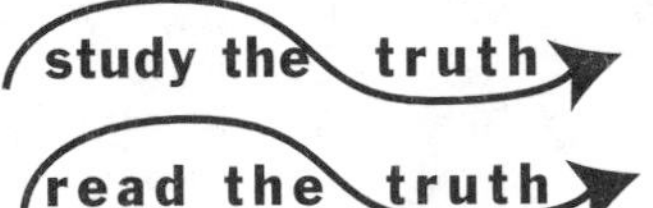
study the truth
read the truth

Ephesians 3:16-21

Numbers 33; John 16

Kenneth

March 15

THE HEART OF THE MATTER

"The Lord does not look at the things man looks at. Man looks at the outward appearance, but the Lord looks at the heart."

1 Samuel 16:7

Too often we ask God to fix the problems *around* us when what He really wants to do is solve the problem *within* us. I used to do that myself when it came to my weight. I prayed and prayed for God to help me lose weight. Yet I kept failing. I lost literally hundreds of pounds, only to gain them right back again.

Finally one day, I made a firm decision. I told God, "I am not going one step further until I find out what to do about this!" Then I shut myself away from everyone, went on a fast and determined to hear from God.

That's when He showed me the real source of my problem. He showed me that I wanted to lose weight, but I didn't want to change my eating habits. I was like an alcoholic who wants to drink all the time and not be affected by it. I wanted to eat nine times a day and still weigh 166 pounds!

Suddenly I realized God wasn't satisfied just to rid me of the extra pounds on the outside. He also wanted to rid me of the sin of gluttony on the inside. So I asked forgiveness and turned away from that sin right then and there. (It was then that I realized just how hard it is for someone who drinks to face the fact that he or she is an alcoholic. It hurts to admit something like that.) Then instead of asking God to rescue me from my weight problem, I asked Him to rescue me from my problem of wanting too much food.

Sure enough, He did.

If your prayers don't seem to be changing the problems around you, maybe it's time to take a look inside. Maybe it's time to ask God to go to work on the heart of the matter.

talk the truth

"The Lord doesn't look at the things people look at. He looks at and works in my heart." (1 Samuel 16:7)

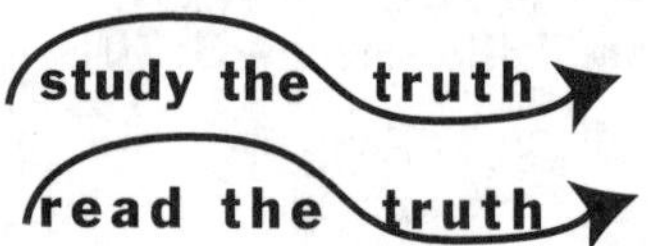
study the truth
read the truth

Psalm 139:1-10; 23,24

Numbers 34,35; John 17

TRAIN YOUR "SELF"

"Anyone who lives on milk is still a baby. He knows nothing about right teaching. But solid food is for those who are grown up. They have practiced in order to know the difference between good and evil."

Hebrews 5:13,14, ICB

You're spiritually "grown up" or mature when, through *practice,* you know the difference between good and evil...when you've practiced following the Holy Spirit daily and have changed your way of thinking by God's Word...when your desires and attitudes have grown accustomed to going His way instead of the world's way.

Stop and think for a moment. Aren't there some things you used to feel pressured to do before you made Jesus the Lord of your life, that now you don't even *want* to do anymore?

There are for me. For example, I used to smoke cigarettes, and I felt sorry for all those Christians who couldn't. But you know what? Now that I'm a Christian, I have no desire to light up. It doesn't even enter my thoughts, let alone my lifestyle.

That's the kind of thing that happens as you study God's Word and change your way of thinking. It doesn't necessarily happen quickly or easily. Your "old sinful self" may fight you for a while because it's been trained to go the world's way for so long. But if you stick with the Bible and keep growing, your "self" can develop habits of right-standing with God just like it used to develop the habits of not standing right with Him.

Don't starve your spirit by trying to get by on just a little spiritual milk now and then. Develop the habit of feeding on the solid food of the Bible every day and find out what real maturity is all about. Your "self" will thank you for it!

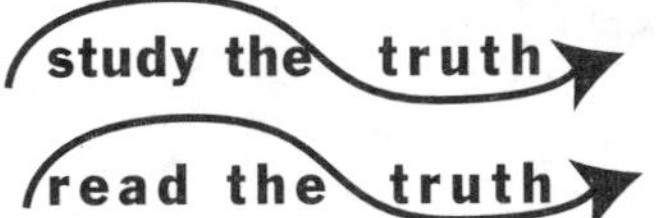

"I am growing up in the Lord. I eat the solid spiritual food of the Word." (Hebrews 5:13,14, ICB)

study the truth **Hebrews 5:11-14; 6:1-3**

read the truth **Numbers 36; Deuteronomy 1; John 18**

Kenneth

March 17

START PLANTING

"For you have been born again, not of perishable seed, but of imperishable, through the living and enduring word of God."

1 PETER 1:23

You won't really get excited about the Bible until you realize that it's more than just a collection of God's promises. God's Word is literally a living force that carries the power to make those promises become real in your life.

Is it tough for you to believe that's possible? It shouldn't be. You see it happen in your backyard all the time.

If I were to put a tomato seed into your hand and tell you that within that tiny, dry seed lies the power to produce a plant thousands of times bigger than the seed, to produce leaves and roots and round, red tomatoes, you wouldn't have any trouble believing that, would you? You know from experience that even though that puny seed doesn't look like a tomato factory, somehow, given the right environment, it will become one.

Jesus says God's Word works the same way. There's miraculous power within it. It's a seed that, once planted in your heart by faith, will produce more good things than you can imagine.

Once you grasp that, you'll get extremely excited about the Bible. You'll want to spend every possible moment in it because you'll want its power inside you more than anything else in the world.

And when you read it, you aren't just reading—you're planting seeds in your heart. You're planting seeds of health, seeds of protection, seeds of wisdom and seeds of victory for every area of your life.

Don't treat the Bible like a book. It's not! It's spiritual seed that has the power within it to produce the harvest of a lifetime. Get excited about it and start planting today!

talk the truth

"I plant the living and enduring Word of God in my heart." (1 Peter 1:23)

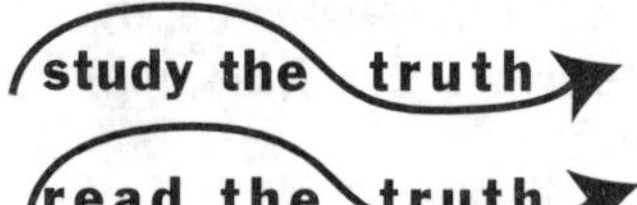
study the truth
read the truth

Mark 4:23-32

Deuteronomy 2,3; John 19

NOTHING TO BE AFRAID OF

Wanting to always be part of the "in" crowd is a major problem. As a Christian, it will keep you from doing the things God tells you to do. Instead of simply obeying Him, it will make you start to wonder, *Now what will people think of me if I do that? What if I pray over my food at lunch and someone laughs? What if I'm not interested in drinking and partying all night and my friends notice? What about that, God? I won't look too good!*

If you've ever wondered things like that, let me tell you something: It doesn't matter how you look! What really matters is that you obey God. When it comes to obeying God, your own reputation doesn't count...and the sooner you forget it, the better off you'll be.

"God has said, 'Never will I leave you; never will I forsake you.' So we say with confidence, 'The Lord is my helper; I will not be afraid. What can man do to me?'"

HEBREWS 13:5,6

But you know what's surprising? Once you do that, your reputation will get better. It's a funny thing. When you lose that desire to protect your image, your image will improve. Why? Because then when people look at you, instead of seeing that struggling little image you have of yourself, they'll see Jesus' image coming through.

So put aside that old self-consciousness and develop God-consciousness instead. Stop being ruled by what others say or think and start being moved by faith in what Jesus can do.

After all, He has promised He will never leave you or abandon you (Hebrews 13:5). Grab hold of that. Believe it. Act on it. Once you do, you'll realize there's really nothing to be afraid of anymore!

talk the truth

"The Lord is my helper. I am not afraid. What can man do to me?" (Hebrews 13:5,6)

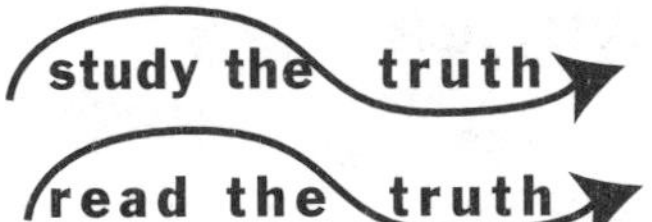
study the truth
read the truth

Romans 8:29-39

Deuteronomy 4,5; John 20

March 19

STAND AGAINST SATAN'S PLANS!

"Leave no [such] room or foothold for the devil—give no opportunity to him."

EPHESIANS 4:27, AMP

If you give Satan any opportunity to make trouble for you, you'd better believe he'll take it. You have to stay alert and keep faith as your shield against him...because if you don't, he'll turn around and steal back from you whatever victory you just had.

Some people receive their healing and then go back into their old way of thinking that God wants them sick. They don't keep their faith strong, and when Satan comes along with a symptom of sickness, they aren't ready. They become his victim on his return attack.

You can stand against Satan's plans! But before you do, you will have to make three decisions.

First, you must make God's Word the final word for everything in your life. Make your thinking line up with whatever the Bible says.

Next, you must decide to live your life by faith in what God has said. The Bible says, "Faith comes by hearing, and hearing by the word of God" (Romans 10:17, NKJV).

Finally, you must decide to live by God's love—because without love, your faith won't work. And you can't even have faith without His Word. So don't try to make one of these decisions without the other two. You need to make all three of them together. This lifestyle of God's Word, your faith and His love keeps you standing strong against Satan!

If you want to stand against him today, get alone with God and pray:

"In the Name of Jesus, I commit myself from this day forward to live by Your Word, my faith and Your love."

Decide today to give Satan no room to make trouble!

talk the truth

"I live by God's Word, my faith and His love. I leave no room or foothold for the devil. I give him no opportunity to work!" (Ephesians 4:27, AMP)

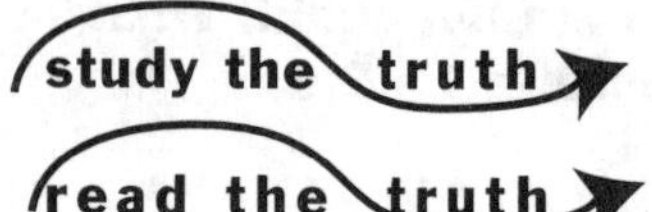
study the truth
read the truth

John 15:7-12

Deuteronomy 6,7,8; John 21; Acts 1

WEAR TRUE HUMILITY

"Clothe yourselves with humility toward one another, because, 'God opposes the proud but gives grace to the humble.' Humble yourselves, therefore, under God's mighty hand."

1 Peter 5:5,6

Most Christians don't know anything about truly being humble. If you tell them they're in right-standing with God, they'll fight to keep from believing it. You can give them scriptures to prove it, and they'll still argue.

"Oh no," they'll say, "I'm nobody special. I'm just a sinner that God has saved." They're really trying to be humble. But they're really wrong. They're so afraid of being full of pride that they let Satan trick them into falling right into it.

Let me show you what I mean. According to the verses above, to truly be humble is to submit to God. That means when God says something, you believe it no matter what people have said they think the truth is. When He says you're in right-standing with Him in Jesus, you say that too. In fact, you wouldn't dare say anything else because to do so would be to disagree with God. And, when you get right down to it, you can't get much more full of pride than that, can you?

Don't let Satan keep you living in false humility. Agree with God. Find out what His Word says about you and then be bold enough to say it yourself. Destroy pride by submitting to His truth. Wear true humility. It's always in fashion.

talk the truth

"I wear true humility. I am humble and submit myself to God." (1 Peter 5:5,6)

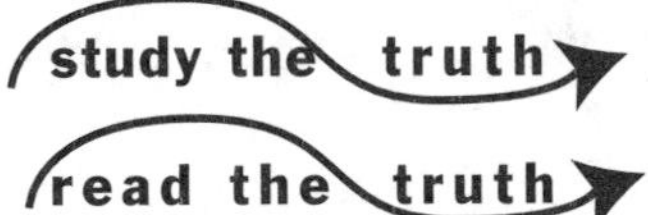
study the truth
read the truth

1 Peter 5:5-11

Deuteronomy 9,10; Acts 2

March 21

ARE ANGELS JUST FOR KIDS?

"Are not all angels ministering spirits sent to serve those who will inherit salvation?"

HEBREWS 1:14

You probably heard about your guardian angel when you were a little kid—and, in those days, it was a comforting thought. With imaginary monsters lurking behind the closet door and creepy things crawling beneath the bed, it was good to know that someone was there to protect you when the lights were out.

But, as you've become a young man or woman, you've outgrown your childhood fears. The imaginary creatures that had once seemed so real disappeared from your mind—and sadly enough, for most people, the angels did too.

But angels are not just baby stuff. They're powerful spirits sent to help you. Just think about that! God has huge numbers of powerful spiritual beings for the single purpose of protecting you and rescuing you from evil.

And remember, according to Psalm 103:20, God's Word is what puts those angels in action. So when you're in trouble, don't hide and cry about how awful things are. Speak the Word! Give your angels something to respond to. Then be patient and let them have time to work. They'll get their job done.

talk the truth

"The Lord's angels camp around me and save me." (Psalm 91:11)

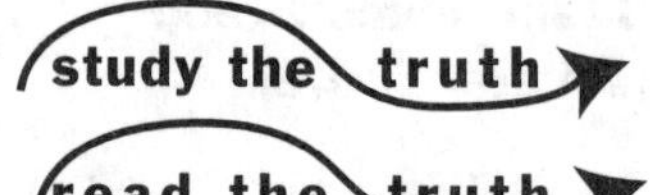
study the truth
read the truth

Psalm 103:17-22

Deuteronomy 11,12; Acts 3

HEALING ALWAYS COMES

"And these signs will accompany those who believe: In my name...they will place their hands on sick people, and they will get well."

Mark 16:17,18

I used to get upset when I'd pray for someone and they wouldn't get well. I was asking God about this one day when He spoke to me and said, *Healing always comes.*

I remember I said, "What do You mean, *Healing always comes?* Not everyone gets healed."

I didn't say they all received it, He answered. Then He spoke very sternly to me. *I do My part. And I said they would recover!*

Those words hit me like a ton of bricks. He said they would recover. He never lies. So if He said they would recover, then that means healing always comes. It's not God who's holding back. It's just that the people aren't receiving.

Since then, I've never had any trouble praying for people and believing for them to be healed. Whether they walk away well or not, I just keep standing in faith for them. In fact, I know that if that person who went away still sick ever lines his faith up with God and me—I don't care if it's five years from now—he'll be healed.

If you've prayed for someone who didn't receive their healing, don't stop God's power by dropping your faith. Keep standing. Keep believing that "healing always comes" and somewhere down the line, that poor, sick person may just decide to stand up and agree with you!

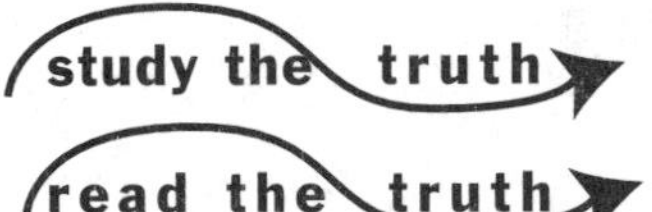

"Signs follow me because I believe. In Jesus' Name, I lay hands on the sick and they recover." (Mark 16:17,18)

study the truth **Mark 10:46-52**

read the truth **Deuteronomy 13,14; Acts 4**

March 23

COMING TOGETHER

"Until we all reach unity in the faith and in the knowledge of the Son of God and become mature, attaining to the whole measure of the fullness of Christ."

EPHESIANS 4:13

You can hear God calling for unity today. He's calling our churches to get rid of our disagreements and come together to get ready for Jesus' return.

How can I agree with someone from another denomination? some Christians wonder. *I can't believe what they do just to be in unity!*

What they don't realize is this: Biblical unity isn't based on doctrine.

Different doctrines, according to Ephesians 4:14, are childish. They don't unify. They divide and throw people in every direction. God's Word doesn't say we will agree in our doctrines. It says we'll agree in our faith.

In the past, we've failed to understand that and tried to demand that all churches believe the same things. We want other churches to have the kind of preaching we have. Or we want other churches to sing the kind of music we sing. But that's not how God works. He only requires us to agree on two things. First John 3:23 tells us what they are: "to believe in the name of his Son, Jesus Christ, and to love one another."

If we all agree on those two things and quit worrying about the rest, we'll be able to forget our denominational fights and come together, unified in faith. We'll grow so strong together that doctrinal differences won't be able to drive us apart.

When that happens, Satan will panic because the unity of God's people is the most powerful thing on earth.

If you look in your school, you may find teens who go to other churches and have made Jesus their Lord. Make an effort to get together with them and take a stand for Christ. If Christian students from all denominations unified in their schools today, just think of what would happen!

Right now all over the world, the Holy Spirit is calling our churches to unite. Hear Him and obey, and you'll be a part of one of the most magnificent moves of God this world has ever seen.

talk the truth

"I unite with my brothers and sisters in Christ, expecting good things to happen!" (Ephesians 4:13)

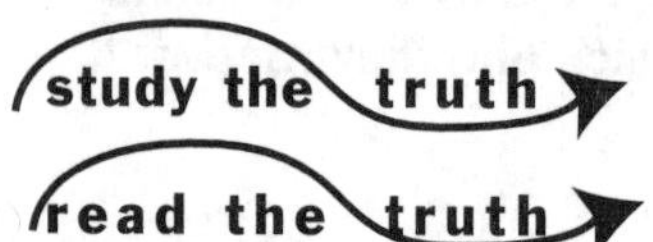
study the truth
read the truth

Psalms 132:13-18; 133

Deuteronomy 15,16; Acts 5

OBEY TODAY

"A man who remains stiff-necked after many rebukes will suddenly be destroyed—without remedy."

PROVERBS 29:1

Some people—young and old—have the idea that when the Holy Spirit gives them direction, they can ignore it for a while if they want, and then obey Him later when they're good and ready. They think, *Hey, I know what I'm doing is wrong, but I'll just do it a little longer. Then I'll straighten things out with God.*

Let me warn you, that is an extremely dangerous thing to do. Because God says that when you refuse to listen to Him, your heart grows hard. It's not that God's compassion isn't there for you anymore. It's not that He wouldn't forgive you if you turned to Him. It's just that sin will block your heart to the point where you can't hear Him calling.

That's what happened to the Israelites. God was trying to bring them into the Promised Land, but they stubbornly refused to do what He told them.

Of course, they thought they had good reasons. They were so full of fear and unbelief that they actually thought if they did what God said, they'd be destroyed. But, you know, it doesn't matter how good your reasons are for disobeying God. Disobedience will still hurt you. It will still harden your heart.

The Israelites ignored God's leading so often that He finally just sent them into the wilderness. They were so stubborn, He couldn't lead them into all the good things He had planned for them, and He had to just let them wander around until all but two of them had died off. He had to raise up a whole new generation of tenderhearted people before He could take them into the land. In the end, it took them 40 years to take what should have been an 11-day trip!

Take a lesson from that and don't play around with sin. When God tells you what you need to do, don't put Him off, thinking it will be easier to do it later. It won't be. It will be harder!

When the Holy Spirit comes to correct you, follow His instructions—and follow them quickly. Keep your heart tender. Obey God!

talk the truth

"I quickly follow the Holy Spirit's instructions when He corrects me. As I obey Him, God's blessings come to me." (Proverbs 29:1)

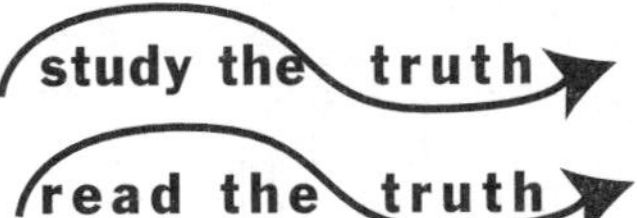
study the truth
read the truth

Nehemiah 9:6-37

Deuteronomy 17,18; Acts 6

March 25

Gloria

COME ALIVE

"Therefore, if anyone is in Christ, he is a new creation; the old has gone, the new has come!"

2 CORINTHIANS 5:17

Resurrection. What do you think of when you hear that word? Most people think of the past. Of a stone rolled away. An empty tomb. And Jesus rising from the dead. *Jesus is alive*—praise God for that.

What we don't fully get is this: He's not the only One Who has been raised from the dead. We have too!

We were *spiritually* raised from the dead the day we made Jesus our Lord. That's when we came alive!

Think about it. When you made Jesus your Lord, the old, sinful person you used to be was destroyed. That old person died. And in his place a new person was created.

Sure, there *will* be a day when your earthly body will be raised up and glorified—but you don't have to wait until then to be free from sin and from the sickness and failure that go with this world. You're free from all that right now!

You may be sitting there thinking, *Well, if I'm so free, why can't I quit smoking? Why can't I lose this weight? Why can't I pass these tests? Why am I always sick?*

Because you've let Satan convince you that you're still under his power. You've let him talk you into living as if you're still spiritually dead!

So, today I want you to begin seeing yourself alive! Begin thinking of yourself as someone who already has God's life instead of someone just waiting around for the resurrection. Consider yourself dead to sin and alive to God's power. You'll find yourself living a whole new life!

talk the truth

"I am a new creation in Christ! The old things have passed away, the new has come!" (2 Corinthians 5:17)

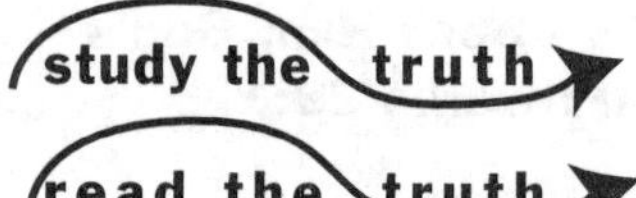
study the truth
read the truth

Romans 8:1-14

Deuteronomy 19,20; Acts 7

SPEAK FOR CHRIST

"So we have been sent to speak for Christ."

2 CORINTHIANS 5:20, ICB

You have been sent to speak for Christ! If you've made Jesus the Lord of your life, you have been sent to be a representative for Him to the world. Just as nations send ambassadors to represent their countries, you've been appointed to represent God to the earth.

Think about that. When you go to your friends' houses, you are representing the King of kings. When you go into the locker room, you represent the Lord of lords. That's a very high honor. It may also seem like a pretty big responsibility. But God has equipped you to do it. He's given you His Name and the power of His Word. He's even put His very own Spirit inside you. And He's given you the ability to hear and obey His directions.

This is no time to be wishy-washy and half-committed. This is the time to follow God no matter what—to give Him your whole life. If you'll do that, He'll give you such help and power and goodness that you'll shine for Him, as Philippians 2:15 says, "like stars in the dark world" (ICB).

Begin to think about yourself today, not as just another ordinary young man or woman, but as an ambassador of Almighty God. Let His interests be most important in your mind and heart. Give yourself to Him and say, "Lord, show me how to be Your representative in everything I do."

You have been sent to speak for Christ. Begin to live like it today.

talk the truth

"I have been sent to speak for Christ. My life speaks His message to the world." (2 Corinthians 5:20, ICB)

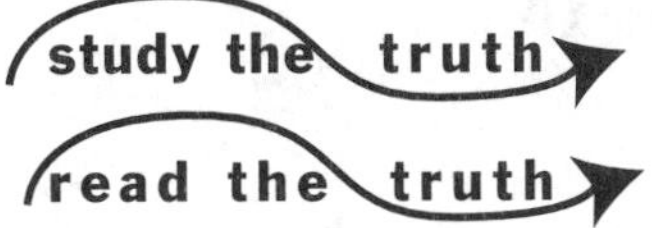
study the truth
read the truth

2 Corinthians 5:10-21

Deuteronomy 21,22,23; Acts 8,9

March 27

Kenneth

FROM BELIEVING TO KNOWING

"In all these things we are more than conquerors through him who loved us."

ROMANS 8:37

The Bible calls us kings (Revelation 1:6, KJV) and world conquerors (1 John 5:4). But for most of us, those are just words. They haven't become real to us. That's why Satan's been able to cheat us into living lives of defeat. We haven't realized who we really are.

In 1 Chronicles 14, you'll see that David had a similar problem. He'd been anointed king by the prophet Samuel when he was a teenager. He'd known for years that someday he'd rule over Israel. Yet somehow, it hadn't really sunk in.

But look what happens in verse 2. "Then David knew that the Lord really had made him king of Israel. And he knew the Lord had made his kingdom very important. The Lord did this because he loved his people, the Israelites" (ICB). Finally, it dawned on him! David knew that the Lord had made him king. I can just imagine David saying to himself, *I am king. I'm actually* king! At that moment, being king stopped being something David had only thought about. It became something he really *was.*

What does that have to do with you and me? Well, just like David, you and I have been given a royal office. We're just having a hard time believing it. But until we do, we can't exercise the power or authority that goes with that office.

Say, for example, you're sick. You can yell, "I'm healed," 50 times a day, hoping for healing. But if you don't really *know* that you're whole and healthy in Jesus, if you don't see yourself as healed instead of sick, you won't get any supernatural help. Yet once the reality hits you that *you are healed,* no one—not even Satan himself—will be able to keep you from getting well.

Don't let Satan cheat you any longer. Step over the line from trying to believe to actually *knowing* by establishing what you know on God's Word. Read it and think about it. Practice seeing yourself as the Bible says until the reality of your royalty in Jesus becomes real to you!

talk the truth

"I am who God's Word says I am. I am more than a conqueror through Jesus!" (Romans 8:37)

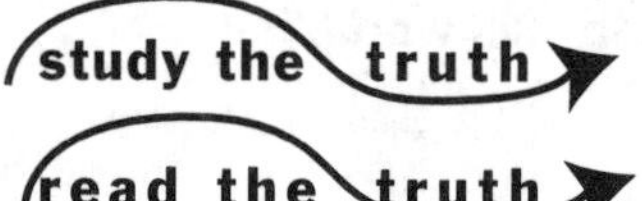
study the truth
read the truth

Ephesians 1:3-23

Deuteronomy 24,25; Acts 10

TURN YOUR LOSSES AROUND

"But the gift is not like the trespass. For if the many died by the trespass of the one man, how much more did God's grace and the gift that came by the grace of the one man, Jesus Christ, overflow to the many!"

Romans 5:15

If you ever feel like a loser and need someone to tell you how to turn things around, go to God. He's an expert on the subject. He's suffered more losses than anyone who's ever lived.

Just think about it. He lost His top-ranked angel, Lucifer (who, of course, is now known as Satan). And when Lucifer fell, God lost at least one-third of His other angels as well. Then He lost the man and the woman He had created (Adam and Eve); and because He'd given them control over the earth, when He lost them, He lost that too. Any way you figure it, that's a lot down the drain!

Yet, in spite of all that, God is no loser. He's the greatest winner of all time. Do you know why? Because He knows how to turn things around. He knows how to use the law of giving and receiving to turn losses into gains.

"Give, and you will receive. You will be given much. Pressed down, shaken together, and running over, it will spill into your lap" (Luke 6:38). That's a powerful principle that breaks all losing streaks.

Now God had every option that exists to recover the things He'd lost. He had all wisdom and all power available to Him. Out of all that, the law of giving and receiving is what He chose to use.

He gave the most irreplaceable thing He had: His only Son. Then He backed that gift with His own faith. And when the law of giving and receiving had done its work, God received not only His Son, but millions of other sons and daughters—like you and me—as well.

Don't get upset over what you've lost. Recover your losses the same way God recovered His. Give. You'll be putting the most powerful principle in the universe to work for you.

talk the truth

"I give. When I do, I will be given much. Pressed down, shaken together and running over, it will spill into my lap!" (Luke 6:38)

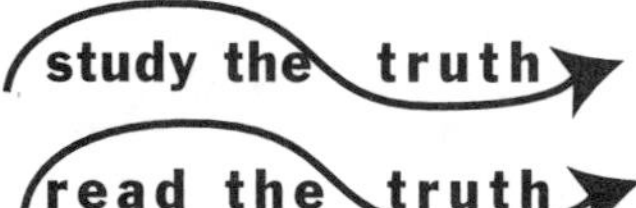
study the truth
read the truth

John 3:12-21

Deuteronomy 26,27; Acts 11

March 29

STOP STRIFE BEFORE IT STOPS YOU

"But if we [really] are living and walking in the Light as He [Himself] is in the Light, we have [true, unbroken] fellowship with one another."

1 JOHN 1:7, AMP

As Christians, there's one area of our lives that we have particularly neglected—the area of our relationships. We simply haven't obeyed the Bible when it comes to relationships. We've criticized our teachers, lied to our parents and fought with our brothers and sisters so much that we've pushed back the forces God has given us to make us successful.

Strife like that causes trouble in our lives. It opens the door to Satan. It keeps our prayers from being answered. It even keeps our angels from working for us!

James 3:16 says, "Where envying and strife is, there is confusion and every evil work" (KJV). So whether it's you and your parents, classmates, boyfriends, girlfriends or members of your youth group, all of us need to wake up to the danger of strife and start loving one another in all we do.

Look to see what the Bible has to say about your relationships. Dig into it and get an understanding of how we are all part of each other. Realize that, as Ephesians tells us, we are one Body and one Spirit (Ephesians 4:3-4).

Let God's power move in all of your relationships. Really work at being understanding, keeping strife away and living together in unity. Learn to walk in the light today!

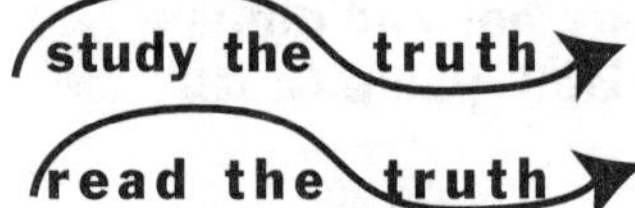

"I have true, unbroken relationships with others because I live and walk in His light." (1 John 1:7, AMP)

study the truth **Romans 15:1-7**

read the truth **Deuteronomy 28,29; Acts 12**

March 30

DIG INTO YOUR COVENANT

"This cup is the new covenant [ratified and established] in My blood."

1 Corinthians 11:25, amp

If we truly understood what the New Covenant meant, every one of us would be faith giants. Instead of "trying" to believe God's promises, we'd be strong in faith, fully persuaded that, what God has promised, He is able also to perform (Romans 4:20-21, KJV).

That's the kind of confidence that jumped up in Abraham when God made the covenant with him. It wasn't a covenant as powerful as ours, yet it totally changed a doubting Abraham into the father of faith—because Abraham understood the full meaning of it.

He knew that entering into the blood covenant with someone meant you were totally giving yourself away to him. All that you were, all that you had or ever would have became the equal property of your covenant partner.

During the covenant ceremony in Abraham's day, the partners exchanged coats, each one giving their authority to the other. They exchanged weapons as a way of saying, "I'll fight your fights and enemies as if they were my own." They walked through the blood of slain animals, announcing their loyalty to one another, even to death.

When God made this covenant with Abraham, God gave him everything He had and bound Himself to Abraham in a relationship that could not be broken. It proved to Abraham that God's promises could be trusted. It became truth to him.

If you want to have giant faith like Abraham, dig into the covenant you have with God. Study it in the Bible. Let the Holy Spirit show you what really happened when your covenant with God became official through Jesus' sacrifice.

Once you realize what Jesus actually meant when He said, "This cup is the new covenant [ratified and established] in my blood," your life will never be the same again.

talk the truth

"Jesus is the mediator of a better covenant established on better promises. I am in this covenant with God!" (Hebrews 8:6)

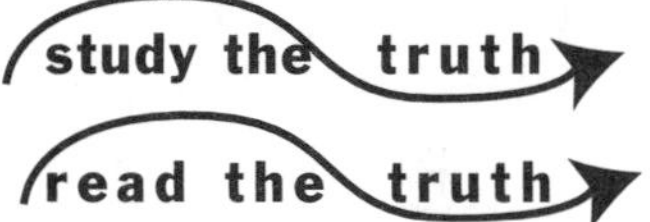
study the truth
read the truth

Hebrews 10:1-23

Deuteronomy 30,31; Acts 13

March 31

FROM SONS TO SERVANTS

"Even on my servants, both men and women, I will pour out my Spirit in those days, and they will prophesy. I will show wonders in the heaven above and signs on the earth below, blood and fire and billows of smoke."

Acts 2:18,19

You and I are living in the most exciting days this earth has ever seen. All around us God is pouring out His Spirit to get ready for the end-time revival that will bring this whole age to a close.

Some of God's children are just standing by watching, like fans watch a high school football game. Others, however, have become a vital part of it all—actually players in the game. They've volunteered for service in this great army. They've become what the Bible calls the "servants of God."

Who are those servants? They are those who have totally committed themselves to their Lord. They are those who—instead of just being happy to be Christians—have gone further, and become servants out of love for God.

The servants of God are those who have said, "I want to be involved in what God is doing today. I want to do whatever He says 24 hours a day."

Those who make that powerful decision are the ones who are experiencing the great outpouring of God's Spirit that Peter spoke of in Acts 2. They are the ones whose words are opening the way for the miracles and wonders.

Do you want to be among them? You can be. God wants you to be. In fact, He needs you to be!

He needs those who will break out of everything that ties them to this world. That's the kind of dedication being a servant requires. It's a demanding role, but its rewards are rich... for those who are willing to fill that role will be God's voice here on earth in these final days. They will be main players in what happens.

Make a decision now to become one of them. Take the step of faith—and become a servant today.

"I am a servant of God and He pours out His Spirit on me." (Acts 2:18,19)

study the truth **Acts 2:1-21**

read the truth **Deuteronomy 32,33; Acts 14**

LET YOUR LIFE SHOUT

Most of us would never dream this verse could apply to us. After all, we're *Christians!* We would never say there is no God.

But maybe we should think again. It's true that we would never say something like that with our mouths...but don't we sometimes say it by what we do?

We say it by sinning just a little here and there and thinking it won't matter. We'll go to an immoral movie or spread gossip about someone, ignoring God's command to the contrary.

With our actions we're saying, "There is no God."

Psalm 14:1 says a person like that is corrupt. Whether you realize it or not, the more you act that way, the more corrupt you will become.

Don't make the foolish mistake of publicly proclaiming Jesus as your Lord, and then privately denying Him with one little action at a time. Be wise in everything you do so that both your heart and your life shout loudly, "My God rules!"

"The fool says in his heart, 'There is no God.' They are corrupt, their deeds are vile; there is no one who does good."

PSALM 14:1

talk the truth

"I have done away with sin. In the middle of a dark world filled with people living crooked lives, I shine like a star." (Philippians 2:15)

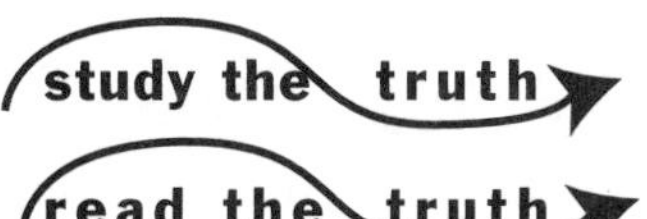
study the truth
read the truth

Psalms 14:1-7; 15:1-5

Deuteronomy 34; Joshua 1; Acts 15

Kenneth

April 2

WHAT A FUTURE!

"And he raised us up with Christ and gave us a seat with him in the heavens. He did this for those of us who are in Christ Jesus. He did this so that for all future time he could show the very great riches of his grace. He shows that grace by being kind to us in Christ Jesus."

EPHESIANS 2:6,7, ICB

All my life people told me the reason God saved us was so that when we got to heaven, we could spend the rest of eternity loving Him and worshiping Him. But that's just not so.

It sounds pretty good, but someone just made that up. God isn't selfish. He's the ultimate giver and He loves us with an ultimate love. He doesn't do anything just so He can get something in return.

Why, then, did He go to the trouble to save us? The Bible tells us He did it so that for eternity, He could show us "the very great riches of his grace."

Think about that! God saved us so He could spend the rest of all time showing us how much He loves us and cares for us.

That's why He sent Jesus into the world. He loved the world so much that He gave His only Son. God gave Jesus so that He *wouldn't be* His *only* son. He sent Jesus so He could have *more* sons and daughters to love and give to—and He plans to spend eternity doing just that.

God says, "For I know the plans I have for you…plans to prosper you and not to harm you, plans to give you hope and a future" (Jeremiah 29:11). As a Christian, you have the best future ahead of you that anyone could ever ask for…start enjoying it now!

talk the truth

"God has plans to prosper me and give me hope and a future. He has great things planned for me." (Jeremiah 29:11)

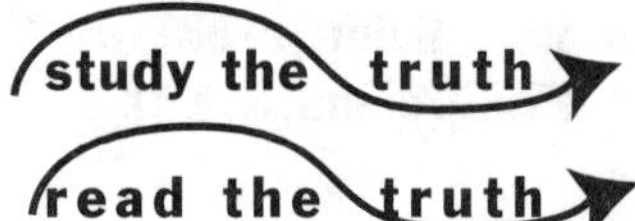
study the truth
read the truth

Ephesians 2:1-8

Joshua 2,3,4; Acts 16,17

BORN AGAIN

> ***"Jesus declared, 'I tell you the truth, no one can see the kingdom of God unless he is born again.'"***
>
> **John 3:3**

Born again. Do you know what Jesus meant when He said those two words to Nicodemus? He was talking about the covenant God has made with us.

Let me paint the picture I believe Jesus was creating. Imagine a little baby born to a single woman. Now imagine no one knows where his father is and no one wants to know. He's the child no one wants. He doesn't belong to anyone.

Now, picture the "perfect" parents. They're confident people who love God. They have a strong marriage and they're financially stable. They love to give and they love people...and they fall in love with this baby. Before long, they adopt him.

What happened? That baby was *born again.* He received a new set of parents. Through adoption, he became part of the family. Why? Well, it wasn't because of anything the baby did. Those parents didn't say, "Look at that baby. He's done so much for us! He has certainly earned our love and respect."

No, he's just a baby. He couldn't do a thing to earn his new life. Out of love, the man and woman agreed together and chose the child for their own. Now that child has access to everything they have.

That's what Jesus was talking about when He said, "You must be born again" (John 3:7). He was talking about entering a new relationship. He was talking about being adopted by a new family. He was talking about accepting God's covenant.

If you feel unworthy to receive all the things God has for you today, think about that. God has made you part of His family. He has made a way for you to stop worrying about the needs in your life and start boldly receiving help from Him.

Discover what it really means to be a child of Almighty God with a big brother like Jesus. Discover what it means to be part of the greatest family around. Discover what it means to be *born again!*

talk the truth

"I am born again, so I will see the kingdom of God." (John 3:3)

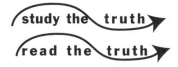

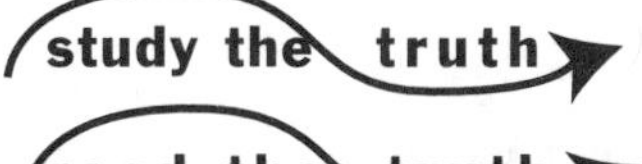
study the truth
read the truth

John 3:1-8

Joshua 5,6; Acts 18

Gloria

April 4

BE LOYAL

"I will honor those who honor me. But I will take honor away from those who do not honor me."

1 SAMUEL 2:30, ICB

God honors those who honor Him. He'll never forget it when you are loyal to Him. He'll bless you for it. And Malachi 3:17 says He will make you a treasured possession—and you'll be one forever.

Forever. Think about that for a moment. By honoring God with how you live and what you say, you're stepping into a place where it will literally take you eternity to explore all the great things He has for you!

Once you begin to look at your life with that in mind, you'll see that it's extremely immature to get mad at God when situations don't work out exactly the way you expected. You'll see that your loyalty must first and foremost be to God, and that you must seek God's ways and do what He wants more than anything else—even when things seem to be going wrong. The Bible says that if you'll do that, all that you need will be given to you.

Remember—God has a perfect memory. If others are giving up in the heat of battle and saying, "This faith stuff doesn't work!" while you are still honoring Him by standing firm and speaking His promises, God won't forget it.

So determine in your heart today to be loyal to God with every word you speak and every action you take. Make up your mind once and for all that nothing in your life is as important as honoring Him. When you do, you'll find that you'll never regret it.

talk the truth

"I honor God and He honors me. I am His treasured possession." (1 Samuel 2:30, ICB)

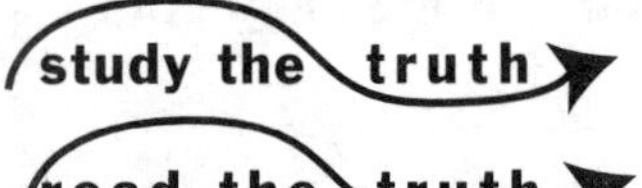
study the truth
read the truth

Psalm 61

Joshua 7,8; Acts 19

April 5

WE NEED EACH OTHER

"That all of them may be one, Father, just as you are in me and I am in you. May they also be in us so that the world may believe that you have sent me."

John 17:21

It's time we began to unify like Jesus prayed in the verse on the right. It's time we stuck with one another in good times as well as bad. It's time we realized that we need each other. We do, you know. Together, we can face anything with faith and win in Jesus.

Let me show you why. In John 3:34, God says Jesus was given the Holy Spirit without limit. That's what made Jesus more powerful than *all* the wicked spirits *combined,* including Satan himself.

Now consider this. We are His Body. We are the end-time generation. And we have a world to win! *We need all the help we can get...and, thank God, we can get all the help we need!*

How? By joining together. Ephesians 4:13 says that when we all unify in our faith, we'll have "the whole measure of the fullness of Christ."

In other words, when Christians come together and begin to function as one Body, we'll have the Holy Spirit without measure—just like Jesus did! We'll begin to see the Holy Spirit move in our lives without limit. We'll see Jesus as we've never seen Him before. Then the world will discover the power of God's Word.

Step into that unity today. Start making a daily effort to pray for others. Start your day by saying, "Holy Spirit, use me to pray for someone today." Then pray for your friends, your pastor, your parents, your teachers, your brother or sister—whomever the Lord may bring to mind.

Once we truly join together in faith, all the wicked spirits of hell won't be able to overcome us!

talk the truth

"I walk in unity of faith with other believers today. We have the whole measure of the fullness of Christ and the world sees Jesus in us." (John 17:21; Ephesians 4:13)

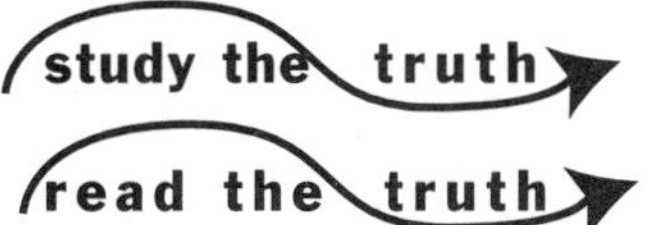
study the truth
read the truth

Ephesians 4:1-16

Joshua 9,10; Acts 20

April 6

SORROW NOT!

"The people the Lord has freed will return. They will enter Jerusalem with joy. Their happiness will last forever. They will have joy and gladness. All sadness [grief] and sorrow will be gone far away"

ISAIAH 51:11, ICB

Did you know that when Jesus died on the cross and rose again, He freed you from grief and sorrow? You don't have to put up with them any more than you have to put up with sin or sickness or disease.

God started teaching me about this several months before my mother went home to be with Him in August of 1988. Every time He'd show me something new about it, I'd put it into practice. (You should do that with anything God is teaching you. Start practicing it now, and you can live in it when the time comes!)

So, 8 1/2 months before my mother left, I began standing against grief and sorrow. I made a decision not to enter into depression. Whenever Satan came to me with depression, I'd say, "No. I won't receive that. I won't put up with depression in Jesus' Name. I belong to the Lord, and I won't receive anything but His joy." Then I'd start speaking scriptures from the Bible and praising Him aloud.

I went through three hard days of resistance until those troubling spirits were gone.

What I'm telling you is this: You will have to stand against grief and sorrow sometime, too. You'll have to stand against depression. It doesn't belong to you. It's not from your Heavenly Father. You may have to stay up and pace all night long. But instead of worrying and crying, walk and quote scriptures until that heavy spirit leaves and the joy of the Lord comes.

Quote God's promises of victory and joy. Quote promises like the one at the beginning of this devotion. Stand and shout that you're the one who will receive joy and gladness. You're the one sorrow and grief will run away from. Stand and let heaven and hell know you are free!

talk the truth

"The Lord has freed me! My happiness will last forever. I have joy and gladness—all grief and sorrow is far away." (Isaiah 51:11, ICB)

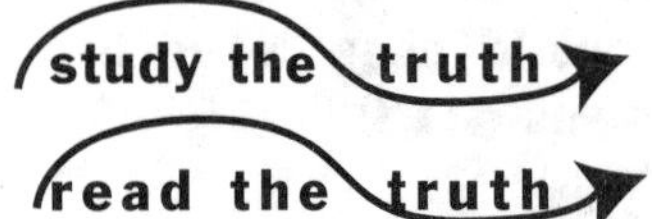
study the truth
read the truth

Psalm 97

Joshua 11,12; Acts 21

RESURRECTION LIFE

"On the first day of the week, very early in the morning, the women took the spices they had prepared and went to the tomb. They found the stone rolled away from the tomb, but when they entered, they did not find the body of the Lord Jesus."

Luke 24:1-3

You know, it's time for us to stop looking for the living among the dead. It's time for us to stop wandering around in the cemetery of sin, sickness and failure—we need to step into resurrection life! As a reborn creation, you're not an accident waiting to happen. Your life isn't just a loose web of events and circumstances. God has specific plans for you (Jeremiah 29:11).

Maybe He intends for you to have the greatest healing ministry of the century, or be the greatest doctor ever. Perhaps He wants to turn you into a successful businessman or woman who knows it's better to give than receive. Maybe He has a revelation or invention prepared for you that will enable you to bless the whole world. But you'll never know what He has in store until you give Him your full attention.

That's why Satan works hard to keep you focusing on life's problems. That's why he tries to keep your attention turned away from God's Word. He doesn't want you to know the life of God is inside you. The thought of your knowing *that* terrifies him.

Why? Because once you truly understand that, you'll begin to act just like Jesus did. You'll pray for the sick and they'll recover. You'll drive out evil spirits. You'll preach God's Word to your classmates. In short, you'll be just what God intended you to be—the Body of Christ on the earth.

Don't let Satan tie you up with the grave clothes of yesterday's sin and defeat. You're not dead anymore. You've been raised with Jesus. Come out from the tomb and start living a resurrection life!

talk the truth

"I have been raised with Jesus. The resurrection life of God is inside me!" (Ephesians 2:6)

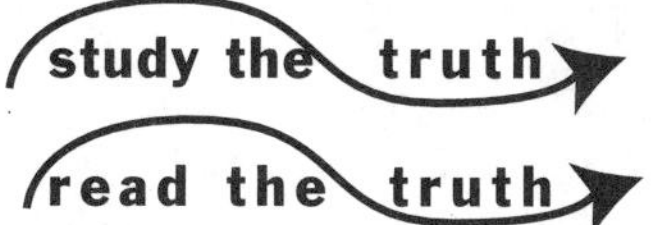
study the truth
read the truth

Acts 17:16-34

Joshua 13,14; Acts 22

April 8

GET ON THE RIGHT ROAD

"This day I call heaven and earth as witnesses against you that I have set before you life and death, blessings and curses. Now choose life, so that you and your children may live."

Deuteronomy 30:19

God's going to get you for that! You've probably said that sometime when you were joking around—most people have said it for years. We may joke about it, but the sad thing is that we've actually believed that God zaps us with pain and punishment whenever we sin. But that's just not true. There are deadly results from sin, but God isn't the one who's passing them out.

You see, the Bible tells us a curse has been in effect for thousands of years. And Satan is the cause of it, not God. God warned us about it in Deuteronomy 30:19. In Deuteronomy 28, God first explained all the benefits available to us if we follow Him. Next He reminded us of the terrible suffering Satan is ready to offer if we'd rather follow him. Then God said, "I have set before you life and death, blessings and curses. Now choose life, so that you and your children may live."

God warned us that trouble is out there and urged us not to travel on the road leading to it. But because He promised to give us freedom, He has allowed us to choose our own way. If we choose to stay on the road to trouble, we will end up in it. Is that because God sent us there? No! He urged us *not* to go.

The important thing to realize is this: At any point in your life—whether you're on the road to trouble or living right in the middle of it—God will save you from it. He'll take you out of there. He'll rescue you from incurable diseases, drug addictions or anything else that's held you captive.

Today if you find yourself on the wrong road and see destruction ahead, just ask God's forgiveness, turn away from that sin and get on the right road. Commit your way to Jesus and He'll rescue you!

Remember this: No matter what you've done, God doesn't want to get you for it, He wants to forgive you of it. He doesn't want to zap you down, He wants to lift you up. Let Him put you on the road of *life* today!

talk the truth

"I commit my way to Jesus and get on the right road today. I choose life!" (Deuteronomy 30:19)

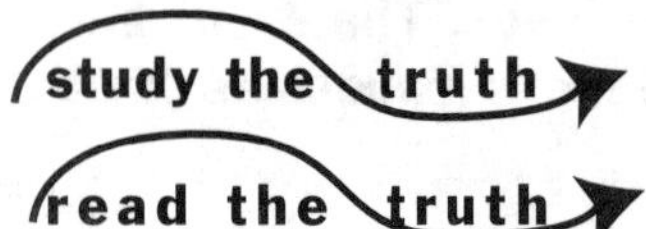
study the truth
read the truth

Deuteronomy 30

Joshua 15; Acts 23

April 9

LEAVE THE PAST BEHIND

"But one thing I do, forgetting those things which are behind and reaching forward to those things which are ahead."

PHILIPPIANS 3:13, NKJV

Failures and disappointments. Emotional aches and pains from the past that just won't go away. Most of us know what it's like to suffer from them, but few of us know what to do about them. We just hope they'll magically stop hurting someday.

But it never happens that way. In fact, the passing of time often leaves us in worse condition—not better. Because, instead of putting those painful failures behind us, we think about them until they become more real to us than God's promises. We focus on them until we become beat down in depression, frozen by the fear that if we go on, we'll only fail again.

I used to get caught in that trap a lot. Then one day when I was battling with depression, the Lord spoke up inside me and said:

Kenneth, your problem is you're thinking about the past instead of the future. Don't do that! Unbelief looks at the past and says, "See, it can't be done." But faith looks at the future and says, "It can be done—and according to God's promises, it is done!"

If depression has caught you in its grasp, break out of it by getting your eyes off the past and onto your future—a future that's been guaranteed by the powerful promises in God's Word (Jeremiah 29:11).

After all, God has forgotten about your failures (Hebrews 8:12). And if He doesn't remember them anymore, why should you?

So, do it! Replace thoughts of yesterday's mistakes with scriptural promises about your future. As you do that, hope will start taking the place of depression. The aches and pains that have crippled you for so long will quickly disappear. Instead of looking behind you and saying, "I can't," you'll begin to look ahead and say, "I *can* do everything through Him Who gives me strength!"

talk the truth

"I forget those things which are behind and reach forward to those things which are ahead." (Philippians 3:13, NKJV)

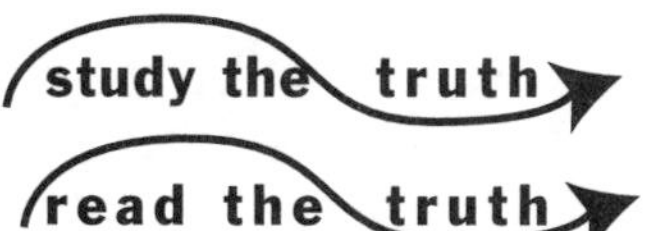
study the truth
read the truth

Philippians 3:1-14

Joshua 16,17,18; Acts 24,25

April 10

FEED ON THE WORD

"Pay attention to what I say; listen closely to my words. Do not let them out of your sight, keep them within your heart."

PROVERBS 4:20,21

Once you've made God's Word the final say in your life, your first step to victory over the enemy's attacks is to go to God's Word and take hold of His promises about your situation.

Notice I said, *"Go* to the Word." It's good to have Bible verses memorized, but don't let that take the place of reading your Bible every day.

Think about it this way. It doesn't do a hungry person any good to think about what a potato tastes like—not even if he can remember it perfectly. The same thing is true with God's Word. It's important to keep it in memory, but it's also necessary to go directly to it and feed your spirit with it. There is power in continually reading and hearing God's Word. That's how it gets in your heart, so you can live by it.

So don't just think about the Bible today, read it. Dig in and find the promises that cover your situation. Place those promises in your heart and grow strong!

talk the truth

"I dig into God's Word and listen closely to what God says. I don't let His Word out of my sight. I keep His promises within my heart." (Proverbs 4:20,21)

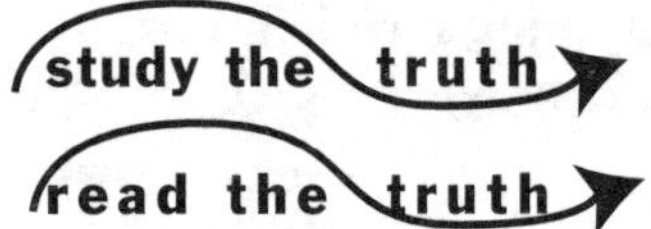
study the truth
read the truth

Deuteronomy 6:1-9

Joshua 19,20; Acts 26

April 11

IT'S NOT OVER TILL IT'S OVER

"Resist him, standing firm in the faith, because you know that your brothers throughout the world are undergoing the same kind of sufferings. And the God of all grace, who called you to his eternal glory in Christ, after you have suffered a little while, will himself restore you and make you strong, firm and steadfast."

1 Peter 5:9,10

No matter how long you've been living by faith, no matter how much you've learned about it, every once in a while you will have a setback. You'll run into something that doesn't turn out the way you expected.

When that happens, remember this: Those setbacks are short-lived. You may have lost a battle, but you won't lose the war. Just get up and go at it again.

"But I don't understand," you say. "I did the best I could. Why didn't I get the victory?"

Because there was something you didn't know! Ken and I have been in the ministry for 30 years. We've spent countless hours in the Bible. Yet it seems like the more we learn, the more we realize we don't know.

So, when we get to a situation where we can't seem to get victory, we ask God for more wisdom. In 2 Samuel 21, you can see a time when King David had to do that. His country had been suffering from a famine for three years and David didn't understand it, so he asked God about it. You know what the Lord told him? He told him the famine had come because of something *Saul* had done! Isn't that wild? Saul had been dead for years, yet what he'd spiritually put in motion was still affecting his country.

David could have just given up when his usual ways of praying didn't drive out that famine, but he didn't. He asked God for more wisdom. He used his temporary setback as an opportunity to seek God for the answer.

Follow his example! Don't quit because of a temporary setback. Refuse to let it knock you out of the game. If professional football teams let setbacks stop them, they'd never make it to the Super Bowl. But they keep believing this fact: It's not over till it's over. So don't give up...because the Bible says when it's all over, you'll have won!

talk the truth

"I resist the devil, standing firm in faith. The Lord restores me and makes me strong, firm and steadfast." (1 Peter 5:9,10)

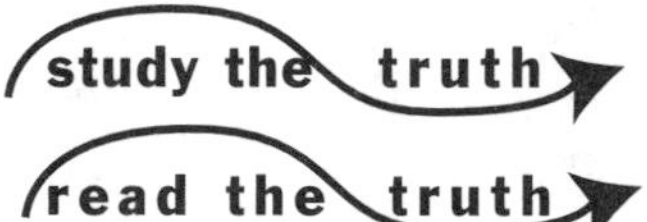
study the truth
read the truth

2 Samuel 21:1-6

Joshua 21,22; Acts 27

April 12

WEAPON OF PRAISE

"I will praise you, O Lord, with all my heart; I will tell of all your wonders. I will be glad and rejoice in you; I will sing praise to your name, O Most High. My enemies turn back; they stumble and perish before you."

Psalm 9:1-3

Never underestimate the power of praise. It's one of the mightiest spiritual weapons you have.

Praise is more than a song or a few kind words about God. It *does* something. It brings God Himself on the scene...and when God shows up, your enemies will take off fast. Sickness and disease can't stay in your body. Insecurity can't stay in your mind. Depression can't stay in your house.

Even physical tiredness has to disappear when it comes face to face with real praise. I know that from experience. Years ago, when I first began teaching Healing School, I had a real battle with getting tired. I'd minister and lay my hands on the sick for so many hours at a time that when the meeting ended, I was sometimes too physically weak even to close the service.

Then, one particular meeting, I discovered the power of praise. I had just finished praying for everyone who came for prayer, and as usual, I was exhausted. But instead of resting, the Holy Spirit showed me that what I needed to do was praise God. So I did. I began to praise Him with everything within me. Do you know what happened? That tiredness left me. And I was energized with the life and power of God!

The next time Satan tries to drain you of the strength and victory that's yours in Jesus, turn him back with a powerful weapon—*praise!*

talk the truth

"I praise God with all my heart and tell of all His wonders. I am glad and rejoice in Him. I sing praise to His Name. My enemies turn back, stumble and perish before me!" (Psalm 9:1-3)

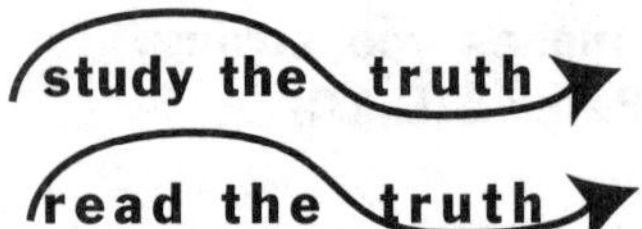
study the truth
read the truth

2 Chronicles 20:1-22

Joshua 23,24; Acts 28

FORGIVE AND FORGET

"Love...is not touchy or fretful or resentful; it takes no account of the evil done to it—pays no attention to a suffered wrong."

1 Corinthians 13:5, AMP

Have you ever tried to forgive someone...and found you simply couldn't do it? You prayed about it and asked God to help you, but those angry feelings just kept burning inside you.

Put an end to those kinds of failures in the future by basing your forgiveness on faith rather than your feelings. True forgiveness doesn't have anything at all to do with how you feel. It's an act of the will—something you *choose* to do. It is based on obedience to God and on faith in Him.

That means once you've forgiven a person, you need to consider them permanently forgiven! When old feelings rise up within you and Satan tries to convince you that you haven't really forgiven them, resist him. Say, *"No, I've already forgiven that person by faith. I refuse to think about those old feelings."*

Then, according to 1 John 1:9, believe you receive God's forgiveness from the sin of unforgiveness, and ask Him to cleanse you from all the sin tied up with it—*including remembering that you were ever wronged!*

Have you ever heard anyone say, "I may forgive, but I'll never forget!" Well, that's not true forgiveness at all—you must forgive supernaturally "just as in Christ God forgave you" (Ephesians 4:32).

You're to forgive as God forgives...to release that person from guilt permanently and unconditionally...to operate as if nothing bad ever happened between you. You are to purposely forget as well as forgive.

As you do that, something supernatural will happen within you. The pain will disappear. God's power will wash away the effects of it, and you'll be able to leave it behind once and for all.

Don't keep account of all the wrongs done to you. Learn to forgive *and* forget.

talk the truth

"The love of God is in me. I am not touchy or fretful or resentful. I take no account of evil done to me. I pay no attention to a suffered wrong. I forgive and forget." (1 Corinthians 13:5, AMP)

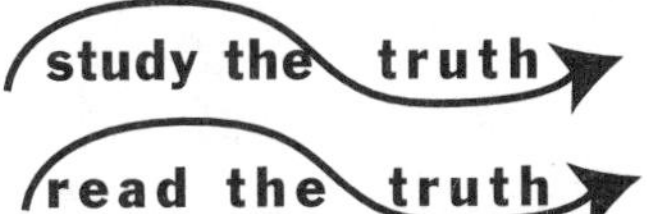
study the truth
read the truth

Luke 6:27-37

Judges 1,2; Romans 1

April 14

Kenneth

USE GOD'S MO

"By faith we understand that the universe was formed at God's command, so that what is seen was not made out of what was visible."

HEBREWS 11:3

God uses words to create. He used His Word to form the universe. Just look in the first chapter of Genesis and count how many times you see the phrase, "God said." It's a lot!

That's because God doesn't do anything without saying it first. That's His MO—His mode of operation. And, if you're smart, you'll use that mode of operation too. You'll take His words and speak them out until they become a reality in your life.

"Well, I tried that and it didn't work. I quoted 1 Peter 2:24 and said, 'By His wounds I'm healed' four times and I'm still not healed."

Big deal. From the time Adam and Eve fell in the Garden of Eden, God started speaking about Jesus' coming (Genesis 3:15). And if you study the Bible, you'll see that He spoke about Jesus' coming again and again throughout the entire Old Testament.

Then finally, after several thousand years, the book of John tells us, "The Word became flesh and made his dwelling among us" (verse 14).

So if you've said you're healed four times and nothing's happened, don't worry about it. Just keep saying it! You might think it's taking a long time to happen, but I'll guarantee you, it won't take thousands of years.

Do you want to operate in God's power? Then use His MO. Speak out His promises about your success in your grades, your relationships and your future. Let those words fill your life with victory!

talk the truth

"I don't doubt in my heart. I believe that whatever I say comes to pass." (Mark 11:23)

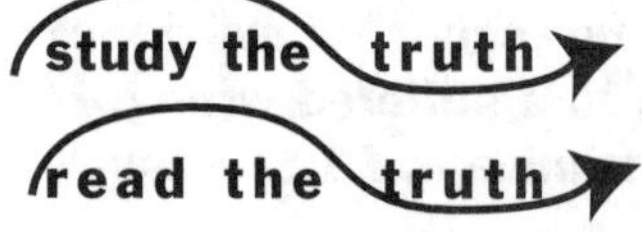
study the truth
read the truth

Genesis 1

Judges 3,4; Romans 2

LIVE THE LOVE LIFE

"But whoever keeps His word, truly the love of God is perfected in him. By this we know that we are in Him. He who says he abides in Him ought himself also to walk just as He walked."

1 JOHN 2:5,6, NKJV

There is nothing—absolutely nothing—more important than learning to love. In fact, how accurately you learn to walk in love will determine how much of God's plan for your life you accomplish. That's because every other spiritual force is activated by love. For example, the Bible teaches us that faith works by love. That's why it's nearly impossible to receive an answered prayer when a Christian steps outside of love and refuses to forgive or is in strife with another Christian. Without love, faith just fails.

So how can you be sure you're walking in love? First Corinthians 13:4-8 paints a perfect picture of true love. It's patient and kind. It's not jealous or proud. It doesn't behave rudely or selfishly and it isn't touchy. Love "bears all things, believes all things, hopes all things, endures all things" (verse 7, NKJV).

Sounds difficult, doesn't it? But don't worry. God has sent His Spirit to live in you and teach you how to love as He loves. With His power, you can live a life full of love.

Start today. Think of a specific way you can love someone and then do it. Maybe you could take the time to help someone who's struggling with their homework. You could ask someone to eat lunch with you who normally sits alone. You could buy someone a candy bar or write someone an encouraging note. You could even do it secretly. Think of some way you can walk in love and then do it in the love of Jesus...it will make your day a day of victory!

talk the truth

"I keep God's Word and His love is perfected in me. I walk as Jesus walked." (1 John 2:5,6, NKJV)

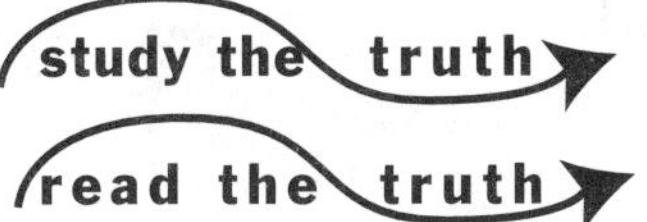
study the truth
read the truth

1 Corinthians 13:1-13

Judges 5,6; Romans 3

April 16

Kenneth

TAKE SOME NEW GROUND

"Again, I tell you that if two of you on earth agree about anything you ask for, it will be done for you by my Father in heaven."

MATTHEW 18:19

As Christians, you and I are part of a conquering army, constantly claiming new ground for the kingdom of God. Right?

Well, yes, that's the way it should be. But just about the time our army makes it over the hill and is ready to advance, Satan pulls out a bazooka—the big gun of *division*—and scatters us in every direction.

Satan's strategy of division takes many facets. He tries to divide us by skin color, culture, age, social status, sex or even popularity. He tries to keep us so concerned with things that don't matter that we never see each other's strengths.

So how can we strike back against Satan's strategy of division? By launching an even more powerful attack of our own. By using one of the most powerful resources given to us by Jesus: the prayer of agreement.

Jesus said that if any two of us will agree about anything we pray for, it *will* be done! That's such a powerful statement, most people don't even believe it...and that's just what Satan wants.

But you can begin counterattacking his strategy of division by finding someone to join with in prayer this week. Put aside your differences and base what you pray for on God's Word. You may have different opinions about everything else, you may not seem to have much in common, but you can be in agreement about what the Bible says.

Then, once you agree, be sure you each keep a watch over what you think and say so you don't drop your faith. "Capture every thought and make it give up and obey Christ" (2 Corinthians 10:5, ICB). And once you've prayed, thank God for the answer.

You'll see that—no matter what your differences—God will answer your prayer if you both keep standing in faith. So get ready...because when we all begin to agree together in faith and start believing God, we'll be taking a lot of new ground for the Lord!

talk the truth **"When I come into agreement with another Christian, anything we ask will be done by our Father in heaven." (Matthew 18:19)**

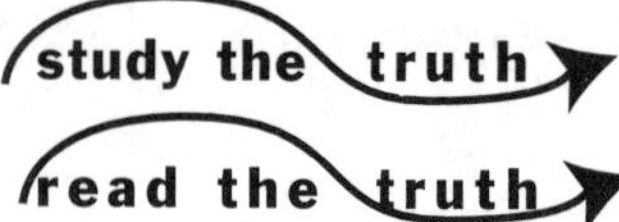
study the truth
read the truth

Acts 4:1-31

Judges 7,8,9; Romans 4,5

NO OFFENSE

> ***"Whoever loves his brother lives in the light, and there is nothing in him to make him stumble."***
>
> **1 John 2:10**

Whenever you find yourself stumbling into failure or sin, check your "love life." Sit down with the Lord and ask Him to show you if you're in strife with anyone, or if you've been offended. If you have, Satan can come in and trip you up.

As a preacher, I've seen that happen countless times. I'll be preaching and some Christian will get upset about something I said. He'll decide I'm wrong and go off angry—and the first thing you know, he's in trouble.

Mark 4:17 tells us Satan uses those kinds of offenses to steal God's Word from our hearts. He causes us to become upset with each other. Then he's able to drain the Word from us like running water from a faucet.

Don't ever let that happen to you. If you hear a preacher or one of your Christian friends say something that rubs you the wrong way, and you catch yourself becoming offended, just say, "Oh no you don't. You're not stealing God's Word out of me, Satan." Then ask forgiveness from God and turn away from thinking like that right then and there.

Search the Bible and listen to the Holy Spirit within you to find out what you should do. If you still feel what that person said was wrong, pray for him or her.

Remember, getting offended never comes from God. He says we're to be grounded and established in love. So refuse to be offended. Pray for that person and love them. Then you'll be able to walk right on through that situation without stumbling at all.

talk the truth

"I love my brother and live in the light. There is nothing in me to make me stumble." (1 John 2:10)

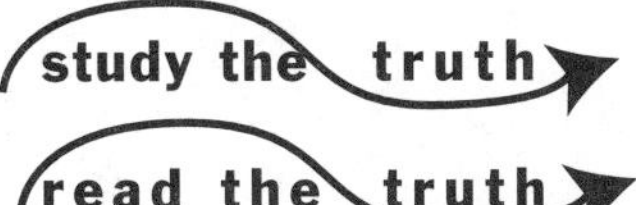
study the truth
read the truth

1 John 2:1-11

Judges 10,11; Romans 6

Kenneth

April 18

THROW OPEN THE DOOR

"Jesus sat down opposite the place where the offerings were put and watched the crowd putting their money into the temple treasury.... A poor widow came and put in two very small copper coins, worth only a fraction of a penny. Calling his disciples to him, Jesus said, 'I tell you the truth, this poor widow has put more into the treasury than all the others. They all gave out of their wealth; but she, out of her poverty, put in everything—all she had to live on.'"

Mark 12:41-44

Have you ever wanted to get God's attention? Well, there's a certain kind of *giving*—giving in boldness and faith—that will get His attention every time.

Read the verses on the left again and just imagine the situation it describes. Jesus was watching as people gave their offerings. I'm sure there were some hypocritical displays going on since He was there watching. Surely, some wealthy leaders looked pretty smug as they walked up to offer their gifts.

Right in the middle of it all, this poor widow walked up and threw in her offering. I can just see her. I can hear her say, "I may be a poor widow now, but I'm not going to be a poor widow anymore. I'm giving Him everything I have!"

Then, wham! She threw the last little dab of money she had into the offering.

That got Jesus' attention.

He said, "Listen up, everyone! Let me tell you about this woman," and He started to preach.

What moved Jesus wasn't just the fact that she gave. It was *how* she gave. She gave in *faith*—not in fear. She didn't stop and calculate what she didn't have and say, "Boy, if I do this, tomorrow I won't eat." She just boldly threw in all she had, knowing God would take care of her.

You and I need to have that same attitude. We need to be confident, throwing our offerings boldly into His service, knowing He will bless us in return.

If you have a need right now, get God's attention by giving with boldness and faith like that widow did. Throw open the door of your life by throwing everything you have at Jesus. Let God know that He is the One you are trusting to take care of you. Before long, the abundance of God will come rushing in!

talk the truth

"I give in faith—not in fear of not having enough. I trust in God to take care of me." (Mark 12:41-44)

study the truth
read the truth

Mark 12:28-44

Judges 12,13; Romans 7

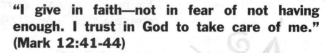

KEEP UP YOUR COURAGE

"But now I urge you to keep up your courage, because not one of you will be lost; only the ship will be destroyed."

ACTS 27:22

What do you do when you're in a really dangerous situation? If you're like I used to be, you desperately cry out to God! One afternoon when I was whining to God about something, He interrupted me and said, *Kenneth, did you know I don't hear the cry of My children when they cry out in desperation?*

"What?!" I said. "I thought You did."

He said, *No, I hear the desperate cry of a sinner because that's all he can cry about—His hopelessness. But once you're reborn, you ought to be crying out of faith. I hear the faith cry.*

What is a faith cry? It's calling things that are not as though they already are (Romans 4:17). It's what the Bible means when it says, "Let the weak say, I am strong" (Joel 3:10, KJV).

The Apostle Paul knew how to cry out in faith. That's why, in Acts 27, he motivated the sailors on that battered, sinking ship to keep their courage. He was telling them to act by faith. Can you imagine what they probably thought when he said that? *Listen to that stupid preacher. We're sinking and he says to have courage. We've thrown everything we own overboard and he says to have courage!*

You may feel just like those sailors did. You may feel like crying out in desperation because your ship's going down. But don't do it. Instead, do what Paul said and keep up your courage!

Cry out to God in faith and say, *"Lord, I will not panic. I'll keep up my courage because the Bible says You'll rescue me from this situation"* (Psalm 34:19).

Then start being courageous. It may take a lot of determination, but God will give you the strength to do it. Instead of desperately crying out, stand in faith. Keep your courage and you can be sure God will bring you through the storm to victory!

talk the truth

"I cry out in faith today, keeping up my courage. I know God can rescue me in *any* situation." (Acts 27:22)

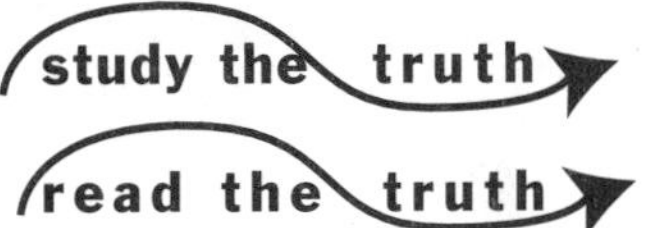
study the truth
read the truth

Philippians 4:4-9

Judges 14,15; Romans 8

April 20

NATURALLY SUPERNATURAL

"Then the Lord said to Moses, 'Why are you crying out to me?... Raise your staff and stretch out your hand over the sea to divide the water so that the Israelites can go through the sea on dry ground.'"

Exodus 14:15,16

If you hang around God very much, it won't be long before you'll start wanting to do some things most people consider supernatural. You'll start wanting to pray for the sick and to see them recover. You'll start wanting to boldly share God's Word with people you don't even know. You'll start wanting to be someone God can powerfully move through—no matter where you are or who you're with.

Furthermore, you can do it if you want to! How? Not by jumping out and "trying" to do supernatural things, but by obeying God one step at a time. By doing the things He's already given you power to do.

That's how it happened with Moses. He didn't have the power to divide the Red Sea. But he *did* have the power to stretch his hand out over it. And when he did that, in obedience to the Lord's command, the Holy Spirit did the rest.

It will be the same way with you. When you start doing your part, the Holy Spirit will do His, and supernatural things will start happening around you.

What is your part? Reading the Bible. Praying. Listening to what the Holy Spirit says to you. As you do those things—as you begin to move as God shows you—and follow His direction, you'll flow in the supernatural as naturally as a bird flies in the air.

You won't struggle and strain to try and "part the sea." You'll just trust the Lord and stretch out your hand...and watch the miracles roll!

talk the truth

"Supernatural signs follow me because I'm a believer. I read my Bible, pray and follow God's direction...and God moves in my life!" (Exodus 14:15,16)

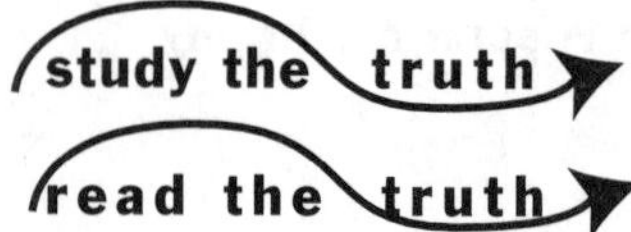
study the truth
read the truth

Exodus 14

Judges 16,17; Romans 9

Gloria

April 21

GOD OF YOUR TROUBLE, GOD OF YOUR HEART

"You are my hiding place; you will protect me from trouble and surround me with songs of deliverance."

PSALM 32:7

In this day and time, trouble seems to surround us on every side. If it's not a failing economy, it's failing relationships or failing health. Yet, in the middle of seemingly overwhelming problems, God has promised to rescue us.

But remember this—if you want God to be God of your trouble, then you must let Him be God in your heart. God honors those who honor Him. So, if you're facing some problems today, don't just start kicking and screaming and begging Him to save you from them. Honor Him by going to the Bible and doing what He says you should do.

Psalm 34 is a good place to start. It says, for example, that if you seek God, He will rescue you.

Secondly, it instructs you to call to the Lord. He will rescue you from *all* your troubles (verse 6).

Next it tells you to fear the Lord. If you don't know how to do that, verses 11-14 will tell you exactly what you need to know. You must keep from speaking evil and lies, turn from evil and do good, seek peace and pursue it.

Remember, if you want God to be God of your trouble, let Him be God of your heart. When you do that, all of heaven will get involved in rescuing you—and your victory will be guaranteed.

talk the truth

"The Lord is my hiding place. He protects me from trouble and surrounds me with songs of deliverance." (Psalm 32:7)

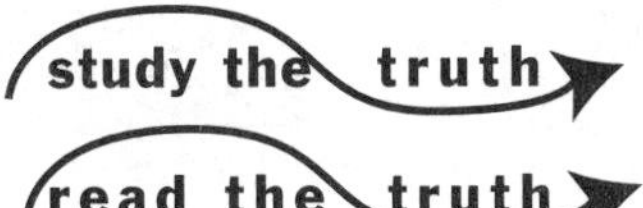
study the truth
read the truth

Psalm 34

Judges 18,19; Romans 10

April 22

HE REALLY CARES FOR YOU

"Cast all your anxiety on him because he cares for you."

1 PETER 5:7

Do you know what it's like to face a problem so big, it seems wrong *not* to worry about it? There may not be a thing you can do about it, but you feel like you need to at least be concerned.

I remember one time in particular I felt that way. I was holding some meetings in Ruston, Louisiana. I had just discovered our budget was $800 short—and in those days, $800 might as well have been $8 million! Satan just kept telling me that I was facing this problem alone.

But instead of giving in to those thoughts, I picked up my Bible and turned to every scripture that promised me my needs were met. Then I promised God that, with the Holy Spirit's help, I would not think about that problem again.

That wasn't an easy promise to keep. I wanted to worry so badly! I went into the courtyard of the motel where I was staying and walked around the swimming pool. Every time I thought about the problem, I would say out loud, "No, I have given that to the Lord. I will not think about it. The budget is met."

After a while, a man drove up in the driveway and began to honk his horn.

I tried to ignore him because I don't like to be interrupted when I'm praying, but he stuck his head out of the window and shouted, "Come here!"

He said to me, "I'm sorry to disturb you, but I'll be late for the meeting tonight. I was afraid I would miss the offering." Then he handed me a check. When I went back to my room and looked at that check, I found it was for $500. Coupled with the offering in the service that night, it totaled the exact amount I needed to meet the budget!

The next time you're facing a problem, give it to God. Let Him be the One Who's concerned about it. He's volunteered for the job and you can trust Him to do it well. After all, He really cares for you!

talk the truth

"I cast all of my cares, anxieties and worries onto the Lord because He cares for me." (1 Peter 5:7)

study the truth
read the truth

Psalm 37:1-11

Judges 20,21; Romans 11

RESIST SATAN

"Submit yourselves, then, to God. Resist the devil [Satan], and he will flee from you."

JAMES 4:7

If you've been crying and asking God to run Satan out of your life, STOP! The Bible says *you're* the one who's supposed to overcome Satan.

How? By resisting him when he tells you to do something… and by doing what God says instead! When Satan tells you a lie, do just like Jesus did in Luke 4—contradict Satan's lie by speaking what the Bible says. According to the verse to the right, when you do that, Satan will flee. He'll literally run away in terror.

That means everywhere you go, as you walk in faith and resist Satan, darkness is pushed back.

So start pushing back that darkness in your school, your workplace and your home. You can do it! God's life is within you. Jesus Himself is living inside you. Everywhere you go, He goes. Every problem that rises up against you, every evil spirit that tries to influence your life, is coming up against God when he comes up against you.

All you need to do is realize that. Begin living your life—moment by moment—knowing that the light of God is in you. The Holy Spirit is in you. Live knowing that Jesus, the Son of God, is in you. Then watch Satan run!

talk the truth

"I submit myself to God. I resist Satan and he flees from me." (James 4:7)

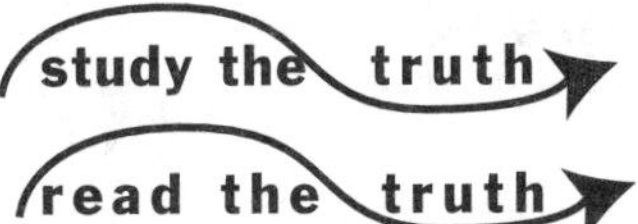
study the truth
read the truth

Ephesians 6:10-18

Ruth 1,2,3; Romans 12,13

Gloria

INSIDE OUT

"Our faces, then, are not covered. We all show the Lord's glory, and we are being changed to be like him. This change in us brings more and more glory. And it comes from the Lord, who is the Spirit."

2 Corinthians 3:18, ICB

Have you ever thought about the fact that humans are the only creatures God created who have to wear clothes to cover themselves? All the other creatures grow their own coverings. Some grow fur, some feathers, others scales or leathery hide. But all creatures are clothed from the inside out!

Most people don't realize it, but in the beginning, man was clothed that way too. The Bible says he was made in God's image (Genesis 1:27). And, if you'll look in Ezekiel 8:2, you'll find that God is clothed in fire. That fire is His Glory flowing out from within Him.

When man was first created, he was like that too. He was covered with the Glory of God. It radiated from the inside out. That's why Adam and Eve didn't know they were naked until after they sinned and the Glory left.

It was a tragic day when man lost that covering. But I want you to know something. It is not lost forever. The Bible says we can get it back.

You see, when you made Jesus the Lord of your life, God's Glory came to live inside you once again. It may be hidden right now, but believe me, it's in there.

And the Bible says that as you gaze into the Lord's face by studying the Bible and spending time with Him in prayer, as you change your thinking to realize who you are in Christ, you'll start showing on the outside what the Glory is like on the inside of you. Little by little, you'll be turned inside out!

Don't just look in your closet each morning, deciding what to wear for school. Look in the Bible, too—and help bring out what's on the inside. Let Him clothe you in His presence. Once His Glory shines through, anything you wear will look more fashionable than ever!

talk the truth

"I show the Lord's glory and I am being changed to be like Him." (2 Corinthians 3:18, ICB)

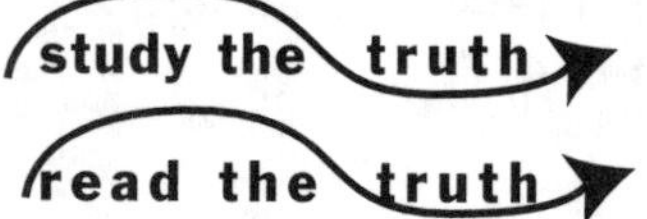
study the truth
read the truth

Psalm 8

Ruth 4; 1 Samuel 1; Romans 14

A FLOOD IS COMING

There's a spiritual flood coming. God promised it in the Bible. He's promised us a flood of the Holy Spirit's power so great that it will result in thousands upon thousands of people choosing Jesus as their Lord. This flood is so great, it will reach the inner-city gangs. It will spread to the guy or girl in your homeroom who's addicted to drugs. It will burst into the lives of those you love the most.

Yet as Christians, we've been looking up, expecting God to pour down this flood from somewhere up in heaven. But you know what? We've been looking in the wrong direction! This flood will come from right here on earth.

Jesus explained it this way—"Whoever believes in me, as the Scripture has said, streams of living water will flow from within him" (John 7:38).

"Be glad, O people of Zion, rejoice in the Lord your God, for he has given you the autumn rains in righteousness. He sends you abundant showers, both autumn and spring rains, as before."

JOEL 2:23

The flood we've been expecting will be made of "living water" pouring out from *Christians.* The Holy Spirit will use *you and me* to deliver God's supernatural power to the world! And as we agree together in prayer, those rivers of living water within each of us will join and become a flood of spiritual power that will cover the earth and touch the lives of everyone we spend time with.

So, start praying every day for your friends, that guy or girl in your homeroom, your family—anyone you can think of...because their lives will be the ones that are changed when the flood sirens sound!

talk the truth

"I believe on the Lord, and streams of living water flow from within me." (John 7:38)

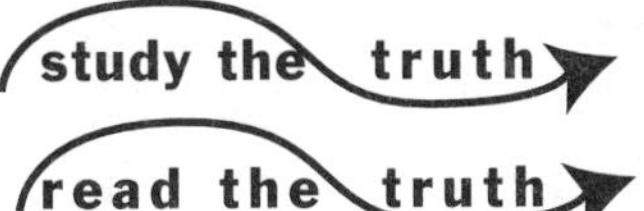
study the truth
read the truth

Joel 2:23-32

1 Samuel 2,3; Romans 15

April 26

Gloria

PRESS ON IN PATIENCE

"We do not want you to become lazy, but to imitate those who through faith and patience inherit what has been promised."

HEBREWS 6:12

You've been walking by faith. You've been believing God to meet your needs. But what do you do when it has taken awhile to see your answer and you are tempted to give up?

Be patient!

There's not much said about patience these days. People want everything fast—from food to computers. But, when it comes to receiving from God, patience is just as important as faith. It will make the difference between your success and failure.

Patience strengthens and supports faith until you see the answer. After you've prayed and read God's promises, patience will encourage you to hold steady until you receive what you're believing for. Patience is power. It has the courage to refuse Satan's lie that says God's Word isn't working for you. Patience knows that His Word has never failed. It will not draw back in fear...it will press forward in faith until you have the answer.

To make your patience strong, practice patience in everyday situations. If you have to stand in long lines at the movies or at lunch, don't get mad—exercise your patience. Every time you do, it will grow stronger, just like a muscle.

And when it takes a long time to see an answer to your prayers, don't give up! Continue to put God's Word first, with patience, and you *will* receive His promise!

talk the truth

"I refuse to become lazy. I imitate those who, through faith and patience, inherit God's promises." (Hebrews 6:12)

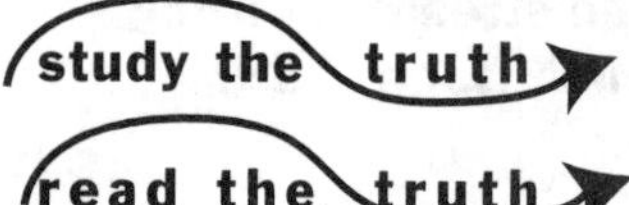
study the truth
read the truth

Hebrews 10:32-39

1 Samuel 4,5; Romans 16

OBEDIENCE—NO SMALL THING

> ***"But the one who hears my words and does not put them into practice is like a man who built a house on the ground without a foundation. The moment the torrent struck that house, it collapsed and its destruction was complete."***
>
> **Luke 6:49**

Do you ever have times in your life when it seems like every time you go to church, spend time in prayer or open the Bible, you receive something special from God? I do. Spiritually, everything will be going great. Then, suddenly, something starts to happen. I start drying up.

It seems like it doesn't make any difference what I pray or how much I read the Bible, I can't get anywhere spiritually.

I never used to understand that. I didn't know what the cause was. I didn't have any sin in my life. I'd taken care of that. I was still praying. I was still acting on God's Word. But I was getting nowhere.

If that's ever happened to you, may I make a suggestion? Think back and find the last thing God told you to do that you didn't do—and *do it!*

It's probably nothing big. But, believe me, minor disobedience will stop the Holy Spirit from flowing in your life just like major disobedience will.

Most of us don't realize that. We'll get on our knees and say, "Oh Lord, I'll do anything for You! I'll go on the missions trip this summer with my youth group. I'll go to Africa. I'll go to Russia. I'll go to China." But when God says, "Go next door," we just ignore Him.

"I can't do that," we'll say. "That guy next door doesn't like me. Besides, I want to preach in front of thousands."

If you've done something like that, repent. Stop and change. Pick up where you left off and do what God directed. And from now on, remember, no matter how minor God's instructions may seem, obeying them is no small thing! It's those simple acts of obedience that will make your spiritual house stand or fall...because all the small things combined become the direction of your life.

talk the truth

"I hear what God says and put it into practice." (Luke 6:47,48)

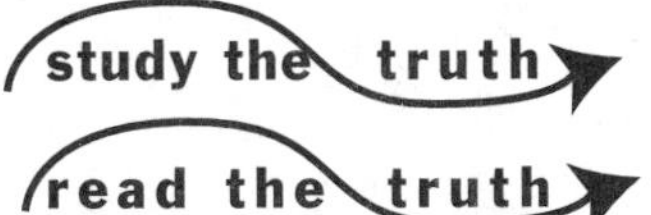
study the truth
read the truth

Luke 16:1-10

1 Samuel 6,7; 1 Corinthians 1

April 28

FOLLOW YOUR DREAM

"But Moses said to God, 'Who am I, that I should go to Pharaoh and bring the Israelites out of Egypt?' And God said, 'I will be with you.'"

Exodus 3:11,12

Have you ever had a dream of doing something really great for Jesus? A dream of being so bold, for instance, that you could lead thousands to the Lord?

At one time or another, you probably have, but then you thought, *Oh, I couldn't do that.*

If so, I have some good news for you. If you'll believe God, something like even a poor self-image won't keep you from success. Look in the book of Exodus and you'll see a man who proved that. His name was Moses.

Moses didn't have a very good self-image. He'd made a terrible mistake when he was young—he actually murdered someone. It was a mistake that drove him to a wilderness hideaway to be a sheepherder for 40 years.

He'd once dreamed of rescuing God's people, but no more. As far as he was concerned, he was finished...a failure...a flop!

But God didn't think so. In fact, when God came to Moses, He didn't ask for his résumé. He didn't mention his shady history. He just told him to go see Pharaoh and tell him to let God's people go.

Moses, however, was still wrestling with his poor self-image. "Who am I, that I should go to Pharaoh?" he stuttered.

You know what God said in response? "I will be with you."

You see, it didn't matter who Moses was. What mattered was that God was with him. The same thing is true for you today. You don't need a history of success behind you to answer God's call. You don't need to be popular and talented. All you need is God's presence.

Think about that when Satan tells you you're a failure, when he says you'll never be able to accomplish the dream God has put in your heart. Put him in his place. Tell him it doesn't matter who you are because God is with you.

Then dare to follow your dream!

talk the truth

"I am a child of God and I have overcome! Greater is He that is in me than he that is in the world." (1 John 4:4)

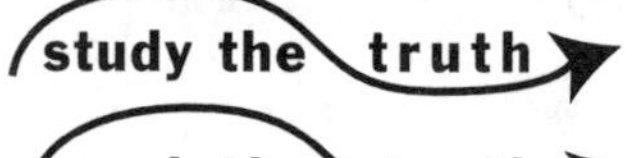
study the truth
read the truth

Exodus 3:1-14

1 Samuel 8,9; 1 Corinthians 2

DON'T LET SATAN PUT ONE OVER ON YOU

"When he [Satan] lies, he speaks his native language, for he is a liar and the father of lies."

John 8:44

Some people find it difficult to believe God's promises because they've seen so many things in the natural world that seem to contradict them. They've seen people faithfully give tithes and then go broke. They've seen sick Christians fail to receive their healing.

Really, it would be more accurate to say that they *think* they've seen those things. Because, you see, there's a deceiver at work in the world. This deceiver is busily doing the same thing he's been doing ever since the Garden of Eden—tricking mankind into believing God's Word isn't true.

And, after practicing for thousands of years, Satan's a master at it. Think about that the next time he tries to make it look as though God's Word won't work for you. Say, "I don't care how things look. I believe the Bible."

Let me show you what I mean. Have you ever seen a magic show where someone crawls inside a box and then is sawed in half? You see it with your own two eyes. The guy's feet are sticking out one end of the box and his head is poking out the other, and the box is plainly cut in two. Then the magician slides the two halves back together and the guy jumps out of the box in one piece.

Tell me, did you really believe that guy was truly cut in half? Of course not! You knew that you'd seen a trick, a deception, something that appeared one way when, in reality, it was a different way altogether. You may not have been able to explain it. But you knew a person couldn't be sawed in half and put back together, so you didn't believe your eyes.

That's exactly the way you need to be with God's Word. You need to learn to trust it to such an extent that when Satan shows you something that appears to contradict it, you just say, "I'm not gullible enough to believe it. I'm sticking with God's promise to me."

If you'll do that, Satan, the father of lies, will never be able to put one over on you.

talk the truth

"Above all, I believe God's Word. I won't be fooled by Satan's deceiving strategies." (John 8:44)

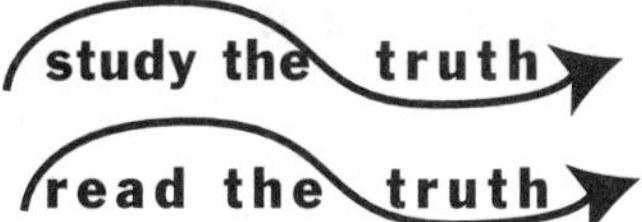
study the truth
read the truth

Psalm 119:89-104

1 Samuel 10,11; 1 Corinthians 3

April 30

BE A CHEERFUL GIVER

"Let each one [give] as he has made up his own mind and purposed in his heart, not reluctantly or sorrowfully or under compulsion, for God loves (that is, He takes pleasure in, prizes above other things, and is unwilling to abandon or to do without) a cheerful (joyous, prompt-to-do-it) giver.... And God is able to make all grace (every favor and earthly blessing) come to you in abundance."

2 Corinthians 9:7,8, AMP

Some people say you should "give till it hurts," but don't you believe it. God doesn't want gifts given in pain. The only kinds of gifts that please Him are gifts willingly and happily given to Him. That's the reason God tacked His promise of abundance onto His command about cheerful giving in the verse above. The two are connected.

Cheerfully giving in faith is the key that unlocks God's promises. Have you ever seen someone give that way? I have. I'll never forget it. I was at a meeting years ago when the offering time became a spontaneous celebration. Ken was singing "Cast Your Bread Upon the Waters," and the people were actually dancing their way down the aisles to give to God. The joy in that place was wonderful. Great healings and miracles happened that night.

But what stood out to me above all was how full of joy the people were as they brought their offerings to God. The offering wasn't pulled from them like a dentist pulls teeth. It was gladly given.

The idea of "giving till it hurts" didn't come from God. He'd rather you give $10 with joy than $20 grudgingly. In 2 Corinthians 8:11-12, the Apostle Paul urges the church in Corinth to give with eager willingness. *Eager willingness*...that's what God looks for!

If you haven't given that way in the past, make a firm decision to start. Ask forgiveness for the times you've given grudgingly. Then spend some serious time with God and His Word, so when you give again, you can give willingly.

Put the "pain" of giving behind. Become a "cheerful, joyous, prompt-to do-it giver"...and believe me—God will bless you richly!

talk the truth

"I am a cheerful, joyous, prompt-to-do-it giver. God is able to bless me with more than enough." (2 Corinthians 9:7,8, AMP)

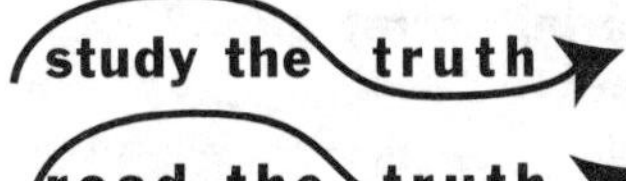
study the truth
read the truth

2 Corinthians 9:6-15

1 Samuel 12,13,14; 1 Corinthians 4,5

BREAK THROUGH THE WALL

"I can do everything through him who gives me strength."

Philippians 4:13

You're running the race of life, moving full speed ahead, and God is blessing your every step. Then suddenly, *wham!* You hit the wall. It may be a wall of sickness, trouble at school or family problems. But, regardless of what kind of wall it is, the effect is always the same. It stops you cold.

The question is, once you hit a wall like that, what will you do? You'll be tempted to quit. But don't do it. God will give you what you need to *break through* that wall.

It's not easy. It's downright tough. But you have to push on through the tough times if you ever want to win.

Ask any athlete. He'll tell you! Because if he's a winner, he's been there. He's pushed his body to what seems to be the maximum. His side has hurt. His lungs have ached. He's had cramps in his legs. And just when he felt like he couldn't go on, he's heard a coach yell, "Come on! Move it!"

Athletes call that "hitting the wall." But the skilled athlete knows that "the wall" isn't the end. It's the signal that he's about to break through. If he'll toughen up and push himself a little more, he'll get a second wind. Suddenly, he'll go faster than before. He'll reach a level of excellence he couldn't have reached any other way.

When you feel the worst, when failure is breathing down your neck, press in to God's Word as never before. All you have to do is punch one little hole in that wall of problems—dig one tiny hole in it with your faith and the Word.

Then keep tearing away at that hole. Don't quit! And, before long, the forces of God will come bursting through, demolishing everything in their path!

Once that happens, you'll never be the same again. You'll be hooked. It will only take one breakthrough like that to make a champion out of you.

talk the truth

"I can do everything through Him who gives me strength." (Philippians 4:13)

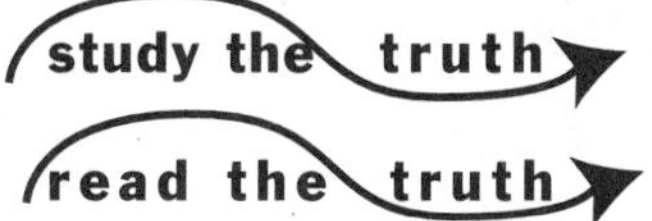
study the truth
read the truth

1 Corinthians 9:24-27

1 Samuel 15,16; 1 Corinthians 6

Gloria

May 2

TRAIN YOUR SPIRIT

"It [Grace] teaches us to say 'No' to ungodliness and worldly passions, and to live self-controlled, upright and godly lives in this present age."

Titus 2:12

When an athlete goes into training, he practices to improve his skills. He works hard, repeating the same motions over and over, until they become what we'd call "second nature" to him.

Most of us understand how important that kind of physical training is. We know that you simply can't be a winner without it. But did you know we can train ourselves that same way in spiritual things?

That's right! Hebrews 5:14 says we can train ourselves to distinguish good from evil. When you train for something, you daily expose yourself to whatever it is you want to become. You practice it over and over until it becomes second nature to you. People who are lazy have practiced being lazy. People who are disciplined have practiced being disciplined.

Spending time with God is "spiritual" exercise. As you spend time with Him regularly, your spirit will grow stronger and will start to overcome bad habits.

If, for example, you have trouble getting up in the morning to spend time with God before your busy day begins, if you've been giving in and staying in bed, then you'll have to start practicing getting up. The more you practice it, the easier it will be.

Don't expect yourself to do it perfectly right from the beginning. Don't get discouraged when you stumble and fail. You're just out of practice. Get back on your feet and go at it again!

Become a spiritual athlete. Put yourself in training by practicing the things of God. Build your spirit muscles by spending time with Him. You will be surprised to find just how much of a winner you can be!

talk the truth

"I say no to ungodliness and worldly passions. I live a self-controlled, upright and godly life." (Titus 2:12)

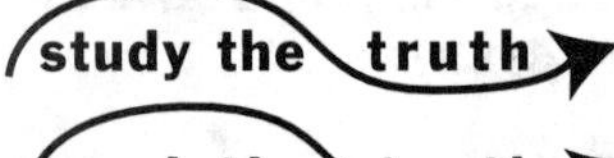
study the truth
read the truth

2 Peter 1:2-11

1 Samuel 17,18; 1 Corinthians 7

CAN HE COUNT ON YOU?

"The Lord said, 'Who is the wise and trusted servant? Who is the servant the master trusts to give the other servants their food at the right time?'"

LUKE 12:42, ICB

We often praise God for His faithfulness. We're thankful that we can always count on Him to be there for us. But we rarely consider the fact that He needs us to be faithful too.

It's true. God needs people He can count on. He needs wise and trusted servants He can entrust over His household. In these last days, He needs faithful young men and women to team up with, so He can show His power and goodness to the world more than ever.

"Oh, God doesn't need me!"

Yes, He does. Ever since Creation, when He put people in charge of the earth, He's needed them to work with Him to get His will done. You can see that all through the Bible. When the Israelites were slaves in Egypt and He wanted to set them free, He teamed up with a man, Moses, to get the job done.

Why did He choose Moses? Because He needed someone who was faithful and would dare to act on His Word. He needed someone He could count on, and He knew Moses was that kind of man.

Psalm 103:7 says, "He made known his ways to Moses, his deeds to the people of Israel." If Moses hadn't been faithful to know God's ways, the Israelites never would have seen God's deeds!

God needs you like He needed Moses. He needs you to be faithful and alert to spiritual things. He needs you to be someone He can trust to know the Bible and obey it. He needs you to be a servant who will believe God like Moses did so that He can miraculously work in this earth.

Will you be faithful? It's a decision you have to make. No one can do it for you. Right now, commit yourself to be that wise and trusted servant. Let God know He can count on you!

talk the truth

"I commit today to be a wise and trusted servant." (Luke 12:42, ICB)

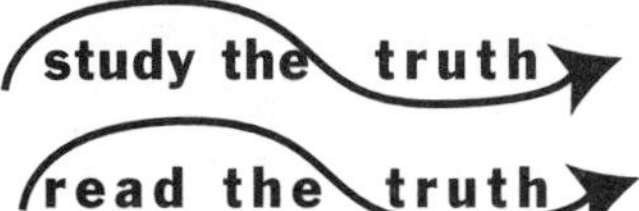
study the truth
read the truth

Psalm 105:23-45

1 Samuel 19,20; 1 Corinthians 8

May 4

NO MORE SURPRISES

"But God has revealed it to us by his Spirit. The Spirit searches all things, even the deep things of God."

1 Corinthians 2:10

God is not full of surprises. He doesn't like to be unpredictable and keep you guessing. Countless Christians, however, have the idea that He does.

"You just never know what God will do," they say. They base that idea on 1 Corinthians 2:9 which says, "No eye has seen, no ear has heard, no mind has conceived what God has prepared for those who love him." They interpret that scripture to mean that God is keeping secrets from His people.

But He isn't!

In fact, the very next verse says He's given us His Spirit to show those secrets to us! He wants us to know everything that's on His heart.

If you're in the dark about God's plans for your life, you don't have to stay that way. He wants you to know all about them. He'll show them to you if you'll let Him.

So, don't depend on guesswork. Determine today that you will start receiving those answers from the Holy Spirit. As you read the Bible, pray in the spirit and ask Him to shine His light on the Scriptures and show you exactly how they apply to you.

Remember—God isn't in the business of keeping secrets from you. He's in the business of revealing them. Take time to listen to Him and you'll never have to settle for living in uncertainty again.

talk the truth

"The Holy Spirit reveals the deep things of God to me." (1 Corinthians 2:10)

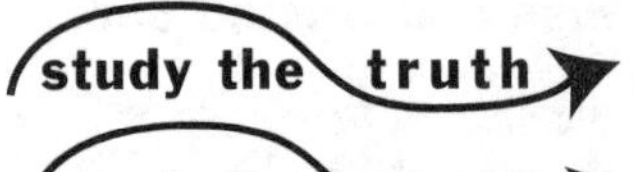
study the truth
read the truth

1 Corinthians 2:1-16

1 Samuel 21,22,23; 1 Corinthians 9

TAKE TIME TO LISTEN

"If any of you lacks wisdom, he should ask God, who gives generously to all without finding fault, and it will be given to him."

JAMES 1:5

When you're facing a problem, the very first thing you should ask God for is wisdom. Not money. Not popularity. Not healing. But wisdom.

God's wisdom is the key that will unlock every door in your life. It will turn any failure into success. So, don't waste your prayer time begging God for things you think you need. Instead, spend some time listening to what He has to say about your situation.

If you've never tried that before, here's what you need to do.

First: Tell the Lord what the entire problem is...not because He doesn't know what you're going through, but because identifying the problem helps *you.* It lets you see things more clearly.

Second: Listen for the Holy Spirit's help. Pay close attention to what He says through the Bible. Most likely, worrying about your problem has squeezed the Word right out of your heart (Mark 4:18-19). If so, you need to get God's Word and begin to put it back in your heart again. Then the Holy Spirit will begin to speak to you through it. And as you're listening, be sure to remain open to what He says. Be ready to accept discipline if necessary.

Third: Act on the wisdom God gives you. Let go of your own way of doing things and do it His way. Be obedient. If you don't, that wonderful wisdom won't do you any good at all.

As you pray today, set aside your own ideas and start looking for His wisdom. It's the only thing that can permanently solve the problems you've been facing. It's truly the most precious gift God has to give.

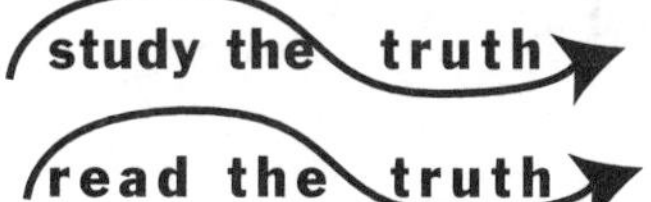

"I ask God for wisdom and He gives it to me generously." (James 1:5)

study the truth **Proverbs 8:10-36**

read the truth **1 Samuel 23,24; 1 Corinthians 10**

May 6

PUT THE WORD INTO ACTION

"Therefore everyone who hears these words of mine and puts them into practice is like a wise man who built his house on the rock."

MATTHEW 7:24

If you want what you do to be blessed by God, if you want to see supernatural results in your life, you'll have to do more than just read the Bible. You'll have to put it into action.

That's what I did. Years ago when I realized God was the One Who had the answers to all my problems—that He was the One Who could supply all my needs—I committed myself to doing everything His Word told me to do. I made a lasting decision to step out in faith on every command I saw in the Bible.

When I found out, for example, that the Bible instructed me to tithe, Gloria and I were already trying to stretch what little money we had further than it could possibly go. We were up to our necks in debt! We couldn't possibly afford to give away 10 percent. But we did it anyway. We stepped out on faith and kept our commitment to do every command we saw. Before long we began to see God blessing us financially.

Keep on reading and studying the Bible. Listen to teaching tapes. Go to church and hear the Word preached. But don't stop there. Go one important step further by taking the Word you've heard and putting it into action!

talk the truth

"I put the Word of God into practice." (Matthew 7:24)

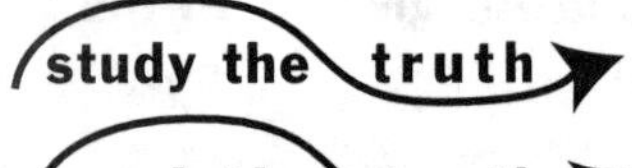
study the truth
read the truth

Matthew 7:17-27

1 Samuel 25,26; 1 Corinthians 11

THE GRACE OF GIVING

"But just as you excel in everything—in faith, in speech, in knowledge, in complete earnestness and in your love for us—see that you also excel in this grace of giving."

2 CORINTHIANS 8:7

How do you give to the Lord? Do you just drop some money in the plate at church without thinking much about it? Or do you just hand money over to God like you'd hand it over for clothing at a department store?

You need to think about that, because *how* you give is very important to God. He won't receive just any old thing in just any old way you feel like giving it.

In Malachi, for example, God refused to receive Israel's offerings. They brought Him their imperfect and injured animals they couldn't do anything else with—and God said it offended Him. He told them, You don't have any reverence or honor for Me, and I won't accept your offering.

I'm sorry to say, but that kind of thing didn't die out after the book of Malachi was written either. Many people today don't have any reverence for God when it comes to giving offerings. Some people won't give unless they feel they absolutely have to give to protect their image. But that's offensive to God.

If we want God to be pleased with our offerings, we will have to do what the Apostle Paul wrote about in 2 Corinthians 8:7. We'll have to learn to "excel in this grace of giving." We have to learn to give with faith and reverence in worship.

Next time the offering plate is passed, don't just drop your gift carelessly in the plate as it goes by. Determine to obey God. Worship Him with your money and be thankful. He'll do more than simply receive it—He'll bless you.

talk the truth

"I am a giver and I excel in the grace of giving." (2 Corinthians 8:7)

study the truth
read the truth

Malachi 1:1-14

1 Samuel 27,28,29; 1 Corinthians 12,13

KEEP QUIET

"A fool gives full vent to his anger, but a wise man keeps himself under control."

PROVERBS 29:11

One of the things that we must learn if we want to be faithful servants of God is how to keep our mouths shut. Very few of us have mastered that skill.

When we get upset about something, we think we have to let everyone know about it. "I'll just give them a piece of my mind," we say.

Don't make that mistake. No one wants or needs a piece of your mind—and if you give it to them, you'll only end up pushing people away from you and bringing harm to yourself. Learn, instead, to keep quiet.

This especially applies when the Holy Spirit shows something to you about a situation. When that happens, don't go spreading it all over school. If you do, you'll come to the place where the Lord can't trust you with insight into situations.

I've seen that happen. I've known people who've prayed and God has shown them something about someone's weaknesses or needs. They've been given insight into the problem in someone's life, so they could pray for that person. But, instead of keeping that information between themselves and God in prayer, they told others about it. As a result, they lost their effectiveness in prayer.

Don't let that happen to you. Learn to be quiet when you need to be, and Satan will find it very difficult to stop your prayer life and ministry to others.

talk the truth **"I keep myself under control, therefore I am wise." (Proverbs 29:11)**

study the truth **James 3:1-13**

read the truth **1 Samuel 30,31; 1 Corinthians 14**

THE FATHER'S HEART

"But while he was still a long way off, his father saw him and was filled with compassion for him; he ran to his son, threw his arms around him and kissed him."

LUKE 15:20

How much love do you have for someone who doesn't follow Jesus? All too often, once we make Jesus our Lord and get our lives cleaned up, we lose our compassion for those who are still lost. We look at the group using drugs, or the girl who cheats on tests, or the guy who tells crude jokes, and we turn up our noses.

But if we ever truly understood the heart of our Heavenly Father, we'd never do that again. Jesus told a story that can give us a glimpse of His heart. It's the story we call "The Prodigal Son" (Luke 15:11-32).

You've probably heard it many times, how the son rebelled and dishonored his father, and how the father, in spite of it all, received him home with joy when he asked forgiveness and turned from his wrong ways. But there's one phrase in it I want to draw your attention to—"But while he [the prodigal son] was still a long way off, his father saw him."

That phrase gives us such a powerful glimpse of the father's heart. It tells us that even before his boy had repented—even when he was swimming in sin—that father was watching for him, longing for him to come home.

Every morning he scanned the horizon, hoping to see the figure of his returning son. And every night, he'd look again...straining his eyes in hope. His son was constantly on his mind, and his heart was always full of love for him.

That's the kind of heart God has for those who are lost. It's the kind of heart that reached out for you while you were still wandering in the world, plunged in sin.

There's a whole world full of tired people out there who are more than just "sinners"—they're our potential family...lost people in serious need of a loving Heavenly Father. God help us to never turn up our noses at them. May He help us instead to start bringing them home.

talk the truth

"The Father has shown me an incredible amount of love—He has made me His child!" (Luke 15:20)

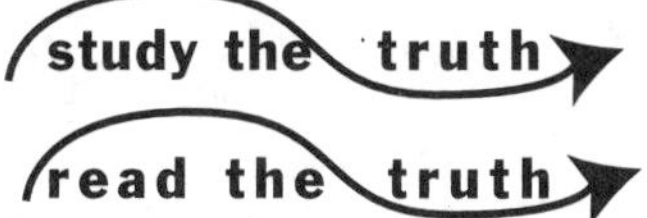
study the truth
read the truth

John 8:1-11

2 Samuel 1,2; 1 Corinthians 15

HEAD FOR THE LIGHT

"And so we have the prophetic word confirmed, which you do well to heed as a light that shines in a dark place, until the day dawns and the morning star rises in your hearts."

2 PETER 1:19, NKJV

So many times when we need the answer to a problem, we try to get it by focusing on the problem. We study it. We think about it. We examine it from every angle. But the Apostle Peter gives us a different approach. He says we should focus our attention on God's Word until the answer to that problem comes to us.

We use the term "seeing the light" all the time. We say, "Have you 'seen the light' on that?" meaning, "Do you know the answer to that situation?" Well, when God's Word enters our heart, it brings light (Psalm 119:130). It brings the answer we need.

Have you ever been in a dark room and tried to find your way out? Or have you ever been lost outside at night? What is the first thing you look for? Light!

That light could be coming from under the door or shimmering from a lamp in a house far away. But either way, you head straight for it. You don't waste your time focusing your attention on the darkness. You fix your eyes on the light because you know it will lead you in the right direction.

If you need the answer to a problem you're facing, pay attention to God's Word. Head for the Light and the answer you need will dawn on you.

talk the truth

"I receive light and understanding for any situation by going to the Word." (2 Peter 1:19, NKJV)

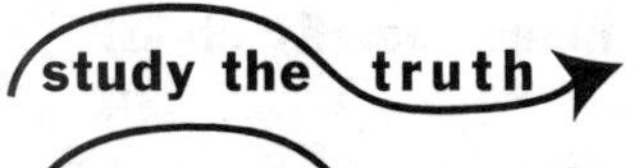
study the truth
read the truth

John 1:1-9

2 Samuel 3,4; 1 Corinthians 16

May 11

NEVER FALL

> ***"Do your best to present yourself to God as one approved, a workman who does not need to be ashamed and who correctly handles the word of truth."***
>
> **2 TIMOTHY 2:15**

A lot of people play spiritual games. They claim to be faith-filled Christians in public. But, in private, they never act like it. They don't read their Bibles. They don't pray. Then, when trouble comes, they fall flat on their faces.

Well, the time for playing games is over. It's time for us to realize that real faith involves action (James 2:20).

First, you need to *study.* You should not only read the Word, but you should also dig deeply into it with devotionals like this and other study guides. And if you have a cassette player, you can listen to teaching tapes.

The second thing you need to do is go to places where God's Word is being preached. When Romans 10:17 says "faith comes by hearing," it's talking about the preached Word.

Whenever I start feeling surrounded by problems and I'm having trouble hearing from God, I find some place where they're preaching God's Word. I've received more answers that way. Some word of Scripture just jumps out at me—even if the preacher isn't talking about my problem! Then I realize, *That's the answer I've been searching for!*

Third, you need to start speaking God's Word. Find a promise of His that applies to your situation and then speak it aloud in faith.

Get serious about the Bible. Study it. Go hear it preached. Speak it. Become so faithful that Satan will look at you with fear and say, "There's one Christian who's not playing games anymore."

talk the truth

"I put action to my faith. I do my best to present myself to God as one approved, a workman who does not need to be ashamed. I correctly handle the Word of truth." (2 Timothy 2:15)

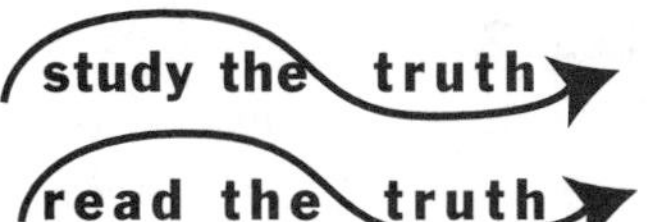
study the truth
read the truth

2 Peter 1:3-10

2 Samuel 5,6; 2 Corinthians 1

May 12

RIVER RUNNING DRY?

"Do not merely listen to the word, and so deceive yourselves. Do what it says."

JAMES 1:22

Have you ever felt like every time you opened the Bible you learned something new? Does it seem lately that that river's run dry? If so, I strongly suggest that you think back to the last time God gave you something new. Back up and see if you did what God showed you to do. If you didn't, dig into that word again and put it into action.

You see, the more I act on what the Bible says, the more I see in it. That's why James 1:22 tells us to not only listen to God's Word but to *do what it says!*

It may seem that the things God has shown you are very minor. But do them anyway! He may have prompted you to give some encouragement to a friend at school. He may have asked you to spend just five more minutes a day in prayer. Those may not seem like life-changing things, but if you could see what God sees, you'd see how important they really are.

Act on God's Word today—don't just listen to it...and your river will *never* run dry.

talk the truth **"I don't deceive myself by merely *listening* to the Word. I do what it says." (James 1:22)**

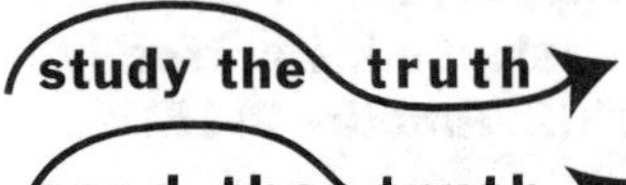

study the truth **James 1:22-27**

read the truth **2 Samuel 7,8; 2 Corinthians 2**

May 13

DISCOVER WHO YOU REALLY ARE

"[For my determined purpose is] that I may know Him—that I may progressively become more deeply and intimately acquainted with Him, perceiving and recognizing and understanding [the wonders of His Person] more strongly and more clearly. And that I may in that same way come to know the power outflowing from His resurrection."

PHILIPPIANS 3:10, AMP

The more you spend time with God and the Bible, the more you'll know the "power outflowing from His resurrection." In fact, you'll start developing God's own characteristics...just by spending time with Him. You'll begin to understand who you really are in Jesus.

I remember one day I was reading the story of the woman who had been bleeding for 12 years—and then she touched the edge of Jesus' coat and was healed (Mark 5:25-34).

I'd read the story many times and pictured myself as almost everyone in the story...just imagining how it would feel to be someone in the crowd or even the one who was healed. Suddenly God spoke to my spirit and said, *Read that again and this time picture yourself as the one wearing the coat.*

I was stunned. "Lord," I said, "how can I do that? I can't take Your place!"

That's what's wrong with the Church, He told me. *That's the reason the world doesn't know anything about Jesus. You identify with everyone except Me. But I sent you to be* My *witnesses, to imitate* Me, *to stand in* My *place...not everyone else's!*

So, I read that story again. This time I pictured myself in Jesus' role. Instead of crawling up to touch the edge of His coat, I was the one wearing the coat, freely giving what God had given me. After all, the Bible does say, "Clothe yourselves with the Lord Jesus Christ" (Romans 13:14).

Do you know who scares Satan most of all? Christians who've found out they can do that. Christians who, instead of begging for a little touch from Jesus, are letting His life flow out to others.

So come on, give Satan a scare. Spend time with the Father in His Word and start discovering who you really are today.

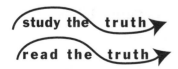

talk the truth **"My determined purpose is to know Jesus more and more each day." (Philippians 3:10, AMP)**

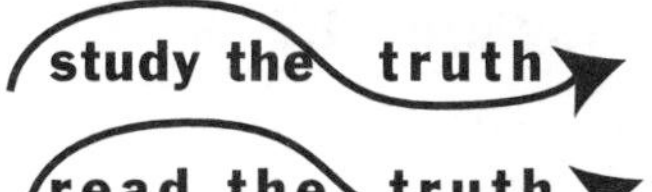

Luke 8:40-48

read the truth **2 Samuel 9,10; 2 Corinthians 3**

May 14

YOUR FIRST PRIORITY

"No one can serve two masters. Either he will hate the one and love the other, or he will be devoted to the one and despise the other. You cannot serve both God and Money."

MATTHEW 6:24

God isn't against your having money. He's against letting money have you. He's against your making it your first priority and putting your trust in it instead of in Him.

Why? Because He knows money makes a lousy god. Its power is limited. It will only buy so much. It will only go so far.

If you need healing from an incurable disease, money won't help you at all. If your relationship with your parents is falling apart, money won't mend it. But if you'll make God your first priority, His life will reach into every area of your life.

God is so generous that He desires you to have the best, just like good parents desire the best for their children. His plan is for you to have more than enough so that *all* your needs are met. Get in on that plan by keeping your priorities straight.

Make pleasing God your number one priority. Set your eyes on Him above all else and you'll find that everything else will fall into place.

talk the truth

"I serve God alone and pleasing Him is my number one priority. I seek Him above all else." (Matthew 6:24,33)

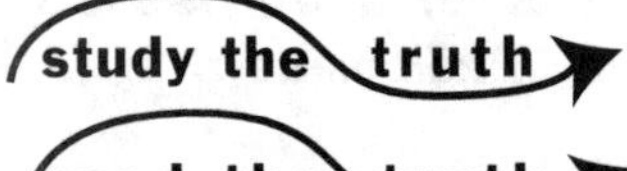
study the truth
read the truth

Mark 10:17-27

2 Samuel 11,12,13; 2 Corinthians 4,5

DON'T FORGET THE JOY

"Rejoice in the Lord always. I will say it again: Rejoice!"

PHILIPPIANS 4:4

Years ago, I decided that I would walk only by what the Bible said. I told God that, as far as I was concerned, the Bible had the first and final say in my life, no matter what.

Not too long after that, I decided that no matter what happened, whether I felt like it or not, I'd walk in love. The Bible clearly says faith works by love. It just won't work any other way.

Those two decisions—to walk only by what the Bible said and to walk in love—are the two most important decisions I've ever made.

Recently, though, God pointed out to me that I left something out—the force of joy. He told me I can't truly walk by faith and love if I forget joy. God showed me that joy is an essential part of a life of victory. Without it, I might have an occasional victory now and then, but it wouldn't stay.

You see, joy is what gives you the strength to hold steady when things get rough (Nehemiah 8:10). It gives you a kind of steadiness that will make you a winner again and again.

So make a commitment to God that you'll walk, not only in faith and love, but in joy as well. Make it a point to rejoice in the Lord always...and there won't be anything Satan can do or say to steal your victory from you!

talk the truth

"I rejoice in the Lord always." (Philippians 4:4)

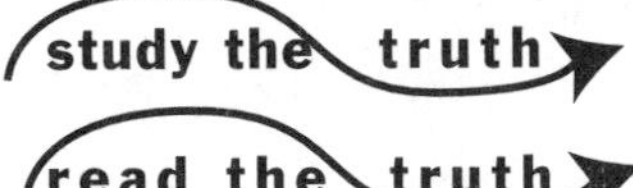
study the truth
read the truth

Psalm 84:1-7

2 Samuel 14,15; 2 Corinthians 6

May 16

STEP OUT OF THE BOAT

"'Lord, if it's you,' Peter replied, 'tell me to come to you on the water.' 'Come,' he said. Then Peter got down out of the boat, walked on the water and came toward Jesus."

MATTHEW 14:28,29

It's easy to be so afraid of making a mistake that you never step out in faith. You can spend all your time wondering, *What if I step out and do something in faith and then find out later I've just made a mistake?*

Don't worry. God can handle any mistake you can make. I know because I've made plenty. If you act on what the Bible says out of the sincerity of your heart and you stay faithful, Jesus will *never* let you down. He proved that the night Peter jumped out of the boat in the middle of the lake.

Have you ever stopped to think about that event? Peter hadn't been praying before he did that. He was just excited and he blurted out, "Lord, if it's you, tell me to come."

Now Jesus could have said, "Wait a minute, Peter. You don't have the faith. You'd better stay in the boat or you'll drown for sure."

But He didn't say that to Peter—and He won't say it to you. If you want to go do something by faith, He'll get out there with you and pick you up when you start sinking.

Remember—it's better to risk making a mistake than to waste your life never stepping out in faith. Don't let fear keep you from taking that first step of faith… C'mon and get out of the boat today!

talk the truth — **"I boldly walk in faith today and not just by what I see." (2 Corinthians 5:7)**

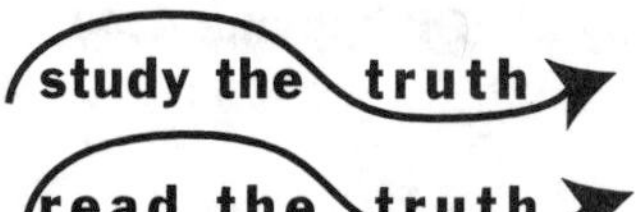
study the truth
read the truth

Matthew 14:22,23

2 Samuel 16,17; 2 Corinthians 7

WALK IN THE LIGHT YOU HAVE

"But as for you, continue in what you have learned and have become convinced of, because you know those from whom you learned it."

2 Timothy 3:14

If you've made Jesus your Lord and you have God's Word in your heart, you can live in victory. Sure, you may not have all the answers. There may be many spiritual things you don't understand. But it's not those things that are most likely to destroy you. It's the things you know to do—but *don't do*—that make you fall.

Just think about walking at night down a dark, unfamiliar path in the middle of a jungle. A guide up ahead has a flashlight to keep you on the right path. But then, you just decide to wander off into the darkness by yourself. What do you think will happen to you? You'll probably stumble, fall and get injured.

That's exactly the same thing that can happen in your walk with the Lord. He knows what's ahead, and He shines just enough light for you to take one step at a time. And you have to continue walking in that light to get where you're going.

It's good to keep studying. It's good to keep learning. But, remember, it's not the great wisdom you haven't learned yet that will cause you the most trouble. It's failing to walk in the wisdom God has already given you.

So be faithful in those things you know day after day after day. Then you'll make it through just fine!

talk the truth

"I will continue in what I have learned. I will walk in the light as He is in the light." (2 Timothy 3:14; 1 John 1:7)

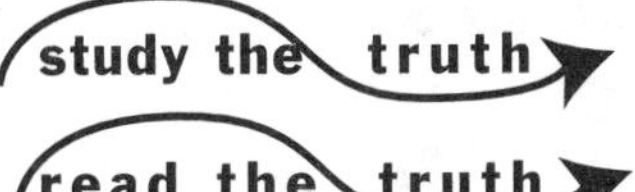
study the truth
read the truth

2 Peter 1:2-11

2 Samuel 18,19; 2 Corinthians 8

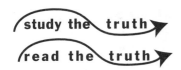

HE'LL BE LISTENING

"Now this is the confidence that we have in Him, that if we ask anything according to [in agreement with] His will, He hears us. And if we know that He hears us, whatever we ask, we know that we have the petitions that we have asked of Him."

1 John 5:14,15, NKJV

Have you ever been in prayer and suddenly wondered if God was even listening? Well, today I want to show you how to know that God is listening once and for all. But let me warn you, I'm not about to slug you on the shoulder and assure you that God will listen to any old doubtful, self-centered thing you say to Him. He won't. He's only promised to listen to prayers that agree with what the Bible says. The Apostle John says when you pray like that, you'll know that you have the "petitions" you desire of Him.

The word petition is defined as "a formal written request addressed to a sovereign superior," and that's exactly what you need when you're praying about something serious.

How do you put together a solid, Bible-based petition?

First, you'll have to roll up your sleeves and dig into the Bible. Find scriptures that apply to your situation and make them the basis for your petition.

Second, get on your knees and talk with the Holy Spirit. Let Him help you with the details. The best way to do that is to spend time praying in other tongues (Romans 8:26-27). And remember—He wants you to know what He desires for you. So, while you're praying, listen!

Last of all, write it down. Make a formal request by writing down every promise you found. Also, as you're listening to the Holy Spirit for the details, write down what He says to you.

Take your time. Let the Holy Spirit develop your prayer. Let the truth He gives to you begin to work in you. Get your petition firmly in mind. Then, when you're ready, present it to God.

Believe me, He'll be listening.

talk the truth

"I have confidence in God, that if I ask anything according to His will, He hears me. I have the petitions I ask of Him." (1 John 5:14,15, NKJV)

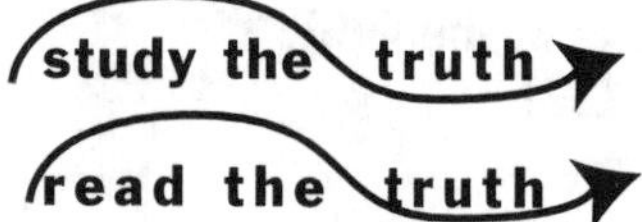
study the truth
read the truth

1 John 5:1-15

2 Samuel 20,21; 2 Corinthians 9

Kenneth

May 19

DON'T WASTE TIME WONDERING

"Therefore do not be foolish, but understand what the Lord's will is."

EPHESIANS 5:17

Have you ever worried about whether or not you're praying in agreement with what God desires? "I certainly can't expect God to do something for me that's the opposite of what He wants," you may say. And you're absolutely right.

But you don't have to waste time standing around looking puzzled. You can grab your Bible and *find out* what God wants!

God has made some very specific promises in His Word, and He wants to fulfill every one of them in your life. Think of it this way. Your Bible is a record of all that God has for you. Everything He's given to you has been written down in that book. So, the smartest thing you can do is find out what's in it. Don't leave it shut up in your locker, and then go home and hit the floor crying, "Oh, God! Help! I don't know what You want me to do!"

Get that Bible out of your locker and find out what His promises are to you! Find out how you need to change to be in agreement with what is written there—because His Word is His will.

But a lot of people don't do that. They try to change God's plans instead of changing their own. But God will never change. The Bible says He's the same yesterday, today and forever. His plans are, too. So don't waste your time wondering if your prayers are in line with what God wants. Get the Book and base your prayers on it. Then get ready—the answer is on the way!

talk the truth

"I will not be foolish. I understand what the Lord's will is by studying His Word." (Ephesians 5:17)

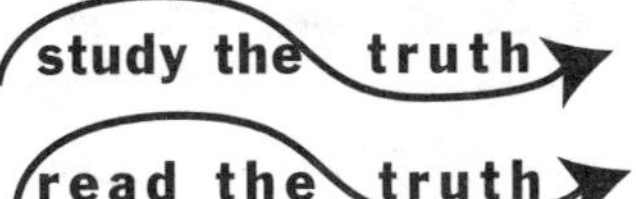
study the truth
read the truth

Proverbs 2:1-12

2 Samuel 22,23; 2 Corinthians 10

May 20

Kenneth

FREE FROM THE TROUBLE

"Christ redeemed us from the curse of the law by becoming a curse for us, for it is written: 'Cursed is everyone who is hung on a tree.'"

GALATIANS 3:13

You know the story. Satan came to Eve and deceived her into disobeying God. Adam, although he was not deceived, followed in her footsteps.

When Satan came into the Garden of Eden that day, he didn't have any power at all. He had to sneak in. Now Adam was standing there, and he should have kicked him out right away. But he didn't. Instead, he ignored the command God had given him and did what Satan told him to do...and when he did that, he made Satan his lord.

He gave Satan the authority that God had given him. He made Satan the illegitimate ruler of the earth. Immediately things changed. Through one man's sin, death came to all people (Romans 5:12).

You may wonder, *Do we have to live under this curse for the rest of our lives? Wasn't there anything God could have done?* Yes! He could and He did! He sent Jesus and set us free from the curse (Galatians 3:13).

The moment you made Jesus the Lord of your life, you were rescued from the lordship of Satan. You were saved from the curse. I didn't say it wasn't out there anymore. It is—you can see it all around you. But now you have a choice. You have authority over it in Jesus' Name, so you can stand against it.

God has done everything that love can do. He sent Jesus to save you from the curse. Now it's up to you to believe His Word, stand against the curse and walk in the victory He won for you—every day!

talk the truth

"Christ has set me free from the curse of the law." (Galatians 3:13)

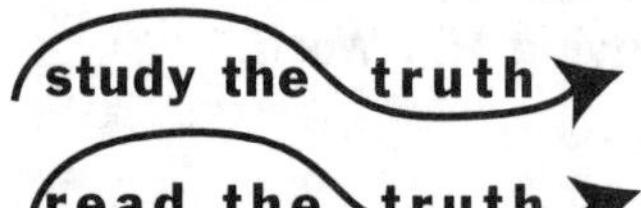
study the truth
read the truth

Romans 5:12-21

2 Samuel 24; 1 Kings 1; 2 Corinthians 11

POSSESS YOUR PROMISED LAND

"When you cross the Jordan into Canaan, drive out all the inhabitants of the land before you... and settle in it, for I have given you the land to possess."

Numbers 33:51-53

God has given you a promised land. It's a place where you can receive everything you need in life. A place where you can keep sin underfoot as you rule and reign with Christ. A place where no weapon formed against you will prosper, where nothing Satan throws at you will harm you.

As you study the Bible, you'll find that's a true description of the kind of victory you should be experiencing in Christ—not when you go to heaven—but right here, right now.

You may say, "That sounds nice, but I'm dealing with real life here. And with all my troubles, this doesn't look like much of a promised land to me."

That's because you're still letting Satan live there with you! He won't just pack up and go home, you know, just because God has promised you victory. You have to kick him out.

But don't let that scare you. God has given you the power to do it. Remember what Jesus said? He said, "I have given you authority to...overcome all the power of the enemy; nothing will harm you" (Luke 10:19).

What's more, Satan is totally unarmed! Colossians 2:15 says, "[God] disarmed the powers and authorities [of Satan], he made a public spectacle of them, triumphing over them by the cross." You have absolutely no reason to cower before Satan. Jesus defeated and disarmed him when He died and rose again. Satan can't defeat you unless you let him. All he can do is make empty threats.

But beware! Empty threats can stop you cold if you believe them. So don't. Believe the Bible instead. Use God's Word and Jesus' Name to drive Satan out of every last detail of your life. Force him to pack up and go home. Start living in your promised land!

talk the truth

"I will go and possess my promised land at once—for the Lord has made the way for me." (Numbers 33:51-53)

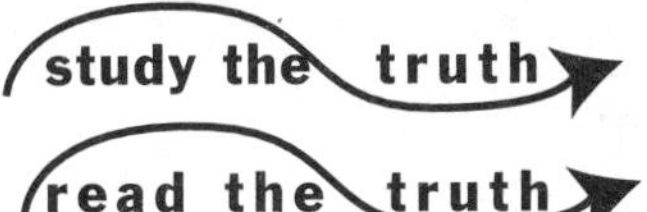
study the truth
read the truth

Mark 16:17,18; James 5:7-9

1 Kings 2,3,4; 2 Corinthians 12,13

May 22

Gloria

SILENCE YOUR CRITICS

"For it is God's will that by doing good you should silence the ignorant talk of foolish men."

1 Peter 2:15

I know from personal experience that when people start to criticize you and harass you because you're a Christian, your natural response is to want to strike back. You want to start dishing out a little criticism and harassment of your own.

But you know what? Your words will just add fuel to their fire, and they'll cause you harder and louder trouble than they did before.

According to the Bible, however, there is a way to silence them. Not by arguing or defending yourself, but by keeping quiet and continuing to do what God has called you to do.

Jesus was highly criticized, but He never fought back. Instead, Acts 10:38 says He simply went around doing good.

When people start getting on your case about being a Christian, be like Jesus and just keep on doing good. Keep on boldly praying for people. Keep on laying hands on the sick and getting them healed. Keep on doing what God has called you to do.

That will aggravate Satan because his primary goal is to make you ineffective. He wants you to get wrapped up in the harassment. He wants to distract you from the job God has given you. He really wants you to quit.

Don't do it! Instead, follow the instructions in 2 Timothy 3:14 and "continue in what you have learned and have become convinced of." Silence the criticisms by continuing to live by faith and do good. And when all their foolish words have faded away, you'll still be standing strong.

talk the truth

"I silence the ignorant talk of foolish men by doing good, for this is God's will." (1 Peter 2:15)

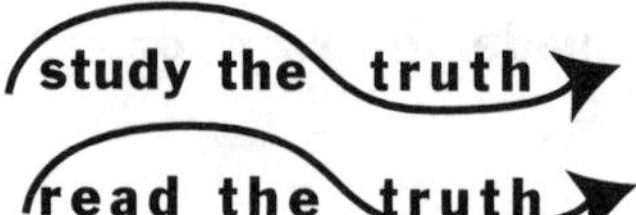
study the truth
read the truth

Luke 23:1-9

1 Kings 5,6; Galatians 1

HE'S RETURNING!

"At midnight the cry rang out: 'Here's the bridegroom! Come out to meet him!'"

MATTHEW 25:6

The Holy Spirit is sending a vital message to us today: *Get ready for Jesus' return!* It's an old message, but there's a new urgency to it that we can't afford to ignore. *Jesus is returning!*

Now, some Christians say, "I just don't think we're supposed to know about Jesus' return. It's supposed to be a mystery. It's supposed to surprise us."

But they're wrong. The Bible says that as God's children we shouldn't be surprised (1 Thessalonians 5:4). We should be so spiritually alert that even though we don't know exactly when, we should sense that the *season* of Jesus' return has come.

First Corinthians 2:10 tells us that God shows His plans to us through the Holy Spirit. I suspect that those who are listening to the Holy Spirit on the day Jesus returns will actually begin to realize that something is about to happen. You may be playing softball or taking a test. You may be riding a motorcycle or plummeting in a roller coaster. Then suddenly, if you're in tune with the Holy Spirit, you'll realize He's coming!

So wake up now and let the Holy Spirit get you ready. Don't get caught sleeping when He returns. Because just as Jesus foretold, there is a cry going out at midnight. The Holy Spirit is announcing His return.

Can you hear it in your spirit? Can you sense the Lord saying, *Get up and come out to meet Me. Spend time with Me. Get ready, and when I return, you'll be right in the middle of what I do!*

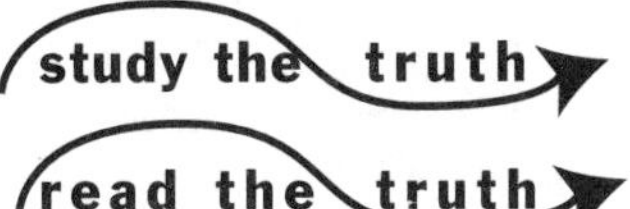

"Jesus is returning and I am ready to meet Him." (Matthew 25:6)

study the truth — **Matthew 25:1-13**

read the truth — **1 Kings 7,8; Galatians 2**

May 24

SURE TO WIN IN HIM

"Therefore, remember that...at that time you were separate from Christ...without hope and without God in the world. But now in Christ Jesus you who once were far away have been brought near through the blood of Christ."

EPHESIANS 2:11-13

Have you ever thought about what it really means to be *in Christ Jesus?* Once you do, it will radically change your life. You see, it's *in Him* that we're saved from our sins. It's *in Him* that we've been set free. It's *in Him* that we have right-standing before God!

If you want those powerful words to explode in you, start searching out scriptures that talk about being *in Christ.* Watch for the words *in Him, with Him, through Him,* or *in Whom.* Mark them and think about them until their truth gets down inside you. They'll give you some powerful bombshells against Satan's attacks.

When he tries to tell you, for instance, that you're just a sinner and God doesn't want to be bothered with your problems, you'll know he's lying. You'll be able to answer him boldly and say, "Thank God, I *was* a sinner, but now I have right-standing with God in Jesus. I'm *in Him* and you can't touch me at all!"

Be prepared the next time Satan comes at you with doubt and unbelief. Be ready to fight back with the scriptures about who you are in Jesus. You're sure to win once you truly know you're *in Him!*

talk the truth

"I have been brought near to God through the blood of Jesus. Now I am *in Him!*" (Ephesians 2:11-13)

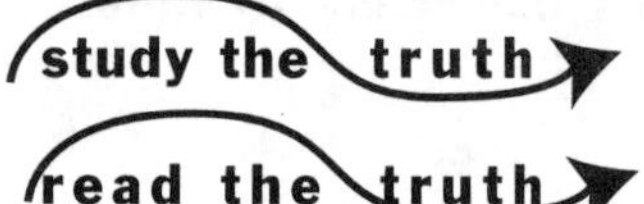
study the truth
read the truth

Ephesians 1:1-14

1 Kings 9,10; Galatians 3

AWAKE TO RIGHTEOUSNESS

"Awake to righteousness, and do not sin."

1 Corinthians 15:34, NKJV

When your alarm clock goes off tomorrow morning, don't just wake up to another day. Do what the Bible says to do and "awake to righteousness"! Awaken yourself to the fact that you've been given right-standing with God.

Why? Because every day Satan will try to convince you that you don't have any right to God's promises. He'll try to make you a slave to sin again in order to control your life. But he won't be able to do it if you'll awaken yourself to who you really are in Jesus.

Here's a prayer to help that understanding come alive in you:

"Father, I say once again that Jesus Christ is my Lord today. Lord, You are the ruler of my life. I completely give myself to You. Whatever You want is what I want. Your plans are my plans.

"As a new creation in Jesus, I accept the gift of right-standing with You and all that gift includes: health, prosperity, peace, joy and life. I won't even put up with any sin that tries to trap me. I look to Jesus, the One Who is the beginning and ending of all that I believe.

"According to the Bible, the power of sin and death in my life has been beaten. I am no longer ruled by the forces of evil but by God Himself. I am more than a conqueror through Jesus.

"I determine today to remember that I am in right-standing with You, Lord. And with every step I will draw closer and closer to You. Thank You for the gift of righteousness. Because of that gift, I can do all things through Jesus Who gives me strength. In Jesus' Name. Amen!"

talk the truth

"I awake to the right-standing I have with God and I do not sin." (1 Corinthians 15:34, NKJV)

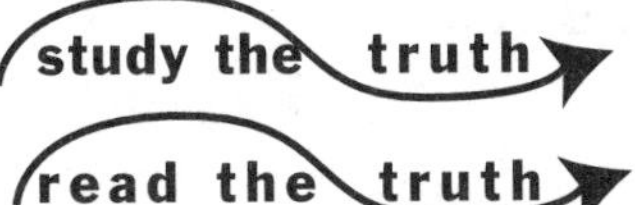
study the truth
read the truth

Colossians 2:9-15

1 Kings 11,12; Galatians 4

May 26

DISCOVER WHAT THE NAME CAN DO

"Therefore God exalted him to the highest place and gave him the name that is above every name, that at the name of Jesus every knee should bow, in heaven and on earth and under the earth."

PHILIPPIANS 2:9,10

Once you make up your mind to keep Jesus' commands and begin to allow His Word to come alive in your life, the Name of Jesus will become much more powerful to you. It will become a force that will cause every circumstance and every demon that tries to stand in your way to bow its knee to your command.

There is far greater power in His Name than any of us have yet realized. In fact, I've discovered that Jesus' Name—just His Name alone—is effective when spoken by a Christian who holds God's Word close to his heart.

In fact, Revelation 19:13 says Jesus' Name *is* God's Word! So, when an evil spirit is trying to bring sickness, depression, poverty or any other garbage into your life, you don't have to quote every scripture you know to stop him. You can just point your finger at him and say, "Jesus!" That's like throwing the whole Bible in his face!

Discover for yourself what His Name can do. Begin to speak it with boldness and authority…because there's power in Jesus' Name!

talk the truth

"God exalted Jesus to the highest place and gave Him the Name above every name. It's full of power and I say it now: *Jesus!* (Philippians 2:9,10)

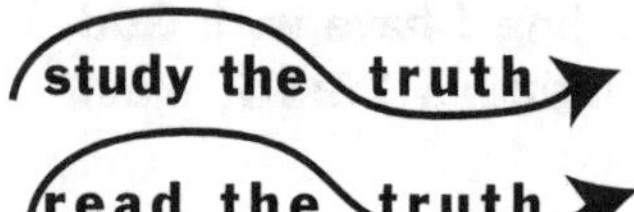
study the truth
read the truth

Acts 3:1-16

1 Kings 13,14; Galatians 5

GOD WANTS YOU HEALTHY

"If you listen carefully to the voice of the Lord your God and do what is right in his eyes, if you pay attention to his commands and keep all his decrees, I will not bring on you any of the diseases I brought on the Egyptians, for I am the Lord, who heals you."

Exodus 15:26

Has Satan ever tried to make you feel guilty when you needed healing by telling you that you're not walking in faith if you go to the doctor or use medicine? If so, here's the first and most important thing you should understand—God wants you healthy.

Now if your faith is strong and you can believe the Bible no matter what circumstances or symptoms come against you, then you'll be able to receive that healing by faith alone.

But that kind of faith takes more than just hearing a few preachers talk about healing. It takes a deep, personal revelation of God's healing power. So, if you haven't yet developed that kind of faith, don't be ashamed to see a doctor.

If you're not certain whether your faith is strong enough or whether you need a doctor's help, follow the instructions of the Apostle Paul and let peace be your guide (Colossians 3:15).

If you feel fear within you when you think about going without medical help, then go to a doctor. And go in faith! On the other hand, if you have solid confidence that you'll be healed by faith alone, let your faith work and receive your healing directly. Whether or not you go to the doctor is not the issue. It is what you do with your faith.

Either way, you can stand in victory knowing that God is working with you and developing your faith. Thank God for your healing—however it comes—and don't let Satan make you feel guilty. It's none of his business!

talk the truth

"I listen carefully to God and do what is right in His eyes. I pay attention to His commands and keep His Word. He is the Lord Who heals me!" (Exodus 15:26)

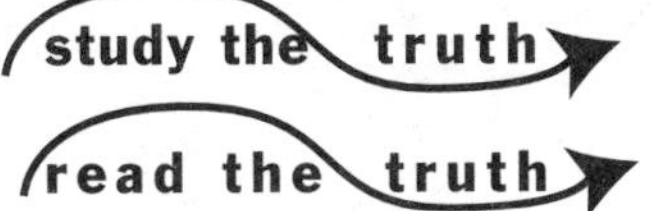
study the truth
read the truth

Deuteronomy 7:8-15

1 Kings 15,16; Galatians 6

Kenneth

May 28

ACCEPT GOD'S MAN

"I tell you the truth, whoever accepts anyone I send accepts me; and whoever accepts me accepts the one who sent me."

JOHN 13:20

I can't tell you how many Christians pick their pastor apart on Saturday night and then expect him to pray in faith for them Sunday morning! They'll constantly make critical comments about the preachers whom God has sent to minister to them and then wonder why the Holy Spirit isn't moving in their churches.

Most of those people would never dream of criticizing Jesus. Yet, according to the Bible, that's exactly what they're doing. You see, Jesus said, "Whoever accepts anyone I send accepts Me."

I know ministers fail sometimes. I know they make mistakes. Jesus knew they would too. But, still, He said, If you receive them, you receive Me.

If you think some preacher is wrong, then pray for him. If you have to, stop listening to him. But the Bible says, "Who are you to judge someone else's servant? To his own master he stands or falls. And he will stand, for the Lord is able to make him stand" (Romans 14:4).

Ministers are not your servants, they're God's servants. Whether they're right or wrong, love them and respect them, if for no other reason than to honor God—the One Who sent them. It doesn't matter if they're the head pastor, an associate pastor, a youth pastor or even the leader of a home group.

Learn to receive the minister Jesus sends to *you* with the same respect and honor you would give Jesus Himself. You'll open the door to God's power, and you'll clear the way for God to meet your needs.

Refuse to let criticism hold back God from moving in your church. Then get ready for Him to move—because He won't hold out on you!

talk the truth

"I accept whoever the Lord sends to minister to me. When I do, I'm accepting the Lord Himself." (John 13:20)

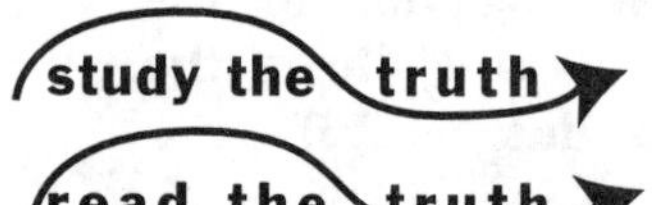
study the truth
read the truth

Numbers 12:1-16

1 Kings 17,18,19; Ephesians 1,2

DON'T HESITATE

"He who doubts is like a wave of the sea, blown and tossed by the wind. That man should not think he will receive anything from the Lord; he is a double-minded man, unstable in all he does."

JAMES 1:6-8

What happens when you hesitate to do something God has told you to do? Satan takes the first step and gets the jump on you.

If you want to live by faith, hesitation is one of the most harmful habits you could ever have. It comes from not making a decision. The Bible says a man like that is "unstable and unreliable and uncertain about everything (he thinks, feels, decides)" (AMP).

If you are double-minded, the decisions you make are split. You try to live by faith and protect your fear at the same time. You make faith statements like "I believe God will heal me." Then your fear whispers, *But I wouldn't want to say I'm well just yet.* You're so busy switching between faith and fear, you can't get anywhere at all.

Kick the habit of hesitation today. Make a solid decision to trust in and act on God's Word. Settle it forever. Decide never to think about those doubts again. When God speaks, don't waste a moment. Step out in faith. That way, you can always keep Satan a step behind you!

"I will not be double-minded and unstable. I believe God's Word without doubting." (James 1:6-8)

study the truth **James 1:1-8**

read the truth **1 Kings 20,21; Ephesians 3**

TELL THE GOOD NEWS

"God was in Christ, making peace between the world and himself. In Christ, God did not hold the world guilty of its sins. And he gave us this message of peace."

2 Corinthians 5:19, ICB

Very few unsaved people have ever really heard the "good news." Why? Because too many Christians are out there telling them that God is mad at them and that they're terrible and wrong. Some call that "good news," but it's not, and it's not what God has told us to share.

He's given us the message of peace!

He's sent us to report that God has brought peace between Himself and mankind. That means between Himself and all people—not just those in one particular church, but everyone everywhere!

That's right. The worst sinner in the world is every bit as at peace with God as we are. Look at Romans 5:10 to see what I mean. It says, "While we were God's enemies, God made friends with us through the death of his Son" (ICB).

God has *already* made peace between Himself and the world. He did it when the entire world was lying in sin. Through Jesus' death and rising again, God has cleansed, forgiven and restored to Himself every adult, teenager and child on the face of this earth. All any of us have to do now is receive it.

That's the good word God has given us. That's the word we need to share with those who are lost. If we'll do it, they won't stay lost very long.

talk the truth **"God does not hold me guilty of my sins. I have peace with Him." (2 Corinthians 5:19, ICB)**

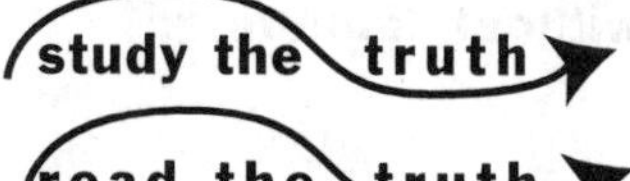

2 Corinthians 5:10-21

read the truth **1 Kings 22; 2 Kings 1; Ephesians 4**

Gloria

May 31

LIVE IN POWER

As a Christian, inside you is the same life God gave Jesus when He raised Him from the dead. The old sinner you once were has died. You've become a new creation on the inside. You are full of the life-giving power of God!

"We were therefore buried with him through baptism into death in order that, just as Christ was raised from the dead through the glory of the Father, we too may live a new life."

Romans 6:4

But sin, disobedience and selfish living will keep that life-giving power from coming out. Sin will separate you from God's power, even though you're a Christian. His power will sit inactive within you if you walk in sin.

So how do you overcome sin? You can't do it by trying to stop sinning. You overcome it by walking in the new life God has put within you, by spending time in the Bible and in prayer. As you do that, the Holy Spirit will strengthen you and enable you to crush that sin.

Remember—the Holy Spirit will not stop those old habits of yours on His own. He'll wait on you to start. Then He will strengthen you to follow through with your decision. He will teach you how to walk in the new life that is on the inside of you.

Take the first step today by asking for His help. Say, *"Lord, I want to experience the power to live this new life every day. I decide today to put away sin. I'm dead to it. In Jesus' Name, I will spend time in prayer and in the Bible today. As I do, I believe I'll begin to live out the life-giving power You've placed in me!"*

talk the truth

"I walk in the new life Jesus gave me when He rose from the dead." (Romans 6:4)

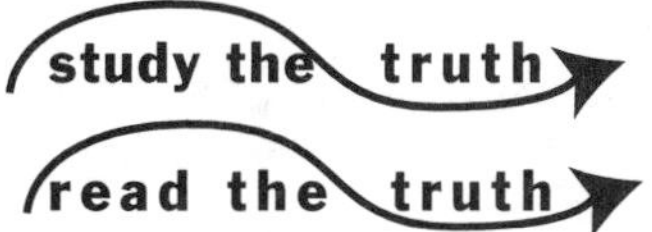
study the truth
read the truth

Romans 7:1-6

2 Kings 2,3; Ephesians 5

Kenneth

June 1

THE GREAT ESCAPE

"Trust in the Lord with all your heart and lean not on your own understanding; in all your ways acknowledge him, and he will make your paths straight."

Proverbs 3:5,6

Once you start stepping out in faith, Satan makes sure you have many opportunities to fall flat on your face. He'll try to get you into some jams where there won't seem to be any way out.

But if you'll look to God and trust Him for wisdom, He'll show you the way of escape (1 Corinthians 10:13).

I remember one particular night in Wichita Falls, Texas, where I was faced with a situation like that. I was preaching and the anointing was especially strong. Just as my message reached its climactic moment, a woman in the audience suddenly started shouting in tongues. I told her to stop three times, but she only grew louder. By the time she hushed, the message was forgotten. So I sternly began to correct her for being out of order.

Then a man sitting next to her spoke up and said, "Mr. Copeland, she is stone deaf. She can't hear a word you're saying."

At that point, I had no idea what to do. Not only had my sermon been shattered, but the whole congregation was mad at me for getting onto that poor deaf woman. (I found out later the man next to her used her to disrupt services and run preachers out of town. When the service reached a high point, he'd punch her and tell her it was her turn to prophesy.)

So I just stopped a moment, got quiet and asked the Lord what I should do. He said, *Lay hands on her and I'll open her ears.*

Talk about a turnaround! When God healed that woman's ears, He turned that disaster into such a powerful meeting—everyone was blessed!

So what's the moral of the story? The next time Satan tries to back you in a corner, get quiet. Ask God to show you the way of escape. He'll bring you out in victory every time.

talk the truth

"I trust in the Lord with all my heart. I don't lean on my own understanding. In all my ways I acknowledge Him, and He makes my paths straight." (Proverbs 3:5,6)

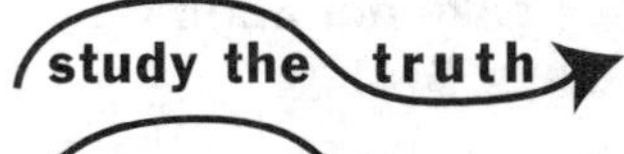
study the truth

Acts 14:8-22

read the truth

2 Kings 4,5; Ephesians 6

BEGIN TO PRAISE

Praise...the Bible says it's a very appropriate thing for a Christian to do.

"Sing joyfully to the Lord, you righteous; it is fitting for the upright to praise him."

PSALM 33:1

Let me warn you though, God's idea of "appropriate" praise and some Christians' ideas of appropriate praise may be two very different things. The praise He calls for is uninhibited and full of joy. And, at times, it's just plain loud!

If you don't believe it, look in the Bible and see the kind of praise that goes on in heaven. Read Isaiah 6 and find out how they act in God's throne room. The angels shout until the door posts shake! And then God's Glory fills the place.

When you get to heaven, you'll be praising like that too. You'll be dancing and praising God with everything you have. But why wait until you get to heaven—begin now!

Decide today that instead of praising God the way *others* like, you will start doing it the way *He* likes. Don't be concerned with what others may think. Let your praise be uninhibited and joyful. Don't wait until you get to heaven. Do it now. He deserves it!

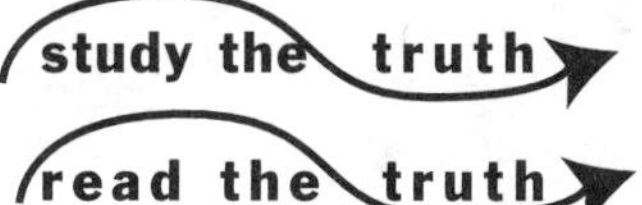

talk the truth **"My praise is uninhibited and joyful—because it's appropriate and it's the way God likes to be praised." (Psalm 33:1)**

study the truth **Isaiah 6:1-8**

read the truth **2 Kings 6,7; Philippians 1**

June 3

Kenneth

FREE FROM FEAR

"For God has not given us a spirit of fear, but of power and of love and of a sound mind."

2 Timothy 1:7, NKJV

What would you think if I told you that you could live without fear? Would you believe me if I said that despite what you hear about gangs around town or the need for metal detectors in school, you could be perfectly at peace? Impossible? Unrealistic? No!

You see, fear isn't just a reaction to what happens around you. It's a spiritual force. It begins inside you. And it is totally destructive. In fact, fear is Satan's main weapon. He moves in response to fear the way God moves in response to faith. He challenges God's promises with it.

An excellent example of this is found in Matthew 14 when Jesus invited Peter to come to Him on the water. "But when he [Peter] saw the wind, he was afraid and, beginning to sink, cried out, 'Lord, save me!'" (verse 30).

What enabled Peter to walk on the water? His faith in Jesus' command, "Come." What caused Peter to sink? His fear when he saw the storm. It wasn't the wind that defeated him—it was his fear of it! He looked at his circumstances, gave in to the fear and was defeated. If Peter had kept his focus on Jesus, his faith never would have been shaken—no matter how hard the wind blew.

Faith comes by spending time in God's Word. Fear is developed by spending time thinking about Satan's lies—also known as "worrying." Don't do it!

God's Word is the sword of the Spirit. Use it to fight Satan every time he comes against you. Hold up your shield of faith and put out all of his fiery darts. You don't have to live in fear of bullets or gangs everywhere you go. When you speak words of faith, the fear will leave.

talk the truth

"God has not given me a spirit of fear, but of power and of love and of a sound mind." (2 Timothy 1:7, NKJV)

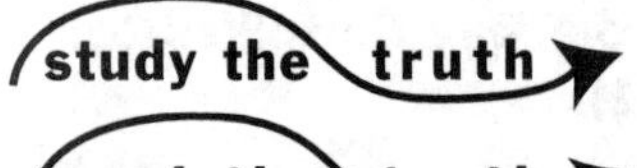
study the truth

Psalm 27

read the truth

2 Kings 8,9; Philippians 2

STRENGTH MADE PERFECT

"But he said to me, 'My grace is sufficient for you, for my power is made perfect in weakness.' Therefore I will boast all the more gladly about my weaknesses, so that Christ's power may rest on me."

2 Corinthians 12:9

When you run into a situation you simply don't have the strength or ability to handle, are you often tempted to simply give up and accept defeat? Well don't—because the Bible says God's power will be "made perfect" in your weakness.

Just think about that. What this scripture is saying is that when your human strength ends, God's miracle-working power will bring you through!

In Acts 14, you can see that promise in action. The scriptures say that the Apostle Paul was stoned by a group of Jews, taken out of the city and left for dead. Paul's human strength had ended. He was absolutely powerless.

But the disciples gathered around him and prayed, and the Lord raised him up and he went on his way. In other words, when Paul didn't have enough human strength to overcome, God's miracle-working power was just what he needed. It enabled him to overcome in spite of his weakness!

So, if you are facing a crisis today...if you're sick and medicine has failed you...if your family is falling apart...if your schoolwork is going down the drain...if drugs or other bad habits have you tied in knots...if you've just done all you know to do and you still haven't won...get excited! For where your strength ends, God's miraculous power comes through!

talk the truth

"God's grace is sufficient for me. His power is made perfect in my weakness." (2 Corinthians 12:9)

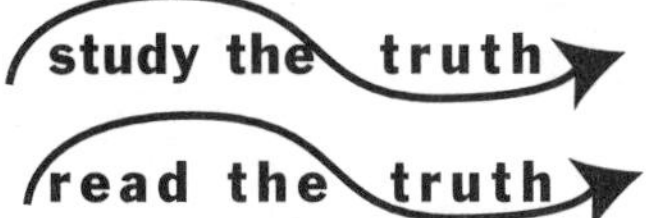
study the truth
read the truth

Acts 14:1-22

2 Kings 10,11,12; Philippians 3,4

June 5

TRUST HIM TO RESCUE YOU

"A thousand may fall at your side, ten thousand at your right hand, but it will not come near you...then no harm will befall you, no disaster will come near your tent."

PSALM 91:7,10

Plainly speaking, this world is not picture perfect. One disaster seems to happen after another. Almost daily we hear about wars, the dangers of nuclear weapons and chemical warfare, about oil spills, earthquakes and floods, about diseases on the rise and gang crime sweeping through our cities.

But in the middle of it all, God promises to protect anyone who will trust in Him. He wants to be your security. He wants to be the first Name you call when trouble comes your way. He wants to be the One you trust in to keep you safe. And if you'll do that, He'll never, never let you down.

He can handle every bit of danger that surrounds you. I don't care how bad it is, He can handle it! He proved that with Shadrach, Meshach and Abednego. They were bound and thrown into a fiery furnace that was so hot, the men who threw them in were killed by the heat. You can't get in any worse trouble than that! But God brought them through...and when they came out, they didn't even smell like smoke.

So, no matter how terrifying things around you seem to get, trust God. He'll never be out doing something else when you need help. He'll be right there to protect you and rescue you.

talk the truth

"The Lord is my protection. No harm or disaster can come near me." (Psalm 91:7,10)

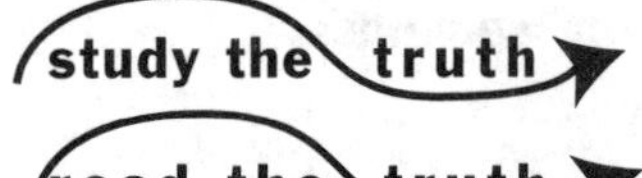
study the truth
read the truth

Daniel 3

2 Kings 13,14; Colossians 1

June 6

OBEY YOUR PARENTS

Well, you knew you couldn't get through this devotional without finding something about obeying your parents! But there's a very good reason for us to bring it up—because the Bible says obeying your parents brings you a special blessing: "that it may go well with you and that you may enjoy long life on the earth."

That's right! God's Word says that honoring your father and mother—obeying them—is the first commandment God gave with a promise attached. That promise is that you will live a long, fulfilled, overcoming life in Him. (Even if you don't live with your birth parents, you can receive this promise by obeying those entrusted with your care.)

Does that mean you should do what your parents say all the time?! Yes—unless it's against what the Bible tells you to do. So, even if you don't enjoy doing the dishes or taking out the trash sometimes, take on those responsibilities with joy knowing that, ultimately, you're obeying the Lord.

"Children, obey your parents in the Lord, for this is right. 'Honor your father and mother'—which is the first commandment with a promise—'that it may go well with you and that you may enjoy long life on the earth.'"

EPHESIANS 6:1-3

Now, some teenagers think it's OK to have a time of rebellion in their lives—to disobey their parents when what their parents ask doesn't suit them. "Oh, it's no big deal. I just want to do what I want to do," they say. But according to the Bible, it's not OK. First Samuel 15:23 says that "rebellion is as the sin of witchcraft" (KJV).

God gave you this promise because He doesn't want you to miss your calling. He wants you to live a long and fulfilled life. So take His advice. And don't worry—if you've blown it in the past, just ask God's forgiveness and turn from those disobedient ways. God will restore you!

talk the truth

"I obey my parents in the Lord, for this is right. I honor my father and mother, it goes well with me and I will enjoy a long life." (Ephesians 6:1-3)

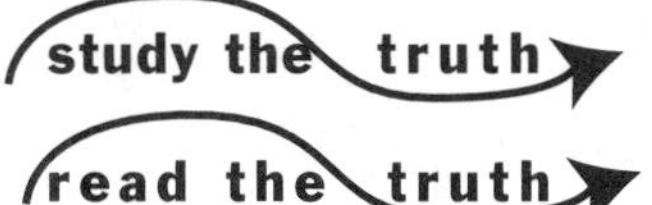
study the truth
read the truth

Proverbs 4:1; 6:20-22; 13:1; Colossians 3:20

2 Kings 15,16; Colossians 2

June 7

PUT THE RUMOR TO REST

"So Moses stretched out his hand toward the sky, and total darkness covered all Egypt for three days.... Yet all the Israelites had light in the places where they lived."

Exodus 10:22-23

Years ago Satan started a rumor. He told a few Christians that they had to live like the world, sharing all the same defeat, heartache and failure. Well, the word spread. You may have heard it yourself. But it's just a lie.

The Bible says in Psalm 91:10 that evil can't even come *near* your house if you are a Christian with your faith in Him. (Of course, if there is currently trouble in your home, you can stand on this promise as you pray for things to change.)

In John 16, Jesus Himself says He has deprived the world of power to harm you. And Exodus 10:23 says that when thick darkness surrounded the Egyptians, the Israelites had light where they lived. They didn't have to live like the world.

You can see that God never intended you to experience all of the junk the world suffers. He's always wanted His children to live above it, to stand out as light in a dark world.

In the Old Testament, God's honor was seen because of the miracles He worked for His children. It should be that way today with you and me. We should give God Glory by the lives of victory we live. People should be coming up to us and saying things like, "I've heard how God healed you," or, "I've heard how your parents' marriage was restored," or, "God has really helped you out in this tough situation."

Can you see now why Satan would spread such a rumor? He doesn't want people asking you where you get your power, peace or health. But that's exactly what God wants to happen.

So put God's Word to work and dare to receive all He has promised you. Let the light of God's power in your life put Satan's dark rumors to rest!

talk the truth

"I am in this world, but I am not of it. Through Jesus, I have the victory!" (John 17:13; 1 Corinthians 15:55)

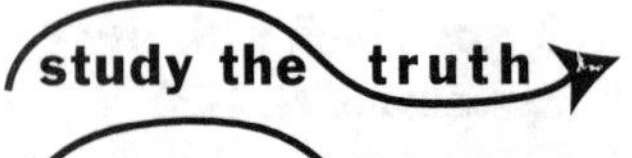
study the truth
read the truth

Philippians 2:1-16

2 Kings 17,18; Colossians 3

ADDICTED TO THE WORD

"Ye know the house of Stephanas...and that they have addicted themselves to the ministry of the saints."

1 Corinthians 16:15, KJV

I want you to begin to develop an addiction today—an addiction to God's Word. That may sound strange to you, especially if you don't have much of an interest in the Bible right now. But, believe me, it's possible. I've done it myself and I've seen others do it, time and again.

All you have to do is make a decision to focus your time and attention on the Word. The more you give yourself to it, the more your desire for it will grow. You'll become addicted.

That happens with anything you totally give yourself to. It happens, for example, with people who give themselves to overeating. As they focus their attention on it, the evil spirit behind it moves in on their mind and eventually draws them from mental activity into physical activity. Finally, they come to a place where they can't get enough. Drugs, alcohol, pornography and stealing are the same way—and I'm sure you can think of many more examples.

But this same principle works on the positive side, too. You can give yourself to God's Word to the point where it totally consumes your life, mentally and physically. The more of it you get, the more you want. The Spirit behind the Bible, the Holy Spirit, will draw you and lead you closer to Jesus than you ever imagined possible.

Every person I've met who walks in faith and power had—at some time—developed that kind of addiction to God's Word by giving themselves totally to it for an extended time. I don't mean just a few minutes here and there. I'm talking about some serious time.

So make up your mind to do that. Determine to become a "Word addict." Once you do, you'll never be willing to live without it again.

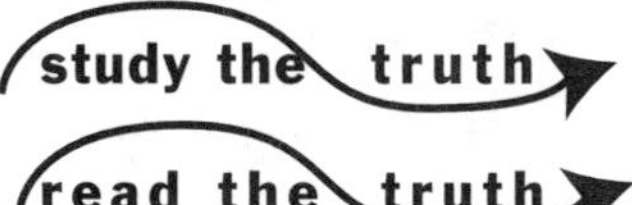

"I am addicted to the Word!" (1 Corinthians 16:15, KJV)

study the truth **Hebrews 4:1-12**

read the truth **2 Kings 19,20; Colossians 4**

June 9

Gloria

GRACE IS ENOUGH

"Lest I should be exalted above measure by the abundance of the revelations, a thorn in the flesh was given to me, a messenger of Satan to buffet me."

2 Corinthians 12:7, NKJV

Years ago, Satan started twisting the above scripture to talk Christians out of victory. He's used it to convince us to freely settle for everything from sickness to sin, making us think that God sometimes sends us a "thorn in the flesh" like Paul had. This may, in fact, be the most destructive and the most widely accepted misunderstanding of Scripture that exists today.

Tradition says *God* gave Paul the thorn in the flesh. What's more, tradition makes the "thorn" into some great mystery. But the Bible doesn't say that at all! It says the thorn in the flesh was a messenger of Satan. Not God—*Satan*. The thorn was just what Paul says it was—not some great mystery!

You see, everywhere Paul went, he preached what Jesus preached and every time he did, he destroyed a little more of Satan's kingdom. So, Satan sent an evil spirit to stop him.

When Paul prayed to God about this thorn (2 Corinthians 12:8-10), God didn't give Paul a negative answer. God said, "My grace is sufficient for you, for my power is made perfect in weakness."

In other words, when Paul didn't have enough human strength to drive out Satan's messenger, God's miracle-working power was just what he needed. It enabled him to overcome in spite of his weakness.

Don't allow Satan to talk you out of your victory when it comes to sharing God's Word, getting good grades, developing a talent or anything else. Throw tradition aside and dare to believe God's Word. Fight the fight of faith, and just like the Apostle Paul, you will see God move in your life!

talk the truth

"God's power is made perfect in my weakness. His grace is sufficient for me!" (2 Corinthians 12:9, NKJV)

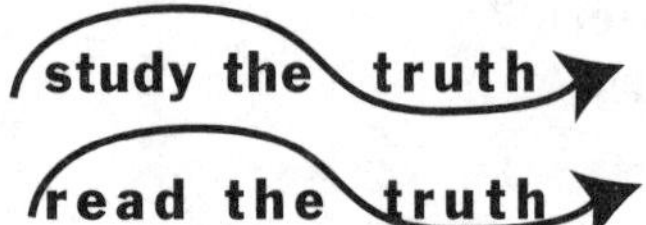
study the truth
read the truth

2 Corinthians 12:1-10

2 Kings 21,22; 1 Thessalonians 1

DEVELOP THE LOVE

God says love is keeping His commandments. And that's exactly what love is. But God has done more than define love for you. He's given you instructions so you can know how to love as He loves. By giving you the Bible, God has spelled it out for you in black and white. All you have to do is what the Bible says, and you'll be walking in love.

If you've made Jesus the Lord of your life, God's love has been placed within you. But, unless you take steps to develop it, that love will remain hidden. Love works in much the same way as the force of faith. Like faith, love becomes active through learning God's Word and living it out.

"And this is love: that we walk in obedience to his commands. As you have heard from the beginning, his command is that you walk in love."

2 John 1:6

Become aware of love by speaking and acting on His Word today. As you focus on these scriptures, see yourself living in love everywhere you go. See yourself led by the commandments of Jesus in school, at home, on the job and when you're out with your friends. Develop the love He has hidden in you.

talk the truth

"I walk in obedience to God's commands by walking in love." (2 John 1:6)

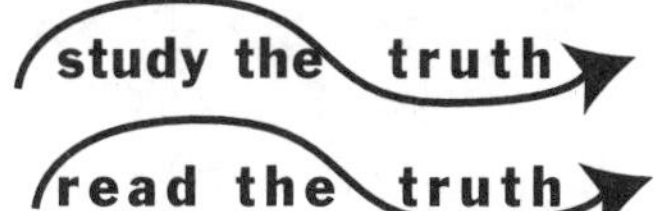
study the truth
read the truth

1 John 2:3-11

2 Kings 23,24; 1 Thessalonians 2

Gloria

June 11

FROM DESPERATION TO DEDICATION

"Set your affection on things above, not on things on the earth."

COLOSSIANS 3:2, KJV

Things, things, things! A hot, new car. Your own apartment. New clothes. A date with the person of your dreams. Tickets to the Super Bowl. Should I go on?

Many of us have learned to believe God for good things...and now we have so many good things, we find them hard to keep up with! We end up spending so much time and energy taking care of the "things" of life that, without even meaning to, we give the attention and affection of our heart to this natural world instead of to God.

When Kenneth and I first heard about living by faith, we were in desperate circumstances. We were sick and broke, so it was easy for us to give ourselves to prayer and to the Bible. And as we honored God's Word, He honored and took care of us. We came to the place where we were no longer desperate. Then came the real test of our faith. Would we serve God out of our love for Him instead of our desperation?

Well, praise God, we did. But in the process we found out one thing: It takes a lot more dedication to serve God when you're doing well than it takes when you're desperate! There's a constant temptation to get so caught up in earthly "things" that your desire for the things of God fades away.

As the material benefits come your way, remember, God has not trained you in His Word so you can use it on your own selfish desires. He has shown His promises to you so you can do the job He's called you to do.

Don't let the things of this world cause you to miss out on the things of God. Get your priorities in line with what the Bible says. Set your mind on the things above, and you'll discover just how good life was really meant to be!

talk the truth

"I set my affection on things above, not on things on the earth." (Colossians 3:2, KJV)

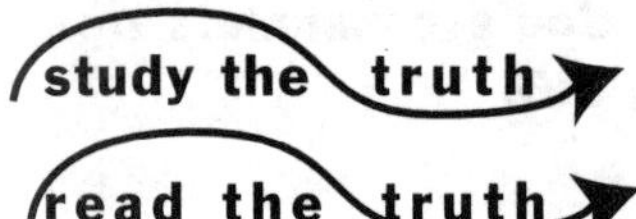
study the truth
read the truth

Colossians 3:1-16

2 Kings 25; 1 Chronicles 1,2; 1 Thessalonians 3,4

PLAY TO WIN

"Who is it that overcomes the world? Only he who believes that Jesus is the Son of God."

1 John 5:5

Any coach will tell you that part of playing the game right is having a winning attitude. And that's what God wants us to have—*a winning attitude.* He wants us to put so much trust in Him that we *expect* to whip any problem Satan brings our way. He wants us to *expect* to win at life.

But most of us don't come by that attitude easily. We're so used to losing that we have to totally change our way of thinking to have a winning mind-set. We need to understand the fact that Jesus has overcome the world.

We need to develop a sense of confidence that says, "I'm determined to live in victory, and there's nothing Satan can do to stop me!"

"But you don't know the kinds of problems I'm facing."

I know I don't, but Jesus does. He said that when Satan comes against you with everything he has, you should be confident—because He's already beaten the enemy!

First John 5:5 puts it this way, "Who is it that overcomes the world? Only he who believes that Jesus is the Son of God." Do you know what that means? It means that if you're a Christian, you have an absolute right to be a winner. Think about that. Start developing a winning attitude today!

talk the truth

"I believe Jesus is the Son of God...and I overcome the world!" (1 John 5:5)

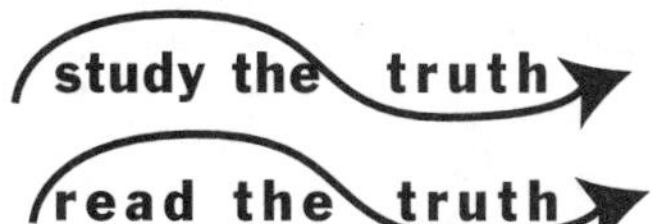
study the truth
read the truth

Romans 8:29-39

1 Chronicles 3,4; 1 Thessalonians 5

Kenneth

June 13

PROMISES BY THE TRUCKLOAD

"'Consider carefully what you hear,' he continued. 'With the measure you use, it will be measured to you—and even more.'"

MARK 4:24

How many promises will you receive from God's Word? It depends on how many you expect to receive. When God measures out blessings to you, He'll be using *your* measuring stick, not His own. He always works that way.

Two people can hear what the Bible says about healing, for example. One will "measure it" with faith. "By His wounds I have been healed!" he'll say. "I believe that with all my heart."

The other will measure it with doubt. "I'll give this healing stuff a try," he'll say, "but I don't think anything will really happen."

Both of those people will get exactly what they expect. God will measure to them just as they measured what the Bible says. One will get healed...the other won't.

I must warn you though, sometimes measuring the Word with faith is hard. Years ago, when Gloria first read the scripture, "Let no debt remain outstanding" (Romans 13:8), it was tempting for her to measure it without faith. See, we were living in a terrible little house at the time, and she wanted a new one more than just about anything.

How could we ever buy a decent house without borrowing money? It didn't seem possible. So, to her, it was as if that scripture had said, "Gloria, you can't have a new house."

But she refused to measure it that way. She grabbed Satan by the throat and said, "No! You won't cheat me out of my house." Then she started believing that somehow God could provide her with a house debt free. Sure enough, He did.

If you want to receive the promises of God into your life by the truckload, start reading the Bible with a big measure of faith. God will measure it back to you with more than you can imagine!

talk the truth — **"I measure God's Word with faith and I receive His promises." (Mark 4:24)**

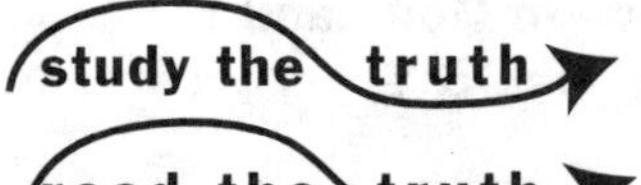

study the truth — **Luke 8:1-18**

read the truth — **1 Chronicles 5,6; 2 Thessalonians 1**

KNOW GOD'S PLAN

"Unless the Lord builds the house, its builders labor in vain."

Psalm 127:1

We're living in a time of big decisions and changes. If there was ever a day when we *must know* God's plan for our lives, it's now.

In fact, nothing else will work! God is changing and rearranging things, getting them ready for a powerful move of His Spirit in the earth. If you want to keep up, you must know God's perfect plan for your life.

How do you do that? Through prayer. In fact, in Colossians 1:9-12, God gave us a prayer that we can use to receive the wisdom we need.

"For this reason...we have not stopped praying for you and asking God to fill you with the knowledge of his will through all spiritual wisdom and understanding. And we pray this in order that you may live a life worthy of the Lord and may please him in every way: bearing fruit in every good work, growing in the knowledge of God, being strengthened with all power according to his glorious might so that you may have great endurance and patience, and joyfully giving thanks to the Father."

God has instructed Gloria and me to pray that prayer for our ministry Partners and for ourselves every day. It's a powerful prayer that will not only enable you to know God's call on your life, but it will also give you the wisdom and understanding to carry it out.

That, by the way, is where most plans fail. We get a small insight into God's plan for our lives, but then we mess things up by trying to make it work on our own. Instead of letting God build the house in His power, we try to build it ourselves and end up doing it all for nothing.

Don't make that mistake. Instead, pray this prayer that God has given us. Put your name in it. It's a prayer you can be sure God will answer—it's *His* Word! Put it to work in your life daily and God will fill you with His wisdom and understanding.

talk the truth

"I am filled with the knowledge of God's will, through spiritual wisdom and understanding." (Colossians 1:9)

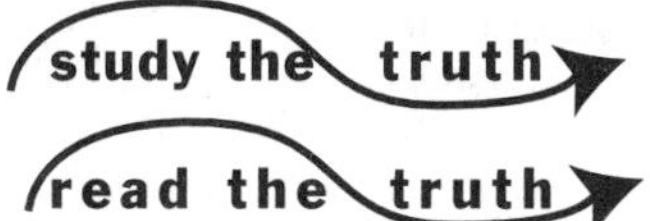
study the truth
read the truth

Colossians 1:9-22

1 Chronicles 7,8; 2 Thessalonians 2

June 15

GIVE YOUR WORRIES TO HIM

"Therefore humble yourselves...under the mighty hand of God, that in due time He may exalt you. Casting the whole of your care—all your anxieties, all your worries, all your concerns, once and for all—on Him; for He cares for you affectionately, and cares about you watchfully."

1 PETER 5:6,7, AMP

When I first learned to give my worries to the Lord, I was in south Texas preaching at a meeting that no one was coming to. After a couple of services with just the local preacher and two others in attendance, I was starting to sweat. But the Lord said, *Cast that concern on Me,* so I did.

I told Satan, "I will not frown or worry. I came here to preach and that's what I'm determined to do. It's God's business whether anyone shows up or not. I couldn't care less!" I was so happy, I felt foolish.

Satan said, *What's the matter with you? Don't you even have enough sense to worry about something like this?* But I just gave my worries to the Lord.

During all the hours I'd spent worrying, I kept hearing 1 Peter 5:6-7 on the inside of me. Finally, I understood that God didn't want me to worry. My part was to preach and pray for the sick, so that's what I did—and left the rest to Him. Once I let Him handle things, we had one of the best meetings of my life—it was the turning point of my ministry!

At the time, I didn't realize what was happening, but being carefree put me in a position where Satan couldn't get me to fear or doubt. He couldn't pressure me and get me to compromise because I wasn't concerned. I'd given all my worries to God!

Are you ready to be free from worry about *everything,* from tests to peer pressure? Then make Jesus Lord over *all* your circumstances—give your worries to Him, and speak this in faith:

"The Word works in me and right now, I humble myself before God. I give all my worries to Him. From now on, I refuse to worry. Instead, I will pray. I will use my faith and believe, and He'll put the problem and the forces of darkness underneath me. I belong to Jesus and He cares for me!"

talk the truth

"I cast all my cares, anxieties, worries and concerns—once and for all—on God. For He cares for me affectionately and watchfully." (1 Peter 5:6,7, AMP)

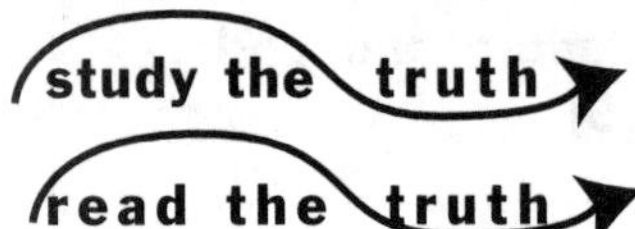
study the truth
read the truth

Psalm 55:16-22

1 Chronicles 9,10; 2 Thessalonians 3

HANG ON

When it comes to any problem—no matter what it is—if you'll hit Satan with God's Word and give your concerns about the situation over to God, you'll win.

Let me warn you though, hanging on to God's promises isn't always easy. Satan knows that if he doesn't steal them from you, you'll use them to defeat him.

So, if you're sick, don't be surprised if he begins to tell you, *You're not healed. It might work for someone else, but healing doesn't work for you.*

When he starts to tell you that kind of thing, don't buy it! Don't start worrying about it and thinking, *What if I don't get healed? I sure don't feel healed. I'll probably just get worse and worse....*

"So is my word that goes out from my mouth: It will not return to me empty, but will accomplish what I desire and achieve the purpose for which I sent it."

ISAIAH 55:11

Remember this: It's God's Word that does the work. And it'll work for anyone. It'll work for you just like it worked for Jesus when He walked the earth.

He told Satan what the Word said. No matter what Satan tries to tell you, refuse to let go of God's promise to you from His Word. Tell Satan what the Bible says about your situation. Find a promise in God's Word about your healing, safety, finances, grades or work, and then let God's Word fight its own fight. It'll whip Satan every time.

talk the truth

"I speak God's Word and it does not return empty. It accomplishes what God desires and it achieves the purpose for which it was sent." (Isaiah 55:11)

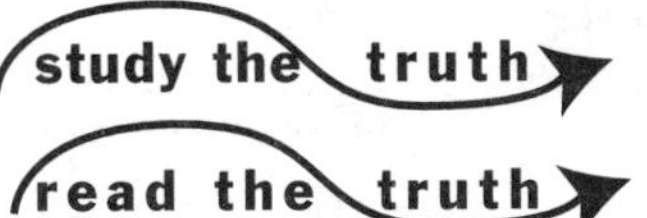
study the truth
read the truth

Psalm 19:7-14

1 Chronicles 11,12; 1 Timothy 1

June 17

OPEN THEIR EYES TO THE LIGHT

"And even if our gospel is veiled, it is veiled to those who are perishing. The god of this age has blinded the minds of unbelievers, so that they cannot see the light of the gospel of the glory of Christ, who is the image of God."

2 Corinthians 4:3,4

Since God doesn't save anyone against their will, does it really do any good to pray for people who refuse to make Jesus their Lord?

Yes. Yes! *Yes! It does!*

You see, most people who refuse to make Jesus their Lord think they've made that decision of their own free will. But the truth is, they haven't. The Bible says Satan has blinded them. He's blocking their understanding of the truth. So their decision hasn't been freely made at all.

That's important for you to grasp. Because through prayer, you can interfere with the demonic forces and help take those blinders off! You can also change circumstances with your prayers and help create situations that will bring them in contact with the Lord.

I prayed with a friend of mine once who'd been praying for his lost brother for years. So we agreed together and bound Satan according to Matthew 12:29. We said, "You blinding spirit, stop what you're doing to keep him out of the kingdom of God. In Jesus' Name, stop *now!*"

Jesus also said in Matthew 9:38, "Ask the Lord of the harvest, therefore, to send out workers into his harvest field." So we prayed, "Lord, send someone to him who knows the Bible. You know who he will listen to. We're believing by faith."

Soon after that, his brother called him. "What have you been doing up there?" he asked. "Everyone I've come across has started preaching to me!"

Our prayers interfered with what Satan was doing to blind this man...and they created the circumstances to help him find out about Jesus. Sure enough, within a few days, he made Jesus the Lord of his life.

Don't sit by and let Satan take your friends and family without a fight. Pray. Pray! *Pray!* Take off the blinders and open their eyes to the truth.

talk the truth

"I pray to the Lord of the harvest to send workers into His harvest field so souls will be saved." (Matthew 9:38)

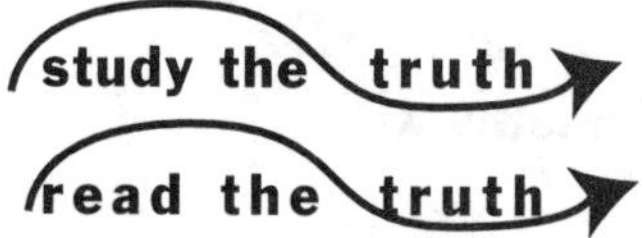
study the truth
read the truth

2 Corinthians 4:1-7

1 Chronicles 13,14; 1 Timothy 2

DISCOVER WHAT GRACE CAN DO

"With great power the apostles continued to testify to the resurrection of the Lord Jesus, and much grace was upon them all."

ACTS 4:33

Most of us don't have any idea what *grace* really is. Sure, we know some basic facts about it. We know we were saved by it (Ephesians 2:8). But we don't even begin to understand the real power it can release in our lives.

If you want to get an idea of what grace can really do, look at what happened to the early Christians in Acts 4. They'd been threatened by the religious leaders of Jerusalem and commanded not to speak or teach in Jesus' Name. So, they prayed about the situation.

Basically, they said, "Lord, we've been threatened, but we aren't about to quit preaching and go hide. Just give us boldness and we'll go on."

As a result of that prayer, verse 33 tells us, "Much grace was upon them all."

Much grace. Grace so powerful that when they received it, the building literally shook. Grace so great it enabled the apostles to work "many miraculous signs and wonders among the people" (Acts 5:12).

That one story alone should be enough to convince you that there's more to grace than meets the eye. *Grace provides the real, supernatural power to make things happen!*

And get this—the Bible says that same grace is available to anyone. That means you and me!

If Satan's been threatening you lately, do what those early Christians did. Pray, "Lord, I don't care what Satan says, I won't back down. I will keep on talking and living by faith! Just give me boldness and I'll go on."

I guarantee you, if you really mean it, He'll do it. He'll give you the strength and boldness you need to live a faith-filled life in front of everyone. And when you receive that strength, you'll discover what *grace* is really all about.

talk the truth

"Great power and *much* grace is upon me!" (Acts 4:33)

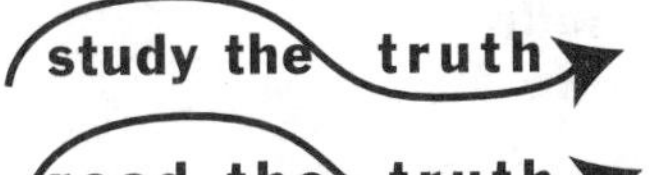
study the truth
read the truth

Acts 4:8-33

1 Chronicles 15,16,17; 1 Timothy 3,4

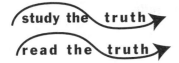

A MIRACLE INSIDE YOU

"'Not by might nor by power, but by my Spirit,' says the Lord Almighty."

ZECHARIAH 4:6

I remember the first time I went with the Oral Roberts crusade team to a healing meeting. I was a student and a member of his aircraft crew. I knew only a little about the things of God, but I was part of the team and eager to learn.

I followed the team inside this huge auditorium. It was filled with sick people. The place was so full of disease, it smelled. Just walking in there sent chills up my spine.

I turned around and headed for the side door as fast as I could. "I don't belong here," I told God. "I'm getting on a Greyhound bus and heading home right now."

Once I was outside the door, suddenly, I froze. My feet wouldn't move. I knew it was God Who'd stopped me. Desperately, I prayed, "Please, let me go! I don't have anything for those people."

That's when God spoke back to me. He said, *I know you don't have anything to give them. But I do and that's why I baptized you in My Spirit.*

Suddenly I knew I had a choice. I could go with what God wanted for my life, or I could go against it. So I turned around and went back.

I was ready to run. But God stopped me. He knew *He* was in me, and if I'd just stay and rely on Him, miracles would happen—and they did.

You have the same miracle-working God inside of you. And there are people all around you who need Him. So quit waiting to "feel" like you have the power—and get out there. Once you do, you'll discover that the power you've been waiting on has been right there inside you all the time...waiting on you.

talk the truth

"I can do what I need to do, not by my own might and power, but by the Spirit of God." (Zechariah 4:6)

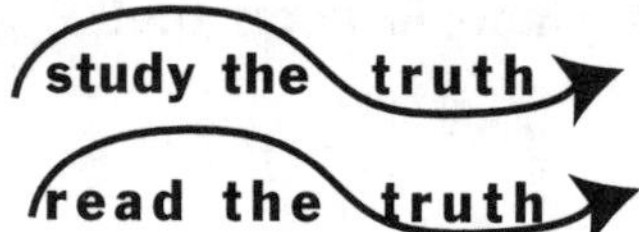
study the truth
read the truth

Exodus 3:1-14

1 Chronicles 18,19; 1 Timothy 5

A HEALTHY DOSE OF LOVE

"Love...is not touchy or fretful or resentful; it takes no account of the evil done to it—pays no attention to a suffered wrong."

1 Corinthians 13:4,5, AMP

Walking in love is good for your health—did you know that?

It's true! Medical science has proven it. Researchers have discovered that hostility produces stress that causes ulcers, tension headaches and many other problems.

When you think of hostility, you probably think of the type of anger you feel when something serious happens. But according to the experts, that isn't what causes the worst problems. It's the little things—when you don't get invited to a party, for example. Or when the coach doesn't put you in the game. Sound familiar?

Just think how much stress you could avoid by being quick to forgive, by living your life according to 1 Corinthians 13 and not counting up the wrongs done to you. That may sound impossible to do, but it's not! As a Christian, you have God's love inside you.

If you'll let love work, it will set you free. Jesus wants that freedom for you. So say to those habits that have you bound, "In Jesus' Name, let me go! I'm putting hostility, unforgiveness and selfishness behind me. I'm going on with God. I'll live a life of love!"

Remember, it doesn't take a miracle to turn your life around. All it takes is a decision to let the force of love work in your life. Do it today!

talk the truth **"I make a decision to let love work in my life. I will not be touchy, fretful or resentful. I take no account of the evil done to me. I pay no attention to a suffered wrong. I walk in love." (1 Corinthians 13:4,5, AMP)**

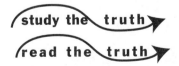

study the truth **Proverbs 4:10-27**

read the truth **1 Chronicles 20,21; 1 Timothy 6**

Gloria

June 21

PUT THE WORD FIRST

"For skillful and godly Wisdom is the principal thing.... Prize Wisdom highly and exalt her, and she will exalt and promote you; she will bring you to honor when you embrace her."

Proverbs 4:7,8, AMP

I want to tell you the only real secret to getting ahead in this world. It's simple. Put God's Word first place in your life.

"Well, that's no secret," you may say. But listen to what I mean.

You see, the Bible is not just a textbook, a storybook or a history book. It's a handbook for living. It's the wisdom of Almighty God written down so that you can apply it to your everyday circumstances.

God says that wisdom is the "principal thing." Principal means "first in importance." That means God's Word should be the most important thing to you—it should influence everything you do. I know from personal experience what an impact that can have on your life.

Years ago I decided to read the books of Matthew, Mark, Luke, John and Acts three times in 30 days. It seemed impossible at the time. With two small children and my house turned upside down from a recent move, I couldn't see how I could spend that much time reading the Bible and still get everything done. But I decided to put other things aside and do it anyway.

To my surprise, at the end of the first day I had accomplished more than I ever expected. And by the end of that 30 days, I had not only read each of those books in the Bible three times, but I had also finished all my regular work, taken care of my kids, and refinished a few pieces of furniture!

That will happen in your life too, if you give God's Word priority. You'll still have time for soccer practice, your job, your homework and your friends. But let me warn you, don't wait until you think you have the time to begin reading the Bible. Satan will see to it that you never find it.

Just do like I did and spend time in God's Word *first.* Soon you'll see it giving back to you in every area of your life.

talk the truth **"I give God's Word first place in my life." (Proverbs 4:7,8, AMP)**

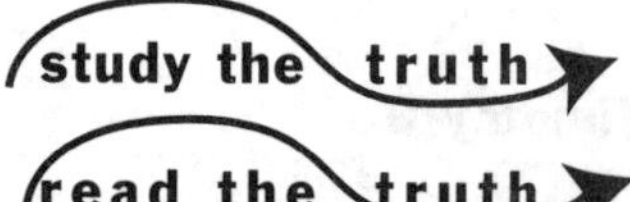

Proverbs 3:1-9

read the truth **1 Chronicles 22,23; 2 Timothy 1**

EXPECT A HARVEST

"Give, and it will be given to you. A good measure, pressed down, shaken together and running over, will be poured into your lap. For with the measure you use, it will be measured to you."

LUKE 6:38

"*Give, and it will be given to you.*" Jesus said that. Yet many Christians refuse to believe it. In fact, they actually think it's wrong to expect to receive from Him when they give. The truth is—it's wrong *not* to!

What would you think about a farmer who planted seeds, then let his crop rot in the field? You'd think he was a fool, wouldn't you? And if he did it when others were starving, you'd think he was a criminal.

Well, it's just as wrong to give and ignore the harvest God promised. Especially when it could help get the message of God's love to people who are starving to hear it.

God wants us to receive from the financial seeds we plant. He wants us to have enough with plenty left over to give "for every good work and charitable donation" (2 Corinthians 9:8, AMP). He wants us to be able to give generously.

Next time you give, don't be afraid to expect a harvest! Then, when it comes, turn right around and plant it again. Keep giving and receiving so the Lord can bless the world through you!

talk the truth

"I give, and I expect the harvest God has for me." (Luke 6:38)

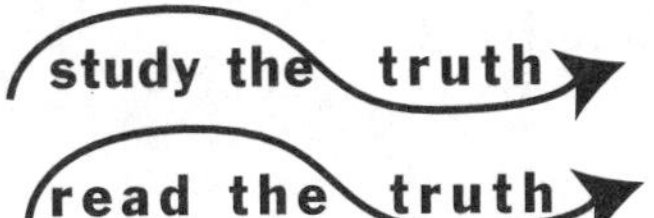
study the truth
read the truth

2 Corinthians 9:6-15

1 Chronicles 24,25; 2 Timothy 2

June 23

Gloria

SEE YOURSELF STRONG

"We seemed like grasshoppers in our own eyes, and we looked the same to them."

NUMBERS 13:33

How does Satan see you? Does he see you as a strong warrior of God...or does he see you as a wimp he can whip in a minute?

The answer to that question depends on you. I realized that one day as I was studying why the Israelites didn't enter into the Promised Land. The key to their failure is found in the words they spoke: "We seemed like grasshoppers in our own eyes, and we looked the same to them."

The reason the Israelites were so terrified to fight the giants in Canaan wasn't because those giants were so big. It was because the Israelites saw themselves as so small!

The same thing is true for you as a Christian. It's what you are in your own sight that will make the difference. If you see yourself as a weak, powerless Christian, Satan will continually run over you. But when you see yourself as God sees you—as a conquering child of the Almighty God, equipped with the very power of God Himself—Satan will want to steer clear of you.

Because he's a coward, Satan would rather do anything than come against someone who's bold and courageous. In fact, ever since Jesus rose from the grave, Satan's heart freezes whenever he hears Jesus' Name used by someone who has faith in it.

If you don't see yourself as strong in the Lord, you need to change that. You need to get so full of God's Word and the Holy Ghost that you walk around like a spiritual giant. Turn the tables on Satan and let him find out what it feels like to be a grasshopper for a change!

talk the truth

"I am strong in the Lord and in His mighty power." (Ephesians 6:10)

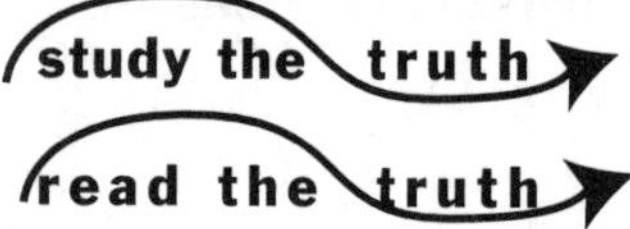
study the truth
read the truth

Numbers 13:17-33

1 Chronicles 26,27; 2 Timothy 3

DON'T TELL IT LIKE IT IS

"The tongue has the power of life and death, and those who love it will eat its fruit."

PROVERBS 18:21

Words are serious business. And, as Christians, we need to get serious about learning how to use them. We need to begin to put them to work for us like God does. The Bible tells us that He uses words to call "those things which be not as though they were" (Romans 4:17, KJV).

Most of us don't know how to do that. We've spent our lives "telling it like it is." We always speak about the bad things going on around us. So, the very thought of calling "things which be not as though they were" seems a little crazy.

"You mean I'm supposed to say, 'I'm healed' when I'm feeling sick? I'm supposed to say, 'I'm smart' when I can't pass a simple quiz in geometry? That sounds like lying to me."

No—there's a big difference between lying and speaking by faith. A lie is meant to deceive someone. It's designed to make someone believe something that's not true. But to speak by faith is simply to speak words that agree with God's Word instead of the circumstances around you.

In 2 Corinthians 4:13, the Apostle Paul said, "It is written: 'I believed; therefore I have spoken.' With that same spirit of faith we also believe and therefore speak." That's important. *I have believed, and therefore I have spoken.*

There are some people who speak, but don't back their words up with faith. So, they fall flat on their faces. Just wishing and hoping won't get the job done. You have to *believe.*

Begin today bringing both what you say and what you believe into line with what the Bible says. Stop "telling it like it is" and start speaking and believing God's promises. Put the power of words to work for you.

talk the truth

"By faith, I call things that are not as though they are." (Romans 4:17)

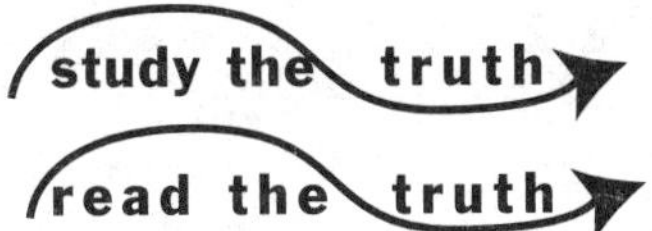
study the truth
read the truth

Proverbs 15

1 Chronicles 28,29; 2 Timothy 4

DON'T GET IN A HURRY

"These commandments that I give you today are to be upon your hearts.... Talk about them when you sit at home and when you walk along the road, when you lie down and when you get up."

DEUTERONOMY 6:6,7

One of the reasons Gloria and I have seen the results we have in our lives and in our ministry is because when we realized what God's Word would do, we plunged into it. We turned off the radio and television, put down the newspaper, and spent nearly every waking moment of our time reading the Bible, listening to tapes on the Bible, or thinking about what the Bible says.

All that time in God's Word eventually had a powerful effect on us. It began to change everything about us. It began to turn failure into success.

All that didn't happen overnight, though. It took time. Many Christians don't realize that. They start out devoting themselves to God's Word, but they make the mistake of expecting instant, miraculous results—and when they don't see them, they get disappointed and fall away. We have to be patient and give His Word time to do its work.

Jesus once said, "Man does not live on bread alone, but on every word that comes from the mouth of God" (Matthew 4:4). God's Word feeds your spirit just as physical food feeds your body. Food has to be built into your body. The vitamins and minerals it contains build up your body over time.

Much the same thing is true with God's Word. He wants you to feed on His Word—then, over time, you'll grow in strength and in faith and produce results. Sure, sometimes God will act instantly and perform a miracle, but only to get things back on track.

So don't get in such a hurry! Stay with God's Word and be patient...the results will come!

talk the truth

"God's Word is in my heart. No matter where I go or what I do, I have His Word on my mind." (Deuteronomy 6:6,7)

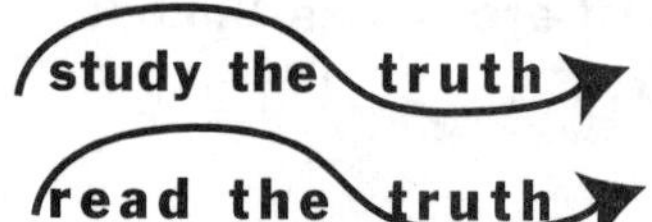
study the truth
read the truth

Deuteronomy 7:11-23

2 Chronicles 1,2,3; Titus 1-2

June 26

TAKE A STAND AGAINST STRIFE

"Starting a quarrel is like a leak in a dam. So stop the quarrel before a fight breaks out."

PROVERBS 17:14, ICB

Throughout Scripture, God warns us about the danger of strife. Yet it's still one of the most common problems among Christians. We let it get into our homes, our friendships, our youth groups...everywhere!

Of course, we don't let it in on purpose. We don't wake up in the morning and say, "I think I'll cause some major problems today." We just let it slip up on us a little bit at a time.

So take a big stand against those little opportunities for strife today. Arm yourself against them by understanding that this world isn't perfect—and there are people in it who will not be nice to you. There are people who will anger and bother you—on purpose or by accident.

Make up your mind that, by God's power, you won't let them get your peace. That peace is important. It will keep your body healthy. It will keep your friendships healthy. It will put you in a place where God can guide your steps and save you from hard-hitting mistakes.

If you're used to getting irritated over every little thing, it may take awhile for you to break that habit. But you can do it—a little at a time.

I know. I used to have the habit of worrying a lot. But when I learned worrying wasn't walking in faith, I had to give it up one minute at a time. With the help of the Holy Spirit, every time a worry came to me, I overcame it with God's Word. And I did it until that worrying habit broke for good.

You can do the same thing with strife. Ask the Holy Spirit to help you notice it and overcome it one moment at a time. Then, every time you start to get upset about something, stop that strife and say aloud, "Oh, no you don't, Strife. I'm walking in the peace of God today."

talk the truth

"I refuse to walk in strife. I let God's peace rule in my heart and life." (Proverbs 17:14, ICB)

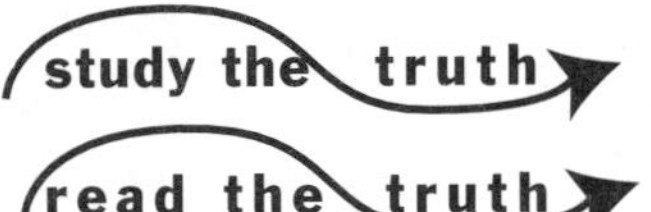
study the truth
read the truth

Matthew 5:21-26,43-48

2 Chronicles 4,5; Titus 3

June 27

Gloria

GOD'S MEDICINE

"The words I have spoken to you are spirit and they are life."

JOHN 6:63

We've seen some incredible medical breakthroughs. We've seen "miracle drugs" developed that can conquer many kinds of sickness and disease.

But, since I've been a Christian, I've discovered another—much more effective—kind of medicine: God's Word. There's never been a miracle drug that could equal it. God's medicine is the answer to every need. It is life. It is health. It is the very power of God. And if you put it in your heart and act on it, you will be healed.

Sometimes people ask, "If God's medicine works every time, why are there so many Christians who are still sick?" There are two reasons. Number one, because they don't take the time to plant what the Bible says about healing deep into their hearts. And number two, because they don't do what the Bible says.

Think of it like this: If a doctor gives you medicine, you have to follow the instructions he gives you if you expect to get well, don't you? In the same way, if you read God's Word and don't act on it, nothing will happen.

Proverbs 4:22 says God's words are life and health to you. So don't wait until you are sick to start using them. Start now. Begin to put His Word in your heart, and it will be hard for you to become sick. That Word within you will constantly keep God's healing power at work in your life.

And don't worry. There's no limit to the amount of God's medicine you can take. You can't overdose. The more you take, the stronger you'll become!

talk the truth

"God's Word is life and health to my whole body." (Proverbs 4:22)

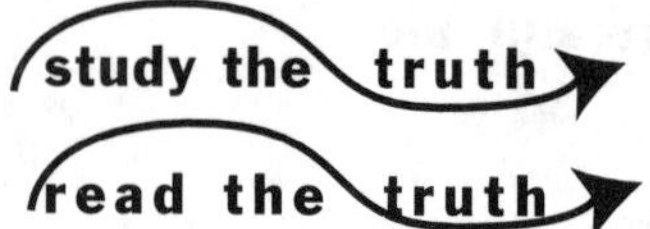
study the truth
read the truth

Proverbs 4:20-27

2 Chronicles 6,7; Philemon

PUT THE DIFFERENCES TOGETHER

"Though one may be overpowered, two can defend themselves. A cord of three strands is not quickly broken."

ECCLESIASTES 4:12

There's power in unity. Satan knows that. That's why he takes the differences between us—differences God put there to make us stronger—and tries to use them to drive us apart.

Take men and women, for example. Satan's tricked us into fighting about which one is superior over the other. But I can settle that argument right now. Women are superior to men. If you don't believe that, you guys try having a baby. But then, men are superior to women. If you don't believe that, you women try having one without us.

It's our differences together that make us strong!

There was a time when I didn't understand that. I got upset with God for giving me a wife who didn't like many of the things that I liked. But I finally realized God knew what He was doing. If He'd given me a woman who loved flying as much as I do, we would have spent the rest of our lives in the clouds. We wouldn't be preaching the Bible. We'd be in some circus air show flying upside down as "The Copeland Duo!" or something.

Do you have people in your life who are irritatingly different from you? Don't let Satan use those differences to drive you apart. Thank God for them! Let Him teach you how to appreciate them. Let Him show you just how powerful you can be...together!

talk the truth

"I will keep unity by walking in peace and love." (Ecclesiastes 4:12)

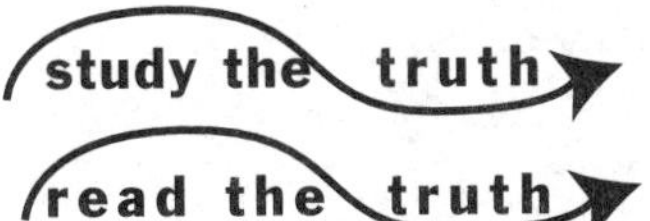
study the truth
read the truth

Ecclesiastes 4:9-12

2 Chronicles 8,9; Hebrews 1

June 29

BE WILLING!

"If you are willing and obedient, you will eat the best from the land."

ISAIAH 1:19

God's promises will not just fall in your lap. You must be obedient *and willing* if you want to receive God's best.

So, *be willing* to receive God's promises in all areas of your life!

Be willing to be well! Don't allow Satan to put sickness on your body. According to the Bible, refuse to accept anything less than divine health.

Be willing to receive God's gift of boldness. With boldness, you'll be able to be obedient to His Word and share His love with those around you. Don't let low self-confidence creep into your life. Read the Bible and find out who God created you to be in Him!

And *be willing* to receive God's best plan for your future and your family. Don't allow Satan to substitute worrying and ulcers for the peace that Jesus bought for you. Be willing and obedient to give all your concerns to Him.

Refuse to let Satan stop God's promises from coming alive in your life. Instead, *be willing* to receive them!

talk the truth **"I am obedient and willing." (Isaiah 1:19)**

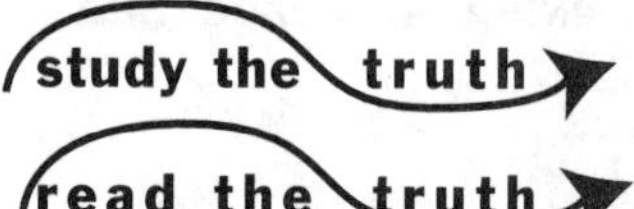
study the truth
read the truth

Deuteronomy 8:5-20

2 Chronicles 10,11; Hebrews 2

NO MORE DYING TO DO

Death isn't a popular topic—even among Christians. In fact, many are just plain scared of it. Sure they talk about living forever with Jesus. Yet when Satan tries to threaten their earthly living with sickness or trouble, they panic.

"But we see Jesus, who was made a little lower than the angels, now crowned with glory and honor because he suffered death, so that by the grace of God he might taste death for everyone."

Hebrews 2:9

Why? Because they haven't learned to look at death through God's eyes. If they had, when Satan tried to push their panic button, they'd just laugh and say, "You can't scare me, Satan. I've done all the dying I'm ever going to do!"

That's true! The Bible says that you, as a Christian, will never see death (John 8:51). Jesus took your place. He went through death, so you wouldn't have to. And when He was raised from the grave, Hebrews 2:14-15 says He destroyed "him who holds the power of death—that is, the devil" and freed "those who all their lives were held in slavery by their fear of death."

If you've made Jesus the Lord of your life, the only death you'll ever experience is over now. Your old self—the one whose nature was to sin and rebel against God—died. Your body didn't die, but your spirit—the real you—died to Satan and all of his works. You became "a new creature," absolutely incapable of spiritual death! (2 Corinthians 5:17, KJV).

When you're finished with your work on the earth, you won't die. You'll simply drop your earthly suit and go to a far better place.

(By the way, that's why Satan tries to talk so many young people into suicide. He doesn't want you to finish your work on earth. He wants to get you back into the grips of death so he can stop your effectiveness and keep you from experiencing God's life.)

So take a look in the Bible and see what God says about death. Once you understand what He has done for you, Satan will never be able to threaten you with it again.

talk the truth

"I don't live in slavery to the fear of death... Jesus destroyed the devil and the power of death!" (Hebrews 2:9)

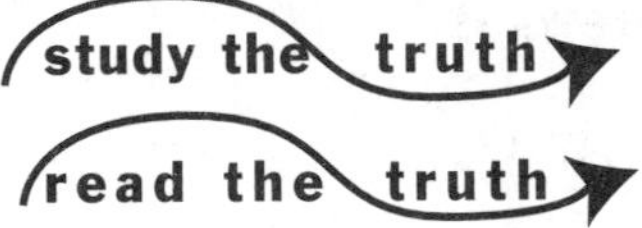
study the truth
read the truth

Hebrews 2:9-15

2 Chronicles 12,13; Hebrews 3

July 1

Gloria

TOMORROW IS HERE!

"Who then is the faithful and wise servant, whom the master has put in charge of the servants in his household?"

MATTHEW 24:45

The Bible tells us that God strengthens the heart of anyone who is "fully committed" to Him (2 Chronicles 16:9).

Who is fully committed? The person who spends his time doing what God asks him to do. Or as Jesus put it, the one who "takes up his cross" and follows Him—the one who puts aside selfish desires and spends his time doing what God desires for him to do.

Maybe God has been asking you to spend more time studying the Bible and praying. Maybe He's been dealing with you about reaching out more to your friends. He may be calling you to pray for the sick or start a Bible study. Perhaps He's asking you to set a better example for your classmates. But you're busy, so you just plan on doing it tomorrow. Well, tomorrow is here!

Decide today that you will be the faithful and wise servant. Figure out how you can spend more time with the Lord and serve His interests instead of your own.

Do you want God's power to show up in your everyday life? Then start living with His purposes and His plans today. Now is the time to be fully committed!

talk the truth **"I am a faithful and wise servant, fully committed to the Lord." (Matthew 24:45)**

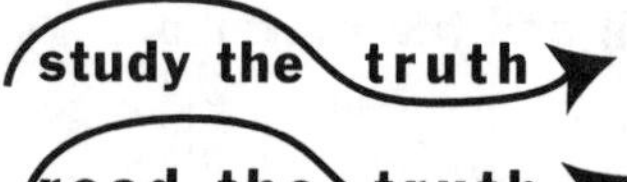

Matthew 24:42-51

read the truth **2 Chronicles 14,15; Hebrews 4**

COMMITTED BEYOND REASON

"Wisdom is supreme; therefore get wisdom. Though it cost all you have, get understanding. Esteem her, and she will exalt you; embrace her, and she will honor you. She will set a garland of grace on your head and present you with a crown of splendor."

Proverbs 4:7-9

If you really want to get the wisdom of God, you'll have to do more than just read the Bible a few minutes a day. You'll have to feed on it continually. You'll have to get rid of the trash you've fed into your mind by thinking in a new way—with the Word of God.

"That's unreasonable!" you may say.

Yes it is. But think about this: A music major in college practices for long periods every day. Olympic skaters spend six to eight hours a day training. They do it because they're unreasonably committed to their goals.

The same is true for you. If you're going to achieve the kind of spiritual excellence you want, you have to be committed beyond reason to God's Word.

That may mean that you'll have to carry your Bible around with you everywhere you go. It may mean that you'll have your toothbrush in one hand and your tape recorder in the other or a devotional in one hand and a fork in the other.

Do whatever it takes to totally plunge into God's Word. I would speak to you no differently if I were your commanding officer in the army and I was about to send you into combat against the best-trained troops of a merciless enemy.

You're in God's army. You have an enemy who is working his hardest to destroy you. In this all-out offensive, Satan will send his best-trained demons to bring you down. If you want to make it through in victory, you'll have to put yourself in training.

Be committed beyond reason today.

talk the truth

"I am committed beyond reason to getting wisdom from God's Word. I want spiritual excellence!" (Proverbs 4:7-9)

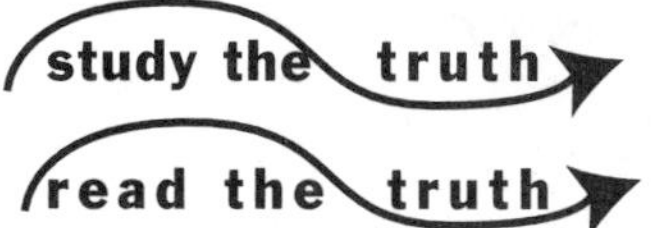
study the truth
read the truth

Proverbs 1:7-33

2 Chronicles 16,17,18; Hebrews 5,6

July 3

GOD'S DISCIPLINE

"'For whom the Lord loves He chastens, And scourges every son whom He receives.' If you endure chastening, God deals with you as with sons; for what son is there whom a father does not chasten?"

HEBREWS 12:6,7, NKJV

There's a terrible misunderstanding among Christians today about how God disciplines His children. Many point to disasters—like tornadoes or car accidents—and say, "I guess God sent that catastrophe to teach us something."

No, He didn't! A loving Father doesn't send death and destruction on His children to instruct them. No, He corrects us with His Word.

Second Timothy 3:16-17 says, "Every Scripture is God-breathed—given by His inspiration—and profitable for instruction, for reproof and conviction of sin, for correction of error and discipline in obedience, and for training in righteousness,...So that the man of God may be complete and proficient, well-fitted and thoroughly equipped for every good work" (AMP).

In 2 Corinthians 7, you'll see an example of this. The Apostle Paul talks about a situation in the Corinthian church that needed correction. That church had gotten out of line and had to be disciplined.

How did Paul do it? He didn't ask God to send an earthquake to shake them up! He wrote them a letter. He wrote them a word of correction. It cut deep into their hearts and caused them to change their ways.

Because God loves you, He will correct you. And He'll use the power in His Word to train you in such a way that you'll come out strong—not weak and hopeless.

So quit giving in to disasters and start giving yourself to God's Word. Let it correct you and trim away your bad habits and selfish desires. Let God use His Word to keep you in line!

talk the truth

"The Lord corrects me with His Word. It strengthens me and makes me more like Him." (2 Timothy 3:16,17)

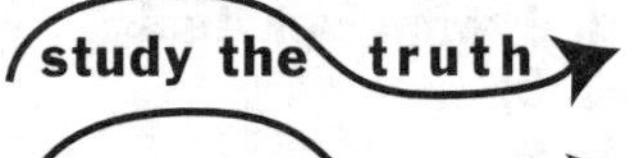
study the truth
read the truth

2 Corinthians 7

2 Chronicles 19,20; Hebrews 7

GOD IS HEALING OUR LAND

"What if some did not have faith? Will their lack of faith nullify God's faithfulness? Not at all!"

ROMANS 3:3,4

Faith-filled words change things. They turn pain into joy. They turn sickness into health. They can turn a sinner into a child of God.

There's something else faith-filled words can do...they can take a sin-filled nation and turn it into God's own country. That's right. If Christians would back up the prayers they pray for their nation with words of faith instead of doubt and discouragement, we'd soon begin to see spiritual revival all around the world.

God promised that if we, His people, would humble ourselves, pray, seek His face and turn from our wicked ways, He would heal our land (2 Chronicles 7:14). And let me tell you, there are prayer warriors in countries all over the world (I hope you're one of them) who are doing just that.

But, even so, you don't hear many people saying, "This is great! God is moving in our land." Instead, you hear them saying, "This place is going downhill" or some other destructive thing. Listen, we need to stop preaching what Satan is doing and start speaking what God is doing!

God said He is healing the land. And no matter what the world says, their unbelief will not stop God's Word from working! That's why Gloria and I have stopped listening to bad news. Instead, we praise and thank God that He's protecting us from evil. And that releases faith in our hearts.

So get determined right now. Take a firm stand with us that things are changing in your country. Settle it in your heart as you pray. The prayers you pray today will determine the kind of country you live in tomorrow!

talk the truth

"I humble myself and pray and seek God's face. I turn from wicked ways and He forgives my sin and heals this land." (2 Chronicles 7:14)

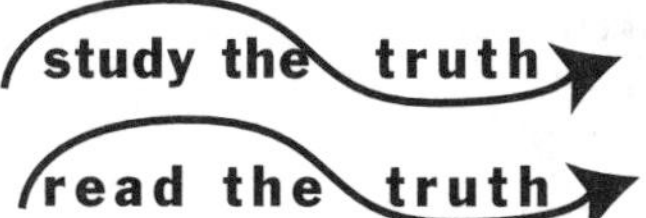
study the truth
read the truth

Nehemiah 6:1-16

2 Chronicles 21,22; Hebrews 8

Kenneth

July 5

DON'T THINK LIKE THE WORLD

"The weapons we fight with are not the weapons of the world. On the contrary, they have divine power to demolish strongholds. We demolish arguments and every pretension that sets itself up against the knowledge of God, and we take captive every thought to make it obedient to Christ."

2 Corinthians 10:4,5

If you think like the world thinks, eventually you will act like the world acts. Wrong thoughts produce wrong acts. So control your thoughts by reading the Bible and bringing them into obedience to God's Word.

Program your mind with the Word of God. The Word is spirit and it is life. When your mind is full of God's Word, you become stronger and you can overcome ungodly thoughts and bad habits.

Don't let Satan trick you into giving up God's power in your life for a few moments of selfishness and sin. Take control of your thought life. Think about what the Bible says instead of thinking sinful thoughts. Keep your eyes on Jesus—and you'll find yourself thinking a whole new way!

talk the truth

"I take every thought captive and make it obedient to Christ. My thoughts match God's thoughts!" (2 Corinthians 10:4,5)

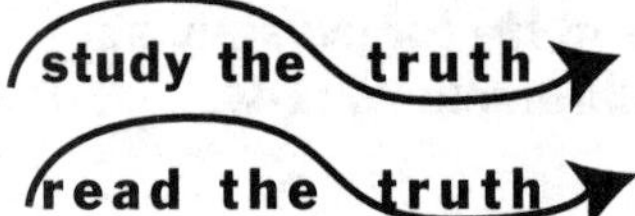
study the truth
read the truth

Psalm 119:11-18; Philippians 4:8

2 Chronicles 23,24; Hebrews 9

UP IN SMOKE

"The tongue is a small part of the body, but it makes great boasts. Consider what a great forest is set on fire by a small spark. The tongue also is a fire, a world of evil among the parts of the body. It corrupts the whole person, sets the whole course of his life on fire, and is itself set on fire by hell."

JAMES 3:5,6

Words. Use them right and they'll change the world around you. Use them wrong and they can cause your entire life to go up in smoke.

"Now, wait a second," you may say, "I find it hard to believe that major catastrophes can be caused by a few simple words. I just can't see the connection."

Look again at the phrase James used. "Consider what a great forest is set on fire by a small spark." Have you ever lit a few little pieces of kindling wood and set them in the fireplace beneath a stack of logs?

What happened?

Most likely, the fire spread from one log to another until finally you had a gigantic blaze going. After it was over, you couldn't go digging around in the ashes and find the kindling that started it all, could you? No—it was burned. There was no trace of it at all.

The tongue is like that. It starts a fire of trouble with a blaze so great that it leaves no trace of its origin. The words that started everything end up so deeply buried in the ashes that you'd never even know they were there.

So, don't underestimate the power of your words. Satan doesn't. He works constantly to get you to say negative things. He'll fire arrows of pain and discouragement at you just to get you to speak faithless words of defeat—words that will eventually send your life up in smoke.

Don't let him succeed. Instead, put out that fire by following the Apostle Paul's instructions in Ephesians 6:16 and "take up the shield of faith, with which you can extinguish all the flaming arrows of the evil one."

Speak words of faith and stop the fire before it starts!

talk the truth **"My tongue has the power of life and death so I speak words of life and faith." (Proverbs 18:21)**

study the truth **James 3:1-10**

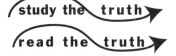

read the truth **2 Chronicles 25,26; Hebrews 10**

Kenneth

July 7

FREE FROM DEBT!

"The borrower is servant to the lender."

Proverbs 22:7

If you've wondered how you can have a good future without going into debt, I have great news for you. God wants you to be free from debt, and He has the power to make a debt-free future possible for you.

I know. He did it for me years ago.

I'll never forget it. We were $22,000 in debt at the time. We'd committed to God to pay it all off and never borrow another dime—though it looked like we'd never be able to do it. But we knew God could.

Day by day we looked to Him to rescue us. We didn't ask Him every day, but we thanked Him because we believed we received when we prayed the first time. Eleven months later, we were out of debt. As we looked back, nothing spectacular happened, but God was continuously faithful, as we were faithful.

God can do the same thing for you if you'll dare to believe His Word and make a commitment to stay free from debt. And if you have some debt right now, He'll be faithful to help you get out from under it if you'll obey Him.

As you look at your situation, you may not be able to see how you could ever go to college, get a car or own your own business someday. But don't worry. I felt that way too, at first. I just didn't see how I'd ever be able to do anything without borrowing money.

But He showed me how—and He'll do the same for you.

There's no dream too big and no business too complicated for Him to handle. If you'll trust Him to manage your finances, He will bring you out on top...and you'll never have to be a slave to debt.

talk the truth

"There's nothing too big for my God to handle. I give Him my finances today." (Proverbs 22:7)

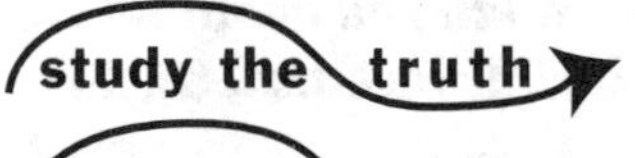
study the truth
read the truth

Psalm 37:21-40

2 Chronicles 27,28; Hebrews 11

PROTECTED BY LOVE

"But I tell you: Love your enemies and pray for those who persecute you, that you may be sons of your Father in heaven."

MATTHEW 5:44,45

Love your enemies...to most people that sounds like a pretty weak way to handle someone who's causing them trouble. But, the truth is, it's the most powerful way there is. It's the way Jesus did it—and His way never fails.

When Jesus said to turn the other cheek, He didn't mean for you to stand there and have your brains beaten out. He meant for you to stand there in love and in faith believing that God's protecting power would keep you safe.

The story of Nicky Cruz as recorded in David Wilkerson's book, *The Cross and the Switchblade,* is a perfect example of that. Nicky was known as the most ruthless gang leader of his time. Yet, when David Wilkerson stood in front of him, telling him about Jesus, Nicky was totally unable to hurt him. He thrust his knife at David several times. But every time he did, David just said, "Nicky, you can cut me into a thousand pieces and every piece will still say, 'I love you and God loves you.'" Because of love, Nicky couldn't hurt him. A supernatural force always stopped his knife short.

"But I don't have that kind of love!"

Yes, you do.

Romans 5:5 tells us that the Holy Spirit put God's love in your heart. All you have to do is make the decision to be moved by that love rather than your own feelings.

Love never fails! You don't have to be afraid of failure anymore. In fact, you don't have to be afraid of anything. If you're walking in the love of God, you're living the most powerful kind of life there is.

talk the truth

"I love my enemies and pray for those who give me trouble. Love never fails!" (Matthew 5:44,45)

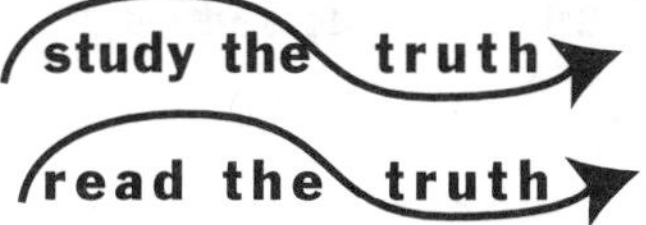
study the truth
read the truth

Matthew 5:38-48

2 Chronicles 29,30; Hebrews 12

Kenneth

July 9

KEEP THE WEEDS OUT

"This is what the kingdom of God is like. A man scatters seed on the ground."

MARK 4:26

Jesus compared God's kingdom with planting seed and receiving a harvest. It's a simple concept we can all understand. But then why aren't we all receiving a harvest of God's blessings every season of our lives? Because we're sitting around waiting for God to do all the work.

He doesn't operate that way. He'll work *with* you, but He won't do it *all.* There are some important things you must do by faith if you want to have a crop of blessings.

First, in faith, you must plant the seed of the Word, expecting it to grow. You must find promises from the Bible and plant them in your heart and life.

Next, you must water the seed every day with praise and thanks to God.

And finally, you have to keep the weeds out! When the weeds of unforgiveness, doubt, fear, discouragement (and all the other junk Satan tries to plant into your life) try to enter in, get rid of them. Immediately pull them up by their roots and fill the space with God's promises.

Don't sit around waiting for God to make your harvest come. Start planting. Start watching over your land (your heart and your mind) to keep it moist, watered with the Word, and free from weeds. Commit to do your part and trust God to do His. You will have a great crop this season!

talk the truth

"I plant seeds and keep them watered. God always brings the harvest!" (Mark 4:26)

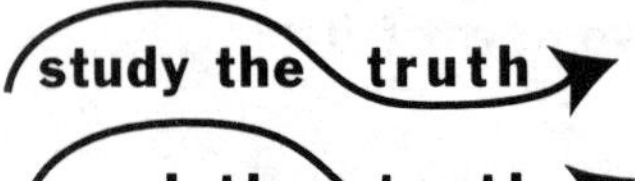
study the truth
read the truth

Ephesians 4:22-32

2 Chronicles 31,32,33; Hebrews 13; James 1

Kenneth

July 10

TURN UP YOUR HOPE

"May the God of your hope so fill you with all joy and peace in believing—through the experience of your faith—that by the power of the Holy Spirit you may abound and be overflowing (bubbling over) with hope."

Romans 15:13, AMP

That's what I want—to be overflowing with hope! I want to throw my whole life and everything I have into building a dream that comes from the heart of God. I want to get out there so far that without God's help, I can't get back.

Most people don't think that way though because they're afraid to fail. Fear of failure is dangerous. If you let it control you, it will cause you to do the one thing that guarantees failure—not trying at all.

How do you stop the fear of failure?

You turn up your hope. You get alone with God and listen to Him. You think about His promises until they are on the inside of you so strong that *nothing* can shake them out of you.

If you're sitting in a wheelchair and the doctor has told you you'll never walk again, instead of holding on to that bad report, start dreaming. Find the promise in the Bible that says those who wait on the Lord shall run and walk and not faint nor be weary (Isaiah 40:31). Look at it until you see nothing else. Picture yourself walking for miles and running from one place to the next, telling everyone that Jesus has healed you.

Maybe your dream is to go to a certain college, enter a particular profession or break some kind of record. If you know that dream is from God, don't let go of it. Picture yourself walking in that dream. Just keep holding onto hope and standing on God's promises until that dream comes true.

That's what hope is all about. It's a divine dream. It's a picture that's bigger than you are because it's built on a promise from God. If you're a Christian, you ought to be a dreamer. So take God at His Word and build some dreams today!

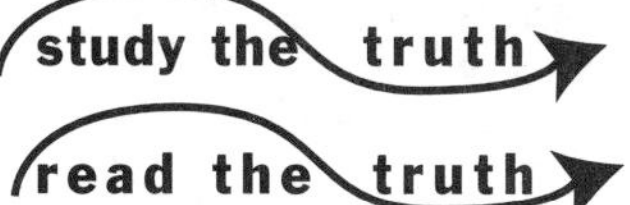

"I build my dreams on God's promises. He is the God Who makes my hopes come true!" (Romans 15:13, AMP)

study the truth — **Psalm 33:18-22**

read the truth — **2 Chronicles 34,35; James 2**

Kenneth

July 11

EXPECT RESULTS

"You do not have, because you do not ask God. When you ask, you do not receive, because you ask with wrong motives."

JAMES 4:2,3

Are all your needs met today? If not, why not? According to the Bible, it's either because you're not praying about them at all or because when you do pray, you're praying wrong.

What does it mean to pray wrong? In many cases it simply means to pray without expecting anything to really happen. Many Christians do that, you know. They act like prayers are just wishes. *This probably won't do much good,* they think, *but who knows? It won't hurt to give it a try.*

If that's been your attitude, then change it! Start getting serious about prayer. Stop praying just because it's the right thing to do, and start praying to get results.

Pray, expecting to receive what you need, not just once in a while, but every time! When prayers do go unanswered, don't just wander away saying, "I guess you never know what God's going to do." Go to God in prayer. Search the Bible to find out where you missed it and get the problem corrected.

When you go to God in sincere, Bible-based prayer, you know what He will do. He'll answer you. Start expecting Him to do it today.

talk the truth **"I pray, expecting to receive what I need." (James 4:2,3)**

1 John 5:4-15

read the truth **2 Chronicles 36; Ezra 1; James 3**

BE SKILLFUL

"The lions may grow weak and hungry, but those who seek the Lord lack no good thing."

PSALM 34:10

Did you know everything we could ever need and every problem we could ever face is covered by God's promises to us in the Bible?

It's true! But it takes skill to apply God's Word and make those promises come alive in our lives. Most of us don't realize that. We just try to use His promises in any old way we can. We pray some faithless prayer and then say, "Oh well, God knows what I mean" and expect it to be answered.

It's funny, though. We'd never stand for that kind of carelessness from others. If our doctor came in and just threw a bottle of pills at us and said, "Here, take that," without even trying to find out what's wrong with us, we'd leave his office and never come back. Yet, we're surprised when that same careless attitude with God keeps our prayers from being effective.

We live in an "instant" society where everything is quick and easy. And too many of us are letting that "instant" mentality spill over into our walk with God. When someone needs healing, we burst through the hospital door, dab a little oil between their eyes and say, "Glory to God!" and out the door we go.

It's time for us to shake off that "instant" mentality and realize that there are situations where we have to take some time and pray. There are times when we have to sit and listen for God's instructions.

If you've come up short in any area of life, determine to develop your "Word skills" where that area is concerned. Get out your Bible and read through God's promises. Find the ones that apply to your situation. Think about them. Ask God to speak to you through them. Spend time with Him and let Him show you how to apply them skillfully...and eventually, you won't be without anything you need.

talk the truth

"I seek the Lord and lack no good thing. I apply His promises to my life." (Psalm 34:10)

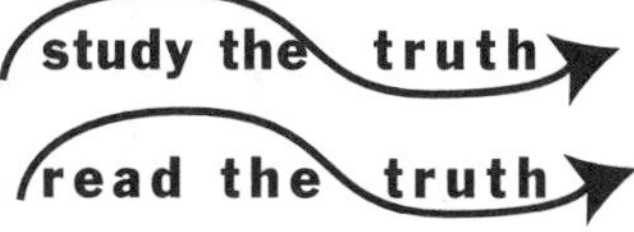
study the truth
read the truth

Psalm 23

Ezra 2,3; James 4

Kenneth

July 13

DON'T OVERLOOK THE BLESSINGS

"For our light and momentary troubles are achieving for us an eternal glory that far outweighs them all."

2 Corinthians 4:17

It's easy to get your eyes so firmly fixed on your problems that you overlook the blessings! As a result, you end up suffering through situations that should have excited you.

Let me show you what I mean. A few years ago, our ministry was facing some serious money pressures. So I stood in faith against them. I battled against them with God's promises and prayer.

What I didn't realize was this: During that time when the problems seemed so great—the blessings were even greater. This ministry was growing faster, we were ministering to more people, writing more letters, printing more publications, sending out more teaching tapes than ever before! It was a breakthrough time...a time to be excited. But I didn't know it because I was too busy thinking about the problems.

I had such tunnel vision, all I could see was the pressure, and I suffered through some hard times when I should have been shouting in victory.

But thank God, He woke me up before it was over. He woke me up to the blessings and reminded me that the problems would change—while God and His Word will never change!

If you've been going through some hard times lately, wake up to the blessings around you. It will be much easier to win over the problems if you're giving God glory for His fulfilled promises along the way. Take your eyes off the trouble and look around you. You'll soon be shouting in victory!

talk the truth

"I do not look at the troubles around me, but at the good things God has in store for me." (2 Corinthians 4:17)

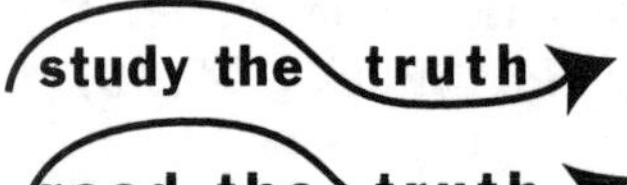
study the truth
read the truth

Psalm 13

Ezra 4,5; James 5

YOUR DEADLY ENEMY

"Brothers, we do not want you to be ignorant about those who fall asleep, or to grieve like the rest of men, who have no hope. We believe that Jesus died and rose again."

1 Thessalonians 4:13

Many people, even though they're Christians, have seen grief and sorrow as such a natural part of life that they haven't even questioned them. Some young men and women have lived for several years grieving over the loss of a loved one—someone who died in an accident or from sickness or some other means. Others live in sorrow over a boyfriend or girlfriend who broke their heart. Still others just can't seem to get over feeling sorry for themselves…feeling bad about grades or relationships or the way they think they look.

But grief and sorrow are dangerous things—they're not just innocent emotions. They are part of the devastating, demonic bombardment Jesus took on Himself when He died on the cross (Isaiah 53). He bore grief and sorrow so we wouldn't have to. If they come knocking on your door, remember they are not innocent emotions. They are deadly enemies that Jesus already carried away for you.

Don't live like someone who has no hope. You're a Christian. You know that Jesus died for you and rose again. That gives you hope in every situation. He whipped those deadly enemies once and for all. So start a new way of living today…because grief and sorrow have no business being in your life!

talk the truth

"I don't grieve or sorrow like those without hope, because Jesus is my hope." (1 Thessalonians 4:13)

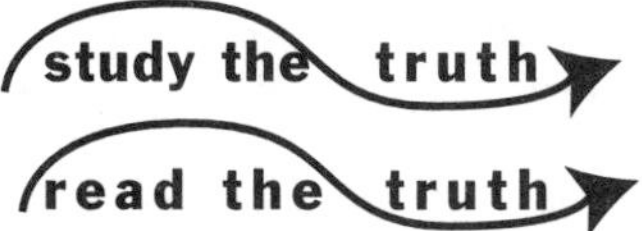
study the truth
read the truth

Isaiah 51:11-16

Ezra 6,7; 1 Peter 1

DISCOURAGE SATAN

"Blessed are you when men hate you, when they exclude you and insult you and reject your name as evil, because of the Son of Man. Rejoice in that day and leap for joy, because great is your reward in heaven. For that is how their fathers treated the prophets."

Luke 6:22,23

Do you want to know how to depress Satan? Just follow the instructions in the verse to the left. When friends or family criticize you because you believe in healing, and when classmates or co-workers call you a fanatic because you love Jesus and aren't afraid to say so, get excited!

That will discourage Satan to no end. He's expecting that mistreatment to hurt you. He's expecting it to damage your faith, wipe you out and leave you hopeless.

I'm not saying you should enjoy being mistreated. But you can learn to overlook the discomfort of those things by focusing your attention on the reward that's coming, and the fact that Jesus said you are blessed.

The Apostle Paul knew how to do that. Satan was constantly stirring up trouble for him. But do you know what he said about all that mistreatment? He said it was not even worth considering compared to the glory that was about to come.

If Paul could have joy in the middle of beatings, stonings, shipwrecks, imprisonment and almost every other kind of mistreatment, you can too!

Just do what he did. When he was told by the Holy Spirit that trouble awaited him, he said, "I consider my life worth nothing to me, if only I may finish the race and complete the task the Lord Jesus has given me—the task of testifying to the gospel of God's grace" (Acts 20:24).

Don't get all caught up in what people think and say. Get caught up in pleasing God. Get caught up in fulfilling your call. Get caught up in the hope that's ahead. For that hope is enough to make anyone—in any circumstance—get excited!

talk the truth

"I take pleasure in others giving me trouble for my stand in Christ. For when I am weak, then I am strong!" (Luke 6:22,23; 2 Corinthians 12:10)

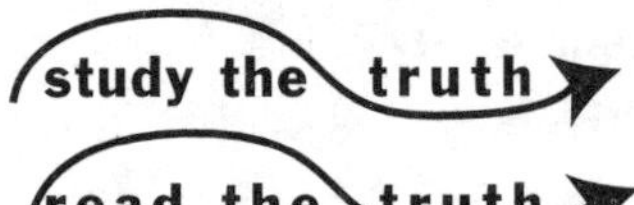
study the truth
read the truth

Acts 16:16-35

Ezra 8,9; 1 Peter 2

Kenneth

July 16

TAP INTO THE TRUTH

Jesus said the Holy Spirit would guide you into all truth. Not just enough truth to get by on. Not just enough truth to give you something spiritual to say in youth group. *All* truth!

At school, that means the Holy Spirit will show you how to excel in classes. At work, that means the Holy Spirit will give you wisdom to do above and beyond the norm. At home, that means the Holy Spirit will show you how to minister to each member of your family.

In fact, as a Christian, inside you is the answer to every problem that exists—even the ones you don't know about yet!

So if you're facing a problem today, don't walk around trying to handle it on your own. Take Jesus at His Word and ask the Holy Spirit to give you the knowledge you need to solve it. Put the wisdom of God to work at school, on your job, in your family and in your world. Tap into the truth!

"But when he, the Spirit of truth, comes, he will guide you into all truth. He will not speak on his own; he will speak only what he hears, and he will tell you what is yet to come."

JOHN 16:13

talk the truth

"The Holy Spirit guides me into all truth." (John 16:13)

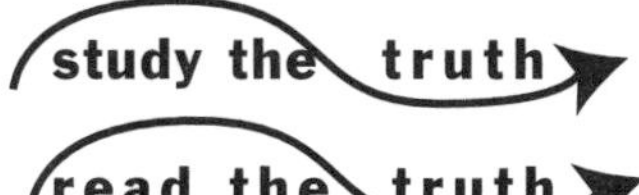
study the truth
read the truth

John 14:6-17

Ezra 10; Nehemiah 1,2; 1 Peter 3,4

July 17

MAKE HELL TREMBLE

"The reason the Son of God appeared was to destroy the devil's work."

1 John 3:8

Is Satan causing trouble for you at every turn?

If so, start making him miserable for a change. You have the power inside you to destroy his works, to heal, to rescue and to set captives free. You have so much power in you that every time your alarm clock goes off, Satan should cry, "Ugh! That troublemaker is up again!"

Several years ago, I got a letter from a little girl who attended one of my healing services in Los Angeles. Although she was far too young to understand theology or anything like that, the Lord showed her something very simple and profound as she watched people being healed.

She said that as she looked up at the platform, she couldn't see me at all. She just saw Jesus. And she also saw Satan. Do you know what Satan was doing? He was lying on the floor crying, "This can't be! This can't be! This can't be!"

Right now, at this very moment, Jesus' power is at work within you. And it's not just there to get you to heaven someday. It's there to make you successful right now. It's there so you can give Satan trouble right here on earth. It's there so you can share your faith with others—while there's still time.

Line up with God's Word and what He wants for your life. Let the power of Jesus come from within you. All of hell will tremble. And you will never be the same again.

talk the truth

"Jesus' power is at work in me right now—and it makes hell tremble!" (1 John 3:8)

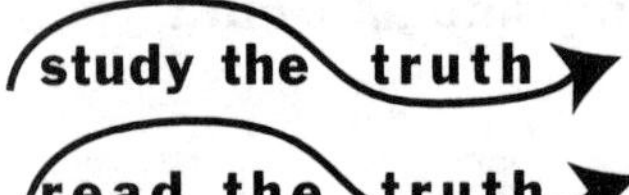
study the truth
read the truth

1 John 5:4-20

Nehemiah 3,4; 1 Peter 5

A LEGEND IN YOUR OWN MIND

"For by the grace given me I say to every one of you: Do not think of yourself more highly than you ought, but rather think of yourself with sober judgment, in accordance with the measure of faith God has given you."

ROMANS 12:3

Do you want to know one of the secrets to staying in God's will and keeping yourself from getting off track? Don't overestimate yourself!

Proverbs 16:18 says, "Pride goes before destruction, a haughty spirit before a fall." How many times have we seen that happen? How many times do we see Christians get into trouble because they think they're super stuff—more special than anyone else? They begin to think they're ultra-smart and that they have it all figured out.

Then, the next thing you know, they think they have to straighten everyone else out. Instead of just letting Jesus be Head of the Church, they feel like they have to step in and help Him out.

Once that happens, it's just a matter of time before they're flat on their face in failure. Why? Because the Bible says God resists the proud (1 Peter 5:5)!

Don't put yourself in a position where God has to resist you. Have a humble attitude. Watch yourself, and if you catch yourself getting filled with your own greatness, turn away from it and remember that every bit of success you've had has come by the goodness and power of God.

Don't become a legend in your own mind. Instead, humble yourself and let God do the exalting. You'll prevent some very painful falls.

talk the truth

"I humble myself under God's powerful hand. He will lift me up when the right time comes." (1 Peter 5:6)

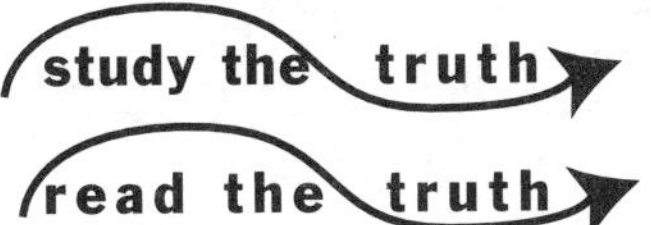
study the truth
read the truth

James 4:6-17; 1 Peter 5:5-7

Nehemiah 5,6; 2 Peter 1

July 19

NO HARD HEARTS

"For the eyes of the Lord range throughout the earth to strengthen those whose hearts are fully committed to him."

2 Chronicles 16:9

The Pharisees had a heart condition that upset Jesus. These religious leaders of Jesus' time had hearts that were hard and insensitive. If you'll look in Mark 3, you'll see what I'm talking about.

God was right there with them, and they, of all people, should have realized it. They knew the Scriptures backward and forward, and Jesus fit every prophecy written in them. But the insensitivity of their hearts blinded them to Who He was.

The hearts of the Pharisees were also hardened to the needs of the people around them. They were criticizing God's ministers, protecting their religious traditions instead of obeying the Bible, and worrying about themselves rather than caring for those around them.

Have you ever known any Christians who fit that description? Sure you have! In fact, every one of us has probably *done* those things at some time in our lives.

I know that's true because if it weren't, we'd be seeing powerful moves of God among us. God wants to move miraculously in His Church. But we've developed a heart condition that's holding Him back.

Today if you desire the Holy Spirit's power to flow through your life everywhere you go, check the condition of your heart. If you find any hardness or insensitivity there, turn away from it and ask God to change you. Ask Him to give you the kind of heart that will allow Him to work mightily through you. He's ready!

talk the truth

"My heart is fully committed to the Lord and He can move through me mightily!" (2 Chronicles 16:9)

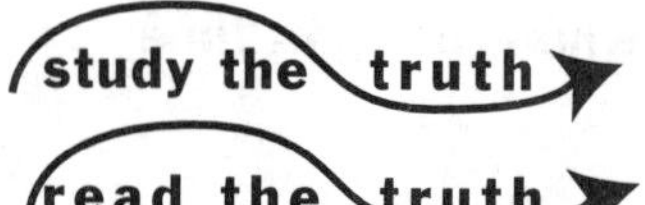
study the truth
read the truth

Mark 3:1-6

Nehemiah 7,8; 2 Peter 2

GIVE MORE—NOT LESS

"One man gives freely, yet gains even more; another withholds unduly, but comes to poverty."

PROVERBS 11:24

When money gets tight, it's always tempting to cut down on your giving. After all, it seems like the logical thing to do—especially if you're in school and without a full-time job. But don't do it! You'll end up cutting off the flow of God's finances for you just when you need them most.

I faced that kind of situation several years ago. This ministry had fallen behind financially. Now, Gloria and I knew firsthand that God would meet our needs—"according to his glorious riches in Christ Jesus" (Philippians 4:19). We'd seen Him prove it over and over again.

Yet this time, all the prayers and faith that brought us victory before just didn't seem to get the job done. Frustrated and tired, I finally went to God one day and laid the situation out before Him. "Lord," I said, "You see the condition of this ministry. I need a million dollars just to break even."

Oh, no you don't! the Lord replied.

I could hardly believe it. How could He possibly be telling me that I didn't need a million dollars? Did I miss something? So I went through it all again.

Again He said, *Oh, no you don't.*

Despite my initial confusion, as I kept asking and listening, I began to understand what the Lord was telling me. He was saying there was something else wrong, other than the debt. There was a bigger problem behind it.

He showed me what I needed to do was to start giving away 10 percent of the ministry's income. To most people, that looked like no solution at all. How do you solve a debt problem by giving away what you have? But when I applied that solution, the debt began to disappear.

Remember that the next time Satan tries to put the squeeze on you. Break his hold on your money by giving *more* instead of less. It won't be long until you'll be doing well in every area of your life!

talk the truth

"I give freely and gain even more!" (Proverbs 11:24)

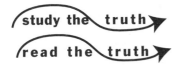

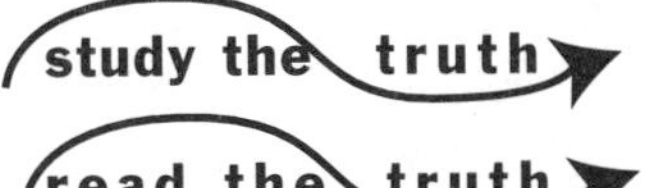
study the truth
read the truth

1 Kings 17:1-16

Nehemiah 9,10; 2 Peter 3

July 21

Gloria

THE KEY TO CONFIDENCE

"Dear friends, if our hearts do not condemn us, we have confidence before God and receive from him anything we ask, because we obey his commands and do what pleases him."

1 John 3:21,22

You can never get away with disobeying God.

Some people think you can. They think that if no one finds out, it won't hurt anything. After all, God is merciful. He won't hold it against them, right? And if no one else knows... what's the difference?

What they don't realize is that their own heart will start giving them problems. Everyone else may think they're great, but when they come before God in prayer, they'll be filled with doubts and fears that keep their prayers from being answered.

That's one of the reasons it's so important to live in obedience to the Lord. A life of obedience will give you spiritual boldness. It will give you boldness in prayer and faith. As the Apostle John says, it will give you confidence toward God that those who are trying to get away with sin don't have.

I'm not saying you have to be perfect, but you *should* obey what you know God has said to you. Take the time to listen and respond to the Holy Spirit. When He tells you to do something, do it.

As you do, your confidence will rise. Instead of having doubts and feelings that the Bible won't work for you, you'll find yourself filled with faith that it will.

Remember this: Even though the eternal price for your sins has been paid, a life of disobedience will still cost you dearly. It will cost you your boldness, rob you of faith and rock you with fear.

So live a life of obedience and honor. Then you'll have confidence with God and stand tall in faith!

talk the truth

"I have confidence before God and receive what I ask, because I obey His commands and do what pleases Him." (1 John 3:21,22)

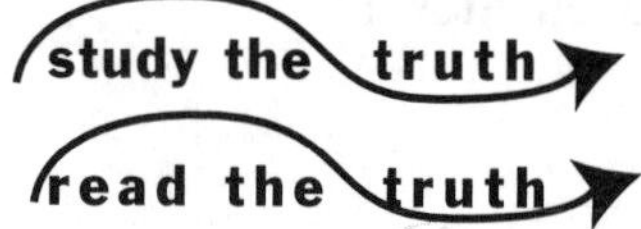
study the truth
read the truth

1 John 3:21,22

Nehemiah 11,12; 1 John 1

NOTHING TO LOSE

"Tell the righteous it will be well with them, for they will enjoy the fruit of their deeds. Woe to the wicked! Disaster is upon them! They will be paid back for what their hands have done."

ISAIAH 3:10,11

Have you ever been afraid to give yourself totally to God because you thought you might lose out on some of life's fun? You probably have felt like that at some time. That's because Satan is working overtime to convince you that he has a way worth living. But don't believe him for a minute. The real truth is, giving yourself completely to the Lord won't cost you anything that's worth having. It will only cause you to live life to its fullest!

Jesus' life on earth was a perfect example of a life totally given to God. He was a walking example of the benefits living for God brings. Everywhere He went, Jesus made the deaf hear, the blind see and the lame walk. He lived in perfect peace and victory. He was entirely healed, entirely victorious and entirely free!

That sounds pretty good to me. All He missed out on was having Satan ruling over Him—killing, stealing and destroying every step of the way. In fact, Satan couldn't do anything to Him until, by the Father's will, Jesus laid down His life.

Do you think you would miss out on a lot if you lived that way? Of course not! And you *can* walk in that same victory and power of God that Jesus did.

Do you have to give up your whole life to do it? Yes! You have to trade your life for God's kind of life. You have to trade your sickness for His healing, your fear for His faith, your insecurity for His peace, your sin for His salvation.

So why wait? When it comes right down to it, you have nothing to lose.

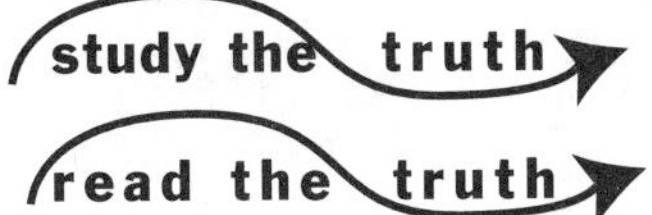

"I give my whole life to living for God." (Isaiah 3:10,11)

study the truth **Psalm 37:7-23**

read the truth **Nehemiah 13; Esther 1; 1 John 2**

July 23

CAN STRANGERS SEE JESUS IN YOU?

"When they saw the courage of Peter and John and realized that they were unschooled, ordinary men, they were astonished and they took note that these men had been with Jesus."

Acts 4:13

How would you like to be so full of God's power that it's unmistakable to those around you? How would you like for people to know just by looking at you that Jesus is with you? Well, that's entirely possible. The same power that changed you inwardly when you made Jesus your Lord can change you outwardly, so even strangers will see Jesus in you.

One of my favorite testimonies is the one my friend Jerry Savelle tells of the time he was in a shopping mall. He was walking from one store to another, when a woman walked up to him and asked him to pray for her. Since he didn't know the woman, he was puzzled. "Out of all the people in this mall, why'd you pick *me* out?" he asked.

She said, "The Lord told me to come to this mall and someone would be here who could pray for me. I came here looking for that person, when I noticed a beam of light. It would go into one store, wander around, then go to another store and wander around some more. I followed the light until I found where it was coming from—and it was coming from you!"

What was that light? The glory of God! It was shining from Jerry much like it shone from the face of Moses when he came down from Mount Sinai (Exodus 34:30). And God's power brought healing to that woman when Jerry prayed.

When you spend time with Jesus, it will be evident. His power and glory will be reflected through you to the world. Take time to be with Jesus today!

talk the truth **"I spend time with Jesus, and as I do, His glory is reflected in me." (Acts 4:13)**

study the truth **Acts 4:1-20**

read the truth **Esther 2,3,4; 1 John 3,4**

YOU HAVE A FUTURE

Spiritual bumps and bruises. Inner aches and pains that just don't seem to go away. Most of us know what it's like to suffer from them, but too few of us know just what to do about them.

We limp along, hoping somehow those sore spots we keep hidden will magically stop hurting—thinking that maybe (with a little extra sleep or an extra helping of dessert) that depression will finally disappear. But does it ever happen that way? No!

I know. I've been there. And I've found out those battles can leave you bruised and beaten on the inside just as surely as a fist-fight can leave you bruised and beaten on the outside.

"I know the plans I have for you," declares the Lord, "plans to prosper you and not to harm you, plans to give you hope and a future."

JEREMIAH 29:11

Before I made Jesus my Lord, I learned just how physically harmful a fistfight could be. Yet as bad as I felt, a few days rest would take care of me.

The healing of a bruised and beaten spirit, however, doesn't come that easily. In fact, the passing of time often actually worsens this condition.

The reason is this: Instead of putting painful failures behind us, we often think about them until those failures become more real to us than God's promises. We focus on them until we slump into depression, frozen by the fear that if we go on, we'll fail again.

Thank God, I'm not there anymore, because there is a way out. All you have to do is get your eyes off the past and onto your future—a future that's been guaranteed by Jesus through the great promises in His Word.

It won't come easy at first, because you've thought about your past failures so long. The key is to purposely focus your attention on what the Bible says. Continually replace thoughts of the past with scriptural promises about your future. Then, instead of being a wounded soldier, you'll become a conquering warrior.

talk the truth

"I forget the things that are past. I strain to reach the goal and get the prize before me. The prize is mine because God called me through Christ to the life above." (Philippians 3:13,14)

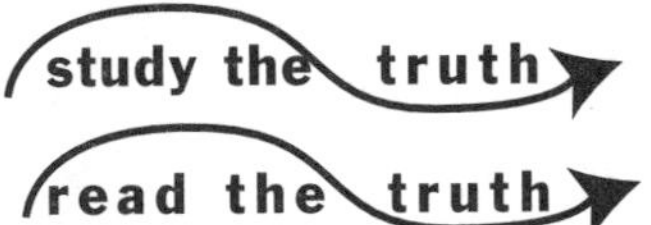
study the truth
read the truth

Philippians 3:12-21

Esther 5,6; 1 John 5

July 25

DON'T LET YOUR FAITH SLIP

"We must pay more careful attention, therefore, to what we have heard, so that we do not drift away."

HEBREWS 2:1

Something very serious has been happening to Christians. We've been letting the message of faith slip. I'm talking about people like you and me—who have known the adventure of living by faith. We've let that faith slip!

In my own life, for example, there have been times when I'd pray for healing. I'd say all the right words, "Thank God, I believe I receive..." and all that. But inside I'd be thinking, *I wonder why God isn't healing me?*

You see, even though I said I believed I was healed, I hadn't really believed God's Word. I believed how my body felt instead of the Bible.

I don't care how long you've been a Christian or how long you've been practicing the principles of faith. You can easily slip into unbelief about God's promises. And, once you do, it will cost you dearly.

So how can we avoid slipping into unbelief? Hebrews 4:11 tells us: "Let us, therefore, make every effort to enter that rest, so that no one will fall by following their example of disobedience."

We must make an effort! Not by working with our hands or struggling to get God to do something, but by spending time in the Bible and prayer—faithfully hanging on to God's promises day after day.

Read it in the morning when you wake up. Read it after lunch. Read it before you go to sleep. Whenever you can, dig more deeply into the Bible than ever. Make an effort! Be diligent to keep your faith from slipping—then you will be able to rest in the Lord, knowing everything He's promised you will happen!

talk the truth

"I pay careful attention to what I hear. I will not let the Word slip away." (Hebrews 2:1)

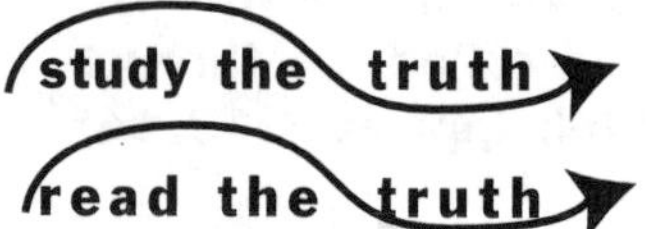
study the truth
read the truth

Hebrews 10:23-39

Esther 7,8; 2 John

FEAST ON THE WORD

God's Word is the same to your spirit as bread is to your body. When you eat food, your body produces a physical power called strength. When your spirit feeds on the spiritual food of the Bible, it produces spiritual power called faith.

Now try this: Close your eyes and see yourself sticking a lemon slice between your teeth. See yourself biting down on it so hard that the juice squirts into your mouth...Yah! You probably have such a vivid memory of what it's like to bite on a lemon that your whole face squinched up at the thought. But let me ask you this—did you receive any nourishment from that memory? No.

In the same way, just remembering what the Bible says isn't enough. You must continually feed on it. Get it out and read it. Go to church and hear it preached. You can't get continued results if you don't spend time in prayer and in the Bible allowing the Holy Spirit to nourish you daily.

Don't try to live on the memory of your last spiritual meal. Fill up the force of faith within you. Feast on God's Word today.

"Man does not live on bread alone, but on every word that comes from the mouth of God."

Matthew 4:4

talk the truth

"I don't live by bread alone, but I continually feed on God's Word." (Matthew 4:4)

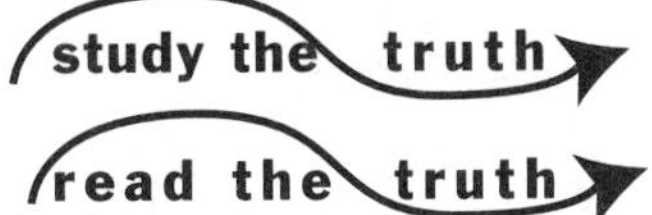
study the truth
read the truth

John 6:48-58

Esther 9,10; 3 John

July 27

BE SEPARATE

"Therefore come out from them and be separate, says the Lord. Touch no unclean thing, and I will receive you."

2 Corinthians 6:17

We're surrounded by a world which, for the most part, is ruled by Satan. How can we avoid getting caught up in it? How can we stand apart?

You'll find the answer in John 17:17. There Jesus was speaking to the Father about all those who would become Christians. "Sanctify them by the truth," He said. "Your word is truth." Now, sanctify means "to separate to." So Jesus is saying, "Separate them by the Word."

When you first believed the Bible, your spirit was reborn. You were spiritually separated *from* the kingdom of darkness *to* the kingdom of light. And that's where a lot of people stop. They let God's Word do its initial separating work and then go right on living like everyone else. Spiritually, they're still separated from death. But physically and mentally, they're up to their necks in it. They're depressed. They're sick. They're worried. They're confused. They're upset. In other words, they're just like everyone else in the world.

But if you'll give God's Word first place in your life, it will continue to separate you *from* the poverty, anxiety, sickness and hatred of the world. It will also separate you *to* the things of God.

You can't simply separate yourself *from* an old destructive habit without separating yourself *to* something stronger...God's Word.

So make a quality decision today—a decision from which there is no turning back. Decide to give the Bible first place in your life. Lock into His Word and let it do its work. Let it separate you *from* the things of the world and *to* the things of God.

talk the truth

"I come out from among the world and I am separate." (2 Corinthians 6:17)

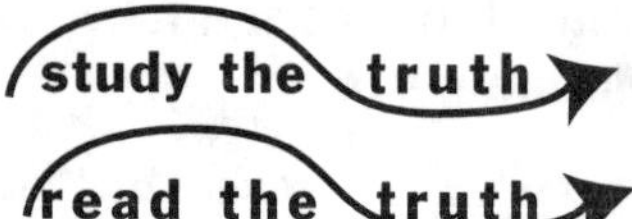
study the truth
read the truth

2 Corinthians 6:14-18

Job 1,2; Jude

WE'RE WINNING

"Only do not rebel against the Lord. And do not be afraid of the people of the land, because we will swallow them up. Their protection is gone, but the Lord is with us. Do not be afraid of them."

NUMBERS 14:9

Thousands of years ago, God told the Israelites to take the land that He had given them. He told them to take it—by force and without fear—from the ungodly ones who were living there.

He is still saying that today. He's still trying to get us to use the power He's given us to run the wicked one out.

You see, this earth doesn't belong to Satan. It belongs to God (Psalm 24:1). Satan's just moved in and taken control of things because we haven't stopped him.

That's our job, you know. Jesus took Satan's legal rights away from him when He rose from the grave, and He has put us in charge of enforcing Satan's defeat. The Bible says that Jesus will sit at the right hand of the Father until His enemies are made His footstool (Hebrews 10:12-13). Do you know what that means? It means Jesus is waiting on us to kick Satan and his crew out of this world's affairs. He's waiting on us to carry out the victory He won at the Cross.

You may not know it, but we're at war. We're in a spiritual battle—and we're winning.

So today if Satan has control of an area of your life or your church or your school, rise up through faith, prayer and God's promises and start taking that territory back in the spirit. Don't be afraid. Satan doesn't have any defense anymore. He can't win!

talk the truth

"The Lord is on my side and I'm winning!" (Numbers 14:9)

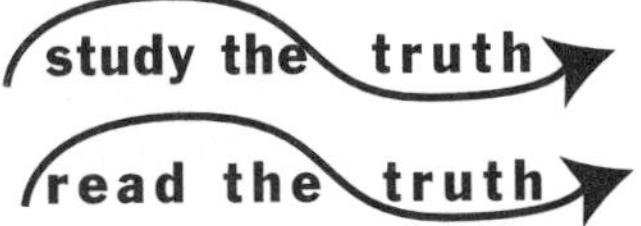
study the truth
read the truth

Exodus 14:10-31

Job 3,4; Revelation 1

July 29

Kenneth

STEP INTO THE LIGHT

"Your word is a lamp to my feet and a light for my path."

PSALM 119:105

As long as you live by God's Word, you never have to be in the dark again. You never have to be confused about which path to take. Isn't it exciting to know that the Bible will give you all the light you need every day of your life?

Build your faith in His Word and renew your commitment to it as you speak this prayer today:

"Father, in the Name of Jesus, I commit to walk the way Your Word says to walk. I know that Your Word is constant, sure and eternal—and I trust my life to its promises.

"You have sent Your Word into my heart. I let its wisdom live powerfully within me. It won't leave—I will think about it and pray day and night so that I will continually act on it. Your Word will always give me life and it's growing in me now, producing Your life inside me.

"I thank You, Father, that Your Word is my instruction, my shield, my strength and my powerful weapon for battle. It is a lamp to my feet and a light for my path. It makes my way straight—and it keeps me from stumbling and falling, for my steps are guided by Your Word.

"I recognize the strategies and tricks of Satan, and I stop them immediately by speaking Your Word out of my mouth in faith.

"I am confident, Father, that You are at work in me, working out Your plans for my life. I love Your Word and give it first place. I boldly say that my heart is firmly established on a solid foundation—the living Word of God. Amen!"

talk the truth

"God's Word is a lamp to my feet and a light for my path." (Psalm 119:105)

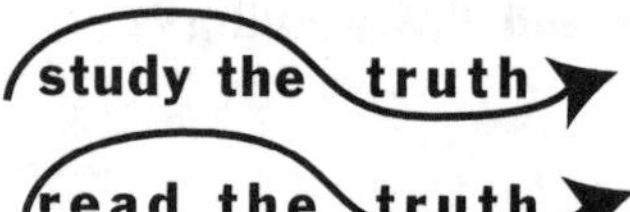
study the truth
read the truth

Psalm 119:89-105

Job 5,6; Revelation 2

YOU DON'T HAVE TO FALL

> ***"Therefore, brethren, be even more diligent to make your call and election sure, for if you do these things you will never stumble."***
>
> **2 PETER 1:10, NKJV**

"You will never stumble." When you think about it, that's a startling statement, isn't it? Most of us have been tripped up by Satan so many times we don't like to think about it. But the Bible says it doesn't have to be that way. It says there's something that can keep us on our feet. What is it? *Diligence.*

You can't have a life of victory without diligence. You can't stand strong on God's Word without picking up your Bible during the week. Yet many young men and women try to get by on Sunday church and the Wednesday night youth group alone. That's why we have thousands of churches filled with young people who could change the world, but they're lacking in faith. Diligence is the key.

Diligence is a daily thing. Satan's out there 24 hours a day coming up with ways to make us fall. Jesus is on the throne 24 hours a day giving us power to resist the enemy, and we need to be exercising our faith all the time.

If you're going to stand every day, you need a lot more than Sunday-morning and Wednesday-night faith. You need some full-grown, mountain-moving faith, and there's only one way to get that: By giving yourself to God's Word more diligently than you ever have before.

So do it. Be diligent...and no matter how slippery the situation gets, you won't have to fall!

talk the truth **"I am diligent to make my calling in Christ sure, therefore I will never fall." (2 Peter 1:10, NKJV)**

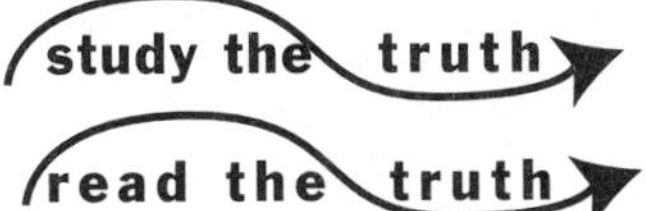
study the truth
read the truth

study the truth **2 Peter 1:3-10**

read the truth **Job 7,8,9; Revelation 3**

July 31

Kenneth

DON'T SERVE THE PROBLEM

"Let the wicked forsake his way and the evil man his thoughts. Let him turn to the Lord, and he will have mercy on him, and to our God, for he will freely pardon."

ISAIAH 55:7

You can't have victory over a problem as long as the problem is the biggest thing in your life!

The Lord showed me that a few years ago. I was facing some difficulties that seemed so big to me, I thought about them from the time I woke up in the morning until I fell asleep at night. Even though I was standing against them, I was thinking more about those problems than about the scriptural promises I was standing on.

Then I saw something in Matthew 6:24-25. "No one can serve two masters.... Therefore I tell you, do not worry about your life."

I'd read that scripture hundreds of times, but that day I saw something I'd never noticed. I saw that right after Jesus said, "No one can serve two masters," He said, "Do not worry." Suddenly it hit me: *We serve our worries!*

That's why 2 Corinthians 10:5 says to cast out thoughts that go against the truth of the Bible. Instead of serving our worries, we need to serve God with our thoughts by making them line up with His Word.

Do you want to be rescued from your problems today? Then quit serving them! Quit allowing them to take over your thought life. Realize that your circumstances won't ever change until you switch to a new way of thinking.

I know that's not easy to do, especially in the middle of heavy troubles. But you can do it if you'll do these three things:

- *Remember you aren't alone.* You have the Bible (God's thoughts). You have the Holy Spirit to strengthen you, and you have the mind of Christ.
- *Get around people who are full of faith.* Instead of talking about your problem again, join your faith with theirs and resist darkness.
- *Praise God.* When you praise, God's presence will turn away those worried thoughts.

Your problems are not the biggest thing in your life. Jesus is. Serve Him with your thoughts and He will set you free!

"Jesus is bigger than any situation I'll ever come up against. I do not worry, but trust in Him." (Isaiah 55:7)

study the truth

Isaiah 55

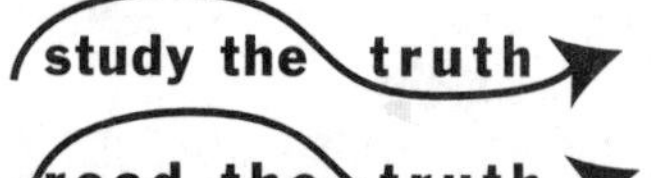

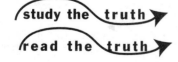

Job 10,11; Revelation 4

RECEIVE YOUR MIRACLE

"For it is with your heart that you believe and are justified, and it is with your mouth that you confess and are saved."

Romans 10:10

Do you need a miracle? Then believe it, speak it and receive it! That's what you did when you made Jesus the Lord of your life—you believed, spoke and received the greatest miracle in the universe, the miracle of a new life! Every other miracle you receive will come in exactly the same way.

You start by simply believing what the Bible says about the kind of need you have, by letting that Word change your heart and mind.

A lot of people try to skip that step. They try to believe for a miracle without spending enough time in the Bible to change their heart and mind. They just want to speak it and have it instantly appear. But that won't happen. It's what we believe in our heart and say we receive that produces results.

If you don't have enough faith yet to believe for the miracle you need, then get it. "So then faith *comes* by hearing, and hearing by the word of God" (Romans 10:17, NKJV). Start filling your heart with God's Word until faith for your miracle comes.

You have the opportunity. God's power is always present. Your faith will bring it into your life. Believe, speak and receive your miracle today!

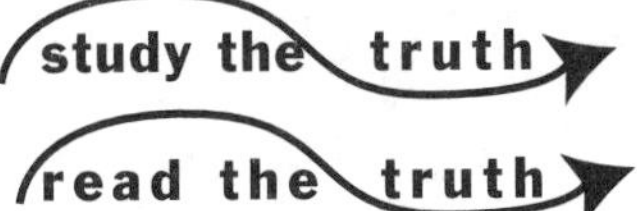

"I believe God's promises in my heart, speak them from my mouth and receive my miracle today!" (Romans 10:10)

study the truth **Matthew 9:18-31**

read the truth **Job 12,13; Revelation 5**

Gloria

August 2

COURAGE COMES FROM FAITH

"Be strong and courageous. Do not be terrified; do not be discouraged, for the Lord your God will be with you wherever you go."

JOSHUA 1:9

Courage comes from trusting God. It comes from believing what God says regardless of what the circumstances look like. Courage comes from faith!

Where does discouragement come from? From fear and unbelief. It comes when you listen to Satan's lies.

As Christians, you and I must shake off discouragement and rise up with courage! We must quit looking at our own abilities and failures and limitations and start looking to God.

If you've been discouraged lately, stop listening to Satan's lies. Whenever someone tells you God isn't going to help you, just tell them, "According to the Bible, He's always present to help me" (Psalm 46:1).

Once you begin to realize who you are and what God has given you, you'll quit letting Satan run all over you. God didn't suggest that you be strong and courageous. He commanded you to be!

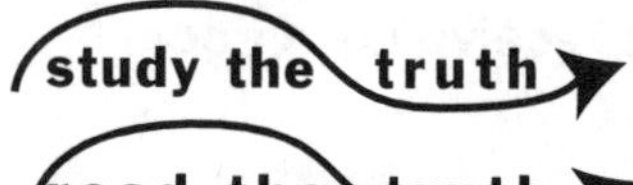

"I am strong and courageous. I refuse to be terrified or discouraged, for the Lord is with me wherever I go." (Joshua 1:9)

study the truth **Joshua 1:1-9**

read the truth **Job 14,15; Revelation 6**

LET IT FLOW

"Whoever drinks the water I give him will never thirst. Indeed, the water I give him will become in him a spring of water welling up to eternal life."

JOHN 4:14

What are the powerful forces the Bible calls the fruit of the spirit? Love, joy, peace, patience, kindness, goodness, faithfulness, gentleness and self-control. They're the character traits of God Himself. And when the Holy Spirit came to live in you, He brought them with Him, so they could become your character traits too.

They're designed to rise up from within you and become part of your life, constantly protecting and cleansing you from the inside out.

Have you ever noticed that you can't put any trash in the mouth of a flowing fountain? When it's shooting water up, the force of its own outflow protects it and keeps it clear of any impurities from the outside. Well, the spiritual fountain within you works the same way. When you're allowing the forces of love, joy, peace, gentleness and all the others to flow out, Satan can't get any junk in.

How do you keep the fruit of the spirit flowing? You pump your heart so full of God's Word that those forces of eternal life start shooting out. Just a little at first...and then stronger and higher.

Choose to keep those forces pouring out of the fountain of your heart. Refuse to let selfishness and sin stop the flow. You have a fountain filled with unbeatable forces inside you. Let it flow!

talk the truth

"As I drink from God's Word, the spring within me shoots out the forces of eternal life." (John 4:14)

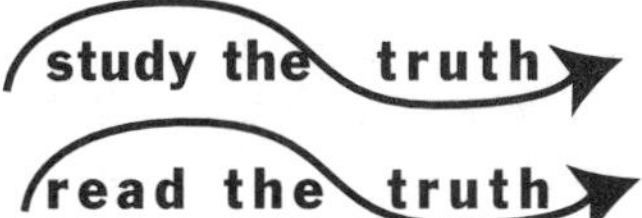
study the truth
read the truth

Jeremiah 17:7-13

Job 16,17; Revelation 7

August 4

RECEIVE HIS MERCY

"Oh, give thanks to the Lord, for He is good! For His mercy endures forever."

PSALM 136:1, NKJV

"His mercy endures forever!" Powerful things happened when Israel said those words. When Solomon finished building the Lord's temple, the singers lifted up their voices with a whole band of musical instruments. They praised the Lord saying, "For He is good! For His mercy endures forever." They said the same thing when they went into battle. Singers marched in front of the troops and cried out, "Praise the Lord! For His mercy endures forever."

His mercy continues to reach you every day. His mercy never runs out or weakens. Whatever you're going through, God still has plenty of love for you. Dare to stretch your faith out, call His Name and take in His everlasting love and mercy. Speak it out loud—"The Lord is good and His mercy endures forever!"

talk the truth

"The Lord is good to me, and His mercy endures forever." (Psalm 136:1, NKJV)

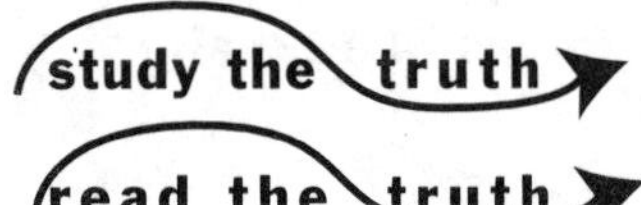
study the truth
read the truth

2 Chronicles 5:1-14

Job 18,19; Revelation 8

CREATED TO PRAISE

"Let everything that has breath praise the Lord. Praise the Lord."

Psalm 150:6

We're created to praise God. Some people don't know that. When the praise service starts in their church, they sit back and say, "I'm not comfortable with all that singing and emotional stuff. Praise just isn't my thing."

Yes it is! According to the Bible, if you breathe, you were meant to praise.

And don't try to slip by with saying, "Well, I'm praising Him in my heart." That's just a cop-out. The Bible says you need to praise with your mouth, too (Psalm 34:1). Psalm 132:9 says, "Let Your saints shout for joy" (NKJV). You can't shout and be quiet at the same time.

When you first begin to truly praise Him, it may seem awkward to you, but if you'll keep it up, it will become a way of life. Why? Because praise causes God to *show up* in your life. It causes you to "walk in the light of His presence" (Psalm 89:15). It will create a surge of life inside you!

"But if I start to praise like that, my friends will think I'm some kind of fanatic."

Well, good! Do you know that every powerful move of God in history started with people the world considered absolute fanatics? God does things differently than the world. So when you set aside your shyness and uncertainty and start letting His Spirit work through you, you'll look strange to those who are strangers to His ways...but you'll look great to God!

Start by praising Him in your own private prayer time and throughout your day. Learn to keep an attitude of praise and thankfulness with you. You'll soon find that you won't even care what your friends or family think—you'll just want to praise Him more. So open your mouth and your heart and do what God created you to do—praise!

talk the truth

"I praise the Lord, and God shows up in my life." (Psalm 150:6)

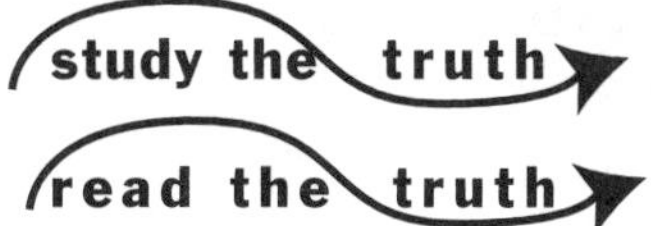
study the truth
read the truth

Psalm 150

Job 20,21; Revelation 9

Kenneth

August 6

LET YOUR LIFE BEGIN AGAIN

"Now is the time of God's favor, now is the day of salvation."

2 CORINTHIANS 6:2

It doesn't matter who you are or what you've done. I don't care if you've been a thief, a murderer, a prostitute, a dope dealer or a churchgoing teenager who's just never made Jesus the Lord of your life. The Bible says that today is the day of salvation. A new life is only a prayer away.

Gloria and I discovered that for ourselves more than 30 years ago. Actually, Gloria took the first step. She found out the Bible said that not even a bird falls without God's knowing about it. *Well,* she thought, *if God cares when a bird falls, He must know what terrible shape my life is in right now. And if He cares, maybe He can do something with it.*

Gloria didn't know anything about the Bible. She didn't even know for sure that God would let her start over. But when she told Him she wanted Him to take over her life, something supernatural happened on the inside of her. She was reborn—totally made new again.

"But what about the awful things I've done?" you say. "I feel so guilty!"

When your spirit is reborn, that past doesn't belong to you anymore. You're like a brand-new baby again in God's eyes—you don't have a past. Your life begins again the day you make Jesus Lord of your life. Then, when Satan tries to remind you of what a worm you used to be, just tell him he's knocking on the wrong door.

You've been kicked around long enough. There's no need to wait any longer. Ask Jesus to be your Lord...and let your life begin again today.

talk the truth

"I am a new creation in Jesus. Old things have passed away and all things have become new." (2 Corinthians 5:17)

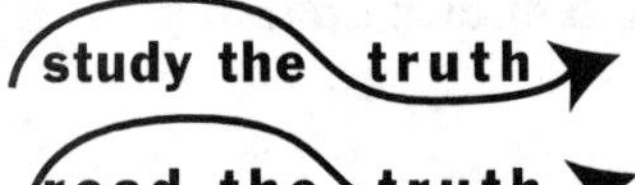
study the truth
read the truth

Matthew 10:29-33

Job 22,23,24; Revelation 10,11

PUT YOUR IMAGINATION TO WORK

"And God is able to make all grace abound to you, so that in all things at all times, having all that you need, you will abound in every good work."

2 Corinthians 9:8

If you have a desire to give to God, yet money problems keep holding you back, you may be surprised to learn that what you need is not more money. What you need is a spiritual breakthrough. You need to take the Bible and destroy any willingness you may have to live with lack. You need to replace that willingness with an understanding of God's provision for you. Then more things, including money, will come.

How? By spending time thinking about the promises God has provided for you in the Bible. By believing you receive those promises. By believing that they are actually being fulfilled in your life.

See yourself, for example, as being able to generously give to people in need. See yourself slipping a $100 bill in someone's locker or secretly purchasing a needy friend's lunch. In your mind, see yourself as giving instead of always needing. When you do, God's promise will become more real to you and your faith will grow.

That's why God gave you an imagination. Working with His Word, your imagination is very powerful. But never forget that without His Word, your imagination will become worldly and starve you instead of feeding your faith.

Let me warn you though, sometimes creating new images of hope is tough—especially when there are old images of doubt blocking the way. If you've been without money most of your life, for instance, it may take awhile for you to see yourself doing well financially. But you can do it if you keep believing His Word.

Eventually you'll be transformed by a new way of thinking. When that happens, money failures will never be able to stop you again.

talk the truth

"I have images of hope within me—I not only see God's promises, but I see them fulfilled in my life." (2 Corinthians 9:8)

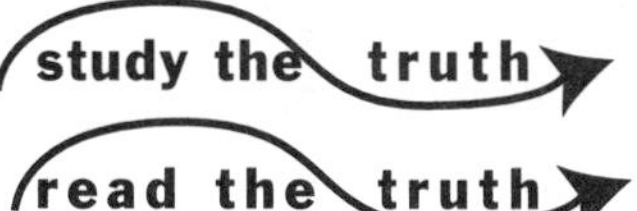
study the truth
read the truth

2 Corinthians 8:1-14

Job 25,26; Revelation 12

August 8

KEEP PADDLING UPSTREAM

"Set a guard over my mouth, O Lord; keep watch over the door of my lips."

PSALM 141:3

Do you really believe that you need to guard your mouth? Most Christians don't. You can tell that just by listening to what they say. They say, for example, "I'm just sure I'll get the flu. I get it every year. I'll be sicker than a dog...."

Do people like that get what they say? Yes! Check with them a few weeks later and they'll be quick to tell you that they got just as sick as they said they'd be. But, if you try to tell them they're sick because they believed they would be, they'll look at you as if you were out of your mind.

Of course, if they would dig into the Bible and find out what it has to say, they'd realize that the words they speak have a tremendous impact on their lives. If you've made Jesus your Lord, you've already experienced the most powerful example of that. You believed with your heart and said that Jesus is your Lord, and you changed the course of your life. You know just how powerful your words are.

Yet, if you're like me, you still find that speaking faith-filled words all the time is tough to do. That's because the world around you is in a negative flow. Like a rushing river, it's always pulling at you, trying to get you to flow with it. Living by faith and speaking faith-filled words is like trying to paddle upstream. You can do it—but it's a lot of work. If you relax a little bit, you'll just start drifting right back down the river of negative speaking.

Make the decision right now to watch what you say. Determine to fill your mouth with God's words...and everything you say will take you a little farther upstream!

talk the truth

"I allow the Lord to set a guard over my mouth and keep watch over the door of my lips." (Psalm 141:3)

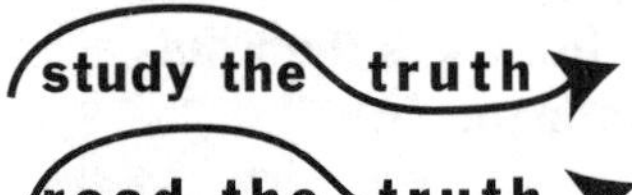
study the truth
read the truth

Romans 10:8-17

Job 27,28; Revelation 13

ENTER GOD'S REST

"There remains, then, a Sabbath-rest for the people of God.... Let us, therefore, make every effort to enter that rest, so that no one will fall by following their example of disobedience."

HEBREWS 4:9,11

God's rest. Between school, peer pressure, work and any other activities you may have, God's rest sounds like a pretty good thing to have, doesn't it? But what is that rest and how do you enter it?

Hebrews 3 and 4 compare God's rest with the Israelites' taking possession of the Promised Land. That land was to be a place where their every need would be met, a place of freedom from their enemies, a place no one would ever drive them from again. All they had to do was go in and possess it. But something kept them from it—unbelief and disobedience.

As a Christian, you also have the opportunity to enter a promised land of peace. A land where you can rest from your struggles and enjoy victory. To enter it you must do what the Israelites failed to do—you must simply trust God and obey His voice.

How do you do that? By getting to know your Father. By spending time with Him in prayer and His Word. *That* is the effort that will bring you into His rest!

I'll never forget when I first discovered that. I'd been learning about faith, but found it hard to keep from doubting. Then, one day, I made an effort to know the Father instead of just knowing *about* Him.

When I did that, He began to show Himself to me. He gave me glimpses of His heart, His nature and His love. As He showed me how much He wanted to do for His children, it changed my striving into peace, my doubt into trust and my fear into bold obedience. It enabled me to enter His rest.

Get to know your Father. Put forth the effort. He has a promised land of rest that is waiting for you!

talk the truth

"I spend time with the Lord and enter into His rest." (Hebrews 4:9,11)

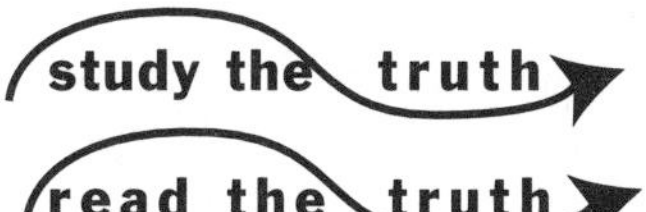
study the truth
read the truth

Hebrews 4:1-11

Job 29,30; Revelation 14

Gloria

August 10

A LIVING EXAMPLE OF LOVE

"And hope does not disappoint us, because God has poured out his love into our hearts by the Holy Spirit, whom he has given us."

ROMANS 5:5

Don't ever worry about not having enough love inside you. The Bible says God has poured His love into your heart by the Holy Spirit. God's love is in you. What you need to do is make a decision to let it show.

Pray this prayer today.

"In Jesus' Name, I make a fresh and strong commitment today to live a life of love, to let God's compassion flow through me and heal the hurting hearts of those I meet.

"Father, teach me to love even when things go wrong...to be patient and kind when friends are impatient and unkind...to overlook the stinging words of an angry family member...to be full of joy when someone else gets something I want. Teach me to walk in love and never gossip.

"Lord, Your Word says that Your love is already inside me...that it has been poured into my heart. So today, I make the decision to remove anything that would keep that love from flowing freely into the lives of others. I put grudges behind me, and I forgive all those who've done me wrong.

"In the days ahead, make me increase with Your love. Help me to be what this world needs most of all...a living example of love."

talk the truth

"God has poured His love in my heart by the Holy Spirit." (Romans 5:5)

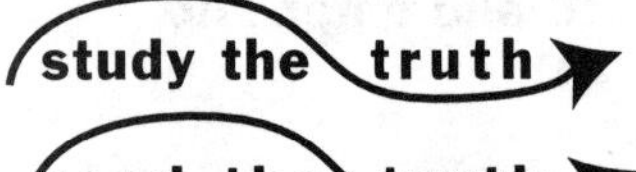
study the truth
read the truth

1 John 4:7-17

Job 31,32; Revelation 15

FOCUS ON HIS WORD

"He took him outside and said, 'Look up at the heavens and count the stars—if indeed you can count them.' Then he said to him, 'So shall your offspring be.' Abram believed the Lord, and he credited it to him as righteousness."

GENESIS 15:5,6

Do you ever have trouble believing the Bible? Not just knowing that what it says is true, but really believing that what it says will work for you?

I do. There are times when the promises in the Bible boggle my mind. There have been times when I've felt so defeated and the circumstances around me looked so bad that it was tough for me to believe I was "more than a conqueror" even though I knew God said I was (Romans 8:37).

What do you do when your mind staggers like that at God's promise? You focus on that promise. You look at scriptures and apply them directly to your circumstances until the scriptures are part of your thinking.

That can affect your life in a way that almost nothing else can. It can, quite literally, change your way of thinking. That's what happened to Abram.

When God first told him that he was going to have a child, Abram was an old man. His wife, Sarai, was old too. What's more, she had never been able to have children! How could an aging, childless couple have a child? Abram couldn't imagine such a thing. It boggled his mind.

But God knew the mental struggle Abram would have, so He didn't just make him a promise and leave it at that—He gave Abram a picture of that promise to focus on. He took him out into the starry night, turned his eyes to the sky and said, "So shall your offspring be."

Can't you just see Abram staring out at the stars, trying to count them?

That's what focusing on God's Word is all about. Taking time to see His promise until it becomes real inside you. It's a tremendously powerful thing to do. By focusing on the scriptural promises God has given you, you can put them to work in your life just as Abram put them to work in his.

Don't just read the Bible. Focus on it today.

talk the truth

"I focus on God's Word and keep it in my heart." (Genesis 15:5,6)

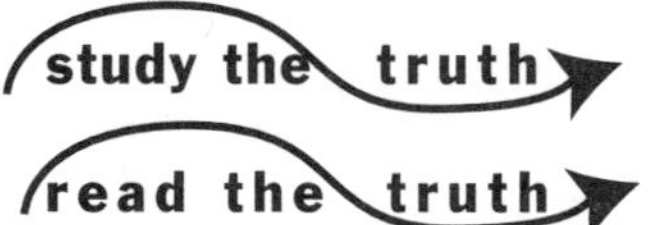
study the truth
read the truth

Romans 4:13-25

Job 33,34; Revelation 16

August 12

A SUPERNATURAL CYCLE

"Cast your bread upon the waters, for after many days you will find it again."

ECCLESIASTES 11:1

One of the most exciting things I ever discovered about God's law of planting and harvesting was the fact that God's harvests are not seasonal. If you give year round, you can be receiving year round.

Don't misunderstand. I'm not saying your harvest will come instantly. It usually won't. You may have to wait for it for a little while. What I'm saying is, if you'll plant consistently, you'll receive just as consistently.

Of course, some people don't give, they just keep waiting to receive. They stand on the beach of life saying, "I wonder where my prosperity is? As soon as it comes, I'll start giving."

God doesn't work that way. He said, "Give, and it will be given to you.... For with the measure you use, it will be measured to you" (Luke 6:38). You have to make the first move. You have to send a ship out before your ship can come in.

Think about that next time you're tempted to complain about the things life brings your way. Remember that whatever you've been casting out there is always what you find on down the road. If you've been giving doubt, unbelief and fear, that's what has been coming to you. If you've been giving nothing, then nothing is what you get.

You're holding the seeds of your future in your hand. Step out in faith and use them to put God's supernatural cycle in motion. Start now planting one good seed after another. Eventually you'll enjoy a good harvest every single day!

talk the truth **"I cast my bread upon the waters—and I know I'll find it again soon!" (Ecclesiastes 11:1)**

study the truth **Luke 6:31-38**

read the truth **Job 35,36; Revelation 17**

HEART TO HEART

Isn't it exciting to realize that you can hold the thoughts and feelings and purposes of God's heart in your own heart?

First Corinthians 6:17 says when you made Jesus your Lord, you were joined to Him. He came into union with you so that He could talk to you, heart to heart.

God wants His thoughts to become your actions. He wants you to walk so closely with Him that you're never without enough power to overcome the evil of this world. He wants you to be so in tune with His Spirit that you are able to feel His love toward those around you who are hurting. He wants to be one with you, so He can reach out through your hands and accomplish His purposes in the world.

Make a commitment today to walk with God everywhere you go—at home, at school, on a date, at a football game, at work, wherever. Determine to follow His voice *only*. Allow His thoughts to become your actions!

"For who has known or understood the mind (the counsels and purposes) of the Lord so as to guide and instruct [Him] and give Him knowledge? But we have the mind of Christ, the Messiah, and do hold the thoughts (feelings and purposes) of His heart."

1 Corinthians 2:16, AMP

talk the truth

"I have the mind of Christ and I hold the thoughts, feelings and purposes of His heart." (1 Corinthians 2:16, AMP)

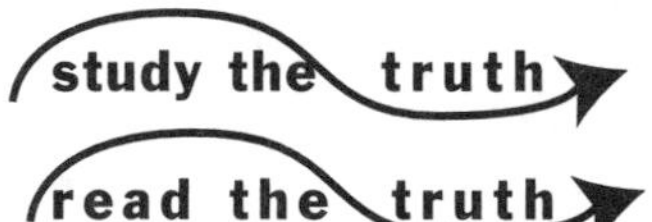
study the truth
read the truth

1 Corinthians 2

Job 37,38,39; Revelation 18,19

August 14

DON'T UNDERESTIMATE YOUR PRAYERS

"I urge, then, first of all, that requests, prayers, intercession and thanksgiving be made for everyone—for kings and all those in authority, that we may live peaceful and quiet lives in all godliness and holiness."

1 Timothy 2:1,2

That verse is clear, isn't it? Yet even when our nations desperately need God's guidance, most Christians don't do what that verse commands.

Why not? I believe it's because most of us are overwhelmed by the problems we see around us. *How could my prayers make a dent in anything?* we think. We fail to pray because we fail to realize just how powerfully our prayers can affect our country.

It's time we realized that if we'd just be obedient to 1 Timothy 2:1-2, there's no king, no president, no ruler, no *anything* that could overthrow God's purpose for His people.

God has called us to pray for those in authority. He has given us His Word, power, Name, authority and faith. We have all the tools necessary to pray effectively for our government and its leaders.

I urge you to pray for them. It is your responsibility as a Christian to get involved in your country. And this is a way you can get involved even if you're not old enough yet to vote or take part in the political process. So pray for your nation every day. And never again underestimate the world-changing power of those prayers.

talk the truth **"I pray for those in authority, therefore I live a peaceful and quiet life in godliness and holiness." (1 Timothy 2:1,2)**

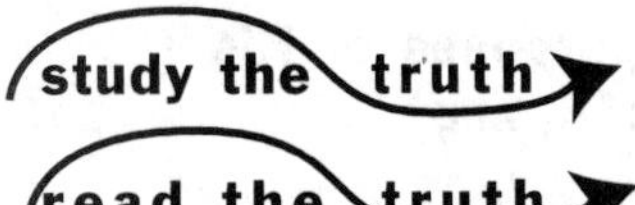
study the truth
read the truth

Daniel 2:1-30

Job 40,41; Revelation 20

CERTAIN ABOUT A MIRACLE

"Now faith is being sure of what we hope for and certain of what we do not see."

Hebrews 11:1

Don't ever stop a miracle by trying to see it in progress! So many Christians do that. They take time to pray for someone else's healing and then, when they don't see any immediate, outward change, they stop using their faith and assume nothing happened.

The Lord taught me an unforgettable lesson about that once when I was in Jamaica. I was preaching to a group of about 150 people in a church that was lighted only by a single kerosene lantern. It was so dark I couldn't see anyone's face. All I could see was my Bible and the feet of the man right in front of me.

Suddenly I realized that I'd always depended on people's facial expressions to determine how my sermon was being received. Knowing what I did about faith, I knew that was dangerous. So I made a decision at that moment never to preach another sermon except by faith. I would not be swayed by the way people reacted.

Before that series of meetings was over, I saw just how important that decision was. The Jamaicans, who tend to show very little expression anyway, sat through every sermon without any outward reaction at all.

One lady was completely healed of blindness during one of those meetings. She never let on that anything had taken place. She was almost rigid when she found me outside and said simply, "Mr. Copeland, I was blind, but now I can see. Thank you." That was all! A miracle had taken place, but by watching, you wouldn't have been able to tell anything had happened at all.

Next time you're tempted to figure out what God is doing by the looks of things, don't do it. Remember instead that it is faith, not appearances, that makes miracles happen. It's the only real proof you need!

talk the truth

"Through faith, I am sure of what I hope for and certain of what I do not see." (Hebrews 11:1)

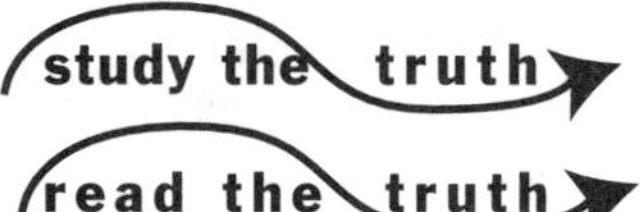
study the truth
read the truth

Hebrews 11:1-13

Job 42; Proverbs 1; Revelation 21

August 16

A FIRM FOUNDATION

"This is my command: Love each other."

JOHN 15:17

In Luke 6:47-48, Jesus said, "I will show you what he is like who comes to me and hears my words and puts them into practice. He is like a man building a house, who dug down deep and laid the foundation on rock. When a flood came, the torrent struck that house but could not shake it, because it was well-built."

That's probably a familiar scripture to you. But today I want you to do something new with it. I want you to put it together with what Jesus said in John 15:17—"This is my command: Love each other."

Love. That one word sums up all Jesus said for us to do. If you'll build your life on it, even the most violent storms of this world will be unable to shake you. It will make you solid in every area of your life.

If you'll build your family and friendships on love, you can win back those Satan has stolen from you. You can win them to Jesus with the love of God.

If you'll build the work you do on love, you'll prosper beyond your wildest dreams. I had a friend who did that. He went into a television and radio business in his church. He wanted to buy a station from a Jewish man and he offered such a good price for it that the owner was stunned. "Why would you offer me such a wonderful price?" asked the Jewish owner.

"Because God's Word says that if I will bless you, God will bless me. So I intend to see to it that you get the better part of this deal," answered my friend.

Before it was all over, that Jewish station owner made Jesus the Lord of his life. He and my friend ended up prospering and preaching the gospel together on the radio. When love rules, prosperity can flow!

Commit to living a life of love today. Commit to building your life on the rock. Then when the storms begin to blow—at home, at school or in any situation—you can enjoy the solid security of knowing that love never fails.

talk the truth

"I love my neighbor as I love myself." (John 15:17)

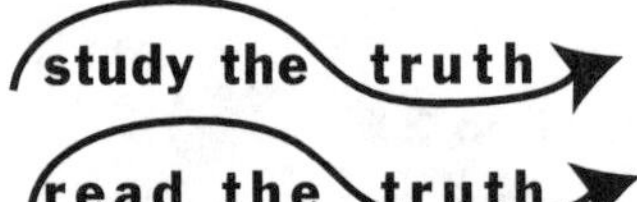
study the truth
read the truth

1 Corinthians 13:8-13

Proverbs 2,3; Revelation 22

GIVE GOD A WAY IN

God is very interested in your finances. He wants to multiply and protect them. But He won't be able to—unless you open the door for Him to do it.

How? Through tithing.

When you give 10 percent of what you make to God, you give Him the right to have a part in your finances, to bless you and to defend you against the destruction Satan brings. When you tithe, you lay your foundation for success.

But don't wait until your back is against the wall to start tithing. Begin tithing when things are going well. Learn to act on His Word now, and when Satan tries to back you into a corner, he'll fail. His power over you will have already been broken.

If you haven't yet opened the door and given God a way into your finances, don't wait any longer. Do it today—even if all you usually have is pocket change or an allowance. Then, when pressures come, you'll be prepared and protected by the special privileges that are guaranteed to those who tithe!

"'I will prevent pests from devouring your crops, and the vines in your fields will not cast their fruit,' says the Lord Almighty. 'Then all the nations will call you blessed, for yours will be a delightful land.'"

MALACHI 3:11,12

talk the truth

"I tithe. I allow God into my finances and He blesses me and defends my finances from Satan." (Malachi 3:11,12)

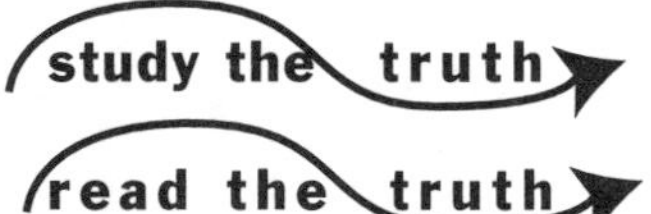
study the truth
read the truth

Hebrews 7:1-9

Proverbs 4,5; Psalm 1

August 18

GET OUT FROM UNDER

"You, dear children, are from God and have overcome them, because the one who is in you is greater than the one who is in the world."

1 John 4:4

Under the circumstances... Have you ever caught yourself saying that?

"I suppose I'm doing pretty well *under the circumstances."*

If you've ever said something like that, I want you to kick those words out of your vocabulary right now. Because you, as God's child, don't have any business living your life "under" your circumstances. You don't have any business letting problems and situations rule over you.

Two thousand years ago, Jesus—the One Who is in you—ruined Satan's kingdom. Through His death on the Cross, He legally entered hell and stripped Satan of everything. He took away all his armor. He took his authority. He bound Satan, spoiled his kingdom and triumphed over all of his power. Then Jesus turned around and gave the victory to you.

Remember that! Because He lives in you, you have the victory. You never have to live "under the circumstances" again!

"I am of God and have overcome the world. For He Who is in me is greater than he who is in the world." (1 John 4:4)

study the truth **Colossians 1:9-15**

read the truth **Proverbs 6,7; Psalm 2**

August 19

SEE YOURSELF RISEN WITH JESUS

"Constantly keep in mind Jesus Christ, the Messiah, [as] risen from the dead."

2 TIMOTHY 2:8, AMP

The scripture to the right is the key to holding onto God's promises. When pressure comes, when troubles are pressing down on you, remember Jesus is risen from the dead!

Remember that when Jesus arose, you arose. When He came out of hell and defeated the enemy, you came out of hell and defeated the enemy. His victory is your victory because you're in Him.

When Satan says you won't get your answer, remember that. When he tells you there's no way out, you remember Jesus is the Ultimate Conqueror!

If there's an image Satan hates more than any other, it must be that image of Jesus, rising from the dead, stripping him forever of his authority, and displaying his defeat to all of heaven and hell. That's the picture you need to keep in front of you. Think about it until it's written in your heart so deeply that nothing Satan says or does can get it out of you.

Keep Jesus in mind—He's risen from the dead!

talk the truth — **"I have been made alive with Christ. I have been raised with Him." (2 Timothy 2:8, AMP)**

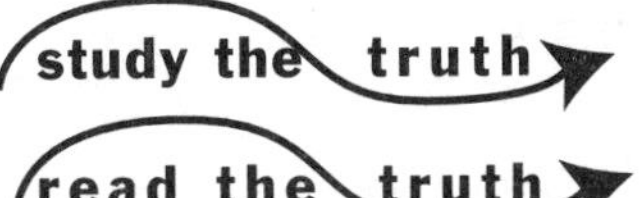

Hebrews 12:1-13

read the truth — **Proverbs 8,9; Psalm 3**

Kenneth

August 20

WHEN SOMEONE DOES YOU WRONG

"I have given you authority to trample on snakes and scorpions and to overcome all the power of the enemy; nothing will harm you."

LUKE 10:19

Sooner or later it happens to all of us. Somewhere along the way, we all get hurt or cheated or lied to or abused. Yet when it happens, most of us find ourselves totally unprepared. If that's true in your life, it's time you found out how to put God's power to work for you when someone does you wrong.

Step one: Identify the enemy! Here's where most of us make our biggest slip. We mistakenly think our enemy is the person who hurt us. Don't waste your energy being angry at people who cause you pain. They're just being influenced by Satan. Aim your spiritual guns at the right target. It's Satan who's behind it all. Go after him!

Step two: Fire! Once you have your spiritual guns pointed in the right direction, fire! Hit Satan fast and hard with God's Word. Speak out some promises from the Bible. In Jesus' Name, bind Satan from doing you any more harm.

Step three: Pray! Pray for the person who did you wrong. In Matthew 5:44-45, Jesus gives us these instructions: "Love your enemies, bless those who curse you, do good to those who hate you, and pray for those who spitefully use you and persecute you, that you may be sons of your Father in heaven" (NKJV).

Crying out for God's vengeance to strike like a lightning bolt when someone does us wrong isn't acting in love. Remember God has great, great mercy. Not just for me and you, but for everyone.

Next time someone hurts you, put God's power to work. Identify the real enemy. Hit him hard with the authority you've been given as a Christian. Then pray for the person who caused the pain. Satan will think twice before he bothers you again.

talk the truth

"Through Him, I overcome all the power of the enemy. Nothing will harm me." (Luke 10:19)

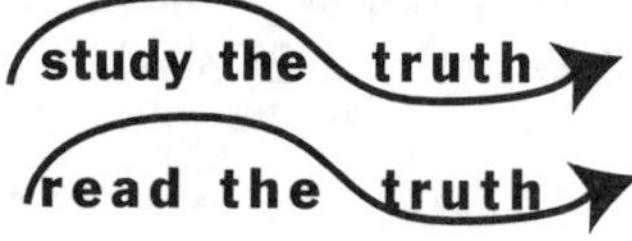
study the truth
read the truth

Matthew 6:6-15

Proverbs 10,11,12; Psalms 4,5

HELL CAN'T PUT OUT THE LIGHT

"In Him was Life and the Life was the Light of men. And the Light shines on in the darkness, for the darkness has never overpowered it."

JOHN 1:4,5, AMP

Whenever things around you get dark and you feel Satan is about to overpower you, remember this: You have the Light of the world in you, and all the forces of hell can't put it out! Even when you're at your weakest, Satan's darkness is no match for you.

Let me show you what I mean. Imagine for a moment that you're in a large gym that has no windows or doors to let in outside light. The place is so black you can't see anything, not even your hand in front of your face. There's nothing around you but complete darkness.

Now, imagine one little lightning bug flying around inside the gym. Your eye would immediately turn toward it. As small as that little light is in comparison to the great darkness around it, you would still be able to see it.

When the circumstances around you begin to get black, think about that lightning bug. Remember the fact that Jesus, the Light of the world, is in you. When the true meaning of that hits you, you'll never again let the darkness back you into a corner. You'll start chasing it down and overcoming it with your light!

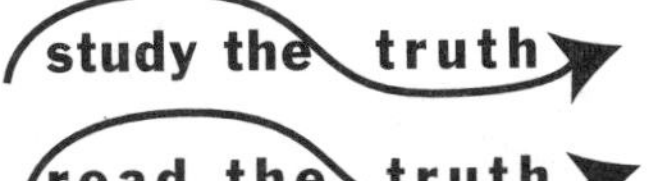

"I am the light in the Lord. I walk as a child of the light." (Ephesians 5:8)

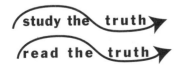

study the truth **Ephesians 5:8-16**

read the truth **Proverbs 13,14; Psalm 6**

August 22

PATIENCE—AN IMPORTANT FORCE

"But let patience have its perfect work, that you may be perfect and complete, lacking nothing."

James 1:4, NKJV

I talk a lot about faith. But there's another force that goes along with it that's just as important. It's patience—the ability to stand on what the Bible says even when your victory takes awhile to come.

Patience is not automatic. It won't go to work unless you put it to work. Many people don't understand that. They think faith and patience will work all by themselves. They just let Satan tear their lives apart and then they say ridiculous things like, "Well, I guess God sent that trial to strengthen my faith."

Don't you ever get caught saying that!

In the first place, the Bible says, "When tempted, no one should say, 'God is tempting me'" (James 1:13). And in the second place, that trial won't make your faith stronger. In fact, it'll destroy it if you'll let it.

If I were to give you a set of weights, would that set of weights make you any stronger? No. In fact, if you dropped one of them on your foot, you could end up painfully weaker. It's what you do with them that counts.

Well, the same thing is true when you run into some kind of circumstance Satan's brought your way. If you just lie down and let it run over you, it will damage you. But if you'll work your patience, trusting in and relying on God's promises, you'll end up "perfect and complete, lacking nothing."

Patience is a first-rate power that will put His promises within your reach. It's a force that will make you a winner!

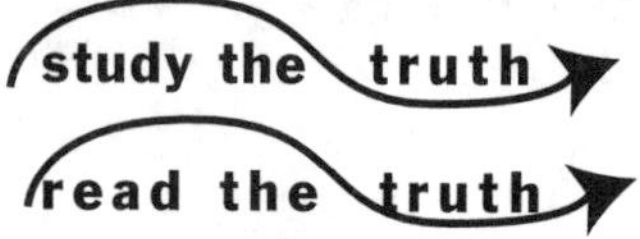

"Patience has its perfect work in me, making me perfect and complete, lacking nothing." (James 1:4, NKJV)

study the truth **Genesis 26:15-22**

read the truth **Proverbs 15,16; Psalm 7**

LEAVING THE LOW LIFE BEHIND

"For whoever wants to save his life will lose it, but whoever loses his life for me will find it."

MATTHEW 16:25

The high life...or the low life? God's kind of life...or the world's kind of life? You can't have them both. It's one or the other. You have to choose.

You may try to hang on to the low life while reaching out for the high life at the same time—just so you can see if it's something you really want before you give up everything the world has to offer. But, you'll never be able to truly sample the high life until you're willing to let go completely, take God at His Word and trust Him to take care of you.

What will happen when you do that? You'll start living the kind of life God describes in Psalm 1. You'll be like "a tree planted by streams of water, which yields its fruit in season and whose leaf does not wither. Whatever he does prospers."

In West Texas talk, that means your roots will go down so deep that no drought can dry you up and no storm can blow you down. No matter what happens around you, you'll have more than enough.

That's what the high life is like—and there's nothing that the world has to offer that can even compare. I know that from experience. Once you dare to let go and trust God, so will you.

talk the truth **"I am like a tree planted beside a river. Whatever I do succeeds!" (Psalm 1:3)**

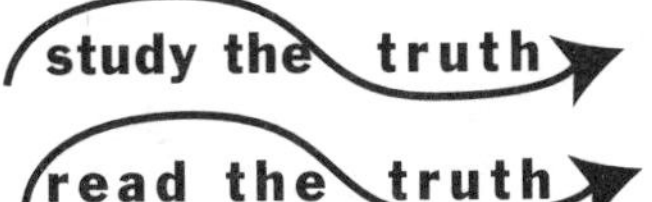

Matthew 16:13-26

read the truth **Proverbs 17,18; Psalm 8**

August 24

Gloria

TRADITION—A KILLER!

"You have made the commandment of God of no effect by your tradition."

MATTHEW 15:6, NKJV

AIDS. Cancer. Heart disease. When we think of killer diseases, those are the names that come to mind. But the truth is, there's a far more deadly killer on the loose today. And it has destroyed more lives than any of us can imagine. It's called *tradition*. Traditions rob Christians of their healing. They steal the power from God's promises. Here are three you should beware of:

Tradition #1—"It's not always God's will to heal you."

It *is* God's will to heal you! It says so in the Bible. If you don't believe that it is, then you can't pray for healing and expect to receive it. You're like the farmer who sits on his porch and says, "I believe in crops, but I'm not going to plant any seed this year. I'll just believe, and if God desires it, my crop will come up." That farmer will never see his crop. Faith is the seed of healing—if you don't plant it, it won't grow. You must know without a doubt that healing is always God's desire for you.

Tradition #2—"Healing has passed away...there are no miracles today."

The Bible proves that's not true. In Exodus 15:26, God says, "I am the Lord, who heals you." He also said He does not change (Malachi 3:6). He has never changed since the beginning of time. For healing to pass away, God would have to pass away...and He's not about to do *that!*

Tradition #3—"God gets glory from Christians being sick."

This tradition totally violates God's Word. The Bible says that people gave glory to God when they saw the lame walk and the blind see. God receives glory from your *healing*—not your pain!

The world is looking for a way *out* of sickness and disease, not a way into it. Let's break down those traditions and rescue a hurting world from the most dangerous killer of all.

talk the truth

"I refuse to let tradition make God's promises ineffective." (Matthew 15:6, NKJV)

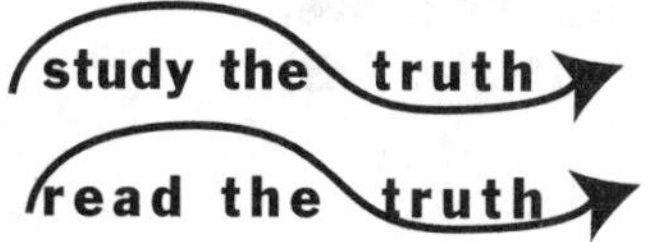
study the truth
read the truth

Mark 2:1-12

Proverbs 19,20; Psalm 9

CHOOSE FRIENDS WISELY

"I wrote you in my [previous] letter not to associate (closely and habitually) with unchaste (impure) people."

1 CORINTHIANS 5:9, AMP

The friends you keep have a big influence on your spiritual life. Spending time with godly people will help push you on to success, while spending time with those who are ungodly will drag you down to failure.

That's why the Bible says to separate yourself from the world...because ungodly companions will corrupt you.

Now, I'm not talking about ministering to others. Jesus Himself ministered to sinners. You have to mix with them to preach to them and pray for them. What I'm talking about here are the people you choose for friends.

If you want to walk in the things of the Lord, don't choose people for friends who walk in the things of the world—people who talk and act ungodly, who don't give God any place in their lives. They'll pull you down. You'll expose yourself to temptation and get so familiar with sin, it will start to appear less repulsive to you. Sooner or later, you'll fall into it.

If you don't know any godly people, pray and ask God to bring some into your life. He will!

So choose your friends wisely. Spend time with those who call on the Name of the Lord out of a pure heart (2 Timothy 2:22). Expose yourself to their love and peace. Let their faith rub off on you!

talk the truth

"I choose my friends wisely. I walk with the wise and become wise." (1 Corinthians 5:9, AMP)

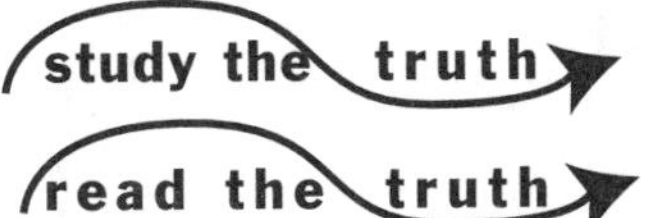
study the truth
read the truth

1 Corinthians 5:9-13

Proverbs 21,22; Psalm 10

August 26

Gloria

TAKE THE FIRST STEP

"The steps of a [good] man are directed and established of the Lord, when He delights in his way [and He busies Himself with his every step]."

PSALM 37:23, AMP

God wants to lead you on a day-by-day basis. He's given His Spirit to guide you every day.

Most Christians don't know that. They expect God to reveal His complete plan for their lives all at once. Don't make that mistake. Don't just sit around waiting for God to show you whether or not He wants you to go to Africa for the rest of your life.

Let Him begin to lead you in little things first, to tell you what you need to do about this situation or that one. He'll show you what you need to change. And, as He does, you'll change one thing at a time.

The truth is, you probably already know one thing God wants you to do. You might not know why He wants you to do it. You may not know where it's leading, but you've heard His voice in your heart. It could be something as small as hearing Him say, *Study for your math test,* or *Take out the trash for your parents tonight.* Many times God will use little, everyday things to prepare you for what's to come.

So spend time in prayer and the Bible. Tune your ear to His voice. He is always ready to give you the idea or answer you need.

Learn to trust Him. Remember that He's smarter than you are and be willing to do what He says whether you understand it or not. Obey even His smallest instructions. If you do, He'll eventually change your whole life...one little step at a time.

talk the truth

"My steps are directed and established of the Lord." (Psalm 37:23, AMP)

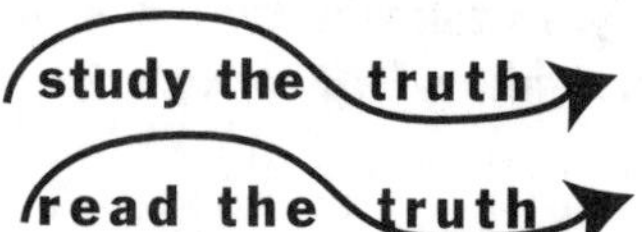
study the truth
read the truth

Genesis 12:1-8

Proverbs 23,24; Psalm 11

NOT OF THIS WORLD

"Whatever is born of God is victorious over the world; and this is the victory that conquers the world, even our faith."

1 John 5:4, AMP

Years ago Satan started a rumor. He told a few Christians that as long as they lived in the world, they had to share the diseases and the defeat, the lack of things they needed and the failure of those around them.

It was a crafty lie—and it worked. You may have even heard it yourself. If so, I want to help you get the facts straight once and for all.

You see, despite what you may have heard, health, prosperity and victorious living aren't concepts some comfort-hungry Christian selfishly dreamed up. They are God's ideas.

You may say, "That sounds good, but be realistic. We live in a world that's full of problems. And as long as we live in this world, we'll have our share."

Yes, that's true. Even Jesus said, "In the world you have tribulation and trials and distress and frustration." But notice, He didn't stop there! He went on to say, "But be of good cheer—take courage, be confident, certain, undaunted—for I have overcome the world. I have deprived it of power to harm, have conquered it [for you]" (John 16:33, AMP).

Most Christians don't have any trouble believing the first part of that verse. They know all too well how many troubles surround them. But they're less certain about the last part. They haven't yet experienced for themselves exactly what Jesus meant when He said He had deprived those things of power to harm them.

Why not? Because they're still living as though they're part of the world. But, listen. Jesus said you and I are to be separated from the evils of this world. How? Through His Word (John 17:17)!

The truths in the Bible will separate you from the world. God's promises will set His victory into motion in your life. They will take you from trouble to triumph. Get to know them today!

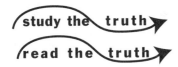

talk the truth **"I am born of God and am victorious over the world. My faith is my victory!" (1 John 5:4, AMP)**

study the truth **John 17:1-17**

read the truth **Proverbs 25,26,27; Psalms 12,13**

Gloria

August 28

ONE SPIRITUAL "DO"

"If anyone does not remain in me, he is like a branch that is thrown away and withers."

JOHN 15:6

If I were to ask you to make a list of a hundred things you need to do to please God today, you could do it, couldn't you? In fact, you probably know so many spiritual "do's" and "don'ts" that you'd hardly know where to start.

But you can relax. I'm not going to suggest you make a list. Instead, I'll help you simplify things by giving you only one spiritual "do": *Remain in Jesus.*

The one thing you're responsible for is your relationship with Him. If you keep a close relationship with Him, everything else will be all right.

"But I'm facing some big problems. My life's so rushed I don't know whether I'm coming or going. I can't afford to spend time with God today."

You can't afford not to! You need to keep your relationship with the Lord going especially when things are tough. I know that's not always easy to do. It's tempting to spend your time trying to fix the problem.

That's what Satan wants. That's the reason he sent that trouble in the first place—to keep you from spending time with God, to draw your attention away from your relationship with Him.

Don't fall into Satan's trap. Instead, find ways to keep your thoughts on the Lord. Read your Bible and pray in the morning and evening. Put some scriptures on your bathroom mirror or in your locker or in your backpack. Listen to some teaching tapes or Christian music on the way to school. Just be creative and find ways to keep your mind on His Word. When you do, you'll find it easier to remain in Him and cut that trouble down to size!

talk the truth

"I remain in Christ and He remains in me." (John 15:4)

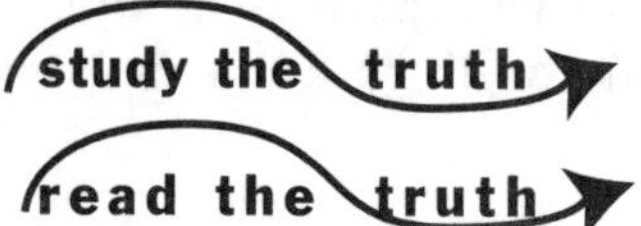
study the truth
read the truth

Philippians 3:1-11

Proverbs 28,29; Psalm 14

YOU HOLD THE KEY

"I will give you the keys of the kingdom of heaven; whatever you bind on earth will be bound in heaven, and whatever you loose on earth will be loosed in heaven."

MATTHEW 16:19

The heaven Jesus was talking about in the verse above isn't the heaven where God resides. He was talking about the battle zone, about the place in the atmosphere where Satan's forces are operating.

He was telling us that God has given us power to bind the wicked spirits in heavenly places and to loose God's angels to work for us.

Philippians 2:9-10 says, "God...gave him the name that is above every name, that at the name of Jesus every knee should bow, in heaven and on earth and under the earth." That covers it all!

As Christians, we have total authority over Satan's powers. It's time we realized how important we are to world affairs. Since the day Jesus gave us the Great Commission, the life or death of the world has been in the hands of the Church. We are the ones who have Jesus' mighty Name and the awesome strength of His Word to bring life to the world. We are the ones whose prayers can change this world—from our governments to our cities to our schools.

It's up to you and me to begin to pray right now. Let's put our angels to work. Let's bind Satan's forces. Remember that Jesus Christ is our Lord and He's given us His power. And that alone is enough to change the face of the earth.

"I have the keys of the kingdom of heaven. Whatever I bind on earth is bound in heaven, and whatever I loose on earth is loosed in heaven." (Matthew 16:19)

study the truth **Acts 4:1-14**

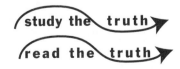

read the truth **Proverbs 30,31; Psalm 15**

August 30

PURE SPIRITUAL POWER

"But the fruit of the spirit is love, joy, peace, patience, kindness, goodness, faithfulness, gentleness and self-control."

GALATIANS 5:22,23

So many Christians don't realize that the fruit of the spirit are more than just good qualities to improve their personalities—they're pure spiritual power!

Love is so powerful, the scripture says, that it never fails. Patience is so powerful it can't be stopped. Self-control is so powerful it can overrule all the desires of your old life.

The fruit of the spirit are not weak; they're strong. So strong that all the evil spirits of hell can't stop them. So strong that if you'll let them flow out of you, they'll correct the problems in your life. They'll keep you steady when all the people around you are falling down. They'll keep you on your feet when troubles come.

We are living in dangerous days. There's only one way you can make it through in victory. You must begin to release the powerful fruit of the spirit God has placed inside you.

Let them come out when you're standing on God's promises for healing from the flu...or when you're studying for a final...or even when you're just standing in the lunch line. Practice love, joy, peace, patience and all the rest of the fruit. Believe me, if you're a Christian, they're there. Learn to let them show, and as 2 Peter 1:10 promised, you shall never fall!

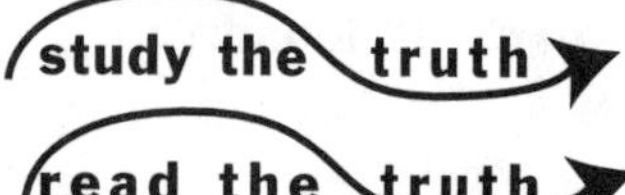
talk the truth
study the truth
read the truth

talk the truth: **"I live by the fruit of the spirit. The spiritual forces of love, joy, peace, patience, kindness, goodness, faithfulness, gentleness and self-control are alive in me." (Galatians 5:22,23)**

study the truth: **2 Peter 1:1-10**

read the truth: **Ecclesiastes 1,2; Psalm 16**

PUT YOUR SPIRIT IN CHARGE

"So too the (Holy) Spirit comes to our aid and bears us up in our weakness; for we do not know what prayer to offer...but the Spirit Himself...pleads in our behalf with unspeakable yearnings and groanings too deep for utterance."

ROMANS 8:26, AMP

As long as you live on this earth, you will have a weakness. What is it? The body you live in. It's a body that can be influenced by the world around you.

Your reborn spirit doesn't want to sin. It wants to completely obey God. But your old nature does tempt you to sin.

Does that mean you're doomed to a life of failure till Jesus comes?

No! It means you need to strengthen your spirit until it rules your body. Praying in the spirit gives you the strength you need. It causes your spirit to rise up and take charge. Just like using barbells strengthens your arms, praying in other tongues strengthens your spirit. You see, your spirit is more powerful than old sinful habits, and as you strengthen it, those old habits will simply have to step aside. Most Christians don't understand that. They'll come face to face with some sin, and instead of conquering it by praying in tongues, they'll keep struggling to overcome. So they end up failing again and again.

If you're caught in that cycle, take heart! God knows your weakness and He's given you a way to overcome it. He's given you the ability to pray in tongues *plus* you can speak God's Word. No matter how badly you're failing in everything else, you can do those two things!

Be warned though, Satan will try to talk you out of it. He knows that once you learn how to bring yourself in line, he'll have no way to get in.

But you can beat him today. Make a decision to follow the command God gives in Jude 20 and "build yourselves up in your most holy faith and pray in the Holy Spirit."

talk the truth

"The Holy Spirit comes to my aid and helps me in my weakness." (Romans 8:26, AMP)

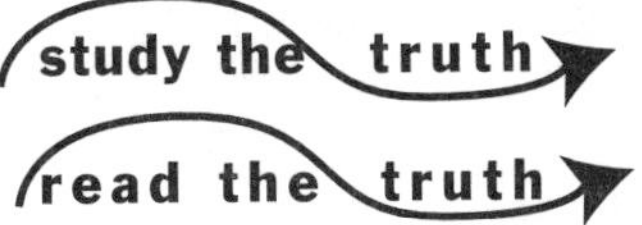
study the truth
read the truth

Romans 8:14-32

Ecclesiastes 3,4; Psalm 17

September 1

Kenneth

PERSISTENCE GETS RESULTS

"I tell you, although he will not get up and supply him anything because he is his friend, yet because of his shameless persistence and insistence, he will get up and give him as much as he needs."

Luke 11:8, AMP

If, as God tells us in 1 Timothy 2:4, it's His desire for everyone to be saved, why aren't we seeing masses of people becoming Christians every day? Why aren't our schools on fire for Jesus? Why aren't the *gangs* out there witnessing? Have you ever wondered that?

I have...and as I've asked God about it, I've come to realize that, many times, it's because those of us who have already made Jesus our Lord don't pray persistently for those who haven't. Instead of persevering—staying before the Father, praying for them to receive the bread of salvation—like the man in Luke 11:8 did for his friend, when we don't see immediate results, we give up.

What we don't realize is this: Persistence is the key to success in prayer!

Why? It's not because you have to change God's mind. He never changes. His mind's made up. He wants everyone to make Jesus their Lord. The reason you have to persist in prayer is to put pressure on the demonic forces that are trying to keep what God desires from being accomplished. Those forces must be broken down through prayer so that the blinders are removed from the eyes of those you're praying for.

You see, God will not go against the will of any person. But He will move through your intercessory prayer to show Himself to them. Through your persistent prayers, He will show them how much they need Him.

If you're sitting around waiting on God to save your parents or your relatives or your best friend...stop sitting around! Get busy praying for them. Be persistent in prayer. Pray the prayer in Ephesians 1:16-23 for them, refusing to give up until they make Jesus Lord of their lives.

Jesus has already laid down His life so that they can become a Christian. The question is, will you?

talk the truth

"I am persistent and insistent, therefore I have success." (Luke 11:8, AMP)

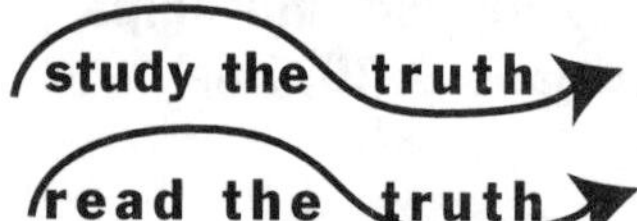
study the truth
read the truth

Luke 11:1-10

Ecclesiastes 5,6; Psalm 18

GO FOR REVELATION KNOWLEDGE

"Grace and peace be yours in abundance through the knowledge of God and of Jesus our Lord."

2 Peter 1:2

If you were to look up the Greek word that's translated "knowledge" in the scripture to the right, you'd find out that it means more than just mentally understanding something. It's actually a precise knowledge that's been revealed directly to your heart by the Holy Spirit. I call it *revelation knowledge.*

The lack of that kind of knowledge has caused more faith failures than anything else I know. That's because most Christians believe the Bible with their minds, but they haven't thought about it enough for it to "light up" in their hearts. If they had, it would absolutely change their lives.

I know a widow who got hold of revelation knowledge one afternoon. She'd been focusing on the scriptures that say if you're a widow, God has become the provider and leader of your household.

She'd been feeling sorry for herself, but when she realized God was the head of her household, she started talking to Him like she would a husband.

"Lord, the plumbing in this house is pitiful. Will You please get it fixed?" she asked Him. From that moment on, she never had any more trouble with her plumbing.

If you need something from God, determine right now that you will do what that widow did. Determine to keep His Word in front of you until you receive revelation knowledge of Jesus as your healer or your rescuer or your tutor—whatever you need Him to be. Don't settle for a slight understanding of Him. Go for *revelation knowledge!*

talk the truth

"Grace and peace are mine through the revelation knowledge of God and Jesus." (2 Peter 1:2)

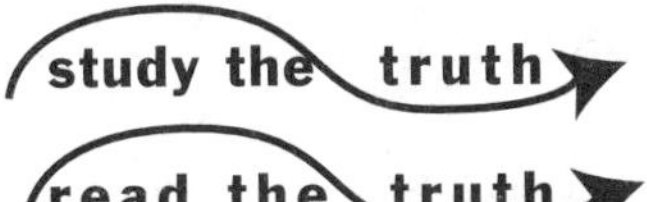
study the truth
read the truth

Psalm 1

Ecclesiastes 7,8; Psalm 19

September 3

Kenneth

GOD'S COUNTRY

"What is impossible with men is possible with God."

LUKE 18:27

Right now we're standing face to face with situations in our nations that need to be changed. Some of those situations look totally impossible. But they're not. Because God is in control of your country.

Looking at the United States, for instance, you'll see that He's the One Who brought it into existence. He had a special purpose for it. He needed a country where the gospel could be preached freely and not silenced.

It was God Himself Who stirred the heart and mind of Christopher Columbus and planted within him the dream of charting a new course to the West. Columbus said so in his own journals. He wrote, "It was the Lord who put into my mind—I could feel His hand upon me—the fact that I could sail from here to the Indies. All who heard of my project rejected it with laughter, ridiculing me. There's no question that the inspiration was from the Holy Spirit because He comforted me with rays of marvelous inspiration from the Holy Scriptures."

Who brought Christopher Columbus to America? God brought him. The United States is God's nation. He raised it up, and it won't be taken away from Him. And your country belongs to Him, too!

So the next time you're tempted to look at situations in your country as impossible, remember Who's in control. The impossible is possible with God!

talk the truth

"What is impossible to me is possible with God." (Luke 18:27)

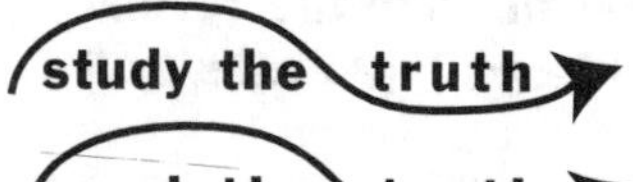
study the truth
read the truth

Psalm 106

Ecclesiastes 9,10,11; Psalms 20,21

LET GOD BE GLORIFIED

"Jesus...had compassion...and healed their sick. Great crowds came to him, bringing the lame, the blind, the crippled, the mute and many others, and laid them at his feet; and he healed them. The people were amazed when they saw the mute speaking, the crippled made well, the lame walking and the blind seeing. And they praised the God of Israel."

MATTHEW 14:14; 15:30,31

Tradition says God gets glory when we go through the pain of sickness and disease. But that's not what the Bible says. It says God gets glory when the blind see and the lame walk!

In India or Africa where many people haven't been taught those kinds of traditions, when someone stands up and announces, "I come to you as a messenger from God," people believe what he has to say. When they hear that Jesus shed His blood for them and that God has sent His messenger to tell them that He'll rescue them from sin and sickness, they get excited. They don't argue with the Bible. So you know what happens?

They begin to get healed. People start throwing away their crutches and flinging off their bandages!

When we learn to hear God's promises like that, the same thing will happen to us. God doesn't have favorites. His Word works for everyone. It's how we receive it that makes the difference!

talk the truth

"I hear God's promises with an open heart—and I believe them by faith." (Matthew 14:14; 15:30,31)

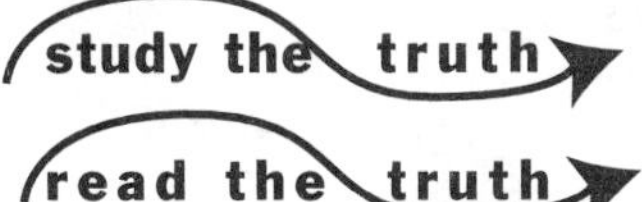
study the truth
read the truth

Acts 17:1-11

Ecclesiastes 12; Song of Solomon 1; Psalm 22

Kenneth

September 5

START SPEAKING FAITH NOW

"Out of the overflow of the heart the mouth speaks. The good man brings good things out of the good stored up in him, and the evil man brings evil things out of the evil stored up in him."

MATTHEW 12:34,35

Words won't work without faith any more than faith will work without words! It takes them both to put the law of faith in motion.

Not realizing that, many Christians will speak words of doubt and unbelief, then jump up one day and say a couple of faith words and expect mountains to move—but they don't. Why not?

Because as Matthew 12:34-35 says, it's the words that come from the heart that produce results. The person who just speaks a couple of words in faith now and then isn't speaking them from what's in his heart, so they're not effective.

Does that mean you shouldn't start speaking words of faith until you're sure you have the faith to back them?

No! Speaking faith-filled words is good spiritual exercise. If you want to receive healing by faith, for example, think about and speak what the Bible says about healing. Instead of talking about how miserable you feel, quote Isaiah 53:5. Say, *"Jesus was pierced for my transgressions. He was bruised for my iniquities. The punishment that brought me peace was upon him, and by his wounds I was healed!"*

If you'll continue to think about those words, and continue to say them, the truth in them will begin to sink in. They'll take root in your heart and begin to grow. And eventually you really will be speaking from what's in your heart.

When that happens, it won't matter what the circumstances look like. You'll know you have what you've been believing for, and Satan himself won't be able to talk you out of it. You'll cross the line from hope to faith, and you'll start seeing those mountains move!

talk the truth **"I have the spirit of faith. I speak what I believe." (Matthew 12:34,35)**

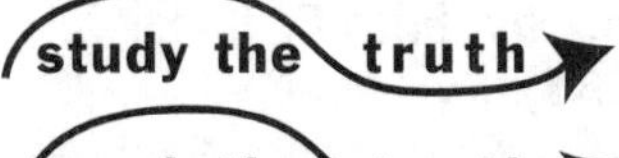
study the truth
read the truth

Matthew 12:33-37

Song of Solomon 2,3; Psalm 23

UNDER PRESSURE? GIVE!

> ***"Do not be deceived: God cannot be mocked. A man reaps what he sows."***
>
> **Galatians 6:7**

If you feel like you're under pressure these days, you're not alone. Satan is pressuring us mentally, financially, emotionally, socially and every other way he can. The pressure has become so great that no one knows what to do...but Jesus does! He says we can give our way out from under any pressure Satan brings.

So, when Satan puts you under pressure, go to Jesus and let Him tell you how and where to give. If you'll do it, it will release you from the pressure Satan's been putting on you.

I've seen it happen. When Jerry Savelle first began to work for our ministry, he only had one suit and one shirt with a pair of slacks to his name. He wore one, then the other, night after night to every service we held. He didn't even have the money to *think* about buying another suit. I'm telling you, he was under pressure for clothes!

Then he found out about giving and receiving. So, he went downtown in the city where we were in a meeting and found a fellow on the street who needed clothes and gave him some. Right after that, people started giving Jerry clothes. It started in that meeting and they've been doing it ever since. Today, there are many preachers around the world wearing Jerry Savelle's suits!

If Satan's pressuring you, don't panic...give! Give your time to help someone else understand biology or English. Give your money to someone who usually doesn't get anything "extra." Give some of your clothes to someone who really needs them. You don't even have to let them know that it was you who gave...God will know.

Then when your needs are met, you can laugh and say, "Hey, Satan, who's feeling the pressure now?"

talk the truth **"What I plant, I will harvest." (Galatians 6:7)**

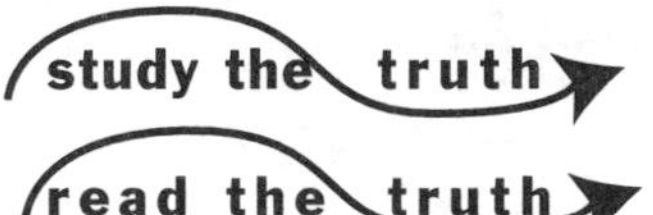

Mark 4:1-20

read the truth **Song of Solomon 4,5; Psalm 24**

Kenneth

September 7

STRIKE IT RICH

"If you belong to Christ, then you are Abraham's seed, and heirs according to the promise."

GALATIANS 3:29

Lack hung around me for years. But I remember the day I decided I wasn't going to live like that anymore. I was reading in the Bible where it says that through Jesus, the blessings given to Abraham are now available to Christians (Galatians 3:14). Then I read verse 29, which says, "You belong to Christ. So you are Abraham's descendants. You get all of God's blessings because of the promise that God made to Abraham." Suddenly the truth hit me. I got so excited I could hardly stand it.

I turned back over to Deuteronomy 28 and—line by line—I read the blessings God promised Abraham...the blessings the Bible says I've inherited: Blessed in the city, blessed in the country. Blessed going out, blessed coming in. Blessed in your barns, blessed in your fields, blessed in all the works of your hands...Man, I had struck it rich!

I'd been going to school in Tulsa, Oklahoma, and I was living in a little house no one would want to live in. But when I read those promises in the Bible, I saw the light. I realized God *already* had saved me from poverty.

Well, that afternoon in my back bedroom, I took my Bible in my hand and I said: "I want to announce to God, Jesus and all the angels of heaven, to all the evil spirits of hell and to anyone else who cares anything about hearing it, that from this day forward my needs are met according to God's glorious riches in Jesus."

I told God, "I'm standing on Your Word, and I'm looking to You to take care of me. I'll never ask a man for a dollar."

That was many years ago—and I've never had to ask anyone for a cent. You know why? Because that decision connected me to God's power. And it'll do the same for you!

talk the truth **"I belong to Christ and am Abraham's seed. His blessings are mine." (Galatians 3:29)**

study the truth **Deuteronomy 28:1-13**

read the truth **Song of Solomon 6,7; Psalm 25**

PLANT A SEED AND WATCH IT GROW!

Jesus compares the workings of God's kingdom to planting seeds in the earth. "When the seed is planted," He said, "it grows...."

Notice He didn't say that it would only grow once in a while or only if God wanted it to grow. He said, "It grows." Period.

God's laws always work the same—perfectly. If you have good earth, good seed and good water, you will have growth. Period.

So, if you're facing a need, don't panic...plant a seed!

That seed may take the form of time, love, money, a thoughtful note, or even taking the time to mow someone's yard for them. But, no matter what it is, make sure you put life in it by giving it in faith. Say, *"Lord, as I bring You this, I bring myself. I give myself to You—spirit, soul and body."* Then plant it. You can rest assured—it will grow up and become greater!

"Again he said, 'What shall we say the kingdom of God is like, or what parable shall we use to describe it? It is like a mustard seed, which is the smallest seed you plant in the ground. Yet when planted, it grows and becomes the largest of all garden plants, with such big branches that the birds of the air can perch in its shade.'"

MARK 4:30-32

talk the truth

"When I plant a seed, it grows." (Mark 4:30-32)

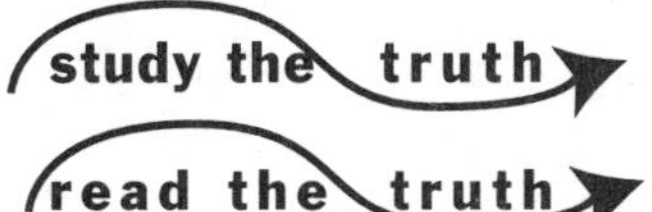
study the truth
read the truth

Genesis 1:11-31

Song of Solomon 8; Isaiah 1; Psalm 26

September 9

Gloria

EXERCISE YOUR RIGHTS

"He was pierced for our transgressions, he was crushed for our iniquities; the punishment that brought us peace was upon him, and by his wounds we are healed."

ISAIAH 53:5

Jesus came to earth and gave Himself as a sacrifice for sin in order to buy back for you everything that Adam lost. He came to destroy all the works of Satan—sickness and disease included. Once you receive Him as Lord of your life, all the rights and privileges God originally intended you to have (like love, health and courage) are restored.

But you are the one who has to exercise those rights and privileges!

You see, even though Jesus has taken away Satan's authority, even though Satan has no legal right to kill or steal from you, he will do it anyway...as long as you let him get away with it.

You must enforce his defeat by speaking God's Word in faith. In Jesus' Name, demand that sickness and disease leave you. Refuse to back off. Resist Satan with all you've got. He might fight you for a while, but he will have to leave!

talk the truth

"I exercise the rights and privileges God has given me by speaking the Word in faith." (Isaiah 53:5)

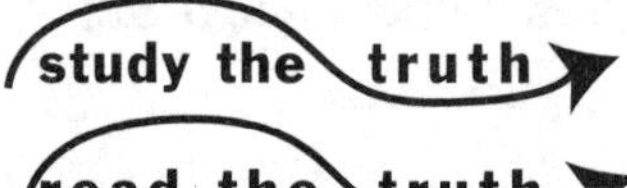
study the truth
read the truth

Matthew 8:1-17

Isaiah 2,3; Psalm 27

HIS STILL, SMALL VOICE

"As for you, the anointing you received from him [God] remains in you, and you do not need anyone to teach you. But as his anointing teaches you about all things and as that anointing is real, not counterfeit...."

1 John 2:27

Have you ever noticed that you sometimes know certain things the Bible talks about even before you see what it actually says about them? That's because the Holy Spirit is inside you teaching you the truth. *I need to forgive that person,* you'll think, or *I need to stop saying those unkind things.*

As you become more aware of the Holy Spirit in your life, you'll be quicker to hear and obey Him. You'll actually get in the habit of allowing the Holy Spirit to show you God's plan for your life, step by step.

One of the first things the Spirit said to me when I began to listen was, *Spend more time in prayer.* After I did that, He showed it to me in His Word (Matthew 26:40). Since then, I have talked with people from all over the world who are hearing the same thing. Other young men and women like you are hearing the Holy Spirit direct them to more prayer. Now that doesn't mean spending long hours cooped up in a closet. It means communicating with God all day long as you tune your ear to His still, small voice within you.

Think about how different your life would be if you knew God's insight into every situation! Honor Him and ask Him to guide you in everything you do. He's ready to speak to you.

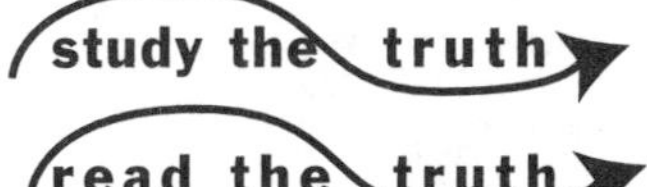

"God's anointing is in me. It teaches me all things." (1 John 2:27)

study the truth **John 15:1-15**

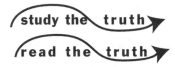

read the truth **Isaiah 4,5,6; Psalms 28,29**

September 11

DON'T BE DISTURBED

"The Lord foils the plans of the nations; he thwarts the purposes of the peoples."

PSALM 33:10

You may be facing trouble today that's caused by people who want to hurt you in some way. They may be trying to steal your ideas, your friends or even your enthusiasm for following God. If so, I have a word of encouragement for you. According to Psalm 33:10, God will stop the plans of those people.

Remember this: When you make God your security in the troubled times, no one can overcome you. No matter how powerful they are, the odds are in your favor because you trust in the Lord. They may think they have an edge over you, but God is on your side, and that gives you the advantage!

Don't worry—you will eventually triumph over this trouble. Meanwhile, God's wisdom will keep you rock solid when all the world around you is shaking.

Don't let the temporary successes of the troublemaker disturb you. Instead, "Consider the blameless, observe the upright; there is a future for the man of peace" (Psalm 37:37).

talk the truth

"I consider the blameless and observe the upright. There is a future for me as I follow after peace." (Psalm 37:37)

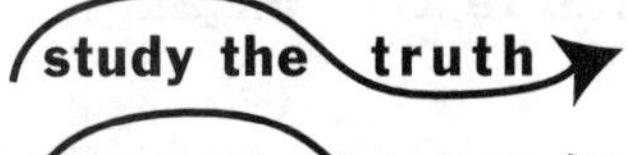
study the truth

Psalm 33:1-10

read the truth

Isaiah 7,8; Psalm 30

CHANGE THE IMAGE

"For in this hope we were saved. But hope that is seen is no hope at all. Who hopes for what he already has? But if we hope for what we do not yet have, we wait for it patiently."

ROMANS 8:24,25

According to Romans, hope is actually looking at something that you can't see. How do you do that? You do it by looking at God's promises in the Bible until a picture is formed with the eyes of your spirit.

For example, one of the hardest things I ever had to do was face the fact that I saw myself as fat...that's the image I had of myself. It didn't matter how hard I tried to change, it wouldn't go away. I was always on a diet. I must have lost (and regained) hundreds of pounds over the years.

I finally had to admit that as long as the image I had of myself was fat, I would be fat. Remember, it's faith that changes things, and without the image of hope to build on, faith can't work.

So I decided to fast for seven days. I searched my Bible for every scripture I could find on food and eating. I concentrated on those scriptures and prayed in the spirit for seven full days. What was I doing? I was creating a different picture inside of me of who I was.

This isn't something you can do overnight. It takes time. Especially if the image you're changing has been there for years. But you can do it. Open your Bible today and begin to change the images inside you. Create a picture of hope and success in your heart and your faith will build on it!

talk the truth **"I patiently wait for what I do not have. I hope and expect it to come." (Romans 8:24,25)**

study the truth **Romans 4:16-21**

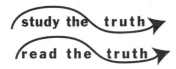

read the truth **Isaiah 9,10; Psalm 31**

September 13

Kenneth

REAL INTERCESSION

"He saw that there was no man, and wondered that there was no intercessor [no one to intervene on behalf of truth and right]."

ISAIAH 59:16, AMP

When someone hurts us, naturally, we want to strike back and ask God to slug 'em good. But that's not what God wants us to do.

I realized that one time when some relatives of mine got robbed. "Lord," I began to ask, "why did You let that happen? Why didn't You just knock that thief upside the head when he tried to do that?"

Suddenly, God enabled me to back up from that situation and see it the way He saw it. Then I knew the answer to my question almost as quickly as I had asked it. It was because of His mercy.

Think about that the next time someone does you wrong. Instead of asking God to knock that person upside the head (like I did), consider the fact that—as bad as he may be—that person may have family somewhere who's praying for him to make Jesus his Lord. Stop and remember that God loved him enough to die for him. He wants to help him—not punish him.

Then you can begin to pray for him instead of against him. You can go to the Lord and pray for mercy for him, and you can go up against Satan on his behalf. That's real prayer, and the forces of darkness have absolutely no defense against it.

The Lord is looking for young people who are bold enough and committed enough to do that. Dare to be one of them. When you're tempted to slug someone, dare to change his life instead. You'll see that as you do, God will take care of you, too.

talk the truth

"I am an intercessor—I intervene on behalf of truth and right." (Isaiah 59:16, AMP)

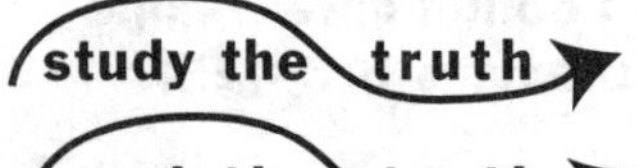
study the truth
read the truth

Luke 6:27-36

Isaiah 11,12; Psalm 32

TAKE CORRECTION

"Reprove not a scorner, lest he hate you; reprove a wise man, and he will love you. Give instruction to a wise man, and he will be yet wiser; teach a righteous man...and he will increase in learning."

Proverbs 9:8,9, AMP

There is one thing you can do that will increase your spiritual growth more than almost any other thing: learn to take correction—from the Holy Spirit and from His people.

So few Christians seem to be able to do that. When their home group leader or youth pastor preaches on something they already have straightened out in their life, they think he's great. They like him because he makes them feel good. But the moment he stands up and begins to preach about something they're doing wrong, they take offense. (Sometimes we do this with our parents, too!)

God says that's foolish. He says, in Proverbs 1:7, only fools hate correction.

So don't be like that. When your pastor, parents or a fellow Christian points out somewhere you've missed it, receive it thankfully. Instead of getting angry, examine yourself and say, *Is that right? Is that what the Bible says? Do I need to make a change there?*

If the answer to those questions is yes, then make the changes you need to make to get your life in line.

I know that's not easy. No one likes to be corrected. But if you'll make up your mind to receive that correction anyway—if you'll be willing to change—you'll be able to grow in spiritual things much more quickly and come out ahead every time.

talk the truth

"I receive correction and instruction and I grow wise. I receive teaching and increase in learning." (Proverbs 9:8,9, AMP)

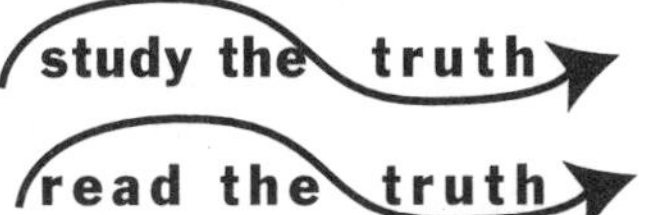
study the truth
read the truth

Proverbs 3:11-24

Isaiah 13,14; Psalm 33

September 15

HOW'S YOUR SPIRITUAL MAINTENANCE?

"The cares and anxieties of the world and distractions of the age, and the pleasure and delight and false glamour and deceitfulness of riches, and the craving and passionate desire for other things creep in and choke and suffocate the Word, and it becomes fruitless."

Mark 4:19, AMP

Did you know that some seemingly innocent things in your everyday life can hurt your spiritual life if you allow it?

A friend of mine said the Lord told her in prayer one day that this nation had become a nation of maintenance men. *You have so many things to maintain,* He told her. *You maintain your house. You maintain your car, your yard, your machines, your hair....*

It's true. You can become a maintainer of so many natural things that you don't have any time left to take care of your own spirit!

When you find yourself in that situation, it's time to simplify your life. I've had to learn that myself. Now when I'm considering something I think I need, I don't just count the cost in dollars and cents. I think about how much time it will take to maintain it. I check to see if I can spiritually afford it.

For instance, if you're looking at buying a new video game, ask yourself, *Will I spend time playing this that I usually spend studying the Bible?* Or if you're interested in trying out for cheerleading, or joining the band or the football team, ask yourself, *Will this take away my time with God?* Of course, there's nothing wrong with these things, but if they interfere with your relationship with your Father, it's time to re-evaluate.

Second Timothy 2:4 says don't get entangled in the affairs of this life. One thing I've learned over the last 30 years: Nothing is as important as spending time in prayer and in the Bible. Absolutely nothing in your life is as vital as that.

talk the truth

"I won't let cares, anxieties and distractions choke the Word out of my life." (Mark 4:19, AMP)

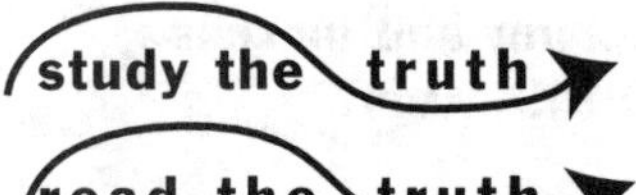
study the truth
read the truth

Mark 4:18-24

Isaiah 15,16; Psalm 34

September 16

STAND UP AND BE COUNTED

God commands us to pray for our nation and our leaders. It's vitally important that the right people be in office—we must see to it through prayer.

But having prayed, God expects us to *act*. If you're old enough and it's part of your country's selection process, register and vote—because elections are critical to the future of your nation. Then, don't wait until election time is upon you before you start asking God for whom to vote. Begin to pray now so that the news media and other voices cannot influence you and draw you in a direction away from what God wants. Pray so that you won't be influenced by natural reactions to cleverly designed commercials and ideas.

Remember: It's essential—no matter how old you are or what kind of selection process your country uses—that you start praying now for the current and future leaders of your country. Then, thank the Holy Spirit for giving you wisdom as you declare, in Jesus' Name, that your nation will have a God-ordained, God-led administration. Who knows—maybe God will call *you* to be a leader in your country someday!

"I urge, then, first of all, that requests, prayers, intercession and thanksgiving be made for everyone—for kings and all those in authority, that we may live peaceful and quiet lives in all godliness and holiness."

1 Timothy 2:1,2

talk the truth **"I make requests, pray, intercede and give thanks for my country's leaders." (1 Timothy 2:1,2)**

study the truth **1 Timothy 2:1-8**

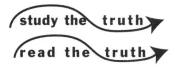

read the truth **Isaiah 17,18; Psalm 35**

Gloria

September 17

BE COURAGEOUS

"Be strong and very courageous. Be careful to obey all the law my servant Moses gave you; do not turn from it to the right or to the left, that you may be successful wherever you go."

JOSHUA 1:7

Living a life of faith takes courage. It takes courage to stand up in the face of sickness and declare you're healed by the wounds of Jesus. It takes courage to believe for prosperity and then give your last dime in the offering plate. There will be days when you'd rather pull the covers over your head and hide than take another stand against Satan. But you can't. Because if you want to keep living in victory, you have to fight again and again.

There's no way around it. Of course, some of God's people still try to find one. The Israelites, for example, thought their battles would be over when they crossed the Red Sea. So when they heard reports of ruthless warriors living in the Promised Land, they decided they couldn't face the fight. They lost courage.

But you know what? They still couldn't avoid that fight. When the time came for the next generation to enter the Promised Land, the ruthless warriors were still there! This time, however, the Israelites found the courage to face them with God's Word.

Their leader, Joshua, had obeyed God's instruction and kept that Word on his mind and in his heart day and night. He'd let it constantly remind him that God was on their side. And with God on their side, they couldn't be defeated!

If you want to fight the fight of faith to the finish, you'll have to do like Joshua did. You'll have to continually draw courage from the Bible. So make up your mind to do it. Let His Word change you from a coward to an overcomer!

talk the truth

"I am strong and very courageous. I obey God's Word and am successful wherever I go." (Joshua 1:7)

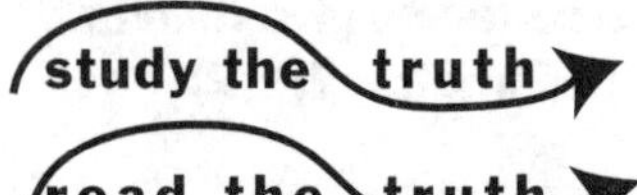
study the truth
read the truth

Joshua 1

Isaiah 19,20,21; Psalms 36,37

WHY DID GOD CREATE YOU?

Man is something really special. He is made in the image of God (Genesis 1:27). He is made to spend time with God.

Some people get the idea that God made man so He'd have someone to rule over. But God is love, and love needs someone to give to. That's why God made man—so He could give him His love.

God could have given His love to the angels, and He did that. But giving to angels didn't provide total fulfillment because angels aren't made in His image.

You're the same way. Let's say, for example, you have a puppy. You can spend time with that little pet, but then there comes a time when you need someone to talk to. There comes a time when you need to have real communication.

The reason you're like that is because you're created in God's image. That's how He is. He has a desire to spend time with someone like Himself.

Dare to believe you're something really special today—a one-of-a-kind creation made by God in His very own image. Dare to receive His love and dare to love Him back!

"What we have seen and [ourselves] heard we are also telling you, so that you too may realize and enjoy fellowship as partners and partakers with us. And [this] fellowship that we have (which is a distinguishing mark of Christians) is with the Father and with His Son Jesus Christ, the Messiah."

1 John 1:3, AMP

talk the truth

"I am created in God's own image." (Genesis 1:27)

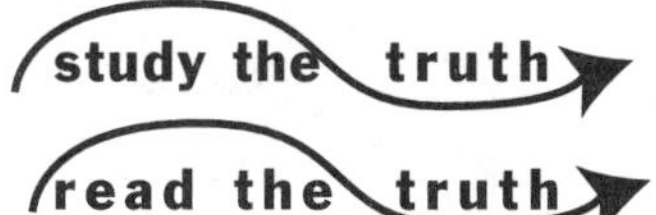
study the truth
read the truth

Genesis 1:26-31

Isaiah 22,23; Psalm 38

September 19

A WORD ABOUT ANGELS

"For he will command his angels concerning you to guard you in all your ways."

Psalm 91:11

It's time to set the record straight. Angels aren't kid stuff. They're not fat, little babies with long, blond hair and bows and arrows in their hands. Angels are big, strong warriors. They are real and powerful. And they are a vital part of your life as a Christian.

We see examples of what angels can do all through the Bible. For instance, when the Israelites were fleeing from Egypt with Pharaoh's army hot on their heels, the Bible tells us that suddenly the wheels on the Egyptians' chariots got fouled up. They just quit rolling!

Who do you think caused that? The angels! And they haven't retired. Angels are at work today just as much as they've always been.

A few years ago in one of Israel's major wars, the enemy had their guns trained on Israeli cities. Those guns were the finest military equipment money could buy. They had a range of at least 20 miles and were equipped with electronic gun sights for accuracy.

But something very odd happened. Every time they fired those guns at the Israelis, they either overshot or fell far short of their targets. We know there was nothing wrong with the guns because later the Israelis captured them and fired them back at the enemy with perfect success.

What happened? Angels, that's what!

That isn't just a fairy tale. That's a real-life example of the involvement of angels in the lives of God's people today. And, as a child of God, you have a right to expect God's angels to do the same kinds of things for you.

So, start expecting—His angels are ready to go to work for you!

talk the truth

"God commands His angels to guard me in all my ways." (Psalm 91:11)

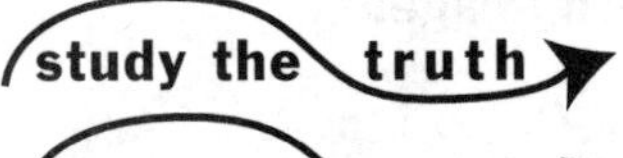
study the truth
read the truth

Acts 12:1-17

Isaiah 24,25; Psalm 39

TIME TO GET SERIOUS

"O God, you are my God, earnestly I seek you.... On my bed I remember you; I think of you through the watches of the night."

PSALM 63:1,6

If you want to live in divine health, there will be times when you'll need more than just reading the Bible for a few moments followed by a quick prayer to receive your healing.

I want to tell you, in very practical terms, what I would do if I were facing a severe sickness.

The moment I woke up in the morning, before I did anything else, I'd take Communion. I'd do it to remember Him—because if you're facing a serious attack of Satan, you need to remember all day and all night the victory Jesus has won for you. You need to think about Him until thoughts of Him push the thoughts of that sickness out of your mind. I'd say, "Lord, I give my body all day today to Your service. I receive Jesus' pure blood shed for me."

Then I'd put Satan in his place. I'd say, "Satan, you're not going to put any sickness and disease on me today. Regardless of how I feel, Jesus overcame this sickness when He was on the cross."

Then, all day long, I'd thank God for my healing. I'd find some teaching tapes that would fill my mind and my spirit with His Word, and I'd listen to them throughout the day. In the afternoon, I'd praise God and receive Communion again to remind myself that Jesus' blood was shed for me, that I'm part of God's family.

That night, before going to bed, I'd receive Communion again, then I'd praise God till I fell asleep. If I woke up in the night, I'd reach over, get my Bible and read healing scriptures. I'd make Satan sorry he woke me.

When Satan launches a serious attack against your body, don't mess around. Get serious with God's Word. Put yourself under its constant care and it will take good care of you.

talk the truth

"I take God's Word seriously. I put myself under the care of His promises and they take care of me." (Psalm 63:1,6)

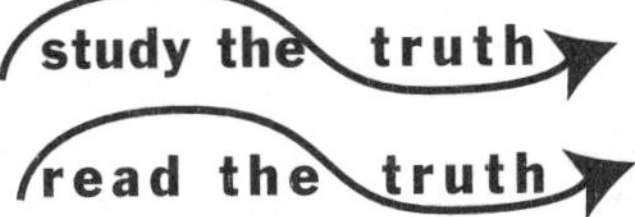
study the truth
read the truth

Hebrews 4:9-16

Isaiah 26,27; Psalm 40

September 21

UNITY OF FAITH

"It was he who gave some to be apostles, some to be prophets, some to be evangelists, and some to be pastors and teachers, to prepare God's people for works of service, so that the body of Christ may be built up until we all reach unity in the faith and in the knowledge of the Son of God and become mature, attaining to the whole measure of the fullness of Christ."

Ephesians 4:11-13

What this scripture means is simply this: If we're ever going to become a truly powerful Church, we have to grow up—together.

It won't be enough for just a few of us to grow up on our own and say, "Too bad" about everyone else. It doesn't work that way. We're a part of each other. The Bible calls us one body...the Body of Christ.

Let me give you an example of what I mean. When I began teaching about how God wants us to live well in every area of life, people started giving me a hard time. Preachers started calling me and chewing me out because I wouldn't borrow money and things like that. Finally, one day in prayer God said to me, *Don't teach on the laws of prosperity anymore until I tell you to.*

"Why not?" I asked.

There's strife in the camp, He told me.

We're not each out here on our own. I can't do anything without affecting you. You can't do anything without affecting me. We're joined together by God and held together by one another (Ephesians 4:16). We can only grow together!

So learn to walk in love. Refuse to be divided. Read your Bible daily and share with others what you find, so we can all grow up to be all God has created us to be.

talk the truth

"I speak the truth in love and I am in unity with God's people. I am maturing in Christ." (Ephesians 4:11-13)

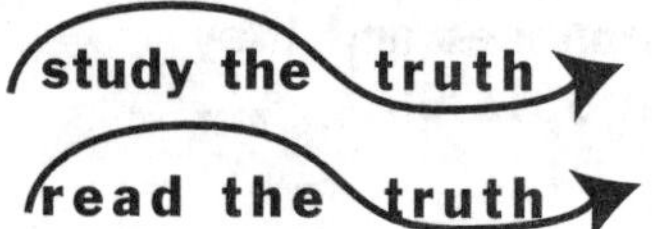
study the truth
read the truth

1 Corinthians 12:13-28

Isaiah 28,29; Psalm 41

A LITTLE EVERY DAY

"What is the kingdom of God like? What shall I compare it to? It is like a mustard seed, which a man took and planted in his garden. It grew and became a tree, and the birds of the air perched in its branches."

LUKE 13:18,19

If you want to grow in God, you will have to do it just like a seed. So how does a seed grow? All at once? No, it grows a little all the time, until it becomes all it was created to be.

Spiritually, most of us don't let it work that way. We read the Bible and pray very hard for a few days and then quit. Then, when some disaster comes, we quickly pray and open our Bible again, realizing that we're just not as strong as we should be.

There's no such thing as an overnight success when it comes to Christianity. Real strength and growth comes as you *constantly* make God's Word your first priority. Not just when you want to or when you feel like it, but constantly—like the seed—a little all the time.

A man once came up to me and said, "Man, your ministry just took off overnight, didn't it?"

"If it did," I answered, "it was certainly the longest night of my life!"

From his perspective, success came quickly for me. That's because he didn't see me during all those hours, weeks, months and years I spent studying, reading and applying the Bible to my life. He didn't see the daily growth behind that success. He just saw the results.

Make up your mind to begin growing a little at a time, each day. Determine to start putting God's Word in your heart consistently.

Live by standing on the truth in the Bible—no matter what comes or how you feel. Eventually, your faith will be bigger than you ever dreamed.

talk the truth

"I continue to put God's Word in my heart. I let it grow in me." (Luke 13:18,19)

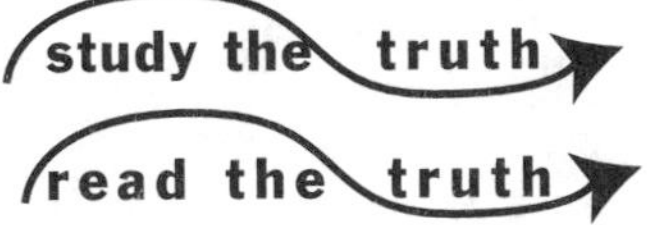
study the truth
read the truth

Luke 13:18-21

Isaiah 30,31; Psalm 42

September 23

Gloria

REKINDLE THE FIRE

"Come near to God and he will come near to you."

JAMES 4:8

Remember when you first made Jesus your Lord and you were so excited? Remember when you could hardly wait to read the next chapter in your Bible or tell your friends about Jesus? There was only one way to describe you—*you were on fire for God!*

When Ken and I first heard about faith, we were like that. We were so on fire that nothing else in the world even interested us. We learned that we could trust God's Word just like we could trust the word of a close friend, and we were hungry to find out everything He had promised us.

Back then, it seemed like all I did was study the Bible, read books about faith and listen to tapes. I was dedicated. All my interest was in God alone.

But slowly that changed. At first I didn't even realize it was happening. Then the Holy Spirit showed me that I had let the fire die down. I still read the Bible, but I had lost my enthusiasm.

If you've had this same experience, I want to tell you how to get the fire back. It worked for me and it will work for you.

The Bible says if you come near to God, He will come near to you (James 4:8). In order to do that, you will first have to drop the things that are stealing your time from studying the Bible. Maybe it's watching TV, reading romance novels or playing video games. If you will spend less time with those things and give more attention to the things of God, soon your desire for God will increase. You get a desire for whatever you spend your time doing.

Also, start building yourself up by praying in tongues whenever you can. And be sure to act on everything God says to you. Before long that spark that's been flickering in your spirit will grow into a raging fire again!

talk the truth **"As I come near to God, He comes near to me." (James 4:8)**

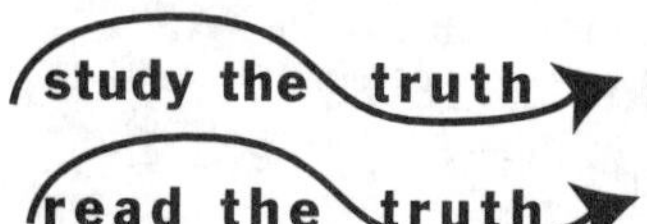
study the truth
read the truth

Revelation 3:13-22

Isaiah 32,33; Psalm 43

Gloria

September 24

GOD DESIRES YOUR FREEDOM

"Now the Lord is the Spirit, and where the Spirit of the Lord is, there is freedom."

2 CORINTHIANS 3:17

Freedom. If you could put God's ultimate desire into one word, that would be it. God wants people to be free—from sin and sickness, poverty and every other trouble.

That freedom is what Jesus came to provide. He said, "The Spirit of the Lord is on me, because he has anointed me to preach good news to the poor. He has sent me to proclaim freedom for the prisoners and recovery of sight for the blind, to release the oppressed" (Luke 4:18). That's what He trained His disciples to do. And if you're a Christian, that's what He wants you to do too!

Two thousand years ago, Jesus' life was a perfect picture of what God wanted to happen on earth—and it still is! That's why He left instructions for us to go and do what He did. That's why He sent the Holy Spirit to give us the power to do those things.

Jesus still wants to accomplish what God wants on earth—but He does it through *us.* We need to start bringing God's freedom to the world. It's time to quit questioning what God wants and start sharing it instead. He said the works that He did we would do—and even greater works (John 14:12). It's time for us to take up where Jesus left off and give freedom to everyone we meet!

talk the truth

"I have freedom because the Spirit of the Lord lives in me." (2 Corinthians 3:17)

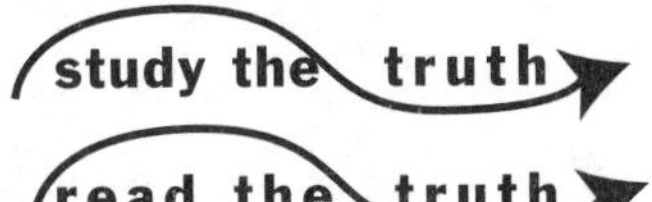
study the truth
read the truth

Isaiah 61:1-11

Isaiah 34,35,36; Psalms 44,45

Gloria

September 25

MOVE CLOSER EVERY DAY

"I am the vine; you are the branches. If a man remains in me and I in him, he will bear much fruit; apart from me you can do nothing."

JOHN 15:5

Remaining in Jesus isn't something that automatically comes to us. It's a lifestyle that involves discipline and effort.

We have to choose to give ourselves to Him—to give Him more attention than anything else. If we want to grow spiritually, we'll have to spend the time it takes to know Him.

That's not something we can do "off and on" either. We must do it every day. For the moment we stop moving closer to Jesus, we always start drifting away.

As you well know, in this world you're surrounded by ungodliness. When you purposely spend time in daily prayer and the Bible, your body and your mind will not give in to the pressures around you and to the world's way.

Right now, make a decision to make the things of God top priority in your life. Keep what the Bible says on your mind with everything you do. Listen to His promises through teaching tapes and music. Listen when you wake up, throughout the day and before you go to sleep. Take every opportunity to fill yourself with His Word...remain in Him today!

"I remain in Jesus and He remains in me. Apart from Him I can do nothing, but through Him I can do all things because He gives me strength." (John 15:5; Philippians 4:13)

study the truth — **John 15:1-11**

read the truth — **Isaiah 37,38; Psalm 46**

LET HIM OUT

When you made Jesus the Lord of your life, you became what the Bible calls a "new creature" (2 Corinthians 5:17). Inside, you're not the same person you were before. God's nature was born inside you. But it's not enough for you just to have that new nature on the inside. You have to let it take over the outside as well.

Don't expect that to happen automatically. You have to make a decision to make your body obey the new nature within you. You must determine to do what Romans 6:12 says and "do not let sin reign in your mortal body."

I know it sounds tough to keep yourself from sin, but remember, you're not in this alone. You have the Holy Spirit to help you to carry out that decision. Listen to His voice inside you, showing you what's right and wrong. He's there to strengthen you. He gives you the power to kick sin out of your life.

Decide to dedicate your body to Him today—and let that new creature that's on the inside of you begin to come out!

"Therefore, I urge you, brothers, in view of God's mercy, to offer your bodies as living sacrifices, holy and pleasing to God—this is your spiritual act of worship."

ROMANS 12:1

talk the truth

"I offer my body as a living sacrifice, holy and pleasing to God." (Romans 12:1)

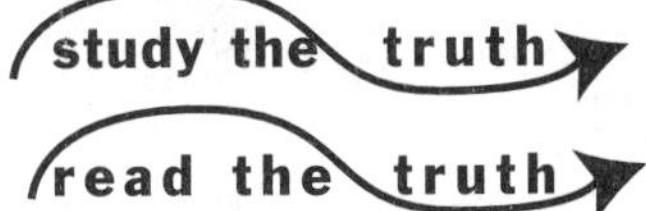
study the truth
read the truth

Romans 6:12-23

Isaiah 39,40; Psalm 47

September 27

SPIRITUAL ARMOR FOR SPIRITUAL WAR

"For our struggle is not against flesh and blood, but against the rulers, against the authorities, against the powers of this dark world and against the spiritual forces of evil in the heavenly realms."

EPHESIANS 6:12

Most of us don't know the first thing about fighting the kind of war the scripture to the left refers to. For, as Ephesians 6:10-12 says, it's not a battle of flesh and blood, but of the spirit.

Most of the time we never even realize where the enemy's attacks actually come from. We blame circumstances and people, and waste our energy fighting natural conditions instead of supernatural causes.

We need to wake up to the warfare that's going on in the spiritual realm!

We can get a glimpse of it in Daniel 10:12-20. There, we find that Daniel had been fasting and praying for 21 days, waiting for a message from the Lord. Then an angel appeared to him 21 days later with the answer. What took him so long? He was fighting the enemy in the heavens.

That confuses some people. They say, "Satan's fighting in heaven? I thought God was in heaven!" What they don't understand is that the Bible teaches there are three different areas called heaven:

1. The heaven where God resides
2. The stellar heavens (what we call "outer space")
3. The heavens around this earth (the atmosphere)

This last heaven—earth's atmosphere—is where spiritual warfare takes place. (That's why Ephesians 2:2 calls Satan the prince of the power of the air (KJV).) "The air" is where wicked spirits operate. And they will operate successfully unless the prayers of God's people keep them from it.

We are God's army. The time has come for us, as Christians, to pray. So, put on your full armor and take your place in the ranks of the faithful today!

talk the truth

"I put on the full armor of God so I can take my stand against the devil's schemes." (Ephesians 6:11)

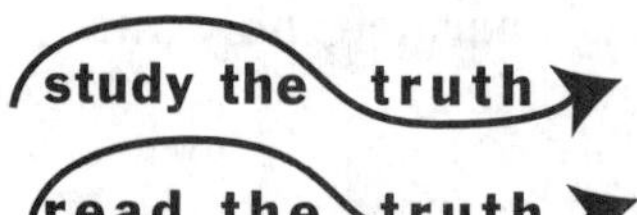
study the truth
read the truth

Daniel 10:1-14

Isaiah 41,42; Psalm 48

NO BURDEN

"For the [true] love of God is this, that we do His commands—keep His ordinances and are mindful of His precepts and teaching. And these orders of His are not irksome—burdensome, oppressive or grievous."

1 John 5:3, AMP

Do you know why the commands in the Bible and the orders God gives to you are not burdens? Because everything He tells you is for your good and for your victory!

God knows what it takes to be a success in this world. In fact, He's the only One Who knows. The people of this world can't tell you how to live victoriously. They don't know how. But God does! He can make things work, even in the middle of darkness. And if we'll follow His instructions and commands in the Bible, we can too!

Let me give you an example. One commandment God gave to us is to love each other and forgive each other, just like He has forgiven us. This command is not a burden because it's the key to your freedom. If you can walk in the love He's put into your heart, you'll have joy every day. But if you don't walk in love, someone will get your joy before the lunch bell rings! God knows that. So, He commands us to love and forgive because it works. Without love, there wouldn't be any joy, and the joy of the Lord is your strength.

Don't resent God's commands. Don't consider His ways a burden to your lifestyle. Receive them with joy and let them lead you all the way to victory!

talk the truth **"I love God and obey His commands. They are not a burden to me." (1 John 5:3, AMP)**

study the truth **1 John 5:1-5**

read the truth **Isaiah 43,44; Psalm 49**

September 29

Kenneth

DARE TO DECIDE

"Be it according to thy word."

Exodus 8:10, KJV

I used to be afraid to step out in faith and do something new that God had shown me to do. I'd think, *What if I fail?* I was so afraid of failing, I wouldn't make a decision about what to do for weeks. Then one day I found out it wasn't my power that was going to do what God asked me to accomplish anyway—it was *His!* But it took a decision on my part to start God moving in the situation. Once I made a firm decision about what I was going to do, God backed me.

What I learned is a biblical truth that, if you'll pay attention to it, will totally change the way you live. It's a truth that carries an awesome responsibility with it, but it's a wonderful thing to realize.

Here it is: The right, the privilege and the power to *decide* has been left in our hands by God.

You have the right, for example, to decide where you will spend eternity. You have a right to make that decision, and God will back your decision.

God has provided His Name, His power and the blood of Jesus. He's even made it so we can share in all of it (Colossians 1:12). But He won't shove that inheritance down our throats—we each have to make the decision to receive it.

Is God leading you in some new direction? Is He leading you to step out in faith for healing or make a decision that could affect your calling in life? Don't let fear stop you. Decide now.

talk the truth

"God did not give me a spirit of timidity, but a spirit of power, of love and of self-discipline. I courageously decide to do my part by moving in faith." (2 Timothy 1:7)

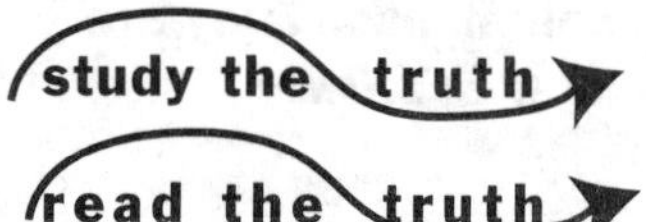
study the truth
read the truth

Romans 4:13-21

Isaiah 45,46; Psalm 50

COMPASSION IN ACTION

"When he saw the crowds, he had compassion on them, because they were harassed and helpless, like sheep without a shepherd."

MATTHEW 9:36

Compassion. That's the one thing people need more than anything else in this world. They need someone to reach out to them with God's compassion.

Compassion is much deeper than sympathy. Sympathy just sits around feeling sorry for people. Compassion does something *for* them.

Jesus' life on earth was a picture of God's compassion in action. It was compassion that caused Him to heal the sick, drive out evil spirits and raise the dead. It was compassion that compelled Him to go to the Cross. And it's that same compassion that He wants to spread through you.

It's staggering to realize that we are the only body Jesus has on this earth. His compassion must flow through our hands and our faith. It must compel us to set the captives free.

"But I don't have that kind of compassion!"

Yes, you do. If you have the Holy Spirit living inside you, you do—because He *is* that kind of compassion! You just need to activate it.

How? Just like Jesus did when He walked the earth—through spending time with the Father in prayer. Look through Matthew, Mark, Luke and John and notice how much time Jesus spent alone with God. That time activated God's compassion within Him. It caused Him to feel what God feels about the suffering of mankind. It stirred Him so much that whenever He found a need, He met it by God's power.

Follow His example. Spend time with your Father. Stir His compassion up inside you until you desire more than anything else to see others set free.

Jesus has sent you to reach out and touch a love-starved world with His compassion. After all...if you don't do it, who will?

talk the truth

"I live in harmony with others and am sympathetic. I walk in love, and am compassionate and humble." (Matthew 9:36)

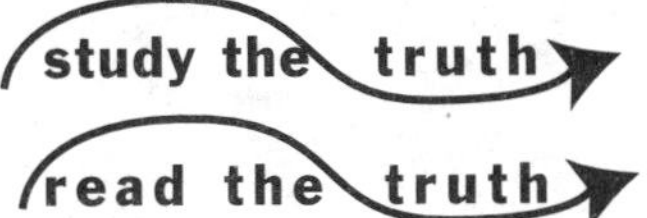
study the truth
read the truth

Mark 6:32-46

Isaiah 47,48; Psalm 51

October 1

Gloria

BLESS THE LORD

"Through Jesus, therefore, let us continually offer to God a sacrifice of praise—the fruit of lips that confess his name."

HEBREWS 13:15

Great things happen when you talk about God's love and mercy. Faith rises up inside you. The reality of His love and compassion comes alive in your spirit.

What's more, it honors God when you think about Him and believe His Word. You honor Him when you speak about His goodness and kindness, when you talk about Him as your loving Father Who only does good. It blesses Him when you praise Him as the great God of the universe Who gave His own Son because He loved the world so much.

So don't be afraid to talk about Him with your friends or family. Don't be afraid to talk about all the good things He's done for you and for others. Who knows—the praise you speak may be just the words someone else needs to hear.

So speak His promises. When you do, you'll not only minister to others, but you'll also begin to realize just how much He really loves you. Your faith will rise to new heights, your Father will be blessed, your friends and family will be blessed...and so will you!

talk the truth

"I speak words that will help others and make them stronger." (Hebrews 13:15)

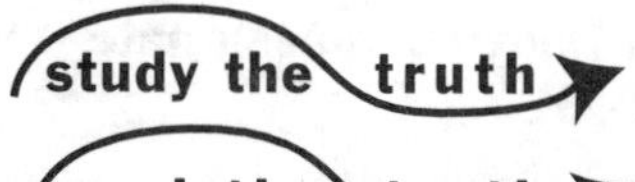
study the truth
read the truth

Psalm 89:1-18

Isaiah 49,50,51; Psalms 52,53

Kenneth

October 2

RUN TO GOD

It's wonderful to know you've been set free from sin and death. But what do you do when, in spite of that wonderful truth, you stumble and fall into sin?

Run to your Father and ask His forgiveness!

That sounds simple. But we often do just the opposite. Instead of running to God, we let guilt drive us further and further from Him. We start thinking, *Well, I've missed it now. I might as well forget it and live like the devil.*

Don't make that mistake. Don't let Satan talk you into sinning in one area of your life just because you missed it in another. When you get off track with God, just admit it and get right back on.

"But I feel so guilty when I tell God what I've done that I don't even want to tell Him at all."

I know. I used to feel that way too. Then, one day, God said to me, *Kenneth, I didn't just find out about that sin when you confessed it. I knew about it all the time! When you confessed it is when you got rid of it, when you were cleansed of its effects in your life.*

When you make a mistake, run to Him! He knows what you're going through. You don't need to be afraid. He didn't tear you apart for the sins you committed before you made Him Lord of your life, did He? Then how much more merciful and loving do you think He'll be now that you're reaching out to Him and have a heart for Him?

Don't run from God. Receive His forgiveness. No matter how badly you've sinned, He wants to restore you. Run to Him!

"If we confess our sins, he is faithful and just and will forgive us our sins and purify us from all unrighteousness."

1 John 1:9

talk the truth

"When I confess my sins, God is faithful and just to forgive me and to purify me from all unrighteousness." (1 John 1:9)

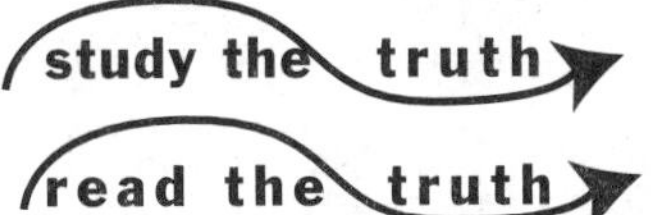
study the truth
read the truth

2 Samuel 11:1-5; 12:1-13

Isaiah 52,53; Psalm 54

October 3

AVOID BIG FAILURES

"This I say therefore, and testify in the Lord, that ye henceforth walk not as other Gentiles walk, in the vanity of their mind, Having the understanding darkened, being alienated from the life of God through the ignorance that is in them, because of the blindness of their heart: Who being past feeling have given themselves over unto lasciviousness, to work all uncleanness with greediness."

EPHESIANS 4:17-19, KJV

There's a subtle strategy Satan uses to take control of our lives. The Bible calls it "lasciviousness." That's a big word that means "to have no restraint."

Lasciviousness has been preached as being extreme immorality, but it doesn't start out that way. It begins with just a few seemingly innocent thoughts. Then those thoughts grow and grow until they begin to produce serious sin.

One afternoon when I was a nine-year-old boy, I just gave in to the desire to cuss. I knew better, but I did it anyway. I had a relative who was so good at cussin', I thought he invented it. I was curious and I wanted to try it.

When I let go of all restraint and began to say those words, something evil moved into my thinking that seriously affected me for some 20 years. A law was set in motion. As a result, my flesh gradually became boss over my entire being.

Don't let Satan use the strategy of lasciviousness on you. Make up your mind and heart today to obey God in even the little things. Avoid big failures by walking in His Spirit one small step at a time. Major victories will eventually be yours.

talk the truth

"I make up my mind to obey God in even the little things. I follow God's direction and don't give in to futile thinking." (Ephesians 4:17-19, KJV)

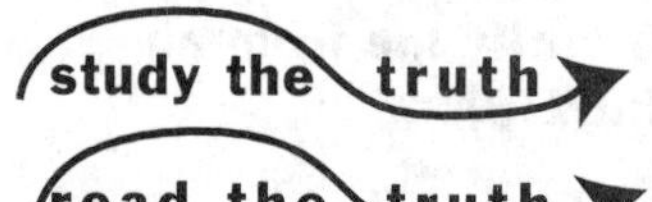
study the truth
read the truth

Ephesians 4:22-31

Isaiah 54,55; Psalm 55

October 4

THE ESTABLISHING WITNESS

"Every matter may be established by the testimony of two or three witnesses."

MATTHEW 18:16

You've been there at a time of decision, standing between victory and defeat. On one side of you is the world saying, "You're a loser. No one likes you because you're worthless." On the other side of you, the Bible is saying, "You are more than a conqueror through God." Who will determine how it all turns out? *You* will. You're the "establishing witness"—the one who establishes what happens.

I remember a guy once who wanted me to pray for him. I said, "The Bible says you're healed." He interrupted me and said, "Yeah, I know it says that, but I've got this terrible pain...."

I looked him in the eye and said again, "The Bible says, 'By His wounds you have been healed.'"

"I know it," he answered, "but I've got this terrible...."

I shook my head. "Listen, the Bible says you're healed!"

He turned beet red. *"I know it says that, but I've got this...."*

Finally, he stopped and stared at me. He didn't realize it, but he'd allowed his physical symptoms to become what he believed. No matter what the Bible said, he believed in what he could see and feel.

But when he got quiet, I said to him, "Look, you're wanting me to agree with you and you're mad because I won't. But if I agree with *you,* you'll die. Now if you'll agree with *me and the Bible,* you can get healed."

Suddenly his eyes lit up. "I see what you mean! I agree with God's Word!"

He was instantly healed. He received it once he decided to become the establishing witness.

Your part is to pray and establish where you stand. If you'll do it, God will back you—and when He backs you, everything else either has to get in line or get out of the way. You're the establishing witness. So what do you say?

talk the truth

"The Word of God is forever established in heaven. I agree with God's Word." (Matthew 18:16; Psalm 119:89)

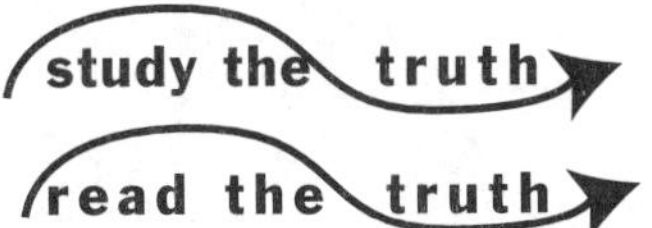
study the truth
read the truth

Matthew 18:15-20

Isaiah 56,57; Psalm 56

October 5

Kenneth

SUBJECT TO CHANGE

"So we fix our eyes not on what is seen, but on what is unseen. For what is seen is temporary, but what is unseen is eternal."

2 CORINTHIANS 4:18

Don't center your attention on what you can see in this natural, physical world. Everything you see is temporary and subject to change. [So] Put your faith in the unseen eternal realm. The things which are eternal will never change.

The Bible—God's Word—is eternal and contains 7,000 promises to cover any circumstance you'll ever face. And no matter what happens in this shifting, changing world you live in, those promises will always be the same.

No matter how bad your body feels, the Bible will always say, "By his wounds you have been healed" (1 Peter 2:24). No matter how empty your wallet looks, the Bible will always say, "And my God will meet all your needs according to his glorious riches in Christ Jesus" (Philippians 4:19). No matter how lonely you may be in a crowd, God will always say in His Word, "Never will I leave you; never will I forsake you" (Hebrews 13:5).

Center your attention on God's eternal truths and don't look to things you can see. After all, they're subject to change!

talk the truth

"I don't fix my eyes on what is seen, but on what is unseen. What I see is temporary, but what I don't see is eternal." (2 Corinthians 4:18)

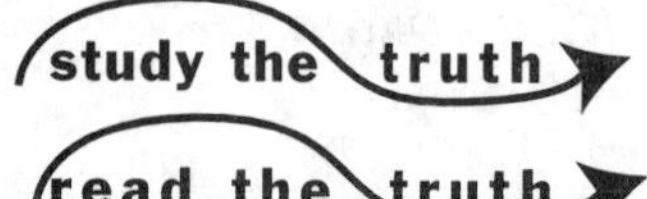
study the truth
read the truth

2 Corinthians 4:8-18

Isaiah 58,59; Psalm 57

EVERYONE WINS

Love never fails. Nothing works without it, and there can be no failure with it. When you live by love, you cannot fail.

It takes faith to believe that love's way will not fail. But when you love others by faith and refuse to be selfish, God acts on your behalf. He sees to it that you succeed. Walking in love is to your advantage!

Godly love is a powerful force. It puts you in charge of every situation. No one even has the power to hurt your feelings because you are not ruled by feelings, but by God's love. You love as He loves.

If we fully understood the great advantages of living in God's love, we'd probably be competing with each other, each of us trying to love the other more. And everyone would win! Love is truly the only sure secret to success.

"Love bears up under anything and everything that comes, is ever ready to believe the best of every person, its hopes are fadeless under all circumstances and it endures everything [without weakening]. Love never fails [never fades out or becomes obsolete or comes to an end]."

1 Corinthians 13:7,8, AMP

talk the truth

"God's love in me bears up under anything and everything that comes. I believe the best of every person. God's love never fails." (1 Corinthians 13:7,8, AMP)

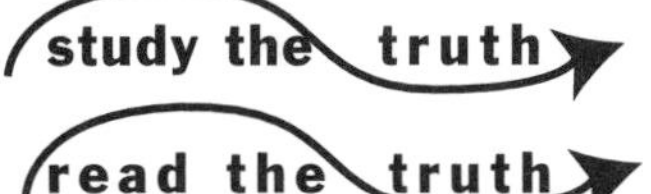
study the truth
read the truth

Romans 12:9-21

Isaiah 60,61; Psalm 58

October 7

LEAVE FOOLISHNESS BEHIND

"Misfortune pursues the sinner, but prosperity is the reward of the righteous."

PROVERBS 13:21

Satan has had us living with less than God's best for so long. It's tough for us to grasp just how much God really *wants* us to live well—spirit, soul and body.

Nonetheless, God has shown us how He desires for His children to live time and again.

God made Abraham extremely wealthy. Genesis 13:2 says he was rich in cattle, silver and gold.

Then, of course, there was Solomon. The Bible says he had more riches and wisdom than all the kings of the earth.

God's servant Job possessed such great wealth that he was called the greatest of all the men of the East. That was before Satan put him through the wringer. Afterward, God blessed him with more than *twice* what Satan had stolen.

The problem is, just the thought of the kind of wealth God gave to those men scares most Christians today. They're afraid it would destroy them.

God has said that "the prosperity of fools shall destroy them" (Proverbs 1:32, KJV). But that doesn't mean you should avoid being prosperous. It means you should avoid being a fool!

I challenge you to go to the book of Proverbs and find out for yourself what God says about the characteristics of a fool. Let the Holy Spirit search your heart. If you see ways in which you've been foolish, ask God's forgiveness and make a firm decision not to be caught in that trap again.

Let the Bible inspire you to leave foolishness behind and stir your faith to reach out and receive what God has promised you—a life entirely full of prosperity!

talk the truth — **"I'm not a fool—I stir my faith to receive what God has promised. He wants me to be prosperous!" (Proverbs 13:21)**

study the truth — **Genesis 15:1-6**

read the truth — **Isaiah 62,63; Psalm 59**

SEED OF FAITH

There's no such thing as someone having "super" faith. God has given everyone the *same* faith—no more, no less. The only reason some people's faith looks like it works better than others is because they use it!

If you've been living in the shadow of a mountainous problem, waiting for God to give you some special faith, make a change today. Step out and put the faith you have to work moving the obstacles Satan has brought against you.

Romans 12:3 says God has given each person a certain amount of faith. Believe Him! Step out in faith about that faith! Say, *"Heavenly Father, through faith in Jesus, I am thankful for the faith given to me as a Christian.*

"I make the decision today to walk in that faith, to put it to work in the situations around me. I make a decision to operate in mountain-moving faith, for I know that it is impossible to please You without it (Hebrews 11:6).

"As I plant this faith and water it with Your Word (Romans 10:17), I expect it to grow and overcome the mountainous problems in my life and in the lives of those I pray for.

"Thank You, Father, that nothing shall be impossible to me! In Jesus' Name. Amen."

"I tell you the truth, if you have faith as small as a mustard seed, you can say to this mountain, 'Move from here to there' and it will move. Nothing will be impossible for you."

MATTHEW 17:20

talk the truth

"I have faith. I speak to a mountain and it is removed. Nothing is impossible for me." (Matthew 17:20)

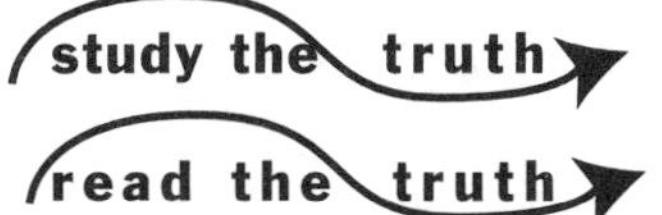
study the truth
read the truth

Luke 8:41-56

Isaiah 64,65,66; Psalms 60,61

October 9

YOUR FIRST AND HIGHEST CALLING

"God, who has called you into fellowship with his Son Jesus Christ our Lord, is faithful."

1 Corinthians 1:9

Do you know what God wants you to do more than anything else today? He wants you to spend time with Him.

He wants you to walk with Him and talk with Him, to discuss the things of life with Him. He wants you to come close to Him.

So many of us get so caught up in striving to please God in the things we do that we forget our first and highest calling is just to spend time with Him.

That's right. God's desire is for us just to want to be with Him.

Have you ever thought about how much it would mean for you to just come to God and say, "Father, I didn't come today to get anything. I've prayed about my needs already and the Bible says they're met according to Your glorious riches in Jesus. So I just came to talk to You. If You have anything You'd like to tell me, I'm ready to listen...and I want You to know that whatever I learn from the Bible, I'll do."

Spend time with Him today. Let Him know how your homework is coming. Talk to Him about your relationships. Listen to what He has to say. He's waiting to spend time with you.

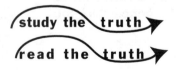

talk the truth **"I am called into fellowship with Jesus." (1 Corinthians 1:9)**

study the truth **1 John 1:1-7**

read the truth **Jeremiah 1,2; Psalm 62**

Gloria

October 10

YOU HAVE PROTECTION—IN HIM

Is it possible to live free from fear in this dangerous and unpredictable world? Is it possible when gang members are in your school and metal detectors are in your halls? Is it possible when classmates are experimenting with Satanism and drunk drivers are commonplace? Yes, it most definitely is! Because protection is a solid promise of God.

But it's not a promise that's offered to just anyone. It is promised to those who *abide* in the Lord. To *abide* is to live in continual union with Him, keeping His Word and obeying His voice. Those who abide in the Lord can live without dread of what Satan will do.

Let me make this clear though—God's promise of protection doesn't mean that Satan will leave you alone! It means that God will give you a way of escape every time Satan comes against you (1 Corinthians 10:13).

If you're afraid of the dangers around you, spend more time in the Bible and in prayer until your trust in God overcomes your fear. Abide in the Lord and—no matter how dangerous this world becomes—He shall surely rescue you.

"He who dwells in the shelter of the Most High will rest [abide] in the shadow of the Almighty. I will say of the Lord, 'He is my refuge and my fortress, my God, in whom I trust.' Surely he will save you from the fowler's snare and from the deadly pestilence."

PSALM 91:1-3

talk the truth

"I dwell in the shelter of the Most High and I rest in the shadow of the Almighty. The Lord is my refuge and my fortress. I trust in Him." (Psalm 91:1-3)

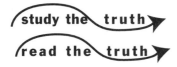

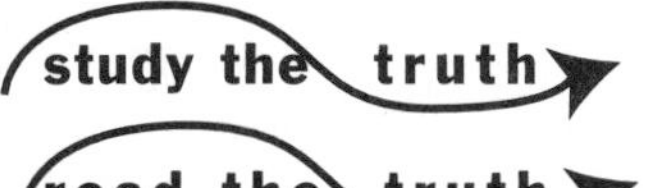
study the truth
read the truth

Psalm 91:1-16

Jeremiah 3,4; Psalm 63

Gloria

October 11

PREPARE FOR MISTREATMENT

"In fact, everyone who wants to live a godly life in Christ Jesus will be persecuted."

2 Timothy 3:12

Did you catch that? The Apostle Paul said all who live godly lives will be persecuted. Not just the "super saints," not just the missionaries in hostile lands—but *everyone.*

If you live for God, you will run into mistreatment—maybe in school, maybe at work, maybe even at home. Satan will make sure of it! I'm not saying that to frighten you or to depress you. I'm saying it because I want you to be prepared.

Second Corinthians 10:4 says, "The weapons we fight with are not the weapons of the world. On the contrary, they have divine power to demolish strongholds." So stay armed and ready for Satan's attack. Then, whenever and however it comes, it won't even slow you down.

That's especially important right now because Satan's time is drawing short. He will do everything he can to stop the Church. But Jesus said the power of Satan would not overcome His Church (Matthew 16:18)!

Remember, the more we grow to be like Jesus and the more God is seen in us, the greater threat we are to Satan's kingdom. But when someone mistreats you, be glad. Jesus said, "Rejoice and be glad at such a time, and exult and leap for joy, for behold, your reward is rich and great and strong and intense and abundant in heaven" (Luke 6:23, AMP).

Do what Jesus said and begin to praise God! There is no way anyone's mistreatment will hurt you if you do that.

talk the truth **"God is on my side. I am comforted and joyful in all tribulations." (James 1:2)**

study the truth **Acts 6:1-15**

read the truth **Jeremiah 5,6; Psalm 64**

October 12

TUNE IN TO THE SPIRIT OF GRACE

Grace teaches us! So let the Holy Spirit—the Spirit of Grace—teach you how to live in this world.

If you listen to the voice of the world, you will be worldly minded, which is death. But, if you tune in to the voice of the Spirit of Grace, you can become spiritually minded, which is life and peace (Romans 8:6). So, when the Holy Spirit speaks to you through that still, small voice inside your heart, listen and obey Him. Trust Him and remember that He wants only the best for you.

Maybe He's asking you to eliminate some activity that's taking too much of your time. Or maybe He's asking you to get up a little earlier and spend more time in the Bible and in prayer. Whatever it is He is telling you to do, if you'll do it, you'll be stronger in Him. So don't hesitate another moment. *Do it now!*

"For the grace of God that brings salvation has appeared to all men. It teaches us to say 'No' to ungodliness and worldly passions, and to live self-controlled, upright and godly lives in this present age."

Titus 2:11,12

talk the truth

"The Holy Spirit—the Spirit of Grace—teaches me all things." (Titus 2:11,12)

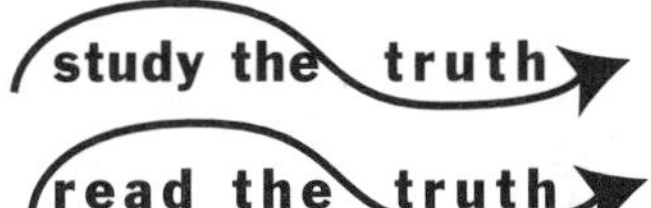
study the truth
read the truth

1 Corinthians 1:3-8

Jeremiah 7,8; Psalm 65

October 13

FROM RELIGION TO REALITY

"God made him [Jesus] who had no sin to be sin for us, so that in him we might become the righteousness of God."

2 Corinthians 5:21

When you made Jesus your Lord, you weren't made half-righteous. The Bible says you became "the righteousness of God!" You were actually made a "joint heir" with Jesus (Romans 8:17). By definition, that means you have "a personal equality based on an equality of possession."

Jesus went to the cross and rose again to give you what He already had. Now you are more than a conqueror in Jesus. John 17:23 actually says that God loves you as much as He loves Jesus.

Once you dare to accept that fact, your life will be changed forever. You'll no longer be satisfied to just sit around hoping things were different. You'll want to step up to the position of authority that Jesus has given you, take your place beside Him and learn to operate the way He does.

As His people, we are everything to God that Jesus is.

If you'll receive that message...if you'll dare to believe it...if you'll dare to put it into action, it will radically change the way you live—from your schooling to your work to your relationships. It will take you from religion to reality!

talk the truth **"I am in right-standing with God. I am a joint heir with Jesus." (2 Corinthians 5:21; Romans 8:17)**

study the truth **John 17:16-26**

read the truth **Jeremiah 9,10; Psalm 66**

THAT GLORIOUS NAME

In Jesus' Name. That's more than a phrase we stick onto the end of our prayers. All that God is and does is represented in the Name of Jesus. *The Amplified Bible* says when you pray in His Name, your prayers are presented to the Father on the credit of *all* that Jesus is. So you can boldly expect to have those prayers answered—not because you're worthy, but because *He is!*

"And I will do—I Myself will grant—whatever you may ask in My name [presenting all I AM] so that the Father may be glorified and extolled in [through] the Son."

JOHN 14:13, AMP

What's more, the Name of Jesus is more powerful than any other name. In Philippians 2:9-11, the Apostle Paul tells us, "God exalted him [Jesus] to the highest place and gave him the name that is above every name, that at the name of Jesus every knee should bow, in heaven and on earth and under the earth."

In spite of all the Bible has to say about the power in the Name of Jesus, most Christians don't seem to believe in it much. They'll pray in the Name of Jesus, then turn right around and say, "I sure hope God answers that prayer." They don't realize that if they only had the faith to believe it, Jesus' Name alone guarantees their prayers will be answered.

Jesus' Name. Dig into the Word and find out just how much power and authority it really holds. Then use that power every time you pray. Stop "hoping" God will answer and start expecting Him to cause every circumstance in your life to bow its knee to His Name!

talk the truth **"Whatever I ask in the Name of Jesus, He does for me, and the Father is glorified." (John 14:13, AMP)**

study the truth **John 16:13-24**

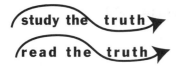

read the truth **Jeremiah 11,12; Psalm 67**

October 15

THE HEART OF THE KING

"The king's heart is in the hand of the Lord; he directs it like a watercourse wherever he pleases."

Proverbs 21:1

Think about that scripture for a moment! God has reserved the right to override the will of a nation's leader, if need be, to see that His people are governed in agreement with what He desires.

What's more, God will hear the prayer of any government leader—even if he's the worst sinner in the whole world. He heard the prayer of old King Nebuchadnezzar, and believe me, that means He'll listen to any leader!

You see, Nebuchadnezzar was king of Babylon. He was an ungodly ruler of an ungodly nation. However, he had some of God's people under his authority. So, God began to deal with him.

Again and again, God warned him, "Nebuchadnezzar, you'll lose your mind if you don't straighten up." And, sure enough, he went just as crazy as could be. He stayed that way for years too. Then one day he cried out to God and God heard him.

Despite the fact that he was a sinful king of a sinful nation, God intervened repeatedly in Nebuchadnezzar's life and heard him when he finally cried out for help. Why? Because he had God's people under his control!

That same principle still holds true today. If we'll open the way through prayer, God will deal with our leaders! If we will humble ourselves and pray, God can change the corruption that exists in our nations. He'll change the hearts of any leader He needs to in order to make sure His children are governed justly.

Make it a point to pray for your leaders today!

talk the truth

"When I pray for my leaders, God moves on their hearts." (Proverbs 21:1)

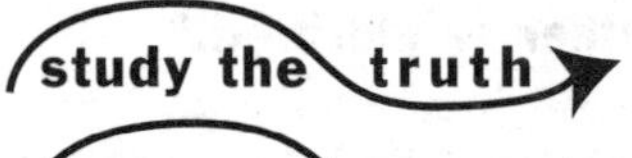
study the truth
read the truth

Daniel 4:1-37

Jeremiah 13,14,15; Psalms 68,69

PUT PATIENCE TO WORK

"Cast not away therefore your confidence, which hath great recompence of reward. For ye have need of patience, that, after ye have done the will of God, ye might receive the promise."

HEBREWS 10:35,36, KJV

Most of us have a mixed-up idea about patience. We think it is something designed to help us gracefully suffer whenever we fail. But according to these scriptures, it will actually put us on the path to success!

Patience and faith work together to see to it that God's promises are fulfilled in your life.

For instance, if you need a part-time job on weekends, you can go to the Bible and clearly see that God promises to provide your needs. You can see it delights Him when you're doing well. Once you see that, faith takes hold and you can say, "I have the job I need."

But what happens to that faith tomorrow evening when you get turned down for three different jobs? Then what? That's when patience has to take over! That's when you have to make a decision to stay constant, to act as if nothing has changed.

The truth is, if you based your confidence on what the Bible says, nothing *has* changed. It says exactly the same thing today as it said yesterday.

So, if you put patience to work, do you know what you'd say after you were turned down for those three jobs? You'd say, "I have the job I need!" just like you did before.

You see, faith opens the door to God's promise for you, and patience keeps it open until that promise is fulfilled. So don't let the delay discourage you. Put patience to work. The Bible guarantees you will receive your reward.

talk the truth

"I walk in patience, and when I have done God's will, I receive what He has promised." (Hebrews 10:35,36, KJV)

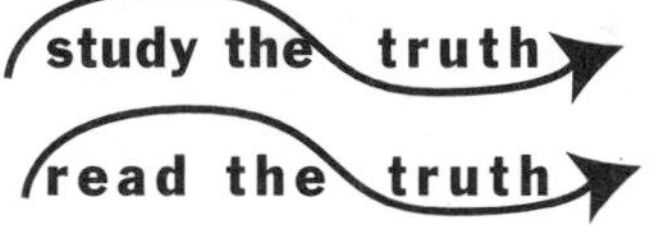
study the truth
read the truth

Hebrews 6:10-15

Jeremiah 16,17; Psalm 70

October 17

LIVING THE LIFE OF LOVE

"Greater love has no one than this, that he lay down his life for his friends."

JOHN 15:13

We often think of the phrase "laying down your life" in terms of dying, because that's what Jesus did. He loved us so much, He laid down His life by dying in our place so we could live.

But now, He's asked us to lay down our lives in a different way. He's asked us to show our love, not by dying for others, but by living for them.

What does that mean? Sometimes it means giving our lives by spending time in prayer for someone. Other times it means giving love and understanding to the person everyone makes fun of and disrespects. Many times it means laying down our own selfish desires—our popularity, our "coolness" or even our time—in order to meet the needs of another.

Romans 15:1 puts it this way, "We who are strong ought to bear with the failings of the weak and not to please ourselves."

When you lay down your life, you live to please God instead of yourself. You allow your life to be guided by His love. Commit yourself today to lay down your own life—and take up the life of love. Say:

"Father, in Jesus' Name, I see from Your Word that You were willing to give Yourself, through Your Son, for all. I know that because Jesus is Lord of my life, I am also called to give myself to others. I accept that calling today.

"I'll give my time. I'll give the love You've put in me. I'll be strong and lift up those who are weak. I'll be available to be used of You so that those around me might experience Your life flowing through me.

"You have loved me, Lord, with the greatest love there is. I count it a privilege to share that love with others. I thank You for it in Jesus' Name. Amen."

talk the truth

"I lay down my life today to share God's love with others." (John 15:13)

study the truth
read the truth

Galatians 5:22-26; 6:1-3

Jeremiah 18,19; Psalm 71

FROM TRADITION TO TRUTH

"Praise the Lord, O my soul, and forget not all his benefits—who forgives all your sins and heals all your diseases, who redeems your life from the pit and crowns you with love and compassion, who satisfies your desires with good things so that your youth is renewed like the eagle's."

PSALM 103:2-5

Is there actually a divine purpose behind the bad things that happen in your life? Could sicknesses and disasters somehow be part of God's plan for you?

Before you can ever experience God's healing and delivering power, you must know the answer to those questions. You have to settle them once and for all. If you even suspect that God is the source of the disasters in your life, you won't be able to believe Him to rescue you from them. Your faith will be crippled because you'll think that by escaping those things, you'll be going against what He wants.

In order to receive all the good things God desires to give you, you must be absolutely sure that He is a good God. You must be certain that what He wants is health, not sickness; abundance, not poverty; joy, not suffering—100 percent of the time! Psalm 103 alone is enough to prove that's true. But if it's not enough to convince you, there are many other scriptures too. One of the best known is Psalm 136:1 that says, "Give thanks to the Lord, for He is good! *For His mercy endures forever"* (NKJV).

If religious traditions have taught you that God brings you trouble so He can teach you something, start washing those traditions away with the truth. Get out your Bible and let God show you in His own Word that He is the God Who heals you (Exodus 15:26). Discover for yourself that He is a God of mercy (Psalm 86:5), kindness (Jeremiah 9:24), and compassion (Psalm 145:8).

Put your doubts to rest and open your heart to receive the truth about your Heavenly Father. It's the only thing that can truly set you free (John 8:32).

talk the truth

"I continue in the Word. Therefore, I know the truth and the truth sets me free." (John 8:31,32)

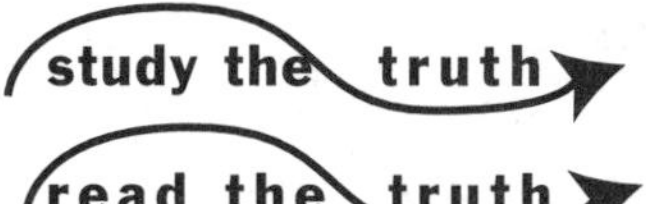
study the truth
read the truth

Psalm 89:1-28

Jeremiah 20,21; Psalm 72

October 19

DON'T LET DIVISION STUNT YOUR GROWTH

"And I, brethren, could not speak to you as to spiritual people but as to carnal, as to babes in Christ. I fed you with milk and not with solid food; for until now you were not able to receive it, and even now you are still not able; for you are still carnal. For where there are envy, strife, and divisions among you..."

1 Corinthians 3:1-3, NKJV

Envy, strife and division brought the early Corinthian Christians back to the sinful state they were in before they made Jesus the Lord of their lives. It hurt their spiritual growth so much till they couldn't understand what the Apostle Paul wanted to teach them.

Satan has sent the same spirit of division among us today. He knows that if we're divided by race, doctrine or anything else, we will crumble. He also knows if we all come together, unified in our faith, we'll become all Jesus has created us to be in Him (Ephesians 4:13). So Satan has assigned a spirit of division to operate in our personal lives, our church lives, our social lives and our family lives. His goal is the same as it was in Corinth—to bring envy, strife and division, and to stunt our spiritual growth.

But we don't have to give in to that spirit. Instead, Paul says, by "speaking the truth in love, we will in all things grow up into him who is the Head, that is, Christ" (Ephesians 4:15).

Compare "speaking the truth in love" to "envy, strife and divisions." Total opposites, aren't they? You can't do both of them at the same time. As you speak the truth in love, you grow up. As you envy, fight and divide, you go back to being an infant.

Don't give in to the spirit of division and let Satan stop your spiritual growth. Instead, speak the truth in love and "in all things grow up into him!"

talk the truth

"I speak the truth in love and grow up into Him in all things." (Ephesians 4:15)

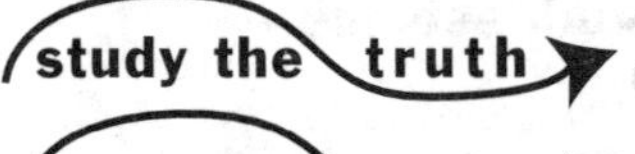
study the truth

James 4:1-11

read the truth

Jeremiah 22,23; Psalm 73

PRESCRIPTION FOR LIFE

"If anyone intends to come after Me, let him deny himself—forget, ignore, disown, lose sight of himself and his own interests—and take up his cross, and...follow with Me.... For whoever wants to save his [higher...] life, will lose ...and whoever gives up his life...for My sake and the Gospel's, will save."

MARK 8:34,35, AMP

When Jesus said these words, He wasn't just giving us a prescription for getting to heaven. He was telling us how to live a superior life right here on earth.

You see, there's a greater life that we can live right here, right now. But to get in on it, we have to lay down the way of life that most of us are accustomed to. We may have to let go of the very things we've been trying so hard to get. Instead, we have to set our hearts on doing what God wants us to do.

That's what Jesus did. He didn't live His life for Himself. He lived it completely for God. He did only what the Father told Him to do—and He lived in total victory.

It's time to realize that making Jesus our Lord is not something we do just to miss hell. Our purpose is to please God, to lay down our lives in order to fulfill His desires, to be His special possessions in the earth and to do whatever He tells us to do. Our top priority is to give ourselves to Him and to spend enough time with Him that we can hear His voice and obey Him.

Only when we do that will we be truly fulfilled. Only when we do that will we be able to live the greater life we've been longing for.

talk the truth

"I live a superior life here on earth because I have given my life for the sake of the gospel." (Mark 8:34,35, AMP)

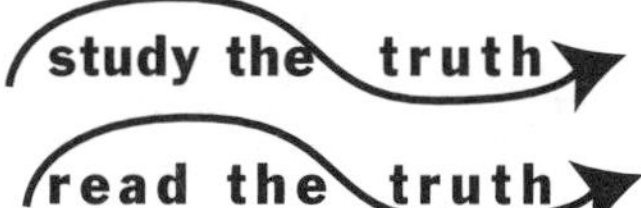
study the truth
read the truth

Acts 20:7-24

Jeremiah 24,25; Psalm 74

Kenneth

October 21

LIVING THROUGH THE COVENANT

"But remember the Lord your God, for it is he who gives you the ability to produce wealth, and so confirms his covenant, which he swore to your forefathers, as it is today."

DEUTERONOMY 8:18

What is God's reason for making sure His people live well? Is it so we can watch the Super Bowl on bigger TVs? So we can buy the hottest clothes and even hotter cars?

Establishing His covenant on the earth and giving to those in need—those are God's purposes for wanting you to live well!

I've had some people tell me, "Well, Jesus' ministry was poor and He got along just fine." That's ridiculous. All the way through the Old Testament God promised material benefits to anyone who would walk upright before Him. If God had failed to bless Jesus financially, He would have been breaking His own Word.

Jesus never built a worldly empire for Himself. But that doesn't mean He was poor. It means He was the greatest giver Who ever walked the face of this earth—and it's about time we started following in His footsteps.

If we'll start giving, if we'll start taking care of others' needs, we'll be far more likely to win their hearts.

Don't ever let anyone tell you it's wrong to want to live well. It's wrong for you not to want to live well, when it can mean the difference between heaven and hell for millions of people.

Forget about your own trivial needs. Raise your vision and set your mind on giving to meet someone else's needs—on establishing God's covenant in the earth. Then stand in faith and get ready to enjoy the greatest living you've ever dreamed of.

talk the truth

"I remember the Lord. He gives me the ability to produce wealth, and so confirms His covenant." (Deuteronomy 8:18)

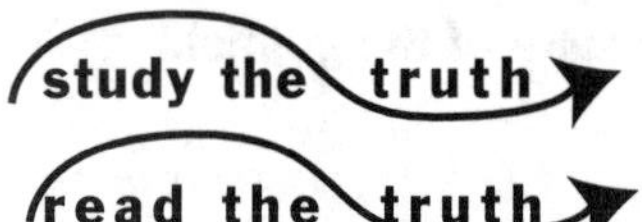
study the truth
read the truth

Deuteronomy 8:11-18

Jeremiah 26,27; Psalm 75

WHEN TOUGH TIMES COME

"Then the church throughout Judea, Galilee and Samaria enjoyed a time of peace. It was strengthened; and encouraged by the Holy Spirit, it grew in numbers, living in the fear of the Lord."

ACTS 9:31

There are times when life is just plain hard. When those times come, you need the comfort that only the Holy Spirit can bring. How do you receive that comfort? By doing just what the Christians in the book of Acts did—by "living in the fear of the Lord."

Now, when I talk about "the fear of the Lord," I'm not saying you should be afraid of God. He's your Father! You should be as secure and unafraid when you come before Him as a child who knows he is loved very much. But you must also have so much respect for God that whenever He shows you something you need to do, you do it immediately—even if it's not really what you want to do. That's living in the fear of the Lord.

Let me show you what I mean. Once, several years ago, I received a very disturbing phone call right before I was to preach at a meeting. It was painful news about a situation in which one of my children had been wronged. It hurt me more than you could imagine.

I cried and wanted to get angry—to strike back. But instead, I began praying in other tongues. As I did, the Holy Spirit prompted me to praise the Lord.

I certainly didn't feel like praising. I felt like losing my temper. But, out of respect to the Lord, I put my feelings aside and obeyed. As I did, I could tell I was being strengthened.

Then suddenly, I realized I was free. By my obedience, I had let the Holy Spirit's comforting power come to me. The anger and pain was gone! They were replaced by the Lord's gentle love and encouragement.

It doesn't matter what tough situation you may be facing—trust and obey the directions of your Father. He will make that same supernatural, Holy Spirit-inspired comfort available to you!

talk the truth

"The Holy Spirit—my Comforter, Counselor, Helper, Intercessor, Advocate, Strengthener and Standby—lives in me." (Acts 9:31)

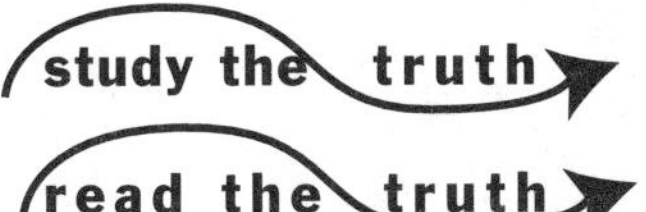
study the truth
read the truth

Matthew 4:1-11

Jeremiah 28,29,30; Psalms 76,77

CHOOSE LIFE

"For to be carnally minded is death, but to be spiritually minded is life and peace."

ROMANS 8:6, NKJV

If you were given the choice between life and death, which would you choose? The answer seems obvious. But it's really not. Choosing death doesn't necessarily mean bungee jumping from the nearest cliff without a cord. It's more subtle than that.

The Bible says death is being worldly minded, being tangled up in the things of this world. The Bible also tells us what life is: "My son...listen closely to my words..." says Proverbs 4:20-22, "for they are life!"

To think like the world is death. To think like the Word is life.

The story of Mary and Martha in Luke 10 demonstrates this principle extremely well. Mary was sitting at Jesus' feet listening to Him teach, while Martha was busy running around in the kitchen cooking dinner for everyone.

Finally, busy Martha couldn't stand it anymore. She came to Jesus and said, "Don't you care that my sister has left me to do the work by myself? Tell her to help me!" Jesus answered, "Martha, Martha...you are worried and upset about many things, but only one thing is needed. Mary has chosen what is better, and it will not be taken away from her" (Luke 10:40-42).

Mary had set everything else aside so she could hear from the Lord. But Martha had let the "important" business of living take priority over His Word. She'd chosen death, not life. You see how easy it is to slip into that?

Don't make the mistake that Martha did. Don't get so tangled up living that you choose death by default. Decide to put God's Word first place. Choose Life!

talk the truth

"God has set life and death before me. I choose life!" (Deuteronomy 30:19)

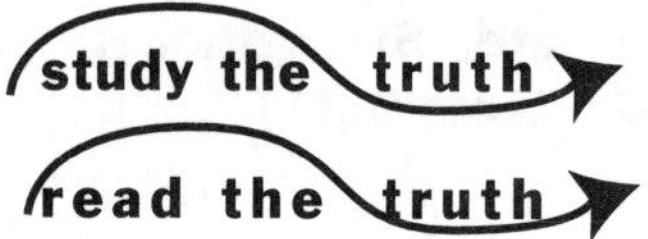
study the truth
read the truth

Romans 8:5-13

Jeremiah 31,32; Psalm 78

GOD GOES TOO!

"But the person who is united to the Lord becomes one spirit with Him."

1 CORINTHIANS 6:17, AMP

I once heard about a great man of God who looked in the mirror every day when he put on his suit and said, "Suit, everywhere you go today, God goes too." And you know, he's right. If you've made Jesus your Lord, everywhere you go today...God goes too!

As Christians, we need to train ourselves to be constantly aware of God inside of us, talking to us, teaching us and strengthening us.

We need to remind ourselves that we are united with Him. That means that every time we face some trouble, God is facing it too. And He's already overcome it!

When you get dressed today, look in the mirror just like that man of God did and say, *"I am united to the Lord. Body, everywhere you go today, God goes too. God is in you. God's power, wisdom and victory is in you!"*

Say that to yourself every day. Say it when you're getting dressed for school, a meeting, football practice or a date. Keep doing it until you develop the habit of thinking that way. Let it come alive in you—God lives in you!

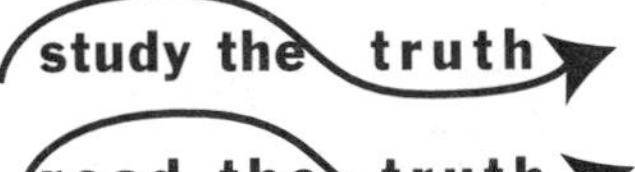

"I am one spirit with Jesus." (1 Corinthians 6:17, AMP)

study the truth **1 Corinthians 6:17-20**

read the truth **Jeremiah 33,34; Psalm 79**

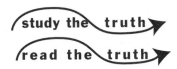

October 25

Kenneth

GET RID OF THE FROGS

"I leave to you the honor of setting the time for me to pray for you and your officials and your people that you and your houses may be rid of the frogs."

Exodus 8:9

Have you ever had a problem that refused to go away? The Bible tells us an Egyptian pharaoh faced just that kind of problem thousands of years ago. He was in a hot dispute with God over the future of the Israelites, and as a result of that dispute, he woke up one morning to find his country swarming with frogs. Slimy, smelly, hopping-all-over-the-place frogs.

It was a serious problem. I'm not talking about a frog or two in the front yard. I mean frogs were everywhere—in their beds, on their tables. Big, old frogs in the ovens. Little bitty frogs in the bread dough and the drinking water. Frogs. Frogs in your hair. Frogs in places you wouldn't even want to think about!

Then God made a move. He sent His man Moses in to ask Pharaoh, "When should I pray to the Lord to get these frogs out of here?"

Do you know what Pharaoh said?

"Tomorrow." Can you imagine that? He could have said, "Right now! Today!" But instead he decided he'd spend one more night with the frogs.

You say, "That's the stupidest thing I ever heard. Why in the world would he do it tomorrow?" I don't know. Probably for the same reason many people want to wait until tomorrow to make Jesus their Lord or to receive their healing.

Here's what I want you to notice. When Moses asked Pharaoh that question and he answered, "Tomorrow," Moses said, "All right. So that you know there's a God in heaven, *let it be done according to what you've said."*

Let me ask you this: How long are you willing to let that problem harass you? When are you planning to get rid of the frogs in your life? Do you realize they'll stay around as long as you'll let them? They'll be there until you finally make a decision to go with God's Word and get them out.

Why not get rid of them today?

talk the truth

"The Lord delivers me out of all my afflictions." (Acts 7:10; Psalm 34:17)

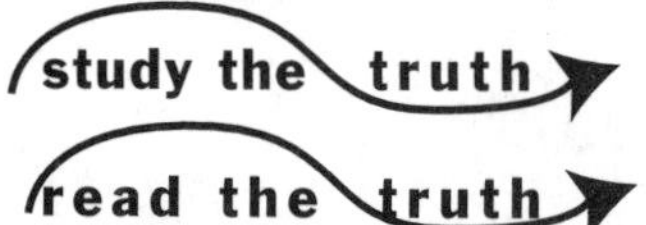
study the truth
read the truth

Exodus 8:1-13

Jeremiah 35,36; Psalm 80

October 26

TAKE YOUR PLACE

God has raised us up to sit with Him in the heavenly realms in Christ Jesus! That's what the Bible says. But very few of us have actually dared to believe it. We've exalted Jesus—and rightly so! At the same time, though, we've belittled what Jesus did by not allowing God to bring us alongside Him.

That was God's purpose at Calvary—to bring us alongside Jesus—to make us what He already was.

You see, Jesus didn't need exalting. He was exalted before He ever came to earth. He was already One with the Father. He came to earth as a man to gain authority over sin and sickness, evil spirits, fear, poverty and all the other troubles that came when the law of death moved into the earth. And He succeeded.

"But because of his great love for us, God, who is rich in mercy, made us alive with Christ even when we were dead in transgressions.... And God raised us up with Christ and seated us with him in the heavenly realms in Christ Jesus."

Ephesians 2:4-6

Before He returned to heaven, Jesus said, "All authority in heaven and on earth has been given to me" (Matthew 28:18). Then He gave that authority to us by giving us His Name.

You and I are the reason Jesus came to earth and died and arose from the grave. He didn't do it for Himself. He did it so He could bring us alongside Him—so we could wear His Name and use His authority on the earth. He did it so that we could stand before God and be everything to Him that Jesus is.

Dare to receive all that Jesus has bought for you and take your place alongside Him!

talk the truth **"I have been made alive together with Christ. I am seated with Him in heavenly places." (Ephesians 2:4-6)**

study the truth **Ephesians 2:1-13**

read the truth **Jeremiah 37,38; Psalm 81**

Kenneth

October 27

DON'T DEPEND ON GUESSWORK

"Call to me and I will answer you and tell you great and unsearchable things you do not know."

JEREMIAH 33:3

Who do you turn to when you need help, when you need an important answer to an important question? Do you turn to God first?

So many Christians don't! They'll stand around worrying and talking to each other all day. They'll talk to their pastor. They'll talk to their parents. They'll talk to their boyfriend or girlfriend. But do they talk to God? No.

Don't make that mistake.

Instead, follow the example of King David. In 1 Chronicles 14, the Bible tells us he was about to face a battle with the very powerful Philistines who had *all* come out against him. The Philistine nation had been an enemy of Israel for years. David probably could have guessed that God would tell him to go to battle against them. But he didn't guess! He went to God and asked, saying, "'Shall I go and attack the Philistines? Will you hand them over to me?' The Lord answered him, 'Go, I will hand them over to you (v. 10).'"

So don't depend on guesswork. When you run into a problem, seek the Lord through searching the Bible and praying and asking Him what the solution is. No matter how much scripture you learn, no matter how much you've grown to know Him, you'll never outgrow your need to talk to Him.

Go to the Lord and find out exactly what He wants you to do. Don't choose your own way and then ask God to bless your plans. Go to Him and say, "Lord, what are Your plans?" His plans are the right ones. If you follow them, your victory is guaranteed.

talk the truth

"I call to the Lord and He answers me. He tells me great and unsearchable things I do not know." (Jeremiah 33:3)

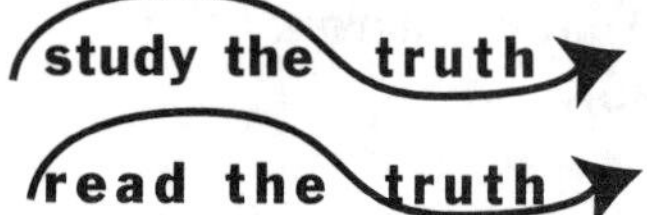
study the truth
read the truth

1 Chronicles 14:8-17

Jeremiah 39,40; Psalm 82

ENJOY THE VICTORY

"But thanks be to God, Who gives us the victory—making us conquerors—through our Lord Jesus Christ."

1 CORINTHIANS 15:57, AMP

Conquerors! That's what the Bible says we are. I know you've heard that many times before, but today I want you to let the reality of it really sink in. I want you to spend some time thinking about what it actually means.

The dictionary says that victory means "final and complete supremacy or superiority in battle or war; success in any contest or struggle involving the defeat of an opponent or the overcoming of obstacles."

To conquer means "to get the better of in competition or struggle; to master, suppress, prevail over, overwhelm, surmount; to gain superiority, to subdue, to vanquish, to crush, to defeat."

Once you get those definitions firmly in mind, you'll realize you have much more than a ticket to heaven. You have the best of this world, too. Through Him, you've overcome the world, mastered it and won over it.

No wonder 1 Corinthians 15:57 shouts, "Thanks be to God! He gives us the victory through our Lord Jesus Christ."

Why don't you shout too! Shout thanks to God today for making you an overcomer. Praise Him that you are joined up with the One Who has conquered the world, sin and Satan. Shout and enjoy the victory!

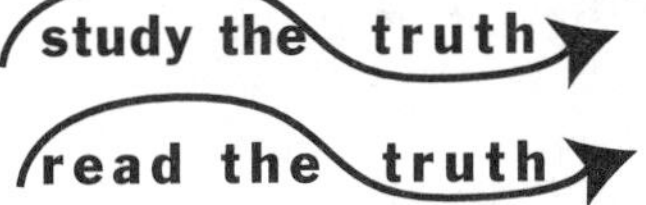

"God gives me the victory—making me a conqueror—through Jesus." (1 Corinthians 15:57, AMP)

study the truth — **Romans 8:29-39**

read the truth — **Jeremiah 41,42; Psalm 83**

October 29

Gloria

COME, LORD JESUS

"Dear friends, now we are children of God, and what we will be has not yet been made known. But we know that when he appears, we shall be like him, for we shall see him as he is. Everyone who has this hope in him purifies himself, just as he is pure."

1 John 3:2,3

Hopelessness. As this age draws to a close, that's a feeling that will be more common among the people of this world. But, you know, it's something we as Christians never have to feel! Because no matter how dark the circumstances are around us, we know that we have hope in Jesus' soon return.

Sometimes we forget that. We get our attention so focused on what's going on around us that we get caught up in hopelessness. But we don't have to let that happen.

A friend of mine once met an Arabian woman who was a Christian in the Middle East. She was living proof of that. The woman was caught in a life most of us would consider unbearable. She was living in a war zone that had been torn up by violence. She faced the danger of bombs and bullets every day.

She had no hope in the world. Her country was being destroyed around her. She had to go to Israel to work and get money for her family because there were no jobs where she lived. Things around her seemed to be going from bad to worse, but she told my friend she had hope because she knew that Jesus was coming back for her. That hope kept her going.

So, if you're feeling hopeless, get your eyes off this world and get them onto the soon return of Jesus. Not only will that encourage you, but the Bible says it will also purify you. It will cause you to live right, to separate you from the sin and failure of the world around you. It will give you joy and let you see the victory.

Think about this. When this old world comes to an end, you and I will just be getting started. We'll be stepping into the most glorious life ever. The people of the world may look back and wish for better days. But for you and me, the best is yet to come!

talk the truth

"The Lord will soon return and I will be like Him. I have this hope and it purifies me." (1 John 3:2,3)

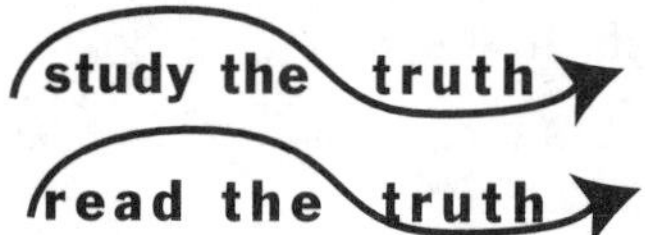
study the truth
read the truth

Revelation 21-22:7

Jeremiah 43,44,45; Psalms 84,85

IT'S YOUR DECISION

"I wonder when God will *do something* about this problem?!" Have you ever asked that? If so, you may be surprised to find out that the answer depends 100 percent on you.

There's an incident in Mark 5 that will show you what I mean. Jesus had just stepped out of a boat and people were pressing in all around Him. They had Him shoved up against the shoreline when suddenly a man came through that crowd to get to Jesus.

Throwing himself at Jesus' feet, he said, "My little daughter is dying. Please come and put your hands on her so that she will be healed and live."

Picture this for a moment. Here's a man that's on the level of a mayor. He is so determined to get to Jesus that he fights his way through the crowd and clears out enough room to fall at Jesus' feet. He's made a decision—and when he gets to Jesus, he says exactly what it is: "Lay Your hands on her and she will live."

"Then one of the synagogue rulers, named Jairus, came there. Seeing Jesus, he fell at his feet and pleaded earnestly with him, 'My little daughter is dying. Please come and put your hands on her so that she will be healed and live.' So Jesus went with him."

MARK 5:22-24

Let me ask you something: In this incident, who do you think is directing the ministry of Jesus? This one man who's made a decision. When he speaks his decision, Jesus doesn't say anything. He just stops what He's doing, turns around, and follows him.

What does that mean to you? It means that if you're sitting around waiting for Jesus to decide to help you and give you victory, you're in for a long wait. Because that's not Jesus' decision. It's yours.

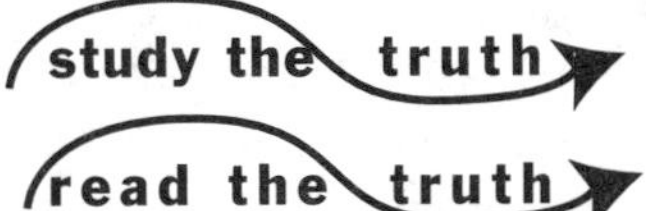

"I decide to obey God's Word and do His will. When I do, He gives me success." (Mark 5:22-24)

study the truth **Mark 5:21-24; 35-43**

read the truth **Jeremiah 46,47; Psalm 86**

October 31

DON'T PLAY DEAD

"From the days of John the Baptist until now, the kingdom of heaven has been forcefully advancing, and forceful men lay hold of it."

MATTHEW 11:12

I want you to get forceful today. Yes, forceful and determined. I want you to get so committed to the things of God that you'll stand against any attempt to take them away from you.

Too many Christians these days are like the Israelites. They're wandering around in a wilderness of defeat because there's an enemy in the promised land. They aren't receiving all God has for them because they're afraid to fight the enemy. They keep hoping that somehow they'll find a way to their victory without using force. But they won't!

When God sent the Israelites in to receive their Promised Land, He told them to send the armed men on the front lines. They were to go in ready for the fight. He knew they'd have to fight to receive the good things He had for them. He never promised them that they wouldn't. What He promised them was that they'd win every time.

The same is true for you. You can't just lie down and play dead when you're dealing with Satan. He won't let you take hold of God's promises without a fight. Satan doesn't want you to become bold, prosperous, successful or healed.

It's up to you whether he's allowed to steal God's blessings from you or not. You have God's permission and His power and His ability to take hold of His promises. So get forceful enough to receive them today!

talk the truth

"I take hold of God's promises by faith...and I won't let go!" (Matthew 11:12)

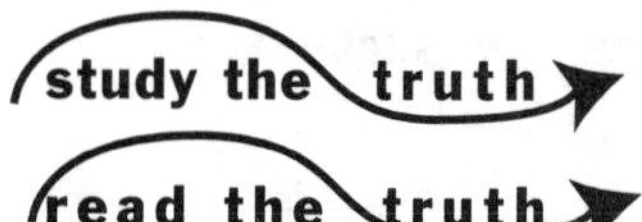
study the truth
read the truth

Deuteronomy 31:1-8

Jeremiah 48,49; Psalm 87

Kenneth

November 1

THE POWER OF LOVE

"But faith... worketh by love."

GALATIANS 5:6, KJV

I used to wonder why we didn't see more of God's power working in His people. With what we know about faith and the Bible, it seemed to me that miracles should be happening in our churches, our homes, our schools and anywhere else God's people go.

So, one day I asked, "Lord, why isn't Your power turned up to a higher volume in us?" Do you know what He said? He told me we weren't walking in enough love yet.

God wants us to have power. But first, He has to be sure we'll use that power in love. He wants to know that we won't take it and mix it with judgment and criticism and start blasting people out of the water.

He reminded me of a time I took my son, John, hunting. He was just a little guy at the time, barely big enough to keep his gun from knocking him on his back every time he'd pull the trigger. I was teaching him how to shoot, and he was doing pretty well.

That day we were at Gloria's grandparents' farm and John spotted one of the biggest tarantulas I'd ever seen. It was clinging to the wall of the barn. When John saw that spider, he took aim. He was about to blow that bug to kingdom come.

If I hadn't stopped him, he would have, too. And it wouldn't have dawned on him until it was all over that he would blow a hole in the barn at the same time. From my grown-up perspective, I could see how foolish that would be. He couldn't. He was looking through the eyes of a child.

Do you want God to put a shotgun of spiritual power in your hand, so you can blow the works of Satan away? Then focus on love. Take hold of it. Practice it. Study it. Operate in it. Then you'll see God's power operating through you.

talk the truth

"God is love and He lives in me. I walk in love!" (Ephesians 5:2)

study the truth
read the truth

Romans 13:8-14

Jeremiah 50,51; Psalm 88

November 2

HE OPENED THE WAY

"In the beginning [before all time] was the Word [Christ], and the Word was with God, and the Word was God Himself.... And the Word [Christ] became flesh (human, incarnate) and tabernacled—fixed His tent of flesh, lived awhile—among us."

JOHN 1:1,14, AMP

The deity of the Lord Jesus Christ is something that can never be questioned by Christians. Our very salvation rests on the fact that Jesus is divine, the second person of the Godhead, God the Son.

The Apostle John forever puts to rest any doubt about that in John 1:1-14. Anyone who doubts what those verses say could not possibly have been born into the kingdom of God. For the deity of Jesus forms the very foundation of our faith in Him.

Yet, if you'll read the Gospels, you'll see that Jesus didn't go around proclaiming Himself as God during His time on earth. He acknowledged that He was the Son of God, the Messiah. He referred to God as His Father, but He never said that He Himself was the Most High God. In fact, He told His disciples that the Father God was greater and mightier than He (John 14:28).

The reason is simple. He didn't come to earth just as God. He came also as man. The Bible says He set aside His divine power and took the form of a human being—with all its limitations. Since God was His Father, He was not born with the sin nature that everyone else has. But by being born of a woman, in all other respects He became a man and called Himself the Son of Man or, literally, the Son of Adam.

How, then, did He do all those mighty works? The same way He expects us to do them today—by the power of the Holy Spirit (Acts 10:38). What does that mean to you? It means that Jesus meant exactly what He said in John 14:12 when He proclaimed that you, as a Christian, would be able to do the works that He did!

It means that you, as a reborn child of God, filled with the same Holy Spirit as Jesus was, have the opportunity to live as He lived when He was on earth. In fact, that is exactly what He wants. He opened the way. Don't just admire Him *for* it...follow Him *in* it today!

talk the truth

"The works Jesus did, I do also—and even greater works!" (John 14:12)

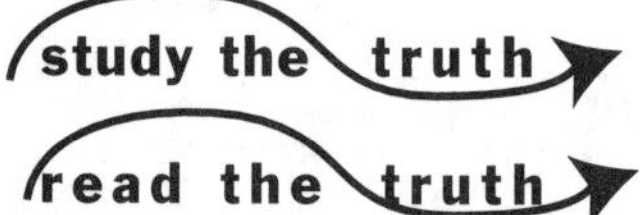
study the truth
read the truth

John 14:1-15

Jeremiah 52; Lamentations 1; Psalm 89

AN EXPERIENCED CHAMPION

"But those who hope in the Lord will renew their strength. They will soar on wings like eagles; they will run and not grow weary, they will walk and not be faint."

Isaiah 40:31

Did you know that the force of faith has the power to refresh your physical body? It's true. You can see that in the life of Abraham's wife, Sarah. Most people don't understand the full extent of what God did in her life. All they know is that He enabled her to have a child in her old age.

But if you'll look closer, you'll see that there was more to it than that.

When Sarah took hold of God's promise by faith, it began to physically restore her to such an extent that when King Abimelech saw her, he wanted her for his wife.

Think about that! At 90 years old, she was so beautiful that a king wanted her as a wife. What's more, after she gave birth to Isaac, the Bible says, she nursed him till he was weaned. Then she kept right on living until he was raised!

Now, I'm not telling you that when you turn 90 you can have a baby like Sarah did. She had a specific promise from God about that. But I am telling you that if you'll believe God for supernatural strength and health, He'll provide it for you. In fact, Psalm 103 says that's one of His promises. It says God will satisfy your desires with good things so your youth is renewed like the eagle's.

That is God's desire for you—to be a powerful, experienced champion of His Word with your strength renewed by faith. You'll still go to heaven when your work on earth is through—but you won't just fade away of old age. You'll fly out of here in a blaze of glory like the conqueror God created you to be.

talk the truth

"The Lord renews my strength. I run and don't grow weary. I walk and don't faint." (Isaiah 40:31)

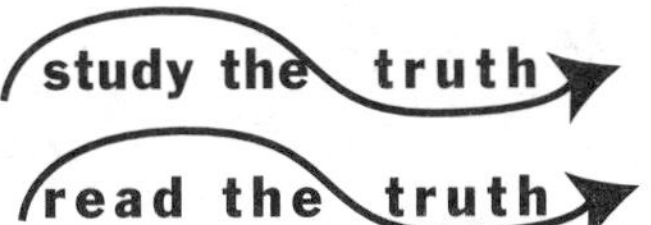
study the truth
read the truth

Psalm 92

Lamentations 2,3; Psalm 90

November 4

Kenneth

IT ONLY TAKES A FEW

"If my people, who are called by my name, will humble themselves and pray and seek my face and turn from their wicked ways, then will I hear from heaven and will forgive their sin and will heal their land."

2 Chronicles 7:14

You may be thinking, *Can only a few people actually change a nation?*

Let me ask you this: Can one demonic person change a nation for the worse? Definitely. Hitler did it in Germany, didn't he?

Then if Satan's power on a man can change a nation for the worse, you can be sure that a group of people with God's power can change a nation for the better. And no nation is so far gone that God cannot change it.

I want you to notice something in today's scripture. It says, "If *my* people, who are called by *my* name...." God didn't say it would take everyone in the nation to get things turned around. He said, "If *my* people..."

Notice also that He didn't say, "If my people will get out there and sign petitions and get enough votes...." He said, "Pray." In other words, we have to quit trying to work things out by ourselves. God Himself will do the healing in your land. Your job is to pray, to believe, to seek His face and to act on His Word. As a young man or woman, your prayers can determine who is leading your nation today and tomorrow. Seek Him today.

talk the truth

"I am God's child and I seek God's face, praying for my nation." (2 Chronicles 7:14; 1 Timothy 2:1)

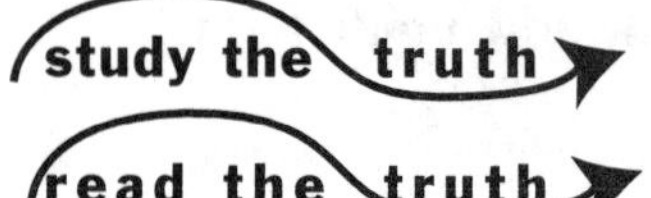
study the truth
read the truth

2 Chronicles 7:1-16

Lamentations 4,5; Psalm 91

FIGHT THE RIGHT FOE

"For though we live in the world, we do not wage war as the world does."

2 Corinthians 10:3

Do you know why so many Christian young people are losing the battles in their lives?

They're fighting the wrong enemy! They've been tricked into believing that just because a person said or did something to hurt them, that person is the one they need to fight. But they're wrong. The Bible says our struggle isn't against people.

"But you just don't know what so-and-so did to me!"

It doesn't matter. If you waste your time fighting so-and-so, your real enemy will get away scot-free.

Who is that real enemy? Look at Ephesians 6:12:,"Our fight is not against people on earth. We are fighting against the rulers and authorities and the powers of this world's darkness. We are fighting against the spiritual powers of evil in the heavenly world" (ICB).

Satan and his evil spirits. They are your enemies! They are behind every personal offense you encounter. The people who hurt you and give you trouble are just Satan's way of getting to you. When he wants to strike out at you, he influences them to do the job. Usually they don't even know it. They're just doing what their old, sinful nature is accustomed to doing.

Remember this: Mistreatment is not the demonstration of another person's hate for you. It's a demonstration of Satan's fear of you. When you dig into the Bible and use it like the sword of the Spirit that it is, Satan gets scared. He doesn't want God's promises coming alive in your life...so he looks for some person he can send in there to stop you.

Next time someone hurts you, don't let yourself get sidetracked into fighting them. Stop the spirit behind them. Put battles with people behind and war with the weapons of the Spirit. Zero in on Satan with authority and with God's Word and bring your real enemy down!

talk the truth

"My fight isn't against people. I fight against the rulers and authorities and the powers of this world's darkness. I fight against the spiritual powers of evil." (Ephesians 6:12)

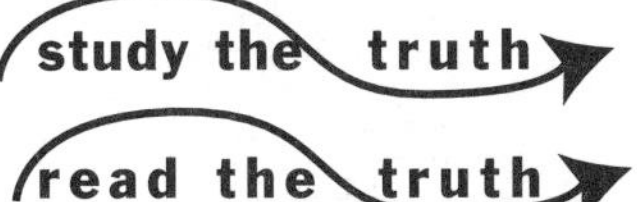
study the truth
read the truth

Ephesians 6:10-18

Ezekiel 1,2,3; Psalms 92,93

November 6

YOU'RE A WINNER

"I write to you, young men, because you are strong, and the word of God lives in you, and you have overcome the evil one."

1 John 2:14

Man was created to be a winner. The Bible tells us in Genesis, for example, that man was put on this earth to rule over it and everything that lived on it.

Man didn't even know what losing was until, through disobedience, he separated himself from God in the Garden of Eden. When that happened, he was forced to accept failure for life, putting himself in a lower position—a position he was never meant to occupy.

It's a sad story. But if Jesus is your Lord, your story has a happy ending. Through faith in Him, you've been made a winner once again!

In fact, God has guaranteed your success. Let me show you what I mean. Imagine you're about to tackle a really tough homework assignment, and before you even get started on it, God speaks to you and says, *I just want you to know, I'm going to personally see to it that this assignment you're working on succeeds.*

Now if He told you that, you'd expect to succeed, wouldn't you? Well, let me tell you something. You do have God's promise that you'll succeed. He said in His Word that in Him you can overcome any problem the world throws your way (1 John 5:1-5). When you face life's troubles, you're not alone!

It doesn't matter how much you feel like a loser. It doesn't matter how many times you've failed. If you believe that Jesus is God's Son, then you've become more than a conqueror in Him (Romans 8:37).

Does that mean you won't have any more trouble? No. It simply means you can go through that trouble and win.

If you've been feeling like a failure lately, let this truth come alive in your heart—*you are a winner!*

talk the truth

"I am strong because God's Word lives in me. I have overcome the evil one." (1 John 2:14)

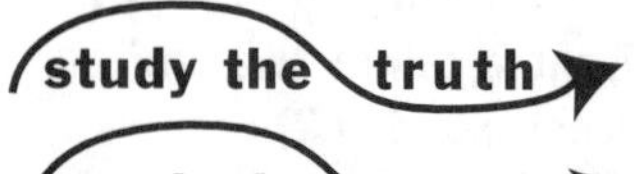
study the truth
read the truth

1 John 5:1-5

Ezekiel 4,5; Psalm 94

A STRONG HEART

"Blessed is the man who fears the Lord, who finds great delight in his commands.... He will have no fear of bad news; his heart is steadfast, trusting in the Lord."

PSALM 112:1,7

The person who delights in God's Word will have a strong, steadfast heart! He can make it through difficult situations without slipping or falling. His mind is made up and he is a winner before he ever enters the battle. A person like that is hard to beat!

The sad thing is that most Christians wait until the disaster hits before they start making themselves strong with the Word. They wait until their back is against the wall. Then, suddenly, they get really spiritual and start praying...and all too often they find they've started too late.

It's like a guy who finds out a burglar is in his house and then starts looking for the barbells, so he can build up enough muscle to throw the burglar out. He won't make it! If he'd been working out instead of watching TV every night, he'd have been ready. But as it is, he's headed for a painful defeat.

Be ready before Satan breaks into your house. Get your heart strong and steadfast. Turn off the TV. Turn off the distractions of the world and turn on God's Word. The time to start working out is right now!

talk the truth

"I delight in God's Word. I do not fear bad news. My heart is steadfast, trusting in the Lord." (Psalm 112:1,7)

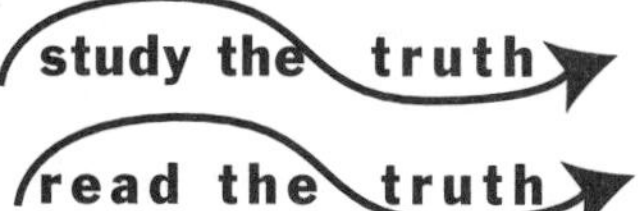
study the truth
read the truth

Job 22:21-30

Ezekiel 6,7; Psalm 95

Kenneth

November 8

THE HIDDEN THINGS OF GOD

"Blessed are you...for this was not revealed to you by man, but by my Father in heaven."

MATTHEW 16:17

Remember when you learned your ABCs? You learned them by using your five senses and your logical abilities to gather information and sort it out. That kind of knowledge is called natural knowledge and it's the only kind most people know anything about.

But for Christians, there's another kind of knowing. It comes from within you instead of from without. It's called *revelation knowledge.*

Jesus spoke about this in Matthew 16. He'd just asked the disciples, "Who do you say I am?" and Peter had answered Him by declaring, "You are the Christ, the Son of the living God" (verses 15-16).

"Blessed are you, Simon," Jesus responded, "for this was not revealed to you by man, but by my Father in heaven" (verse 17).

In other words, Jesus was saying, "Peter, you didn't learn this information through your physical senses. You received it directly from God."

If you've ever had knowledge like that, you know that when it comes, it changes things. It makes you see things in an entirely new light. It gives you such confidence that, as Jesus said to Peter, even the power of hell can't overcome it.

But knowledge like that doesn't come easy. You have to search out what the Bible says. You have to pray in the spirit because this kind of knowledge is "hidden" in Him. The Bible says God has hidden His wisdom *for* the saints (1 Corinthians 2:7-9). He wants you to have it. But to get it, you have seek Him.

If you're hungry for revelation knowledge, get ready to receive it by focusing on what the Bible says, praying and spending time with the Lord. Begin to receive His knowledge...it's the most exciting kind of learning there is.

talk the truth

"I have received the Holy Spirit, so I can know the things freely given to me by God." (1 Corinthians 2:12)

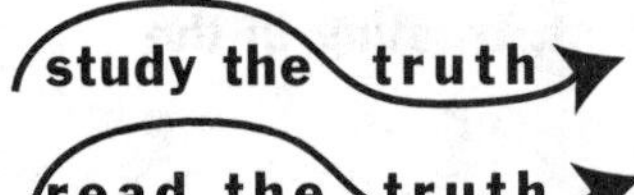
study the truth
read the truth

1 Corinthians 2

Ezekiel 8,9; Psalm 96

STOP THE PRESSURE

"Rejoice and exult in hope; be steadfast and patient in suffering and tribulation; be constant in prayer."

ROMANS 12:12, AMP

Facing a difficult situation? Feeling under the pressure of homework assignments, family problems, or friends who want you to join them in doing something wrong? Then take hold of this mighty promise of God...

"Rejoice and exult in hope."

When Satan comes to steal your victory and tell you that God won't help you, just think about what the Bible says. You can get excited because your hope is in Him and heaven is your home. You can shout because the One inside you is greater than the evil one. You don't have any reason not to be overjoyed! So don't hold back!

"Be steadfast and patient in suffering and tribulation."

Now, the word "tribulation" in this verse means "being under pressure." This verse is saying that when pressures come, you don't have to cave in. Instead, you can be patient and boldly go to God in Jesus' Name to get the help you need. He is always there for you, ready for you to give your worries to Him.

"Be constant in prayer."

Remember this: When things start to become difficult, don't think it's time to give up on God's promises. That's when it's time to double up on them. That's when you need to consistently be in prayer so that you are immovable. Open your Bible, find the promise from God that you need and then pray it. God's promises spoken out of your mouth will not return without an answer! (See Isaiah 55:11)

Release your joy. Be patient under pressure. Be constant in prayer. Satan won't be able to steal a thing from you!

talk the truth

"I rejoice and exult in hope. I am steadfast and patient in suffering and tribulation. I am constant in prayer." (Romans 12:12, AMP)

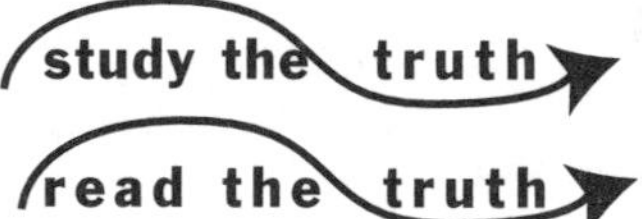
study the truth
read the truth

Romans 5:1-5

Ezekiel 10,11; Psalm 97

November 10

THE INNER WITNESS

"The Spirit Himself bears witness with our spirit."

ROMANS 8:16, NKJV

Do you ever have trouble hearing from God? Even after praying and reading the Bible, do you find that you're still not sure what God wants you to do?

I've had that happen before. I knew His Word, but I was uncertain when I had to make decisions about things the Bible didn't specifically talk about, things such as what college to attend, for example.

The answer lies in understanding that God gives us direction in two ways—His written Word, the Bible, and the "inward witness." They are both very important in our walk with God and they *never* contradict each other.

We can see these two types of direction in the Bible. God expected the Israelites to obey His written Word, but He also said to them, "Obey my voice" (Jeremiah 7:23, KJV) because He wanted them to know His will in certain situations. That's what happened when the Israelites invaded Jericho (Joshua 6). They heard God's voice. Where else do you think they would have gotten that strange battle plan? It wasn't written in the Law of Moses. And certainly, no human being would suggest a seven-day march around a city as the most effective form of invasion!

So how does God speak to us? Romans 8 says the Holy Spirit "bears witness" with our spirit. That means that God's directions come from inside, not outside, of us. He speaks to us with an "inward witness."

Tune in today to that inward witness, to that quiet knowing, that urging, prompting and leading within you. If, when you hear it, it sounds like you, don't be surprised. It *is* you! It's your spirit influenced by the Holy Spirit. After Jesus is your Lord, your spirit is a safe guide because you now have God's nature. So listen to what He's telling you today!

talk the truth

"I am led by the Spirit of God. He bears witness with my spirit and leads me by the inward witness." (Romans 8:16, NKJV)

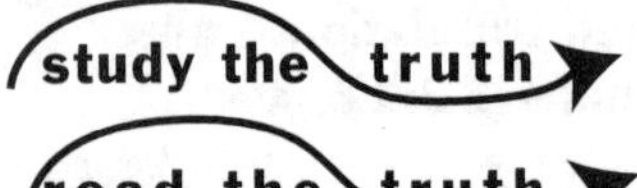
study the truth
read the truth

Joshua 6:1-20

Ezekiel 12,13; Psalm 98

A POWERHOUSE OF PROTECTION

"'No weapon forged against you will prevail, and you will refute every tongue that accuses you. This is the heritage of the servants of the Lord, and this is their vindication from me,' declares the Lord."

Isaiah 54:17

"No weapon forged against you will prevail." Isn't that great news?! Isn't it good to know that no sickness, no circumstance, no pressure that rises against you can successfully bring you down?

Some years ago, one of our friends was facing a lawsuit. So, we prayed together and agreed that this promise was the final word in the situation—not what was spoken against him. We stood in faith, believing that lawsuit had to fail.

Sure enough, when my friend went to court, they just couldn't beat him. He didn't win that case because of smart lawyers. He won because he was innocent, and because he had believed that powerful promise from God.

Follow his example. When Satan attacks you, don't sit around begging God to save you. Open up your Bible to Isaiah 54:17 instead. Remind yourself of what God has promised you. Use that promise to strengthen you against sin and whatever Satan would like to use to keep you bound.

Then stand on it in prayer. Say, *"Lord, I refuse to be afraid of this weapon Satan has brought against me because I know that according to the Bible, it cannot win. I trust You to protect me, and I thank You for it now. In Jesus' Name. Amen."*

Don't let the powerhouse of God's protection go to waste. Put it to work in your life when faced with peer pressure, mistreatment or another problem. It's your God-given right!

talk the truth

"No weapon formed against me will prevail." (Isaiah 54:17)

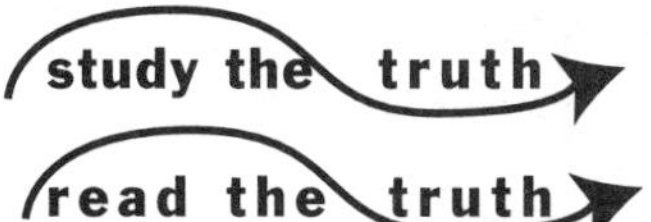
study the truth
read the truth

Isaiah 54:10-17

Ezekiel 14,15; Psalm 99

November 12

OPEN THE FLOW

"Therefore, since we are surrounded by such a great cloud of witnesses, let us throw off everything that hinders and the sin that so easily entangles, and let us run with perseverance the race marked out for us. Let us fix our eyes on Jesus, the author and perfecter of our faith...."

Hebrews 12:1,2

Many Christian teenagers know that disciplining themselves to stay away from sin is important—the Bible clearly teaches that. But they're not sure exactly how to go about it.

Some have given up, shrugging off such discipline as impossible. Others are still fighting to get themselves under control—and losing one battle after another. But it doesn't have to be that way. In fact, we can't afford to let it be that way. It will cost us too much.

We're part of the generation that will see the miracles and wonders which the prophets of long ago wished they could have seen. We will see the Holy Spirit moving throughout the earth. But sin hinders the Holy Spirit's flow. And only as we rid ourselves of it will God's power be seen through us. Only then will we experience the wonderful things that were prophesied would take place.

So put your failure behind you. Start by making a firm decision that you won't let sin rob you of God's power in your life. That's the first step to setting yourself up for victory.

Then, day by day, spend time filling yourself with God's Word. Replace the desire to sin with a desire to know God more and more. Soon you'll find yourself reaching for your Bible instead of reaching to that sin you've been struggling with.

It's possible to step out of sin and live under the Holy Spirit's control. Look to Jesus...He will show you the way.

talk the truth

"I throw off everything that hinders and the sin that so easily entangles me. I run the race marked out for me with perseverance." (Hebrews 12:1,2)

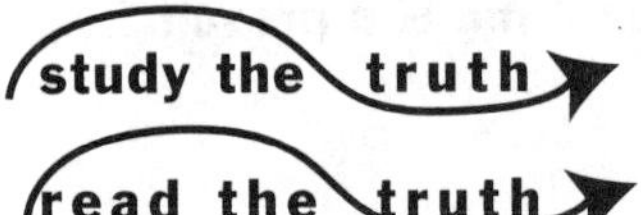
study the truth
read the truth

2 Timothy 2:19-23

Ezekiel 16,17,18; Psalms 100,101

STAKE YOUR CLAIM

"Praise the Lord. Blessed is the man who fears the Lord, who finds great delight in his commands.... Wealth and riches are in his house, and his righteousness endures forever."

PSALM 112:1,3

I'll never forget the time Gloria discovered that scripture. We didn't have any money at the time, and the walls in our house were as bare as they could be. But she was ready to decorate. So she took that promise, "Wealth and riches are in his house" and believed in it by faith. Suddenly, everywhere we went, someone was giving us a painting or something else for our house.

Sadly, most Christians aren't as quick to believe God for that kind of thing. Some even say God doesn't promise us physical blessings, just spiritual. But the truth is, you can't separate the two. That's why Jesus says, "Seek first his kingdom and his righteousness, and all these [material] things will be given to you as well" (Matthew 6:33). He knows the spiritual and the physical are connected.

The physical world cannot operate independently from the spiritual world. What happens in one is just a reflection of what happens in the other.

Obviously, your standing with God greatly affects every part of your life. That's why, when you get hold of God's Word and begin to prosper spiritually, you can begin to prosper physically as well.

Don't let anyone talk you out of any of God's promises. You don't have to choose between physical and spiritual blessings. God's promised both to you. Take hold of them by faith. Dare to reach out and receive the riches God has given to you!

talk the truth

"I am blessed because I fear the Lord and love His Word. Wealth and riches are in my house." (Psalm 112:1,3)

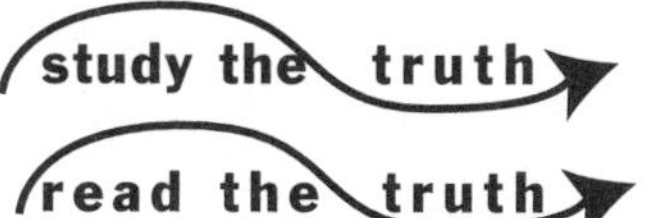
study the truth
read the truth

Deuteronomy 7:8-13

Ezekiel 19,20; Psalm 102

November 14

WHEN THE PRESSURE IS ON

"Then those who feared the Lord talked with each other, and the Lord listened and heard. A scroll of remembrance was written in his presence concerning those who feared the Lord and honored his name."

MALACHI 3:16

Have you ever noticed that those who have the most exciting, faith-inspiring testimonies are those who've been under pressure at some time in their lives? They're the people who remained faithful when the pressure was on...people who believed God's promises of protection in the middle of dangerous situations or people who trusted God for healing in the face of a terminal disease.

When you get into a difficult spot, that's not the time to step back and wonder if God will come through. When the situations around you seem to refuse to get in line with God's promises, don't re-evaluate God. He's not failing.

If you re-evaluate anything, re-evaluate yourself! Look and see where you may have failed. If you still can't find out what the problem is, just say, "God, I don't know what's wrong here, please show me. But one thing I know, the problem's not with You, and I continue to be moved by the promises in Your Word and not by circumstances." Then, when He reveals something to you, quickly make changes.

I encourage you to stand firm and to keep honoring God with your life. And when the pressure is on, realize that the Lord is listening. What's He going to hear?

talk the truth — **"By faith, I stand firm in God's promises to me. I do not stagger." (Romans 4:20)**

study the truth — **Psalm 62**

read the truth — **Ezekiel 21,22; Psalm 103**

PUT LOVE TO WORK

What do you do when you're facing a stubborn problem? Put the power of love to work! The power of love is the greatest power in the universe. It *never* fails (1 Corinthians 13).

"And now these three remain: faith, hope and love. But the greatest of these is love."

1 Corinthians 13:13

Now, the Bible says God *is* love. So when you put love into a situation, you bring God right into the middle of it. Think about that! When you walk in love in any situation, Jesus becomes responsible for your success.

What is this love I'm talking about?

First Corinthians 13 tells us it's patient and kind. It does not envy or boast, and it's not proud or rude. It isn't self-seeking or easily angered. And it keeps no record of wrongs. Love rejoices when truth wins and it hates evil. It always protects, always trusts, always hopes and always perseveres.

The person who refuses to love is missing out on the very best God has to offer. So don't you miss out. Put love into every situation, every relationship, every prayer and every thought until it totally takes over your life. It will strengthen you and drive out every fear. It will drive Satan out of your life and set you free from every torment of darkness.

Put love to work on the stubborn problems in your life. It's the one solution they'll never be able to resist.

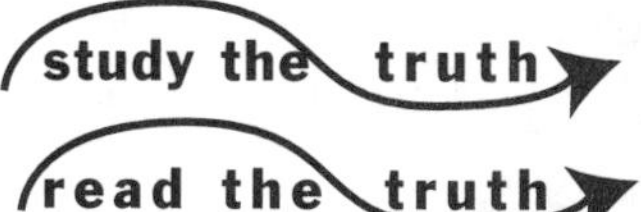

"The love of God in me never fails." (1 Corinthians 13:13)

study the truth **1 Corinthians 13**

read the truth **Ezekiel 23,24; Psalm 104**

Kenneth

November 16

PICK UP YOUR SWORD

"Fight the good fight of the faith."

1 TIMOTHY 6:12

When you're up against the wall, don't start begging God to break through it for you. That's not the way He works. He'll give you the plan and the power and guarantee your victory. But *your* hand, not His, is what He will use to get the job done. *You're* going to have to act on His promises.

God showed me that through a vision many years ago. I was spending some time in prayer when suddenly I saw myself standing at the front of a church. I looked up and saw a horrible, ugly dragon poke his head through the front door.

As he came in, his body expanded like a balloon, filling the whole room. He was snorting fire and smoke. Then, in the vision, he turned on me and almost burned my clothes!

As I fell back onto the floor, I saw Jesus standing nearby with a sword in His hand. *Why doesn't He do something about this?* I thought.

But He didn't move. He just stood there frowning. I could tell He wasn't pleased with me lying there in defeat. Then Jesus held out the sword to me and pointed at the dragon. The look on His face said, *Get up!*

I reached up to take hold of the sword, and an instant before I touched it, Jesus turned it loose. The sword stayed in midair on its own. I grabbed it and began to pull myself up. Not only did it hold its place, but it began to lift me!

I stood and touched the dragon's chin with my sword and it split him from one end to the other. It laid him open right before my eyes. In amazement, I looked down at the sword. *Why haven't I used this before?* I thought.

So what's the meaning to this vision? Simply this—don't wait for God to slay the dragons in your life. You have the sword of the Spirit, the all-powerful Word of the living God, at your fingertips. Pick it up and use it today!

talk the truth

"I fight the good fight of faith. I have the sword of the Spirit, which is God's Word." (1 Timothy 6:12; Ephesians 6:17)

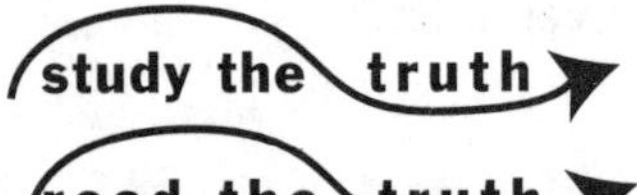
study the truth
read the truth

Joshua 11:5-23

Ezekiel 25,26; Psalm 105

THE POWER TO CREATE

Creating new things, changing old things. Because you and I are made in God's image, that's something we're always supposed to be doing. But if we're to be successful at it, we need to learn a lesson about it from the Creator Himself.

"Therefore be imitators of God—copy Him and follow His example—as well-beloved children [imitate their father]."

EPHESIANS 5:1, AMP

You know, God didn't just start creating everything by accident. He didn't say, "POOF! Well, what do you know! Look at that!" No, before He made His universe, He had an idea inside Himself of what He wanted to create. Then He said, "Light be!," and light was.

If we're going to imitate Him, we need to put this principle to work too.

"But that's God," you say. "Surely you don't expect me to try to act like God." I most certainly do. Ephesians 5:1 says to!

If you're a reborn child of God, He has given you this principle and the power to make permanent changes in your life and in your circumstances.

Think again about creation. God wanted light. So He said, "Let there be light" (Genesis 1:3). The words He spoke were directly related to the idea He had inside Him. He used His words to get that image from the inside to the outside.

You can use the Bible as the foundation for the ideas inside you. God's Word has supernatural power. And if you believe His Word by faith and speak it out, it will work to change your life and circumstances as surely as it did for your Father.

Find out what real creativity is all about. Dig into the Bible and start rebuilding your world today.

talk the truth

"I imitate God, copying Him and following His example." (Ephesians 5:1, AMP)

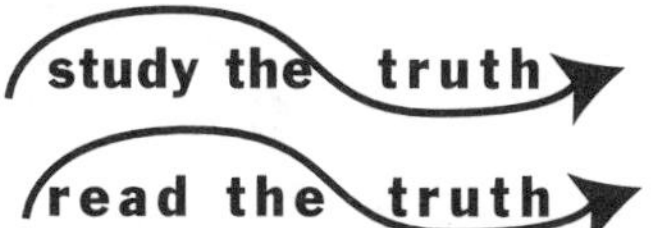
study the truth
read the truth

2 Corinthians 4:6-13

Ezekiel 27,28; Psalm 106

November 18

DO YOU KNOW WHAT TO ASK FOR?

"'What do you want me to do for you?' Jesus asked him. The blind man said, 'Rabbi, I want to see.'"

Mark 10:51

All of us know what it's like to go around in circles...to receive one answer to prayer only to find another problem waiting for us.

We pray in faith, but we keep getting caught in the same old problems over and over again. Why? Because all too often, we don't really know what it is we need to be praying. Too many times we pray for the wrong thing.

Look with me at Mark 10 and you'll see what I mean. Blind Bartimaeus sat by the roadside begging when Jesus passed by. "When he heard that it was Jesus of Nazareth, he began to shout, 'Jesus, Son of David, have mercy on me!...' [Then] he jumped to his feet and came to Jesus. 'What do you want me to do for you?' Jesus asked him. The blind man said, 'Rabbi, I want to see.'

"'Go,' said Jesus, 'your faith has healed you.' Immediately he received his sight and followed Jesus along the road" (verses 47, 50-52).

Now think about this. From what the Scriptures tell us, how many needs did Bartimaeus have? Just one? No! He wasn't only a blind man—he was a beggar. He probably had more problems than you could imagine, and every one would have seemed like a logical need. But if Bartimaeus could receive his sight, all the rest would fall into line. It was sight he *needed*...and Bartimaeus knew it.

So, when Jesus asked how He could help, Bartimaeus knew exactly what to ask for—and he got it.

Jesus is just as willing to meet your need today. The question is, do you really know what to ask for? Think and pray about that. Let Jesus show you what you really need. If you do, your prayers will take on a whole new power. Instead of hitting around at the edges of your problems, they'll go straight to the heart. And you won't have to waste your life running in circles anymore.

talk the truth

"Jesus meets my needs. I take time to find out what I *truly* need. Then, when I pray in faith, I receive my answer." (Mark 10:51)

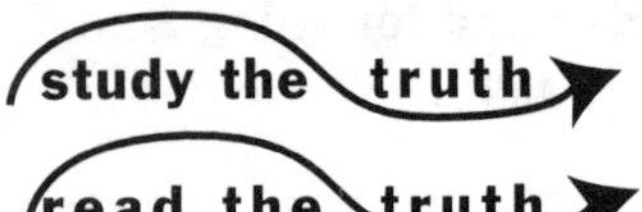
study the truth
read the truth

Mark 10:46-52

Ezekiel 29,30; Psalm 107

FROM MILK TO SOLID FOOD

"In fact, though by this time you ought to be teachers, you need someone to teach you the elementary truths of God's word all over again. You need milk, not solid food!"

Hebrews 5:12

Do you know why the Church has been in such a mess over the past few years? Do you know why Satan has been able to make a public display of our weaknesses? Do you know why instead of being unified and strong, we've often been torn apart by division and criticisms that come from within?

It is because God's people need to learn the elementary truths of the Bible all over again. For the most part, God's people don't know His ways. When it comes to living by faith, they're just like babies. That's why He's made it my job and yours to train Christians up and help bring them to maturity.

Well, what can I do? you may wonder. You'll find your answer in Hebrews 3:13. "Encourage one another daily, as long as it is called Today."

That's not just a Bible verse. It's a direct command from the Lord.

"Encourage one another daily." Pray about that scripture today, won't you? Spend time talking about it with God. Ask Him how He wants you to fulfill that command. He may tell you to help support ministries. He may tell you to spend some quality time with your brother or sister. He may tell you to fill yourself so full of His Word that it spills out on everyone you meet and encourages them to go on—and grow on—in Jesus.

Whatever He says, do it! There's a Church full of spiritual babies out there and more are being born all the time. You can help bring them from milk to solid food. Begin to encourage them. Today.

talk the truth

"I encourage others daily." (Hebrews 3:13)

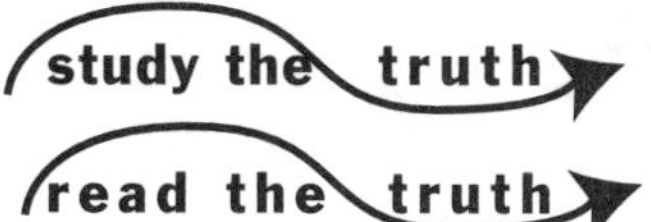
study the truth
read the truth

Hebrews 3:7-19

Ezekiel 31,32,33; Psalms 108,109

November 20

GET OUT OF PRISON

"Then you will know the truth, and the truth will set you free."

John 8:32

You may be reading this devotional in a juvenile detention center. Or, you may be reading it in the comfort of your own living room. No matter where you are, it's possible to be in a prison whether you're under guard or not. Whether you're bound behind locked doors or by increasing troubles, realize this: God wants you completely free from the inside out! If you want a way out of the prison you're in, here is the best place to begin...

1. Start Where You Are Right Now

It doesn't matter how you got where you are. What's important is that you start believing God from there—even if you're right in the middle of growing troubles. Don't think you have to wait until you're in a better place. Just start getting real with God immediately. When you do, you'll be freer where you are right now than you ever were anywhere else.

2. Find Out Who You Are in Jesus

What matters is not who you are, what you are or where you've been, but who you are now in Jesus. Through reading the Bible, you can find out who you are now—a reborn child of God, with a call on your life.

3. Learn How to Pray

No situation in which you find yourself disqualifies you from prayer—it's available to everyone. Even sinners in the deepest sin can pray and make Jesus their Lord. The only situation that keeps you from getting help is absolutely refusing to pray at all. So learn how to pray and let God run things. Then you can be free even in the midst of trouble.

It doesn't matter what kind of situation you're in—God wants you free! Just honestly lay everything out before Him and start praying and acting on His Word. You can be free, regardless of the situation you're facing. Let God prove it to you today!

talk the truth

"I know the truth, and the truth sets me free." (John 8:32)

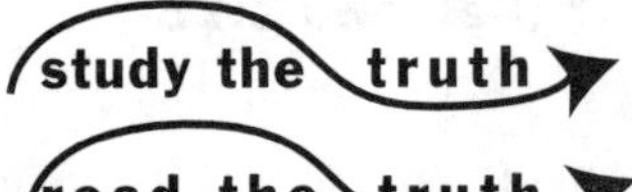
study the truth
read the truth

John 8:31-36

Ezekiel 34,35; Psalm 110

GIVE GOD THE GLORY

"This is to my Father's glory, that you bear much fruit, showing yourselves to be my disciples."

JOHN 15:8

There's an old tradition that says God gets Glory from the wonderful way His children bear pain and hurt and that the world is impressed by that. What a lie! That's simply a tool of Satan to keep God's children from being all God created them to be.

People of the world already have all the pain and hurt they want. They are looking for a way out of it. They don't care what you preach. All they care about are the results. That's why they'll come to your church when they hear people are getting healed and set free from suffering.

The Bible says that God gets Glory when they see the lame walk and the blind see (Matthew 15:31). Jesus said, "This is to my Father's glory, that you bear much fruit..." (John 15:8). What is that fruit? Lives being restored and healed by God's power.

There was a man who came to one of our healing meetings who was so far gone with cancer, he had almost no life in him. He didn't even know the Lord, but he came believing for a miracle. During the service, the Lord told Ken someone was being healed of cancer. When the man came up and received his healing, he said, "I left the hospital this morning with cancer, and I'm healed." He went back to the hospital that afternoon and the doctors checked and dismissed him. As a result, the man received Jesus as his Lord, and later that day he and his wife—who were separated—got back together.

Now that's fruit! That brings God Glory. Let's do away with religious tradition and go with what the Bible says. Let's impress the world with Jesus and give God the Glory today!

talk the truth

"God is glorified when lives are restored and healed by His power." (John 15:8)

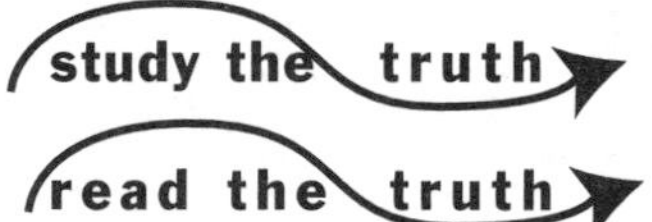
study the truth
read the truth

John 15:1-16

Ezekiel 36,37; Psalm 111

November 22

BECOME SENSITIVE

"Get rid of all bitterness, rage and anger, brawling and slander, along with every form of malice. Be kind and compassionate to one another, forgiving each other, just as in Christ God forgave you."

Ephesians 4:31,32

A few years ago I was in Detroit, and I met a woman who was raised in a Communist-bloc country. While I was visiting with her, a news broadcast came on. And as we sat there listening to it, suddenly tears came to her eyes.

"What's the matter?" I asked.

Although I hadn't noticed it, the news commentator had said something derogatory about the president. "I don't like to hear anyone talk about this country like that," she said. "I don't care whether it's true or not. I don't want to hear it."

The newscaster's comment had slipped right by me. But it brought tears to her eyes. Why? Because she had a sensitive heart for this country.

We need to be more like that. We need to realize that our own insensitivity has driven the Holy Spirit's power from our lives, our schools and our churches. We need to realize that the license we've given ourselves to criticize others has weakened us all.

What will strengthen us again? The power of the Holy Spirit that falls on every sensitive and seeking heart.

I urge you to repent, forgive anyone who's offended or hurt you, be devoted to the Word and spend time with the Father. Commit yourself to walking with a tender heart everywhere you go. Watch what you say—even when you're joking—so that you don't offend a classmate or someone else you know. Be sensitive to the needs of others when you pass them in the hall or when you're out with your friends. You never know when your example might affect someone's life.

So don't allow the condition of your heart to hold back the Holy Spirit. Become sensitive!

talk the truth

"I am kind and compassionate to others, forgiving, just as God has forgiven me." (Ephesians 4:31,32)

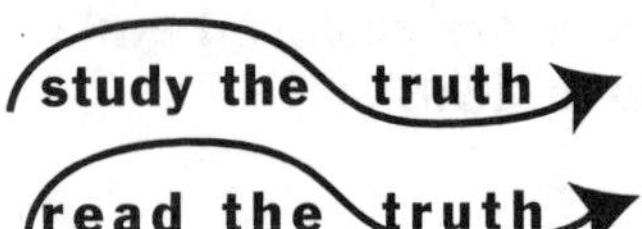
study the truth
read the truth

Ephesians 4:1-13

Ezekiel 38,39; Psalm 112

OBEY HIM IN THE LITTLE THINGS

"He who is faithful in a very little [thing], is faithful also in much..."

LUKE 16:10, AMP

Have you ever wanted to do something really big, but it seemed the Lord wouldn't let you? If so, there's probably a good reason why.

You'll see what I mean when you notice what God did with the Israelites after He rescued them from Egypt. He wanted to take them into the Promised Land. But before He could, God had to know if they would obey Him. Because if they wouldn't, the enemies they were about to face would wipe them out.

Do you know what He did? He tested them in a small matter.

Exodus 16:4 tells us about this simple test. "Then the Lord said to Moses, 'I will rain down bread from heaven for you. The people are to go out each day and gather enough for that day. In this way I will test them and see whether they will follow my instructions.'"

God took a little, insignificant matter—the food they ate—to see if they would listen to Him. He told them how much of it to pick up, when to pick it up and what to do with it after they brought it in.

And the Israelites went right out and disobeyed those instructions. Their actions showed God that what He said was not important to them. They weren't even willing to obey His simplest commands.

God works the same way today. Before He sends you on a major mission, He gives you the opportunity to prove you can be trusted with small instructions.

But most of us miss that opportunity. We pray, "Lord, I'll do anything You say." But then when the Lord says, *I want you to get up and pray for one hour every morning,* we never quite get around to it.

Start obeying God in little things. Let Him know you'll be faithful to obey His Word and the voice of His Spirit. Once He knows you won't let disobedience wipe you out, He'll start sending bigger and better assignments your way.

talk the truth

"I am faithful in the very little things, and I will be faithful also in the big things." (Luke 16:10, AMP)

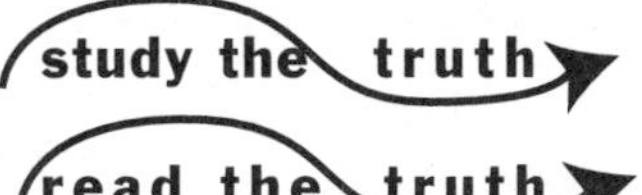
study the truth
read the truth

Exodus 16:1-28

Ezekiel 40,41; Psalm 113

Gloria

November 24

LET YOUR LIFE SHINE

"Don't let anyone look down on you because you are young, but set an example for the believers in speech, in life, in love, in faith and in purity."

1 TIMOTHY 4:12

The world needs to see good examples. *Your friends* need to see good examples. They need to see Christians walk in love and purity and faith in their homes, in their schools and on their jobs.

The Apostle Paul encourages us in Romans 12:17 to live above reproach in the sight of all people. Other scriptures teach us to avoid all appearances of evil. So, when you go after God, don't walk on the edge, trying to see how much you can get by with. Conduct yourself in a way that will put to rest any question about whether or not you're a Christian. Let the people around you see your love, faith and purity in every situation.

Your example will go a lot further than your words. When our son, John, was a little boy, we were spending time with my grandparents. John was sleeping with my granddaddy and he woke him up in the night and said, "Pop, I have an earache. Would you pray for it?" Well, my grandparents were raised in a church that didn't believe in healing. I don't know what Pop did, but it didn't work. So, John just got up and said, "I'm going to go get in bed with my mother. When she prays, it stops hurting." You see, I had set an example of faith and love and John remembered it.

Now, in day-to-day living, your friends might forget some of the Bible verses you've told them or act like they're not interested in the things of God. But they'll never forget your example.

Don't let little sins and spiritual compromises cast a shadow over your example. Live right and let the light of Jesus shine brightly through you.

talk the truth **"I set an example for others in speech, in life, in love, in faith and in purity." (1 Timothy 4:12)**

study the truth **Romans 12:9-21**

read the truth **Ezekiel 42,43; Psalm 114**

STIR UP THE POWER

There are times when you know what God has called you to do, but you just don't feel you have the resources inside you to do it. The Bible tells us how to handle those situations through a clear command: "Stir up the gift of God which is in you."

You stir *yourself* up! Everything you need is already in you. Jesus put it there. Everything you'll ever need to accomplish what God has called you to do has been placed inside you by God Himself.

Faith is in there. Power is in there. Love is in there. Courage is in there. Believe that. Speak it aloud right now:

"In the Name of Jesus, I stir up the gift of God that's within me. I won't wait until I feel stirred up. I'm stepping out by faith—and letting my feelings follow!

"I'm stirring up the faith, love, power and courage of God that's in me. I'm stirring myself up and running Satan out of my life. I am stirred up!"

"Greatly desiring to see you, being mindful of your tears...I remind you to stir up the gift of God which is in you.... For God has not given us a spirit of fear, but of power and of love and of a sound mind."

2 Timothy 1:4,6,7, NKJV

talk the truth

"I stir up the gift of God in me!" (2 Timothy 1:6, NKJV)

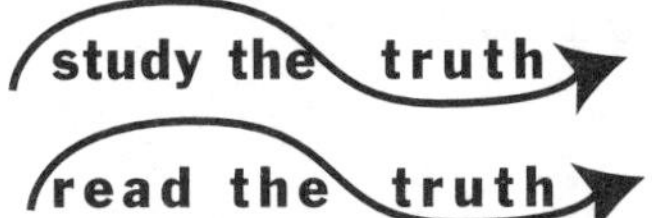
study the truth
read the truth

2 Timothy 1:1-8

Ezekiel 44,45; Psalm 115

Kenneth

November 26

WHAT'S YOUR NAME?

"And whatever you do, whether in word or deed, do it all in the name of the Lord Jesus, giving thanks to God the Father through him."

COLOSSIANS 3:17

Did you know your name has been changed? It's no longer the same as it was before you became a Christian. When you entered your covenant with God, you gave yourself completely away. You are no longer your own. Your strengths and your weaknesses belong forever to Jesus—your covenant partner. And in this blood covenant, you take each other's names.

When you received Jesus as your Lord, He took your name! Your name was sin, weakness, fear, poverty and every other evil thing you inherited from Adam. Jesus took those names from you and gave you His own in exchange. That's right! Ephesians 3:15 says that the whole Church has been named after Him. That means you have been given Jesus' Name—and the power and authority that goes with it!

Just think about Whom you're named after:

Jesus, Mighty God, Lion of the Tribe of Judah, Wisdom, Rescuer, Word of Life, Defender, Provider, The Great I Am, Helper, Savior, Prince of Peace, Wonderful Counselor, Lamb of God, Lord of Hosts, Root of David, Author and Finisher of Our Faith, The Way, Healer, Son of God, The Truth, Chief Cornerstone, King of kings, Light of the World, Chief Shepherd, My Strength and Song, Righteous Judge, Son of Righteousness, Resurrection and Life, The Alpha and Omega.

Those names cover any need you'll ever have!

You can't call yourself discouraged anymore. That's not your name. You can't answer when Satan yells, *Hey, loser!* That's not your name. Jesus has taken those old names of yours. They're gone. So take time to consider all the names of the Lord. Each one is wrapped up in the Name of Jesus, the Name above all names!

talk the truth

"Everything I do or say, I do in the name of the Lord." (Colossians 3:17)

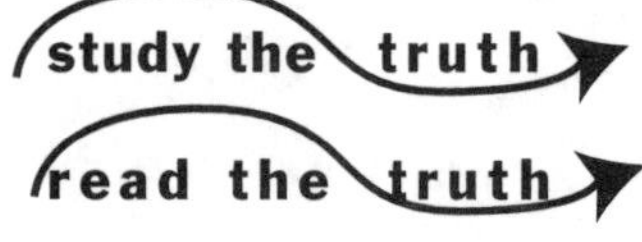
study the truth
read the truth

Ephesians 3:16-21

Ezekiel 46,47,48; Psalms 116,117

November 27

OCCUPY TILL JESUS COMES

The Bible teaches that as Christians, you and I are to occupy until Jesus comes. "Occupy" is a military term meaning to hold possession, or control, of conquered troops and territory. If we're to hold possession of the promises God has given us in Jesus, and if we're to stay in control of conquered sins in our lives, then most of us will have to change our attitudes. We have to recognize that Jesus has already won the victory.

That's right. Satan is already defeated. He was whipped when Jesus died and rose again. We're not on the defensive, he is!

What's more, Jesus has given you His very own armor and sword to use to keep that defeated devil in line. You may be a 90-pound weakling on your own, but if you'll put on God's armor, Satan will never know it. He'll run from you just like you were Jesus.

Think about it. What would you do if you were Satan and you came face to face with some guy wearing God's armor with God's weapons in each hand? As long as he only spoke what God says, you would think that must be God inside!

Don't overlook any of the armor you've been given. Wear it all. Keep Satan on the defensive—and occupy till Jesus comes!

"Therefore put on the full armor of God, so that when the day of evil comes, you may be able to stand your ground, and after you have done everything, to stand. Stand firm then, with the belt of truth buckled around your waist, with the breastplate of righteousness in place, and with your feet fitted with the readiness that comes from the gospel of peace. In addition to all this, take up the shield of faith, with which you can extinguish all the flaming arrows of the evil one. Take the helmet of salvation and the sword of the Spirit, which is the word of God."

EPHESIANS 6:13-17

talk the truth

"I will 'occupy' until Jesus comes, not letting go of God's promises." (Ephesians 6:13-17)

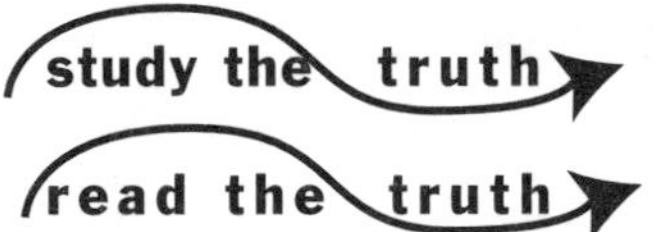
study the truth
read the truth

Luke 12:35-44

Daniel 1,2; Psalm 118

November 28

IMITATE THE FAITHFUL

"Remember your leaders and superiors in authority, [for it was they] who brought to you the Word of God. Observe attentively and consider their manner of living...and imitate their faith...."

HEBREWS 13:7, AMP

Apart from God's Word and prayer, nothing can do more for you than imitating a real man of faith. I found that out many years ago when I was a student at Oral Roberts University. As co-pilot on the airplane that took Oral Roberts and his staff to meetings, I had the opportunity to study him closely. I heard him preach. I watched him pray for the sick.

I'll never forget the day I had the opportunity to put some of what I'd learned into action. Spiritually, I wasn't that mature. But I'd been assigned to help the people in the "invalid room" get ready for Oral Roberts to pray for them. I was standing there surrounded by every kind of sickness and disease you can imagine. And when Oral Roberts came in, he caught me by the coat sleeve and said, "You're going to do the praying. You're going to lay hands on them."

I know all the blood must have drained out of my face because about the only things I'd ever prayed for were a headache and a serious hangnail!

The first lady we approached had cancer of the stomach. She weighed less than 80 pounds. She was just the picture of death. I walked over toward her and before I could open my mouth, I heard a voice from behind me say, "In the Name of Jesus, take up your bed and walk." She instantly spit that cancer out on the floor. Then she jumped off that bed and screamed, "I'm healed!" and started running around the room.

Let me tell you, that moment changed me. When I stepped up to the next person and raised my hands, I could see the healing coming. I'd seen Jesus heal through Oral Roberts, so I could see Him heal through me.

You can do the same thing. Find someone who's operating in more faith and power than you are and learn from them. Sit under them. Watch Jesus in them, and then copy Him. Sooner or later, others will start seeing Jesus in you.

talk the truth

"I remember my leaders who brought me the Word. I observe them attentively and consider their manner of living. I imitate their faith." (Hebrews 13:7, AMP)

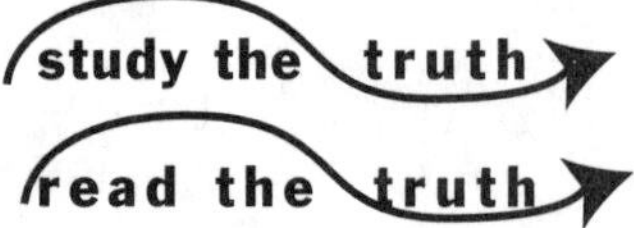
study the truth
read the truth

2 Kings 2:1-15

Daniel 3,4; Psalm 119:1-24

DON'T BUY A LIE

"All these blessings will come upon you and accompany you if you obey the Lord your God."

DEUTERONOMY 28:2

"Well, in the end I'm sure you'll see that being broke is actually a blessing in disguise." Have you ever heard anyone try to comfort someone by saying that? You probably have. The problem is, honestly, it's a lie from Satan.

As a result, many Christians are suffering one financial defeat after another. So let's look at the Bible and get the issue of prosperity and poverty straight once and for all. Let's find out which is good and which is bad.

You can find the answer to that question in Deuteronomy 28. What God describes in verses 1 through 14 is what's good—prosperity. In verses 15 through 31, God describes poverty—and He calls it a curse.

A curse is meant to destroy. Not to teach people a lesson. Not to make them more spiritual. But to destroy them.

Satan has gone to great lengths to convince God's people that poverty is a blessing in disguise. But don't buy into his lie. Get your thinking in line with God's Word. If you're a Christian, you no longer have to live under the curse of poverty or any other curse, for that matter. According to Galatians 3:13, you've been redeemed!

talk the truth

"All God's blessings come upon me and overtake me because I obey the Lord." (Deuteronomy 28:2)

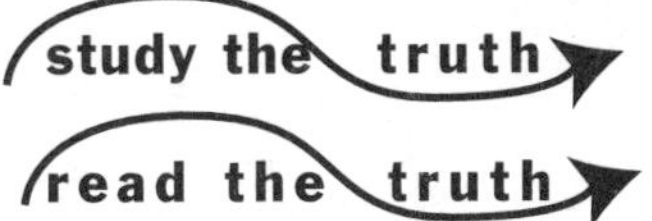
study the truth
read the truth

Deuteronomy 28:1-31

Daniel 5,6; Psalm 119:25-49

November 30

REMAIN IN THE WORD

"If you remain in me and my words remain in you, ask whatever you wish, and it will be given you."

JOHN 15:7

That word "remain" is so important. When Jesus told us to obey His commandments and keep His Word, He wasn't just telling us to follow a bunch of rules and regulations.

He was telling us to allow His living Word to make its home within us. He was telling us to spend time with it, to think about it, to fill our minds and our mouths with it, and to let it guide our every action.

The Apostle Paul put it this way, "Let the word of Christ dwell in you richly..." (Colossians 3:16). Most Christians don't have any idea what that means. That's one of the reasons they're so short on power.

Oral Roberts once said that when God's Word is really remaining in you, when it's alive and producing like it should, you can hear it. You know what it's like when you get a song on your mind and you just keep hearing it over and over inside you? Well, when you remain in the Word, you'll probably hear it in the same way.

Many times I've been in desperate situations, wondering what I should do, when suddenly a scripture would come up from inside me. Suddenly, I'd know exactly what the answer to my situation was. I'd be rescued by the Word of God that remained in me.

So, invite the Holy Spirit to go to work on your behalf. Just keep telling Him, "Whatever You help me remember from the Bible is exactly what I'll do. I'll be obedient to every command of Jesus that You bring to mind."

Make a decision to remain in the Word...and you'll soon discover that the Word is remaining in you.

talk the truth

"I remain in the Lord and His Word remains in me." (John 15:7)

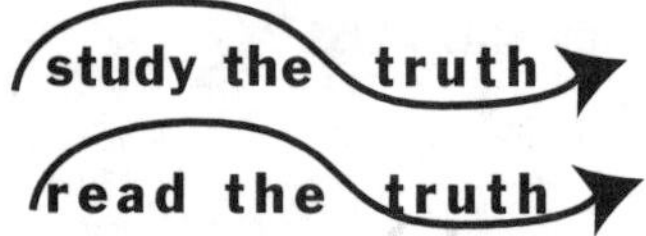
study the truth
read the truth

Colossians 3:1-16

Daniel 7,8; Psalm 119:50-72

MOVING FORWARD OR DRIFTING BACK?

"We must pay more careful attention, therefore, to what we have heard, so that we do not drift away."

Hebrews 2:1

It's happened to all of us. Our lives are going great for the first time in months, when suddenly we slip into a moment of sin and everything falls apart. We have to start all over again.

That's what happened to the people to whom the book of Hebrews was written. They made great spiritual progress, but then drifted back so much till they needed the basics of the Bible again (Hebrews 5:12).

What caused them to fall so far? They let things get in the way of their faith. They let God's promises slip, so they slipped.

That's happened to Christians a lot lately.

"Well," they say, "I just don't have much time to spend reading the Bible."

They've turned their attention away from God's promises. It's not that they didn't believe them anymore. It's just that they gave their attention to other things. They let their Word level drop, and since low Word level equals low faith level, they soon began to be defeated in areas where they once had victory.

Don't let that happen to you. When things are going well, dig even deeper into what God has for you. Concentrate on becoming so strong that not only can you get your own needs met, but you can meet others' needs also!

Don't get so busy enjoying today's victory that tomorrow ends up in defeat. Give God's Word more of your attention—not less. And grow from faith to faith.

talk the truth

"I pay careful attention to God's Word, so it won't slip away." (Hebrews 2:1)

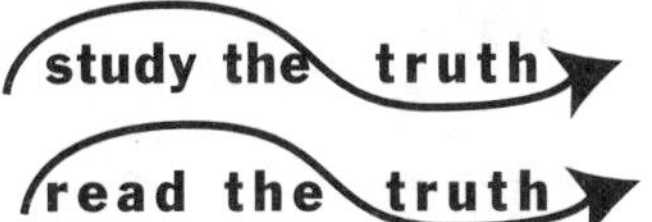
study the truth
read the truth

Hebrews 5:11-14; 6:1-12

Daniel 9,10; Psalm 119:73-96

December 2

FREE YOUR FAITH

"And when you stand praying, if you hold anything against anyone, forgive him."

MARK 11:25

Few people realize just how closely connected faith and forgiveness are. Jesus taught about that connection in Mark 11:22-26.

He said, "Whatever you ask for in prayer, believe that you have received it, and it will be yours. And when you stand praying, if you hold anything against anyone, forgive him."

Jesus put those two thoughts together on purpose. He wanted us to know that forgiving those who have wronged us is fundamental to receiving from God. He wanted us to know that we cannot have our prayers answered and hold grudges at the same time.

Unforgiveness stops your faith and keeps you powerless!

If you're praying for something and you can't seem to get an answer, check your heart for unforgiveness. Ask the Holy Spirit to bring any hidden grudge to light. Make sure you're not angry at your locker mate for the way he hangs up his coat—or upset at your parents for not letting you see a certain movie. Examine yourself for "little grudges," as well as the big ones, and then free your faith. You will soon see the things you're praying for!

talk the truth

"When I pray, I forgive anything I've held against anyone. When I forgive, my faith is set free." (Mark 11:25)

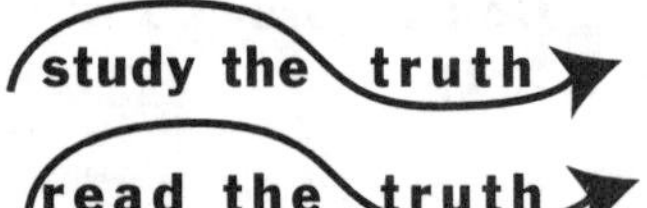
study the truth
read the truth

Matthew 18:21-35

Daniel 11,12; Psalm 119:97-120

TALK LIKE GOD!

"If anyone says to this mountain, 'Go, throw yourself into the sea,' and does not doubt in his heart but believes that what he says will happen, it will be done for him."

MARK 11:23

Jesus didn't say, "If anyone speaks to God about this mountain...." He said we should speak directly to the mountain—or the problem we're facing—and that we should tell it what to do.

From a worldly point of view, that sounds ridiculous. But 1 Corinthians 1:27 explains that God has chosen the foolish things of the world to shame the wise. It will always sound foolish to the world when a Christian talks as if what God has promised is reality...especially when those promises seem to contradict what's happening around us. But if you want to keep the enemy defeated, that's the kind of talking you'd better be doing.

The Bible says God Himself talks that way! In Romans 4:17, it says, "God...calls things that are not as though they were." God doesn't wait for everything to line up before He speaks. He *causes* them to line up *because* He speaks. You can do the same thing if you'll make your words agree with His and speak them by faith.

"But what if nothing happens right away?" you may ask. "What if the circumstances don't immediately change?" When Jesus spoke to the fig tree in Mark 11:14, He didn't go back and check to see if anything had happened to it. No, once He had spoken it, He considered what he said to be done.

Follow His example. Let your faith speak. Agree with God's Word!

talk the truth **"I speak to the mountain and it is removed. I believe what I say will happen." (Mark 11:23)**

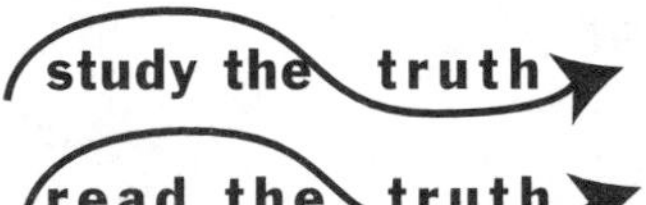

study the truth **Mark 11:12-23**

read the truth **Hosea 1,2,3; Psalm 119:121-144**

December 4

HONOR GOD AND HE'LL HONOR YOU

"Honor the Lord with your possessions, And with the firstfruits of all your increase; So your barns will be filled with plenty, And your vats will overflow with new wine."

PROVERBS 3:9,10, NKJV

The book of Proverbs gives us a very basic principle of success. It is this: If you want God to honor you and bless you in any area of your life, you will have to honor Him in that particular area.

If you want God to bless you financially, you have to honor Him with your money, or as this verse puts it, with the firstfruits of all your increase. In other words, you have to tithe.

Ken and I know that from experience. When we made Jesus the Lord of our lives, we were in terrible shape financially. And we stayed that way for several years because we failed to tithe consistently. Sure, we tithed once in a while, but we never stuck with it.

Then, one day, we decided once and for all that we would tithe no matter what. That's when we started coming out of financial trouble. When we began honoring God with our money by tithing, He began to help us in miraculous ways financially.

You may say, "Well, I don't make that much. I'll start tithing when I get out of school and into the full-time work force. I just can't afford to tithe right now."

But let me tell you, you can't afford not to! Whether you're receiving an allowance or working odd jobs or have a regular job, you need to tithe if you want God to bless you financially.

So do it—even if it looks like you can't afford to. God is faithful! If you'll honor Him by giving Him the 10 percent that belongs to Him, He'll help you with the rest.

Give your tithe to God *first.* Do it in faith, expecting God to bless you. As you tithe, worship Him and be thankful for what He has already done in your life. You'll be amazed when you see what He can do.

talk the truth

"I honor God with my tithe—and His blessings overflow toward me!" (Proverbs 3:9,10, NKJV)

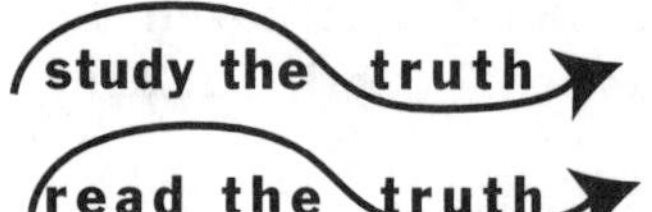
study the truth
read the truth

Malachi 3:8-12

Hosea 4,5; Psalm 119:145-176

WHAT RICHES WERE MEANT TO DO

"He who has been stealing must steal no longer, but must work, doing something useful with his own hands, that he may have something to share with those in need."

EPHESIANS 4:28

It always amazes me when I preach about financial prosperity and then someone says, "I don't need much money. I have a simple life. I just ask God for enough to meet my needs."

They think that's humility, but it's not. It's selfishness! They don't realize it, but they're actually saying, "All I care about is getting enough for me. I don't care about helping anyone else."

Instead, they should ask God for a million dollars, and then give whatever they don't need away. But they don't think about that. They've been brainwashed by a world that says if you have it, you've got to keep it.

That way of thinking has hindered ministries worldwide. It has stunted the growth of ministries that could have reached thousands more for the Lord. But let's face it—it takes money to preach the gospel. Jesus knew that, and contrary to what some people think, His ministry was not a poor one. He had so much money going through His ministry that He had to appoint a treasurer named Judas.

Jesus didn't store up all that money for Himself. He gave it to help meet others' needs. In fact, He had such a reputation for giving that on the night of the last Passover when Judas left so abruptly, the disciples assumed that Jesus had sent him out to give to the poor (John 13:27-30). Can you imagine how much and how often Jesus must have given to the poor for the disciples to assume that?

Jesus wasn't poor. He was the greatest giver Who ever walked the face of this earth, and it's time we started following in His footsteps.

Don't turn down wealth God has for you just because you don't "need" it. Dare to accept it, then pass it along to someone who does need it. Stop working to live and start working to *give*. Discover what riches were *really* meant to do.

talk the truth

"I work and believe for God's blessings, so that I may have something to share with those in need." (Ephesians 4:28)

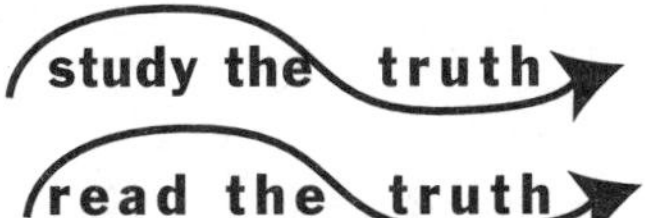
study the truth
read the truth

Luke 12:15-31

Hosea 6,7; Psalm 120

December 6

GOD WILL PROMOTE YOU

"In all the work you are doing, work the best you can. Work as if you were working for the Lord, not for men."

COLOSSIANS 3:23, ICB

Whether you work right now or are just looking forward to earning a paycheck, you need to know that you can be promoted! Now, depending on where you work, that may not seem easy. But know this: God has equipped you. He has already given you everything you need to prosper. All you must do is follow a couple of simple steps to develop what's inside.

First, start right where you are and begin to be diligent and faithful about your job. Proverbs 12:24 says that the hand of the diligent shall bear rule (KJV). That means that if you start applying the principle of diligence to your life, you will prosper. It may not happen tomorrow, but you need to start where you are today. Make sure you show up to work on time. Do what you're asked to do—and more. And work consistently. When you do, your actions will speak for you.

Then, be sure to put your heart into your job. Do your job unto God and you *will* be promoted. It doesn't matter if your boss is a mean and angry person. It doesn't matter if you're cleaning dishes and you want to be the one who owns the restaurant. Remember—promotion comes from God (Psalm 75:6,7, KJV). Just clean the pots and pans until they shine and do it with a smile. In everything you do say, "I'm doing this as unto You, Lord"—and from the Lord you'll receive your promotion. Believe Him for it!

So stir up your faith. And if you're looking for a new job, do the best you can at your present place of employment while you're looking. Then get ready...because God Himself *will* promote you!

talk the truth

"When I work, I do the best I can. I work for the Lord, not for men." (Colossians 3:23, ICB)

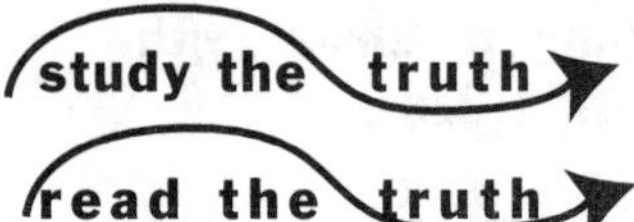
study the truth
read the truth

1 Thessalonians 4:11,12; 1 Peter 5:5,6

Hosea 8,9; Psalm 121

PRESS IN

"Let the word of Christ dwell in you richly."

Colossians 3:16

Things in this world aren't getting any better, and recently, the Holy Spirit has been speaking an urgent message to my heart. He's been saying, *Press in. Draw in to a more intimate relationship with your Heavenly Father. If you don't, you won't make it. If you do, you will see more miraculous wonders of God than you can imagine.*

That message isn't just for me. It's also for you. We are in the last of the last days. Jesus is coming soon. It's an exciting time, but it's also a dangerous time. Those who don't press in to know the Lord will go from trouble to trouble. But those who do will defeat the troubles and turn them into successes!

Your first step in drawing closer to God is to realize that you can know God through His Word. Time spent praying and reading the Bible is time spent with Jesus. Most people don't realize that. So, instead of getting to know Him through His Word, they try to know Him through feelings—and that just won't work.

Remember this: The first chapter of John tells us that Jesus is the Word. That means, when you spend time in it, you're spending time with Jesus. When His Word is living in you richly, then Jesus is living in you richly too!

Don't go from trouble to trouble. Take those troubles and turn them into successes. Press in to Jesus. Press in to the Word and you'll make it through these dangerous days just fine!

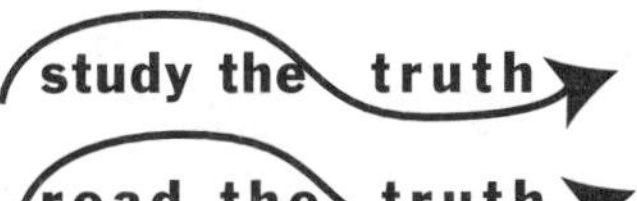

"The Word of Christ dwells in me richly!" (Colossians 3:16)

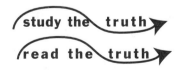

study the truth **John 1:1-14**

read the truth **Hosea 10,11; Psalm 122**

Kenneth

December 8

GET THE TWO TOGETHER

"As you received Christ Jesus the Lord, so continue to live in him. Keep your roots deep in him and have your lives built on him. Be strong in the faith, just as you were taught. And always be thankful."

Colossians 2:6,7, ICB

Strong in the faith and thankful. These days that's a rare combination.

A lot of people have been taught about faith over the last several years, and a lot of people have been taught to always be thankful. But it's been hard to put the two together. Faith people want to speak God's Word all the time, but they don't praise God very much. And those who like to praise God just want to have a good time in the Lord. You can't get them to be very serious about God's Word.

Success comes from combining the two.

So, do it! Put them together. When you run into a challenge, don't just stand there holding on to your faith until your knuckles turn white. Raise your hands high and praise. Start thanking God in the middle of what's happening. Keep thanking Him for the answer until it comes.

Instead of just standing on God's Word, let His joy enable you to live in praise. It will get you where you're going a whole lot faster...and you and God both will have a much better time on the way.

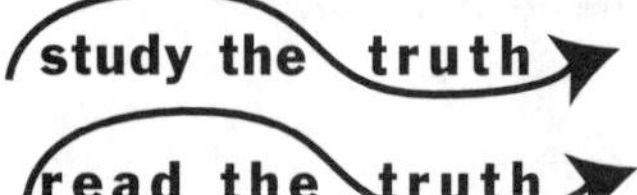
talk the truth

"I am strong in the faith and thankful." (Colossians 2:6,7, ICB)

study the truth

Colossians 2:1-10

read the truth

Hosea 12,13; Psalm 123

LOVE—THE SECRET OF SUCCESS

"Love never fails."

1 CORINTHIANS 13:8

Fear of failure. It's haunted all of us at some time. Popular psychology tells us to adjust to it. But the Bible tells us that there is a failureproof way to live without it. It is the way of *love.*

If you want to know real success, you must learn to be moved and motivated by love. That's how Jesus was when He was on the earth.

Even when John the Baptist was brutally murdered and Jesus went away to be alone, He didn't stop loving. Matthew 14:6-14 says that even then, in that emotionally draining time when the people wouldn't leave Him alone, He was moved with compassion and healed the sick.

I used to wonder how Jesus could just turn away from that terrible crime and not avenge. What I didn't realize was that He *did* avenge. He overcame the works of Satan with compassion. He defeated hatred with love. He attacked Satan by destroying his works of sickness and disease.

Compassion doesn't strike at the surface of things. It goes straight to the root of the problem. That's why it always succeeds.

"But wait!" you may say. "I'm not sure I can love like that. I'm not Jesus."

Yes, you can, because the Bible says that His love has been poured into your heart! (See Romans 5:5). And 1 John 2:5 says His love is made complete in you as you keep His Word.

Commit to living the life of love today. Watch God turn failure into success at home, at school, at work...in any situation. *Love never fails!*

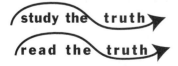

talk the truth

"I walk in love and I always succeed because love never fails." (1 Corinthians 13:8)

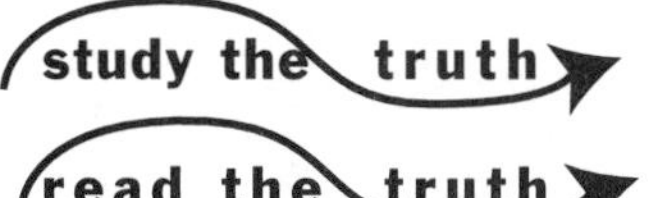
study the truth
read the truth

Matthew 14:1-14

Hosea 14; Joel 1; Psalm 124

Gloria

December 10

SEEK GOD FIRST

"Seek ye first the kingdom of God, and his righteousness; and all these things shall be added unto you."

MATTHEW 6:33, KJV

I know that some people must think it's easy for Ken and me to be Christians because we're preachers. They think we've got it made. In some ways, we do. Our calling demands that we give God our attention, which always brings success.

But it hasn't always been that way. In fact, the first time I saw Kenneth Copeland, he was about as far from a preacher as I figured you could get. He flew planes and sang in nightclubs. I was a college girl who said she would never marry a preacher and who had never heard about making Jesus the Lord of my life.

Right after we got married, I quit my job because Ken went into a business enterprise that we thought was sure to make us rich. Two weeks later it folded.

We ended up sleeping on a rented rollaway bed that sagged in the middle. We had a wrought-iron coffee table Ken had made in high school and a black-and-white TV. Nothing else. No refrigerator. No stove. I cooked in my coffeepot and an electric skillet, and I used a cardboard box on the porch to keep our food cold.

We were broke, unemployed, deeply in debt and had nowhere to go.

Then one day I picked up the Bible Ken's mother had given him. In the front she'd written the verse, "Seek ye first the kingdom of God, and his righteousness; and all these things shall be added unto you." I turned and read Matthew 6. It said God cared for the birds. For the first time in my life I realized God cared for me personally. I figured if He cared for birds, He cared for me! I knelt and told Jesus that if He could do anything with my life, He could have it.

I had no idea I had just become a Christian. Two weeks later Ken found a new job. We moved to a new, furnished apartment and bought a better car. In the midst of it all, something else happened—Ken made Jesus his Lord.

So don't worry if you don't "have it made." We certainly didn't when we started. Just stick with God and make a decision in your heart to seek *Him* first. Then *all* the other things will be added.

talk the truth

"I seek God and His righteousness first. All that I need is given to me." (Matthew 6:33, KJV)

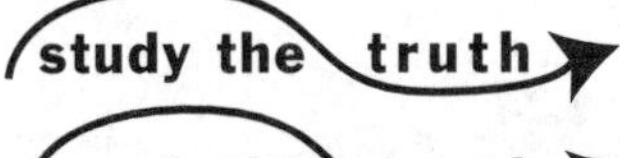
study the truth
read the truth

Psalm 128

Joel 2,3; Amos 1; Psalms 125,126

SPREAD PEACE THIS CHRISTMAS

Christmas is a wonderful time of year. It's a time when the whole world is hearing the message of Jesus' birth. It's a time when people are tenderhearted...the perfect time to plant seeds of love in the lives of those you meet.

Sometimes those seeds may just be kind words in the middle of rush-hour shopping. Other times, you may get the opportunity to pray and minister to someone. But whatever the situation, keep a sharp eye out for even the smallest chance to help someone.

I've had some outstanding experiences giving a few dollars to someone in need. As they are taking the money, I tell them, "This money is from the Lord Jesus Christ. I serve Him. He is the One Who instructed me to help you."

"Suddenly a great company of the heavenly host appeared with the angel, praising God and saying, 'Glory to God in the highest, and on earth peace to men on whom his favor rests.'"

LUKE 2:13,14

It's amazing how many people are ready to hear what you have to say when you speak in love. They're starving for someone to really care. Be someone who cares this Christmas season. Spread the Word about the peace that's available in Jesus.

Who knows—some of those small seeds may spring up and show someone the way to heaven!

talk the truth

"I plant seeds of love in everyone I meet." (Luke 2:13,14)

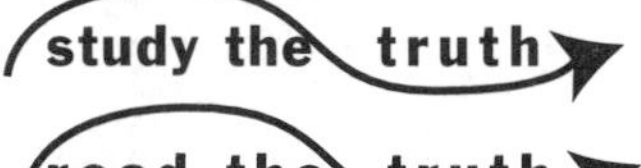
study the truth
read the truth

Luke 2:1-20

Amos 2,3; Psalm 127

December 12

TUNE IN

"One who has the gift of speaking in a different language [tongues] is not speaking to people. He is speaking to God. No one understands him—he is speaking secret things through the Spirit."

1 Corinthians 14:2, ICB

Have you ever looked around and wondered why it's taking the Lord so long to get things in order? If so, let me tell you something I learned a few years ago. He's not the one who's slow. We are!

It's not God's fault that we're not living in total victory. He's always ready. He's the great "I AM." We're the ones who fall short.

It's like turning on a radio. If you don't have it tuned to exactly the right frequency, you won't be able to hear the station. It's not the station's fault. It's sending out signals perfectly. The problem is, you haven't tuned in to it.

That's what's happening with Christians today. We haven't fine-tuned our spirits. We pick up a few things from the Holy Spirit now and then, but mostly, we just fade in and out. We don't stay on God's wavelength.

How do you stay in tune with God? By praying in the spirit. Praying in tongues is the fastest, most effective method I know to tune in to God—because instead of praying your own thoughts and plans, you're praying His!

The Bible says that when you pray in tongues, you're speaking mysteries to God. In the spirit, you're praying for parts of God's plan you don't even know about. Through the Holy Spirit, you're praying for exactly what God wants.

You see, God knows how to rescue His people. He has a plan. And if we'll tap into that plan and start praying in the spirit in agreement with what *He* desires, there will be an explosion of God's power that will turn this world around!

Get in tune with God today. Spend an hour praying in tongues. Set your spirit on God's wavelength and just see how quickly victory will come.

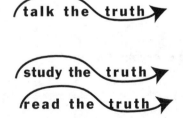

talk the truth — **"I build myself up in faith and tune into God by praying in the spirit." (1 Corinthians 14:2, ICB)**

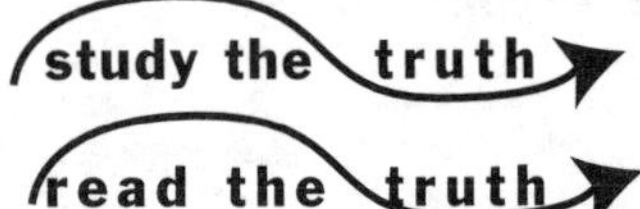
study the truth
read the truth

study the truth — **1 Corinthians 14:1-19**

read the truth — **Amos 4,5; Psalm 128**

DON'T PANIC

Right now you may be on the edge of a major decision...and you know you need divine guidance. You're desperately hoping to hear from the Lord. You may need to decide about what college to attend or where to spend this Christmas season.

"Roll your works upon the Lord—commit and trust them wholly to Him; [He will cause your thoughts to become agreeable to His will, and] so shall your plans be established and succeed."

PROVERBS 16:3, AMP

If you have a situation like that, don't panic. Being led by the Lord isn't some complicated process that only the spiritual "pros" can master.

When I was a new Christian, I found that out. I wanted to please God, but I didn't know how to make decisions that would be pleasing to Him.

Then one day as I was studying *The Amplified Bible,* I came across Proverbs 16:3. Immediately, I latched onto this verse and began to use it in my life—and now I can tell you from experience, it works!

It will work for you too, if you'll do what it says. Give everything you do to God. Trust Him entirely. Your thoughts will start being like His until, at some point, you'll just know the right thing to do. Of course, you have to have faith in Him—and you get that by reading the Bible. Then as you practice committing what you do to the Lord and trusting Him, you become more confident in your ability to hear Him. Start now with whatever problem is bothering you. Pray and trust God with it. In other words, believe you receive the answer when you pray. Stop worrying and begin believing.

Learn to live this way and it won't matter whether you've been a Christian 15 minutes or 15 years, God will show you the successful way!

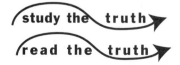

"I roll my works upon the Lord. I commit and trust them wholly to Him. He causes my thoughts to agree with His will and my plans to succeed." (Proverbs 16:3, AMP)

study the truth **Psalm 37:1-7**

read the truth **Amos 6,7; Psalm 129**

December 14

NO DEPOSIT—NO RETURN

"Blessed is the man who fears the Lord, who finds great delight in his commands.... He will have no fear of bad news; his heart is steadfast, trusting in the Lord."

Psalm 112:1,7

Are you ready to face a crisis? Well, don't wait until one hits to find out. Prepare yourself now. That's what a couple of my Partners did. They faced a situation that would have made many people panic. But when the crisis hit, they were so deeply rooted in God's Word that their first response was one of faith.

What affected me most when I heard their story was one particular phrase they kept using: *No deposit—no return.*

What they meant by that was that if you don't take the time to deposit God's Word in your heart now, it won't be there later when you really need it. You'll end up in a crisis with only unbelief instead of the faith and power you need to see you through. In a situation like the one this couple faced, that could be deadly.

You see, their two-year-old son had suffered a fall that had cracked his skull and critically injured his neck. He had no feeling in his arms and legs and was unable to move. Yet as they rushed him to the emergency room, a great sense of peace rested on them. Rather than crying with fear, they prayed in faith and declared, "By Jesus' wounds, our son is healed!"

Sure enough, within hours, their boy was totally healed. Even the X-rays proved that a miracle had taken place.

What's important to understand about that story is this: The victory was not won when the damage to that little boy's body disappeared. It was won during the days and weeks and months before when his parents were studying the Bible and praying in the spirit. It was won because these people spent time building a strong foundation on God's Word so that when the storm came, they stood strong.

Now is the time for you to build a rock-solid foundation! Don't wait around until you're faced with a crisis. Get God's Word in your heart now, so when you really need it, it will flow out in power.

talk the truth **"I deposit God's Word in my heart now, and it is always there when I need it." (Psalm 112:1,7)**

study the truth **Psalm 112**

read the truth **Amos 8,9; Psalm 130**

December 15

A CAREFREE CHRISTMAS

"Do not worry about anything. But pray and ask God for everything you need. And when you pray, always give thanks."

PHILIPPIANS 4:6, ICB

Can you really have a merry Christmas even when you have a thousand and one pressures coming down on you? Yes, you can—and you don't have to thumb a ride out of the country to do it. No matter how intense or how trivial the problems are that you're facing right now, you can have the most wonderful, most carefree Christmas season you've ever had—and you can start having it today.

As a Christian, you're probably familiar with that scripture that says not to worry about anything. But, have you ever taken it seriously enough to put it into action? There's a good chance you haven't because you haven't understood just how dangerous worries are. You probably haven't realized that they're a deadly part of Satan's strategy against you.

That's right. Worry is one of Satan's chief weapons. If he can get you to worry about them, he can use the pressures of finals, peers and family that are just a "normal" part of everyday life to weigh you down and drag you into a heap of trouble.

Medical science tells us that a high percentage of the people hospitalized in America are there with illness caused by worry and tension. Yet, a great many Christians worry without even thinking about it. They'll worry about being too short or not looking like a magazine model. They'll fuss over this and that and not even realize they've been sinning.

"Sinning?"

Yes! For the reborn, Spirit-filled Christian, worrying is a sin. So, even if you haven't started your Christmas shopping and finals are creeping up like a stalking cat, don't worry. Instead, do what the Bible says. Pray, asking God for everything you need...and give Him thanks for the answer. Then you'll have peace.

Now, go ahead and have a truly merry Christmas!

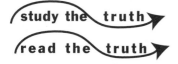

talk the truth **"I refuse to worry about anything. I pray and ask God for everything I need." (Philippians 4:6, ICB)**

study the truth **Matthew 6:24-34**

read the truth **Obadiah; Jonah 1; Psalm 131**

Kenneth

December 16

RUN HIM OUT OF TOWN

"Stand therefore... having shod your feet in preparation [to face the enemy with the firm-footed stability, the promptness and the readiness produced by the good news] of the Gospel of peace."

EPHESIANS 6:14,15, AMP

Preparation. When it comes to fighting spiritual battles, that's a word you ought to remember. Most Christians don't prepare themselves in advance. They twiddle their thumbs until Satan makes his move. Then they jump up and try to fight him with God's Word...and they usually lose.

I used to do the same thing until the Lord taught me differently. I used to wait until my meetings began before I'd pray for their success. Then one day the Lord showed me that by waiting until the last minute to take my stand, I was giving Satan time to build up his forces against me. Consequently, I was losing many of my battles.

Then the Lord said something to me I'll never forget. He said, *If they had kicked Al Capone out of Chicago when he was just a small-time operator, he wouldn't have been so hard to handle; but they waited until he became a first-class criminal with his forces built up. Then it took an army to bring him down.*

When I heard that, I made up my mind never to be caught unprepared again. I started praying about those meetings weeks in advance, getting ready spiritually before they ever began. Instead of letting Satan get his forces secure, I threw him out before he got a single foothold. When I did, I saw more victories than I ever had before.

Don't let Satan catch you off guard. Be prepared! Start praying and speaking the God's promises over your family, your school and your church. Get your feet "shod with the preparation of the gospel of peace" (KJV). Then if Satan causes trouble, you'll be well-equipped to run him out of town.

talk the truth

"I stand, having my feet shod in preparation to face the enemy with firm-footed stability of the gospel of peace." (Ephesians 6:14,15, AMP)

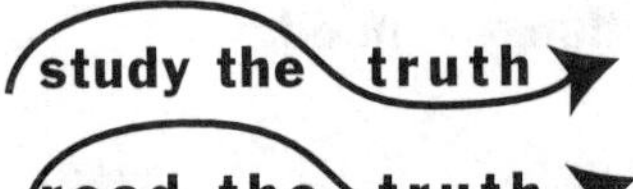
study the truth

1 Samuel 17:12-51

read the truth

Jonah 2,3; Psalm 132

December 17

DARE TO TAKE YOUR PLACE

"But then the kindness and love of God our Savior was shown.... God poured out to us that Holy Spirit fully through Jesus Christ our Savior. We were made right with God by his grace. And God gave us the Spirit so that we could receive the life that never ends."

TITUS 3:4,6,7, ICB

An everlasting, unbreakable promise of grace—that's what you and I have with God. If you could truly grasp that, you'd never be the same again.

What exactly *is* this grace? It's a relationship of favor that gives you access to someone else's power. An illustration of this is the agreement the old Sicilian "family" members have with the "godfather" of the family.

In that group, a weak person might come in and ask the head of the family for a favor. The head of the family would say, "I will grant this favor and I will ask a favor of you, and when the time comes, I will collect it."

Once that was said, the weak person would become excited. Suddenly he knew he would no longer have this problem because anyone who tried to rough him up would now have to face the godfather, the one with all the power. He would have the full assurance that he didn't have a thing to worry about. He was no longer small and powerless. He had gained favor (grace) with the powerful.

He'd walk out thinking, *Everything is handled. All I have to do now is whatever the head of the family asks me to do. And he knows I don't have anything, so He'll provide everything I need to do what He asks me to do.*

That's grace. God's willingness to enter into a blood covenant with you and give you everything He has in exchange for everything you have.

He took your sin and gave you right-standing with Him. He took your sickness and gave you His health. He took your poverty and met all your needs with His riches. Whenever He asks you to do something, He provides everything you need to carry it out.

If you've made Jesus your Lord, you've been made a covenant child of the most powerful being in the universe. He's Almighty God, the Head of the family. Dare to take your place in the family today!

talk the truth

"I have been made right with God by His grace." (Titus 3:4,6,7, ICB)

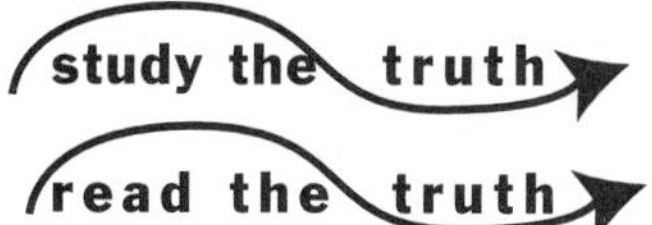
study the truth
read the truth

Luke 4:14-21

Jonah 4; Micah 1,2; Psalms 133,134

Gloria

December 18

EXTREMELY BLESSED

"A present is a precious stone in the eyes of its possessor; Wherever he turns, he prospers."

PROVERBS 17:8, NKJV

If I could give you a gift this Christmas, I'd give you God's Word. I'd rather give you His Word than a check for a million dollars. You can run through a million dollars like lightning, but the truth of God's Word never stops—and it will get you out of situations that a million dollars never could.

Ken and I are just ordinary people. But when we took hold of God's Word, we latched onto something that changed every part of our lives.

Nothing good has happened to us because of us. It's happened because of God's Word. I promise you this: If you'll give the Bible your full attention—and not be afraid of what God wants for your life—you will be happier and doing better than you could ever dream.

Of course, if you do that, your classmates may call you extreme. But don't mind that. You *are* extreme when you set your faith on what the Bible says. You're extremely well. Extremely happy. And extremely blessed.

talk the truth **"God has blessed me with every spiritual blessing through Jesus." (Ephesians 1:3)**

study the truth **Psalm 119:56-65**

read the truth **Micah 3,4; Psalm 135**

December 19

DON'T SETTLE FOR SECOND BEST

"My brethren, count it all joy when you fall into various trials, knowing that the testing of your faith produces patience."

JAMES 1:2,3, NKJV

I admit it's tough to be enthusiastic about going through tests and trials. But can you get excited about having everything you need? Well, according to the Bible, if you'll use your trials to develop patience, that's exactly the position you'll be in!

You see, patience doesn't mean what you thought it meant. It doesn't mean standing by while Satan tramples all over you.

No, patience is a powerful word. The New Testament meaning of it, translated literally from the original Greek text, is "to be consistently constant or to be the same way all the time, regardless of what happens."

To understand how much power is involved in that, you have to realize that it's one of the most outstanding qualities of God Himself. The Bible says He's the same yesterday, today and forever (Hebrews 13:8).

Think about that for a minute. Someone who absolutely cannot be changed by anyone or anything is extremely powerful, wouldn't you say? Obviously, God has that much power. But you know what? You do too!

By the power of the Holy Ghost working within you, you can be the same every day, no matter what happens. If you'll put your trust in God's Word and let your patience work, it won't matter what happens. You won't ever have to accept anything less than victory again.

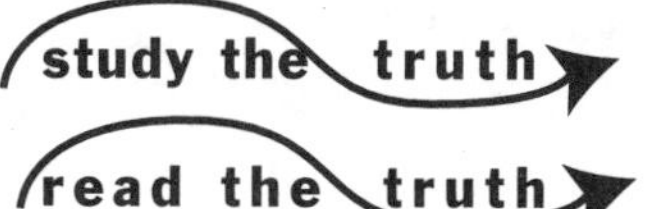
talk the truth
study the truth

talk the truth **"I count it all joy when I fall into various trials, knowing that the testing of my faith produces patience." (James 1:2,3, NKJV)**

study the truth **2 Timothy 3:10-17**

read the truth **Micah 5,6; Psalm 136**

December 20

A LITTLE BIT OF HEAVEN ON EARTH

"Therefore, as God's chosen people, holy and dearly loved, clothe yourselves with compassion, kindness, humility, gentleness and patience. Bear with each other and forgive whatever grievances you may have against one another. Forgive as the Lord forgave you."

COLOSSIANS 3:12,13

Living in a home filled with God's love and peace is almost like living in heaven on earth. We all know that's true. We all want to live in such a home. Yet, time and again, we short-change our families. We use our kindest words and most winning smiles on those beyond our front door. Have you ever wondered why?

The answer is simpler than you might suspect. Spiritually speaking, your family is under attack. You see, it is not only one of your most precious gifts, but when it's operating in harmony, it's also one of your most powerful resources. Satan knows that, even if you don't—and he's out to destroy it.

His battle plan is simple. He will do everything he can to create conflict in your home. He'll stir up feelings of self-pity and jealousy. He'll encourage you to become resentful and bitter. And through it all, his purpose remains the same...to divide and destroy your home.

When family members agree, they create an atmosphere in which God's miracle-working power is free to flow! So Satan is constantly tempting us to ruin that atmosphere through strife. All too often we fall to his tactics simply because we don't realize just how dangerous discord really is. James 3:16 says, "For where you have envy and selfish ambition, there you find disorder and every evil practice."

Don't open your home to Satan by allowing a few quarrels to come in. Stop the destruction before it starts. Anchor yourself to God's Word. Start seeing your family from God's perspective—as a powerhouse! Determine right now to pray for, support and love your family. Bring them together, so you can all enjoy a little bit of heaven on earth.

talk the truth

"I pray for, support and love my family. I won't allow strife in my house!" (Colossians 3:12,13)

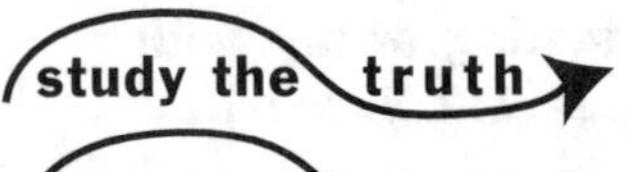
study the truth
read the truth

Colossians 3:12-25

Micah 7; Nahum 1,2,3; Psalm 137

STICK TO YOUR CALLING

"Therefore I remind you to stir up the gift of God...who has saved us and called us with a holy calling, not according to our works, but according to His own purpose and grace which was given to us in Christ Jesus before time began."

2 Timothy 1:6,9, nkjv

Are you doing what God called you to do?

If you haven't ever thought about it before, that may sound like an odd question to you. You may be tempted to shrug it off and say, "Oh, I'm not really called to do anything. I'm not going to be a pastor or a minister or anything like that. Besides, I'm not even a full-fledged adult yet."

Let me tell you something: No matter who you are or what your age is, God has put a calling in you. He's called you to meet a need in the Body of Christ that no one else can meet quite like you can. He's given you special gifts and abilities.

You may be called to be so successful in business, you can finance the gospel worldwide. You may be called to a ministry of prayer. You may be called to a ministry of healing right there in your own neighborhood. God needs Christian schoolteachers, doctors, lawyers and policemen. No matter what your calling is, it's important and you need to follow it! God has a call for you to meet even now—and it will determine whether you continue to meet the full potential of your calling in the future.

If you're like many Christians I know, you may have let your life become so busy with other things that you just don't have time to pursue your calling. You may be so overwhelmed with everything you "need" to do that you can't imagine how you can fit anything else in.

I've had to deal with that in my own life. I've had to quit doing things just because they "need" doing. I've had to discipline myself to sticking to what I'm called to do.

Make up your mind to prayerfully trim away the extra things you've added to your life. Stir up the gift God has placed inside you. Get back on the path to what He has called you to do. After all, that calling is important. It's holy...and it's yours. Don't ever let it slip away from you.

talk the truth

"I stir up the gift of God within me and don't let my call get pushed aside. I will do what God has called me to do." (2 Timothy 1:6,9, nkjv)

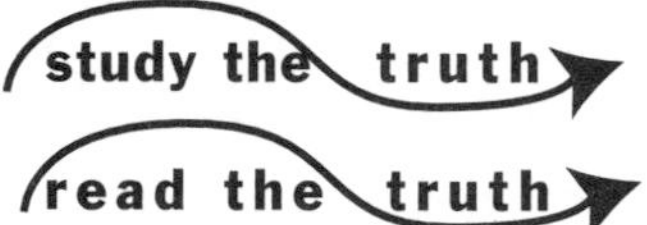
study the truth
read the truth

Acts 9:1-20

Habakkuk 1,2,3; Psalm 138

December 22

DON'T JUST SIT THERE...ARISE!

"Now there were four men with leprosy at the entrance of the city gate. They said to each other, 'Why stay here until we die?... So let's go.... At dusk they got up and went to the camp of the Arameans....'"

2 Kings 7:3-5

No matter how bad the problem is that you may be facing today, no matter how far under the pressure you may be, in 24 hours you can be back on top!

"Oh, that would be impossible!"

That's what the Samaritans thought in 2 Kings 7. Their land was being devastated by a famine. Enemy troops had surrounded them and cut off all source of supply. And as disgusting as this may sound, mothers were eating their own children just to survive.

But right in the middle of that, the Lord told the prophet Elisha that in 24 hours the whole situation would change, that flour and barley would sell for just a few pennies and there would be more than enough for all.

What did God use to turn that situation around?

Four lepers! Four lepers who, instead of sitting around feeling sorry for themselves, decided to go take their chances in the enemy camp. When they got there, they found it *empty*. All the warriors had been frightened away by angels, and they'd left enough food behind to feed all of Samaria!

Sometimes you and I are like the Samaritans in that story. We focus on the problem instead of what the Bible says. When that happens, faith and power begin to drop by the wayside and life caves in on us.

If that's happened to you, stop whining about it. Stop looking at your problem and feeling sorry for yourself. That won't change anything!

Just like He did for Elisha, God's given you a word. He's promised you victory. He's promised to make you a winner. So don't just sit there till you die. Don't accept defeat. Rise up in faith. Stand on God's promises and fight for your life. Get mad at Satan. Drive him out. Get mad at that crisis. Get angry with loneliness and start loving. Rise up and watch the Lord rescue you!

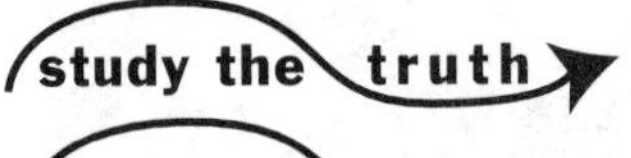

"I stand on God's promises to me today. I refuse to just sit back and die!" (2 Kings 7:3-5)

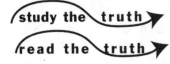

study the truth **2 Kings 6:24-33; 7:1-20**

read the truth **Zephaniah 1,2,3; Psalm 139**

December 23

YOU DON'T HAVE TO DIE YOUNG

"With long life will I satisfy him and show him my salvation."

PSALM 91:16

Did you know that God doesn't want you or anyone else to die young? His desire is for you is to live the full number of your days. You ought to live 70 or 80 years, and if you are not satisfied, live awhile longer! The Bible says that when Abraham died, he died at a good old age, *full* of years. That's the way it ought to be with all of us.

Some Christians don't realize that and they've gotten themselves in a mess. When they get sick, instead of just believing for healing, they start wondering if it's "their time" to die. This even happens with young people. They may get depressed and start thinking, *Maybe this is God's way of telling me my work is done.*

Don't ever put up with thoughts like that. If God has His way, He won't call you home until you're good and ready and *full* of years. The Apostle Paul understood that. In 2 Timothy 4:6-7, he said, "For I am now *ready* to be offered, and the time of my departure is at hand. I have fought a good fight, I have finished my course, I have kept the faith" (KJV). Paul didn't die until he and Jesus were ready for him to go.

If Satan is telling you it's time for you to go home, he is lying to you. God promises in Psalm 91:16 that if you are living under the shadow of the most High—living in Him—He will satisfy you with long life. (John 15 talks about living in Him.)

It's not time for you to die until you have finished your course and calling on this earth. So ignore Satan and keep right on living. Resist sickness, disease and depression in Jesus' Name. Stand on God's promise!

Then, after you've lived a long life on earth and you're ready to go on to heaven, go! But don't go until you've lived a long, fulfilled life, and you're ready!

"The Lord satisfies me with long life and shows me His salvation." (Psalm 91:16)

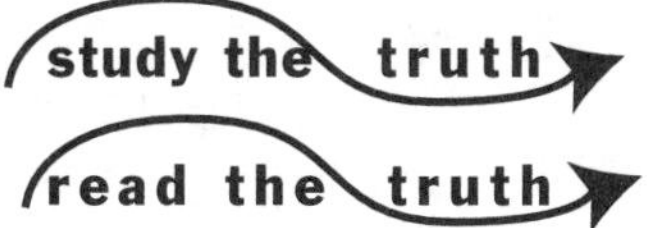

Deuteronomy 34

Haggai 1,2; Psalm 140

GOOD SUCCESS

"Do not let this Book of the Law depart from your mouth; meditate on it day and night, so that you may be careful to do everything written in it. Then you will be prosperous and successful."

JOSHUA 1:8

Success is a way of life that comes from being established in what the Bible says. It comes from spending so much of your time and your thought life on God's Word that it becomes "second nature." Success comes from hearing and obeying the Bible so consistently that it begins to guide your actions even when you're not making it a point to think about it.

When I started flying airplanes, I trained myself by getting the handbook for a certain airplane and reading it over and over again. In my mind, I'd visualize everything that could happen in that airplane. I trained myself by reading over and over what I needed to do and thinking about it.

And that's exactly what I started doing with the Bible. I thought about what it said day and night. Before long, I started getting excited about what I was reading. I'd sit at home and think about how I'd apply God's promises in different situations. His Word became "second nature" to me.

Practice thinking, reading and praying God's promises. Let them become part of you. See yourself obeying His Word in every possible circumstance. It will guarantee your success!

talk the truth **"I study God's Word day and night and obey everything written there. As I do, I become wise and successful." (Joshua 1:8)**

study the truth **Psalm 1**

read the truth **Zechariah 1,2,3; Psalms 141,142**

A TIME TO FORGET

"'Lord, how many times shall I forgive my brother when he sins against me? Up to seven times?' Jesus answered, 'I tell you, not seven times, but seventy-seven times.'"

Matthew 18:21,22

Most people love thinking about fond memories at Christmastime. But sooner or later, we all stumble across some we'd rather forget. Suddenly, the pain comes rushing back. The sting of a parent's criticism, the broken promise of a friend, the rejections, the disappointments, the heartaches....

What should we do with memories like that? Do we have to drag them along from year to year? No. We can leave them behind. In fact, we *must* leave them behind. And there's only one way to do it—through forgiveness.

Forgiving someone sounds simple. Yet few of us really do it. We treat forgiveness like an option, something we can take or leave. But it's not. It's a basic requirement for every Christian.

In Matthew 18, Jesus tells a parable about a servant who owed his master millions of dollars. But the master—moved with compassion—canceled the entire debt. Soon after, however, the servant sought out a man who owed *him* only $15. Finding him unable to pay, the servant ignored the man's pleas for mercy and had him thrown into prison. When the servant's master heard about it, he was furious. He called him a wicked servant and had him imprisoned until he could pay all that was due.

Look again at the size of that unforgiven debt. *Fifteen dollars.* The little debts are the ones that trip us up the most. It's the little resentments between you and your mom or dad or between you and your brother or sister that seem too insignificant to bother with. But beware. Those are the kinds of debts Satan uses to torment you. After all, Jesus paid off a mountain of debts for you. You can afford to be generous about the "nickel-and-dime" debts of others.

Spend time with the Holy Spirit, allowing Him to reveal any unforgiveness in you. Then ask God's forgiveness and release it. Make this Christmas more than just a time for remembering. Make it a time to forget.

"I forgive others as God forgave me." (Ephesians 4:32)

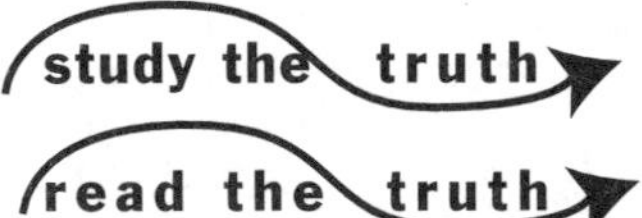

Matthew 18:21-35

Zechariah 4,5; Psalm 143

Kenneth

December 26

KNOW HIM AS DADDY

"For you did not receive a spirit that makes you a slave again to fear, but you received the Spirit of sonship. And by him we cry, 'Abba, Father.'"

ROMANS 8:15

One night after a worship service a friend of mine and I stepped outside and were suddenly awed by the beauty around us. It was one of those crisp, clear winter nights when the brilliance of the moon and stars nearly takes your breath away. I said to my friend, "Tommy, will you look at that!" Then he looked up with a big smile and with a voice full of tenderness said, "My Daddy made that!"

"My Daddy...." I'll never forget the way he said that.

Some people might think he shouldn't have been talking in such familiar terms about God, but they'd be wrong. It's scriptural to talk that way about Him. In the New Testament there's a Greek word for father—*"Abba."* The most accurate translation for that word in English is "Daddy." It's a word that means closeness. It's a relationship that's been developed through time spent together.

"Father" is one thing. "Daddy" is another. Growing up, my father was sometimes my "Father" and sometimes my "Daddy." When we were out duck hunting, he was "Daddy." When he gave commands he meant to be obeyed instantly, he was "Father."

God is like that too. He's your Father and He's your Daddy. There are times you'll be very serious and down to business with one another. Other times you'll be more lighthearted. But either way, once you spend enough time with Him to get to know Him, I guarantee you'll want to be close to Him all the time.

"God has made me His child. He is my Father...and my 'Daddy.'" (Romans 8:15)

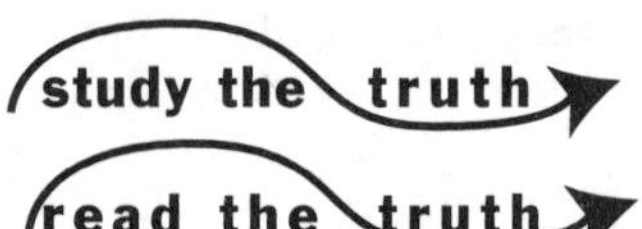

Romans 8:14-18

Zechariah 6,7; Psalm 144

A WORLD OVERCOMER

Do not let yourself become like the world. If you live like the world, you'll be beaten by its system. It's as simple as that. So don't let the world squeeze you into its own mold.

Instead..."be transformed" by the entire "renewing of your mind." Overcome the world by thinking in a new way—like God thinks. In other words, when you see something in the Bible, say, "I agree with that. From now on I'm believing that instead of what I used to think."

For example, when locker-room talk starts, don't give in to the temptation to join in. Agree with the Bible instead and say, "I'm dead to that, Satan. You can't pull me into it anymore!"

Soon you'll find yourself changing. You will find yourself living like a world overcomer!

"Do not conform any longer to the pattern of this world, but be transformed by the renewing of your mind. Then you will be able to test and approve what God's will is—his good, pleasing and perfect will."

ROMANS 12:2

"By my faith, I am a world overcomer!" (1 John 5:4)

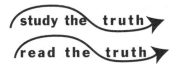

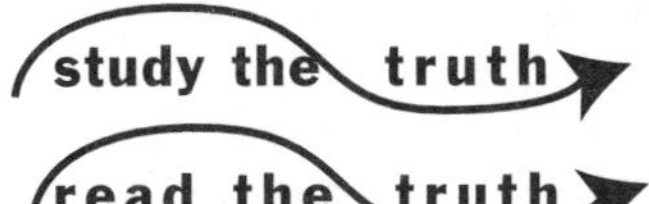

Romans 6:1-11

Zechariah 8,9; Psalm 145

Kenneth

December 28

MAJOR IN MERCY

"Then Moses said, 'Now show me your glory.'"

EXODUS 33:18

What would you say is the single, most outstanding thing about God? What's His most important characteristic? Some people would say it's His power. Others, His holiness. But God Himself would give a different answer.

You can find that answer in Exodus 33. There Moses is asking God to show him His Glory.

Now the word "glory" could literally be translated "heavy weight." It refers to the heaviest, biggest thing about someone. It's the totality of their worth.

So what Moses was actually saying was, "Lord, I want to see the biggest thing about You. I want to know Your greatest attributes." What did God say to him in response?

Chapter 34:6-7 tells us, "The Lord passed in front of Moses and said, 'I am the Lord. The Lord is a God who shows mercy and is kind. The Lord doesn't become angry quickly. The Lord has great love and faithfulness. The Lord is kind to thousands of people. The Lord forgives people for wrong and sin...'" (ICB).

Just think about that! When Moses asked God to show him the most important thing about Himself, God showed him His mercy.

That means if you and I are to imitate God (Ephesians 5:1) we must major in mercy too. Mercy, goodness, forgiveness and compassion must mark our behavior above all else. When someone talks about you behind your back, you should major in mercy and forgive them immediately. When you see someone who is picked on, you should major in mercy and lift them up instead of putting them down.

You'll see—major in mercy and others will see God's Glory in you!

"I imitate God—His mercy, goodness, forgiveness and compassion mark my life." (Exodus 33:18)

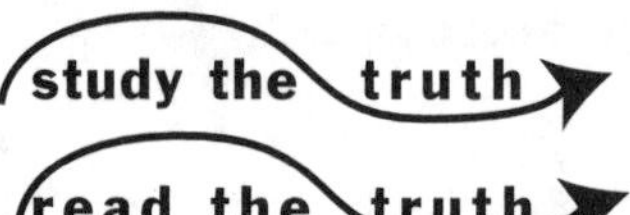

Exodus 33:7-23; 34:5-10

Zechariah 10,11; Psalm 146

REMEMBER NOAH

"So the Lord said, 'I will wipe mankind, whom I have created, from the face of the earth—men and animals, and creatures that move along the ground, and birds of the air—for I am grieved that I have made them.' But Noah found favor in the eyes of the Lord."

GENESIS 6:7,8

One of the dirtiest, most damaging lies that Satan ever told you was when he said, *You aren't important.* Don't you ever believe that.

You *are* important! Every Christian has a part to play in God's plan. God has something for you to do that no one else can do like you can. If you don't take your place and do your part, things won't be quite right.

I can just hear you thinking, *Oh, I'm just one person. What could I possibly do that could be so significant?*

Look in Genesis 6, and you'll see the answer to that question. There you'll see that the people on earth had become so wicked that God regretted that He'd made them. He was ready to wipe them all out—but He didn't. Why? Because of one man: Noah! *One* obedient man saved the human race.

Think about that. What if Noah had said, "Well, this is just too much pressure. I can't live godly in the middle of this ungodly generation. I mean, everyone around me is living the other way. Besides, I'm just one person. I can't make any difference in this dark world."

Thank God, Noah didn't say that. He didn't see himself as an insignificant man whose life didn't matter. Instead, he saw himself as a man to whom God had spoken—and by faith he obeyed God. Because of that, he alone prevented total destruction.

Next time you're tempted to shrug off God's instructions and be disobedient, next time you catch yourself thinking, *It doesn't matter what I do*—remember Noah. Remember that God is counting on you to carry out your part of His plan. Live like you're someone important in God's plan. And sooner or later you'll realize you are.

"God has great plans for me and my future!" (Genesis 6:7,8)

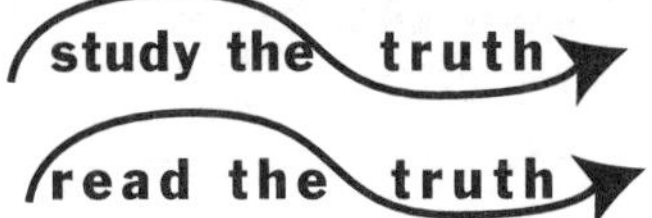

Genesis 6

Zechariah 12,13; Psalm 147

December 30

BORN TO VICTORY

"I have told you these things so that in Me you may have perfect peace and confidence. In the world you have tribulation and trials and distress and frustration; but be of good cheer...I have overcome the world."

JOHN 16:33, AMP

Jesus said as long as you live in the world, you will have trouble. But you're not just in the world. You're *in Jesus* in the world, and that makes all the difference. You're in Him and He's overcome every kind of trouble there is.

As God's child, you're not a defeated person trying to get victory. You're the winner, and Satan's trying to rob you of the victory that already belongs to you. When you made Jesus the Lord of your life, you were born into victory... because the Victor came to live in you. Think about it. The Ruler of the universe lives in you.

So cheer up! Have "perfect peace and confidence." Jesus lives in you!

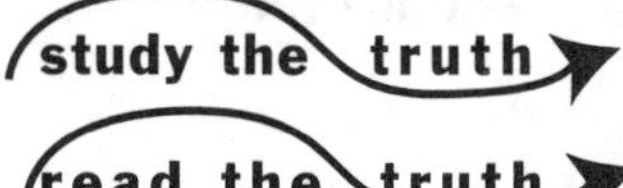

"In the world, troubles may come, but I have perfect peace and confidence. I am cheerful—for Jesus, Who has overcome the world, lives in me!" (John 16:33, AMP)

study the truth **John 16:15-33**

read the truth **Zechariah 14; Malachi 1; Psalm 148**

DON'T SPEAK—SHOUT YOUR VICTORY!

"From the rising of the sun to its going down The Lord's name is to be praised."

PSALM 113:3, NKJV

Praise God. Praise Him in the morning. Praise Him in the afternoon. Praise Him at night. If you've never praised God in your life, then get started right now. Praise Him for freedom. Praise Him for healing. Praise Him for the Name of Jesus.

You ought to be praising Him on your way to school and praising Him on your way back home! If there's anything Satan can't stand, it's praise.

Now is not the time to sit down and whine about how things aren't working out. It's not time to start wondering if God is doing anything in your life.

It *is* time to get into God's Word and get yourself established in His promises. It's time to keep them on your mind and in your heart. It's time to pray and believe because of what He's done for you. It is time to continue to do the things you know to do.

When Satan starts shaking you up, don't take off and run for cover. Speak to the problem with the authority you hold in the Name of Jesus. Then, when you're done with that, start to praise and shout the victory.

You don't have to be afraid of Satan. He'll be afraid of you!

"I praise the Lord all the time, for He is worthy to be praised. He gives me the victory!" (Psalm 113:3, NKJV)

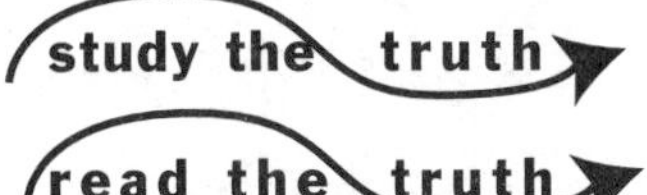

Psalm 50:1-23

Malachi 2,3,4; Psalms 149,150

OVER THE EDGE TOPICAL INDEX

Searching for Answers?

The Word of God has the answers you need for every circumstance in life. And the *Over the Edge Topical Index* is your quick reference guide! Study these devotions and let God show you what to do, every step of the way.

Angels
March 21
September 19

Being in Christ
January 26
March 25
May 24
May 31
August 21
October 24
December 30

Calling
December 21

Choices
February 25
April 8
June 9
August 23
August 25
October 4
October 23
October 30

Christian's Authority
January 14
January 22
January 25
January 28
February 1
February 5
March 2
March 19
April 23
May 21
June 19
July 17
July 28
August 29
September 9
September 24
October 25
October 31
November 2
November 16

Compassion
September 30

Consistency
March 5
September 22

Courage
August 2
September 17

Covenant
March 30
December 17

Death
February 27
June 30
December 23

Dedication
January 9
March 9
March 26
March 31
April 4
May 31
June 11
July 1
July 2
July 22
July 23
July 25
July 27
August 3
August 13
August 23
September 15
September 23
September 25
September 26
October 3
October 20
November 12
November 14
November 24
December 1
December 6
December 29

Diligence
July 25
July 30

Dreams
April 28
July 10

Encouraging Others
November 19

Faith
January 8
January 11
January 18
January 31
February 6
March 13
May 16
May 29
June 3
July 25
August 1
August 15
September 22
October 5
October 8
November 16
December 2
December 8
December 10

Faithfulness
May 3

Family
December 20

Fear
March 18
June 3

Fear of the Lord
October 22
November 7
November 14
December 14

Forgetting the Past
April 9
July 24
December 25

Forgiveness
February 3
February 15
April 13
May 30

October 2
December 2

Freedom
January 13
January 16
January 29
February 10
February 29
April 19
April 21
April 23
May 20
June 4
June 5
September 24
November 20
December 22

Fruit of the Spirit
August 3
August 30

God's Discipline
July 3

God's Rest
August 9

God's Word
January 30
February 6
February 16
February 19
March 4
March 8
March 17
April 10
April 29
May 10
June 8
June 13
June 16
June 21
June 25
July 3
July 12
July 26
July 29
September 4
November 30
December 7
December 14
December 18
December 24

Grace
February 15
June 4
June 9
June 18
October 12
December 17
December 29

Guidance
January 7
January 17
February 4
February 28
March 7
April 20
May 4
May 5
May 17
June 1
June 14
July 29
August 26
September 10
September 29
October 12
October 27
November 10
December 10

Hardness of Heart
July 19

Healing
January 27
March 22
May 27
June 20
June 27
September 20
October 4
October 18

Holy Spirit
March 14
July 16
September 10
October 12

Hope
January 12
July 10
September 12

Humility
March 20
July 18

Following the Faithful
November 28

Imitating God
November 17

Joy
February 20
May 15

Long Life
November 3

Love
January 20
February 14
February 24
March 11
March 29
April 13
April 15
April 17
May 9
June 10
June 20
July 8
August 10
August 16
August 20
September 28
October 6
October 17
November 1
November 15
December 9

Mercy
January 10
August 4
October 1
December 28

Moving of the Holy Spirit
April 25

Name of Jesus
May 26
October 14
November 26

Nations
July 4
September 3
September 16
October 15
November 4

New Way of Thinking
February 21
April 24
June 23
July 5
August 11
December 27

Obedience
March 18
March 24
April 27
May 3
May 6
May 12
May 17
May 22

June 6
July 21
November 23
December 21

Patience
February 22
April 26
June 25
August 22
October 16
December 19

Peace
February 4
February 7
February 24
June 26
December 11

Persecution
February 17
July 15
October 11

Praise
March 6
April 12
June 2
August 5
October 1

Prayer
January 24
February 9
February 23
March 29
April 16
May 18
May 19
June 17
July 11
August 14
September 1
September 13
September 16
September 27
November 5
November 18

Praying in Tongues
January 6
February 11
August 31
December 12

Preparation
December 16

Promotion
December 6

Protection
February 5
October 10
November 11

Remaining in Jesus
August 28
September 25

Representing Jesus
March 26

Revelation Knowledge
September 2
November 8

Right-Standing
January 5
February 18
March 20
May 25
October 13

Salvation
January 1
April 3
June 17
August 6

Seated With Christ
April 2
August 19
October 26

Second Coming
May 23
October 29

Sensitivity
November 22

Serving God
March 31

Sorrow and Grief
April 6
July 14

Speaking God's Word
January 19
January 31
April 14
June 16
June 24
August 1
September 5
December 3

Spending Time With God
August 9
August 28
September 18
October 9
December 26

Spiritual Growth
January 18
January 23
March 1
March 3
March 5
March 14
March 15
March 16
April 1
April 20
May 2
May 11
May 13
May 28
July 3
July 9
September 14
October 19
November 19

Stirred Up
November 25

Strength
June 4

Thoughts
July 31

Tradition
June 9
August 24
October 18
November 21

Unity
January 4
March 23
April 5
June 28
September 21
October 19

Victory
January 2
January 30
February 2
February 13
March 3
March 13
March 27
March 28
April 7
April 11
May 1
June 7
June 12
June 29
July 13

August 18
August 21
August 27
September 11
October 28
November 6
November 9
November 11
November 27
December 30
December 31

Well-being
January 3
January 21
February 8
February 26
March 12
March 28
April 18
April 30
May 7
May 14
June 22
July 7
July 20
August 7
August 12
August 17
September 6
September 7
September 8
October 7
October 21
November 13
November 29
December 4
December 5

Wisdom
May 5
July 2

Words
February 7
February 22
March 10
May 8
May 22
July 6
August 8
November 11
November 14

Worry
January 15
February 12
April 22
June 15
December 13
December 15

PRAYER FOR SALVATION AND BAPTISM IN THE HOLY SPIRIT

Heavenly Father, I come to You in the Name of Jesus. Your Word says, *"Whosoever shall call on the name of the Lord shall be saved"* (Acts 2:21). I am calling on You. I pray and ask Jesus to come into my heart and be Lord over my life according to Romans 10:9-10. *"If thou shalt confess with thy mouth the Lord Jesus, and shalt believe in thine heart that God hath raised him from the dead, thou shalt be saved."* I do that now. I confess that Jesus is Lord, and I believe in my heart that God raised Him from the dead.

I am now reborn! I am a Christian—a child of Almighty God! I am saved! You also said in Your Word, *"If ye then, being evil, know how to give good gifts unto your children: HOW MUCH MORE shall your heavenly Father give the Holy Spirit to them that ask him?"* (Luke 11:13). I'm also asking You to fill me with the Holy Spirit. Holy Spirit, rise up within me as I praise God. I fully expect to speak with other tongues as You give me the utterance (Acts 2:4).

Begin to praise God for filling you with the Holy Spirit. Speak those words and syllables you receive—not in your own language, but the language given to you by the Holy Spirit. You have to use your own voice. God will not force you to speak. Worship and praise Him in your heavenly language—in other tongues.

Continue with the blessing God has given you and pray in tongues each day.

You are a born-again, Spirit-filled believer. You'll never be the same!

Find a good Word of God preaching church, and become a part of a church family who will love and care for you as you love and care for them.

We need to be hooked up to each other. It increases our strength in God. It's God's plan for us.

ABOUT THE AUTHORS

Kenneth and Gloria Copeland are best-selling authors of more than 60 books, such as the popular *Hidden Treasures, Managing God's Mutual Funds—Yours and His,* and *God's Will for You.* Together they have co-authored other books, including *Family Promises* and their soon-to-be-released devotional *Pursuit of His Presence—A Daily Walk in the Presence of God.* As founders of Kenneth Copeland Ministries in Fort Worth, Texas, Kenneth and Gloria are in their 31st year of circling the globe with the uncompromised Word of God, preaching and teaching a lifestyle of victory for every Christian. They are committed to reaching entire families—grandparents, parents, young men and women, and children.

Their outreach to families includes:

- The production of the *Commander Kellie and the Superkids*SM adventure movies, audiotapes and books including *The SWORD, Armor of Light* and more
- The production of the Wichita Slim western movie series including *The Treasure of Eagle Mountain* and *Covenant Rider*
- *Baby Praise* video, music cassette and board book
- *Shout! The Voice of Victory for Kids* monthly magazine
- *The Shout! Super-Activity Book*
- The new teen devotional *Over the Edge*

Their daily and Sunday *Believer's Voice of Victory* television broadcast now air on more than 500 stations around the world, and their *Believer's Voice of Victory* and *Shout!* magazines are distributed to 1 million adults and children worldwide. Their international prison ministry reaches an average of 60,000 new inmates every year and receives more than 17,000 pieces of correspondence each month. With offices and staff in the United States, Canada, England, Australia, South Africa and Ukraine, Kenneth and Gloria's teaching materials—books, magazines, audio and video—have been translated into at least 22 languages to reach the world with the love of God.

Learn more about Kenneth Copeland Ministries
by visiting our website at **WWW.KCM.ORG**

OTHER BOOKS AVAILABLE

by Kenneth Copeland

* * A Ceremony of Marriage
* A Matter of Choice
* Covenant of Blood
* Faith and Patience—The Power Twins
* * Freedom From Fear
* Giving and Receiving
* Honor—Walking in Honesty, Truth and Integrity
* How to Conquer Strife
* How to Discipline Your Flesh
* How to Receive Communion
* Living at the End of Time—A Time of Supernatural Increase
* Love Never Fails
* Managing God's Mutual Funds
* * Now Are We in Christ Jesus
* * Our Covenant With God
* * Prayer—Your Foundation for Success
* Prosperity: The Choice Is Yours
* Rumors of War
* * Sensitivity of Heart
* Six Steps to Excellence in Ministry
* Sorrow Not! Winning Over Grief and Sorrow
* * The Decision Is Yours
* * The Force of Faith
* * The Force of Righteousness
* The Image of God in You
* The Laws of Prosperity
* * The Mercy of God
* The Miraculous Realm of God's Love
* The Outpouring of the Spirit—The Result of Prayer
* * The Power of the Tongue
* The Power to Be Forever Free
* The Troublemaker
* * The Winning Attitude
* Turn Your Hurts Into Harvests
* * Welcome to the Family
* * You Are Healed!
* Your Right-Standing With God

by Gloria Copeland

* * And Jesus Healed Them All
* Are You Ready?
* Build Your Financial Foundation
* Build Yourself an Ark
* Fight On!
* God's Prescription for Divine Health
* God's Success Formula
* God's Will for You
* God's Will for Your Healing
* God's Will is Prosperity
* * God's Will Is the Holy Spirit
* * Harvest of Health
* Hidden Treasures
* Living Contact
* * Love—The Secret to Your Success
* No Deposit—No Return
* Pleasing the Father
* Pressing In—It's Worth It All
* The Power to Live a New Life
* The Unbeatable Spirit of Faith
* * Walk in the Spirit
* Walk With God
* Well Worth the Wait

Books Co-Authored by Kenneth and Gloria Copeland

Family Promises
Healing Promises
Prosperity Promises

From Faith to Faith—A Daily Guide to Victory
One Word From God Series
- One Word from God Can Change Your Destiny
- One Word from God Can Change Your Family
- One Word from God Can Change Your Finances
- One Word from God Can Change Your Health

Over the Edge—A Youth Devotional
Over the Edge Xtreme Planner for Students
Pursuit of His Presence—A Daily Devotional
Pursuit of His Presence—A Perpetual Calendar

Other Books Published by KCP

The First 30 Years—A Journey of Faith
The story of the lives of Kenneth and Gloria Copeland
Real People. Real Needs. Real Victories.
A book of testimonies to encourage your faith.

John G. Lake—His Life, His Sermons, His Boldness of Faith

The Holiest of All, by Andrew Murray
The New Testament in Modern Speech, by Richard Francis Weymouth

Products Designed by KCP and Heirborne™ for Today's Children and Youth

Baby Praise Board Book
Best of *Shout!* Adventure Comics
Noah's Ark Coloring Book
Shout! Super-Activity Book
Superkid Novels
- Escape from Jungle Island
- In Pursuit of the Enemy
- Mysterious Presence, The
- Quest for the Second Half, The

SWORD Adventure Book

*Available in Spanish

Available from your local bookstore.

HARRISON HOUSE
Tulsa, OK 74153

WE'RE HERE FOR YOU!

Join Kenneth and Gloria Copeland, and the *Believer's Voice of Victory* broadcast, Monday through Friday and on Sunday each week, and learn how faith in God's Word can take your life from ordinary to extraordinary.

It's some of the most in-depth teaching you'll ever hear on subjects like faith and healing, deliverance and prosperity, protection and hope. And it's all designed to get you where you want to be—*on top!* The teachings are by some of today's best-known ministers, including Kenneth and Gloria Copeland, Jerry Savelle, Charles Capps, Creflo A. Dollar Jr., Kellie Copeland and Edwin Louis Cole.

Whether it's before breakfast, during lunch or after a long day at the office, plan to make *Believer's Voice of Victory* a daily part of your life. See for yourself how one word from God can change your life forever.

Catch the *Believer's Voice of Victory* broadcast on the following cable and satellite channels:

Sunday 9-9:30 p.m. ET
Cable*/G5, Channel 3—TBN

Monday through Friday 6-6:30 a.m. ET
Cable*/G5, Channel 7—WGN

Monday through Friday 6:30-7 a.m. ET
Cable*/G5, Channel 20—BET

Monday through Friday 7-7:30 p.m. ET
Cable*G1, Channel 17—INSP

Monday through Friday 11:11:30 a.m. ET
Cable*/G5, Channel 3—TBN

Monday through Friday 6:30-7 a.m. ET
Cable*/W1, Channel 7—Cornerstone TV

*Check you local listing for more times and stations in your area.

The Harrison House Vision

Proclaiming the truth and the power

Of the Gospel of Jesus Christ

With excellence;

Challenging Christians to

Live victoriously,

Grow spiritually,

Know God intimately.

WORLD OFFICES
OF KENNETH COPELAND MINISTRIES

For more information about KCM and a free catalog, please write the office nearest you:

Kenneth Copeland Ministries
Fort Worth, Texas 76192-0001

Kenneth Copeland
Locked Bag 2600
Mansfield Delivery Centre
QUEENSLAND 4122
AUSTRALIA

Kenneth Copeland
Post Office Box 15
BATH
BA1 1GD
ENGLAND

Kenneth Copeland
Private Bag X 909
FONTAINEBLEAU
2032
REPUBLIC OF SOUTH AFRICA

Kenneth Copeland
Post Office Box 378
Surrey
BRITISH COLUMBIA
V3T 5B6
CANADA

UKRAINE
L'VIV 290000
Post Office Box 84
Kenneth Copeland Ministries
L'VIV 290000
UKRAINE